JEWISH CULTURAL STUDIES

VOLUME SIX

The Jewish Cultural Studies series is sponsored by the Jewish Folklore and Ethnology Section of the American Folklore Society in co-operation with the Council on the Anthropology of Jews and Judaism of the American Anthropological Association.

For more information on the Section see <http://www.afsnet.org/?page=JewishFLE>.

For information on other titles in the series visit <https://liverpooluniversitypress.co.uk/collections/series-jewish-cultural-studies>

D1598080

THE LITTMAN LIBRARY OF
JEWISH CIVILIZATION

*The Littman Library of Jewish Civilization is a registered UK charity
Registered charity no. 1000784*

Jewish Cultural Studies

VOLUME SIX

Connected Jews
Expressions of Community in Analogue and Digital Culture

Edited by

SIMON J. BRONNER AND
CASPAR BATTEGAY

London

The Littman Library of Jewish Civilization
in association with Liverpool University Press

2018

The Littman Library of Jewish Civilization
Registered office: 4th floor, 7–10 Chandos Street, London WIG 9DQ

in association with Liverpool University Press
4 Cambridge Street, Liverpool L69 7ZU, UK
www.liverpooluniversitypress.co.uk/littman

Managing Editor: Connie Webber

Distributed in North America by
Oxford University Press Inc, 198 Madison Avenue,
New York, NY 10016, USA

Catalogue records for this book are available from
the British Library and the Library of Congress

ISBN 978–1–906764–86–9

Publishing co-ordinator: Janet Moth
Copy-editing: Lindsey Taylor-Guthartz
Proof-reading: Norm Guthartz
Index: Bonnie Blackburn
Production, design, and typesetting by Pete Russell, Faringdon, Oxon.

Printed in Great Britain on acid-free paper by
TJ International Ltd., Padstow, Cornwall

The editors dedicate this volume to

DAN BEN-AMOS

champion of communication-centred approaches
to culture, on the occasion of his 50th year of
teaching Jewish studies and folklore at the
University of Pennsylvania

Editor and Advisers

Acknowledgements

THIS VOLUME, apropos of our theme, represents a global effort that benefited from media technology to connect editors and authors. A conference on the idea of the Jewish community at Haifa University in 1999, organized by Haya Bar-Itzhak, sowed the seeds of a project to re-examine the concept of community in light of changing media through time. The idea then took form from face-to-face discussions in central Pennsylvania between Simon Bronner at the Pennsylvania State University and Andrea Lieber at Dickinson College on research projects related to the effects of the Internet and social media on the Jewish community close to home. Aware of scholarship on the advance of 'digital culture' in the twenty-first century, they considered the special case of Jews, who were usually left out of the lively discourse in media studies on cyberspace. Lieber's publication of 'Domesticity and the Home (Page): Blogging and the Blurring of Public and Private among Orthodox Jewish Women' in the second volume (2010) of the Jewish Cultural Studies (JCS) series set the stage for wider listserv discussions and eventually panels at the Association for Jewish Studies, the World Congress of Jewish Studies, and American Folklore Society meetings on broader historical enquiries into the role of media and communication in the formation, or dissipation, of Jewish community.

Back from academic meetings in the reality of everyday life, we benefited from the co-operation of Sally Jo Bronner, a teacher in the local yeshiva, Hebrew high school co-ordinator, and BBYO adviser, as well as an admitted Facebook addict. She helped educate us about the processes of mediation among today's Jewish youth and the thinking of community leaders about the challenges of shaping Jewish identity in a digital age. Simon Bronner's children were also happy to instruct him on the ins and outs of Jewish online communities. The archives and programming staff of the Center for Holocaust and Jewish Studies at Penn State, the Jewish Studies Program at the University of Pennsylvania, and the Schusterman Center for Jewish Studies at the University of Texas were incredibly helpful.

Caspar Battegay in Switzerland had a similar path to this project from discussions with JCS board member Joachim Schlör on the globalization of Jewish popular culture. Bronner and Battegay were able to connect at conferences and via email, joining their different disciplinary as well as geographical perspectives towards an understanding of Jewish uses of media through time and space. Although other obligations prevented Lieber and Schlör from contributing to the present volume, we are grateful to them for their support and encouragement of the project all along the way, including serving as readers for several papers. We also want to acknowledge other readers and consultants: Haya Bar-Itzhak,

Dan Ben-Amos, Dov-Ber Kerler, Anthony Buccitelli, Harvey Goldberg, Itzik Gottesman, András Kovács, Nathanael Riemer, Dani Schrire, Dani Shavit, Steve Siporin, and Assaf Zilbering.

We are grateful to Timothy Lloyd, Executive Director, and Lorraine Cashman, Associate Director, of the American Folklore Society for support of the Society's Jewish Folklore and Ethnology Section, which sponsors the Jewish Cultural Studies series. At Pennsylvania State University, we benefited from the capable editorial assistants Brittany Clark and Cory Hutcheson, and supportive professorial colleagues Anthony Buccitelli, Gregory Crawford, and Charles Kupfer. We especially owe much gratitude to Penn State administrative assistants Hannah Murray, Cindy Leach, and Rachel Dean for an organizational job well done.

We dedicate this volume to Dan Ben-Amos for his years of writing, mentoring, and lecturing on the importance of Jewish cultural studies. His ideas on communication, mediation, and the performance of cultural expression have inspired us, and after fifty years of teaching at the University of Pennsylvania, have influenced countless students and scholars around the world and in many fields.

Contents

Note on Transliteration

THE transliteration of Hebrew in this book reflects consideration of the type of book it is, in terms of its content, purpose, and readership. The system adopted therefore reflects a broad approach to transcription, rather than the narrower approaches found in the *Encyclopaedia Judaica* or other systems developed for text-based or linguistic studies. The aim has been to reflect the pronunciation prescribed for modern Hebrew, rather than the spelling or Hebrew word structure, and to do so using conventions that are generally familiar to the English-speaking reader.

In accordance with this approach, no attempt is made to indicate the distinctions between *alef* and *ayin*, *tet* and *taf*, *kaf* and *kuf*, *sin* and *samekh*, since these are not relevant to pronunciation; likewise, the *dagesh* is not indicated except where it affects pronunciation. Following the principle of using conventions familiar to the majority of readers, however, transcriptions that are well established have been retained even when they are not fully consistent with the transliteration system adopted. On similar grounds, the *tsadi* is rendered by 'tz' in such familiar words as barmitzvah.

The distinction between *ḥet* and *khaf* has been retained, using *ḥ* for the former and *kh* for the latter; the associated forms are generally familiar to readers, even if the distinction is not actually borne out in pronunciation, and for the same reason the final *heh* is indicated too. As in Hebrew, no capital letters are used, except that an initial capital has been retained in transliterating titles of published works (for example, *Shulḥan arukh*).

Since no distinction is made between *alef* and *ayin*, they are indicated by an apostrophe only in intervocalic positions where a failure to do so could lead an English-speaking reader to pronounce the vowel-cluster as a diphthong—as, for example, in *ha'ir*—or otherwise mispronounce the word. An apostrophe is also used, for the same reason, to disambiguate the pronunciation of other English vowel clusters, as for example in *mizbe'aḥ*.

The *sheva na* is indicated by an *e*—*perikat ol, reshut*—except, again, when established convention dictates otherwise. The *yod* is represented by *i* when it occurs as a vowel (*bereshit*), by *y* when it occurs as a consonant (*yesodot*), and by *yi* when it occurs as both (*yisra'el*).

Names have generally been left in their familiar forms, even when this is inconsistent with the overall system.

Media, Mediation, and Jewish Community

SIMON J. BRONNER AND CASPAR BATTEGAY

THIS VOLUME grapples with the common assumption that media-driven popular culture has weakened ethnic-religious ties of community with each advance in communication technology, and has been especially detrimental to tradition-centred groups such as Orthodox Jews. Popular culture theorists have long asserted that the very notion of 'popular' works against the survival of ethnic-religious groups socially interacting in locally bounded areas (Nye 1970: 6). A leader in this school of thought, Russel Nye, asserted that the idea of popular culture, associated with urbanization and industrialization, depends on artists and agents who exploit media and create cultural standards. He proclaimed that in order to create for a mass audience made possible by communication technology, 'the popular artists cannot take into consideration the individualities and preferences of minority groups'. Nye explained that 'since the popular arts aim at the largest common denominator, they tend to standardize at the median level of majority expectation', and that objective of standardization typically cut out marginalized Jewish urban enclaves in the diaspora (1970: 6).

Importantly for the discussion among authors in this volume, Nye theorized that the process of popularization depends on a mass audience, consuming secularized cultural expressions that became accessible in Western societies through communication media on a national and even global scale after the eighteenth century. To establish this audience, composed of strangers to one another, institutions as well as industries often function in the areas of entertainment to convince a populace whose primary social frame of reference is the localized face-to-face community that benefits accrue from consumption and communication through mass media, rather than localized, often oral conduits. These promised benefits might include more individual freedom and mobility, coupled with diminished control by an elite class or local religious authorities. The advent of popular culture purportedly diminishes the need for public space and peer pressure, since consumers can make private choices about what and when information is consumed. Brokers for popular culture implied that the embrace of mass market products was progressive, in the sense of fostering change in the future by erasing the hold of elders and emphasizing imaginative, trendy possibilities for the individual desires for gratification of urbanizing, 'modernizing' youth. Whereas tradition held that members of groups should follow practices and guidelines of the past, monitored by elders and conceptualized as 'culturalism', texts and trends of popular culture generated by youth often emphasized breaks with tradition and community, in pursuit of determining one's own future path. In the Jewish liturgy, emphasis on continuity and community is expressed as *ledor vedor* (generation to generation) in the Kedushah (third blessing of the Shemoneh-Esrei prayer), and is extracted frequently as a guiding ethical saying in Judaism. Many Jewish community centres and synagogues also use the maxim 'Do not separate yourselves from the community', attributed to Hillel in the mishnaic tractate *Pirkei avot*.

The pitch to consumers to think and act globally and break from the past was not an easy sell. Conflicts among supposedly progressive and conservative factions arose in tradition-centred communities with the popularization of magazines, phonographs, and photography during the nineteenth century, and particularly with cinema, radio, and television in the twentieth century. A prominent symbol of this conflict for Jewish communities, and the response of popular culture brokers through media, is the release by Warner Brothers in 1927 of *The Jazz Singer* as the first 'talkie', or feature-length film with synchronous speech and music. Before its release, the studio was associated with adventure films with decidedly non-ethnic themes, featuring Rin-Tin-Tin, 'the famous police dog' (Hoberman and Shandler 2003: 78). Jews were not common characters in popular films up to that point, and when they did appear, they were usually unflattering characters from well-known literary adaptations such as Dickens's *Oliver Twist* and Shakespeare's *Merchant of Venice* (L. Friedman 1987: 17).

Edison Studios, which dominated the film industry in the early twentieth century, was outright hostile to Jews as subjects, filmmakers, and cultural brokers. When Edison's white Protestant producers featured Jews, they intended to demean them to a popular Christian audience and to reinforce the image of a white Protestant majority at the heart of popular culture. As film historians Harry M. Benshoff and Sean Griffin point out, Edison Studios 'featured grotesque stereotypes of Jews as hunchbacked, hook-nosed, and greedy cheats. Such sub-human depictions, found in films like *Levitsky's Insurance Policy* (1903) and *Cohen's Advertising Scheme* (1904), presented an image of Jews as money-grubbing and untrustworthy' (2011: 65–6). One response to these depictions, they surmise, was the creation of films made by and for Jews, particularly in urbanized ethnic neighbourhoods, where immigrant Jews began breaking religious taboos on partaking in popular entertainment. Indeed, some cultural historians, such as R. Laurence Moore, counter Russel Nye's account of immigrants swayed to a Christian-produced version of popular culture by arguing that urban entertainment was a 'non-Protestant and ethnic working class accomplishment' (Moore 1994: 202). Religious historian Mark Massa has broken down the 'ethnic working class' into Catholics and Jews relocating during the global Great Wave of immigration between 1880 and 1920, and comments, 'Catholics were far less important in crafting the twentieth-century mass-culture vision than second- and third-generation American Jews' (2004: 114; see also Buhle and Pekar 2007: p. ix; Schmalzbauer 2010: 259–60). One of the purported Jewish goals was to deracialize depictions of Jews by characterizing them as ordinary citizens able to blend into mass society, rather than by distinguishing, and hence marginalizing, them by repulsive bodily features, clannish residence, and old-fashioned, even cultish dress. Yet in recasting, or simply omitting, their image through the media, assimilating Jews arguably lost their ethnic visibility and participation in a multicultural politics. According to many cultural critics, Jews hid or denied their ethnic or community identities in the name of subverting embodied stereotypes in popular culture (Brodkin 2010; Fingeroth 2007; Pearse 2008, 2014; Zurawik 2003).

The association of Jews with popular culture largely derives from their conspicuous involvement as producers in the early movie industry in the United States. Film critic Neal Gabler's best-selling book, *An Empire of Their Own: How the Jews Invented Hollywood* (1988), and the spinoff film documentary written and directed by Simcha Jacobovici (1998), drew attention not so much for its claim that the culture industry of 'Hollywood' owed its existence to first- and second-generation Jewish entrepreneurs, but more to the psychological interpretation that they were motivated by their alienation as Jews and immigrants. Aspiring to join the mainstream, according to this view, the Jewish studio moguls created movies that by appealing to the non-ethnic 'largest common denominator', in Nye's words, proclaimed their inclusion in society and the endorsement of assimilation by the masses. Yet at the same time, non-Hollywood Jewish producers sent out messages of ethnic persistence in silent films with Yiddish intertitles, such as *Mizrekh un Mayrev* (East and West, 1923) directed by the prolific Odessa-born Sidney Goldin (born Samuel Goldstein) and featuring the budding Jewish star Molly Picon, who attracted young Jews in places such as the Lower East Side of New York, despite religious prohibitions on movie-going. Other metropolises with major Jewish districts in London, Paris, and Berlin gave rise to Jewish theatres whose productions often spilled over into popular culture, but it was the Lower East Side of New York that came to represent the Jewish imagination in the popular culture of the early twentieth century. Social historian Hasia Diner writes that 'Pictures—moving ones—linked the immigrant Jews all over America and in eastern Europe through the neighborhood as a spatial icon' (2000: 144). She points out that films, with their obligatory background shots of bustling street life, forged a 'constantly recycling diaspora culture' because they played across America to immigrant audiences and were screened in eastern Europe.

In addition to connecting Jews culturally across continents, the films contributed what Diner calls 'a cinematographic element to the inner Jewish debate'
about defining one's Jewish identity through a separatist religious community.
The Yiddish films made in New York suggested that, in a new urban maelstrom,
it was possible to forge a cultural identity in which people could live comfortably
in an ethnically mixed social environment and retain continuity through Jewish
cultural expressions of literature, drama, music, and food, rather than by means
of traditional dress and worship. Jewish-made movies of this era, according
to literary historian Donald Weber, 'depict the combustible reaction of street
versus home, English versus Yiddish (or "potato Yiddish", as the less than perfect
rhetoric of *shund* [trashy] theater was derisively styled), of "civilized" America and
the nation's linguistically mongrel future. Out of that exhilarating encounter
much popular culture in America was forged' (2003: 131).

Diner asserts the significance of popular culture arising out of and symbolized by the Lower East Side: 'In that imaginary world made by the movies and
other cultural products America emerged as a liberating land of opportunity yet
one that shook the foundations of communal and familial coherence' (2000:
145). Theatres were the main source of entertainment for working-class Jewish
immigrants in urban locales. The movies were more than cultural products in
their ethnic language; they also had the psychological function of anticipating
the future. While many of the films were sympathetic to the bonds of heritage
in the Old World, they typically showed America as a place to break the hold of
ancient, and apparently superstitious, customs. Basing his claim on recollections
of immigrant commentaries about the allure of ethnic stage and screen, Weber
concludes that 'audiences watched their deepest anxieties and desires literally
enacted, displayed before their eyes' (2003: 131). Audiences tended to see transitions to America and the apparently strange ways of popular culture as difficult,
but inevitable. Thus the source of production as well as the setting in America for
Jewish viewers advanced the acceptance of popular culture as future-oriented and
potentially progressive.

Although so far we have focussed on the culture industries of the United
States, we should not overlook developments in other countries that tied Jewish
creative endeavours (not always successfully) to a broad-based popular culture
that would be tolerant of Jewish contributions. In Germany, successful Jewish
artists, such as the director Ernst Lubitsch, worked for the major German production company Universum Film-Aktien Gesellschaft (UFA) before coming to the
United States. Moreover, there is a long list of Jewish songwriters producing
Schlager music (later this term became a loan word in other languages for a musical 'hit'), and of Jewish composers and cabaret singers in the urban scene of
Berlin and Vienna in the 1920s and 1930s. Some of them—including the actor
Kurt Gerron and the legendary comedian and cabaret artist Fritz Grünbaum—
were murdered in German concentration camps. Others were able to escape to

the United States or other countries and resume their careers. A prominent example of this transnational experience, who affected the development of popular culture in both the United States and Germany, is the composer Robert Gilbert (born Robert David Winterfeld), who was one of the composers of the 1931 operetta *The White Horse Inn* (*Im weißen Rössl*). This musical comedy enjoyed international success, with long runs in Vienna, Paris, and New York. Gilbert's works were discredited by the Nazis, who banned works by Jewish writers and composers. He managed to emigrate to New York, where he unsuccessfully tried to work in English-speaking Broadway theatres. He continued to write in German, however, influenced by the 'big revues, chorus lines, and dancing troupes' of Broadway musical comedy (Schlör 2014a; Schlör 2014b). Gilbert connected to an émigré artist community through the publication *Aufbau*, founded by the German-Jewish Club in 1934 in New York. In New York, he befriended and was influenced by other contributors, including the writer Hannah Arendt, the poet Heinrich Blücher, and the composer Hermann Leopoldi, while some of his Jewish countrymen, such as his former composer partner Werner Richard Heymann, went across the country to Hollywood to compose music for the studios there (his musical film credits include *Ninotchka* (1939) and *To Be or Not to Be* (1942)) under the direction of another German Jewish émigré, Ernst Lubitsch (see Schlör 2016). Gilbert's lyrics for *The White Horse Inn* did not have explicitly Jewish content, but reflected the show's theme of ethnic–class conflict between a privileged urban gentry and rural folk that results in a happy ending of a triple marriage representing social conciliation. Gilbert returned to Europe in 1951 (the same year that Heymann returned), where, according to cultural historian Joachim Schlör, 'he came to play an important (yet forgotten) role in the translation and transfer of American popular culture to Europe' (Schlör 2014b). Gilbert was welcomed into the reviving post-war theatre and film industry in Munich, where a German-language film version of *The White Horse Inn* (1952) was produced, along with *The Forester's Daughter* (1952), featuring compositions by Gilbert. Revivals of the stage production of *The White Horse Inn* continued to be popular throughout the 1950s and 1960s, and a new film version was released in 2013 as *Im weißen Rössl—Wehe Du singst!*

To be sure, the imaginary and real connection between Jews and the media was mostly located in 'Hollywood', after immigration to New York sharply declined during the 1920s in the wake of American governmental efforts to stem the tide of east European Jews and other groups from southern and eastern Europe. Movies in the early twentieth century as the main, technologically advanced popular entertainment (especially historically in the transition from neighbourhood theatre), sparked conversation—and debate—about the sustainability of Jewish community and tradition in a popular culture world generated out of, or largely modelled on the creative industries of, the United States (Barth 1982: 192–228). Yet since the finances and social capital to produce movies and television shows have developed in different centres around the world, often with the intention of creating a distinctive popular culture within global regions and ethnic diasporas, textual and contextual analyses of language and performances within media productions involve not only aesthetic judgements but also cultural, and political, considerations. Thus German, Polish, and Russian productions of films on the Jewish experience are often couched within Holocaust histories and the relative absence of Jews in the present (Dorchain and Wonnenberg 2013; Gershenson 2008; Prawer 2007; Stradomski 1989). And when productions are adapted in, or distributed to, new locations, commentaries often look for social and political reasons for changes. The popular Israeli television series *Srugim* (broadcast 2008–12) was the first to focus on religious nationalists in the Katamon neighbourhood of Jerusalem, nicknamed 'the swamp' for its dense population of unmarried religious Jews hoping to find spouses (Weiss 2016: 69). The title refers to the crocheted skullcaps commonly worn by men in this group. When distributed to American audiences watching it on the streaming services of Amazon Prime and Hulu, commentaries from Jews noted the connection of other 'modern Orthodox' communities to the dilemmas of young adults negotiating modernity and tradition. Non-Jews posted reactions that tended to overlook issues of community and nationalism and focused more on the love plot of religiously motivated young people, and interpreted the glimpse provided of this community as somehow representative of Israeli daily life (Weiss 2016: 81–4).

In this volume, contributors treat conversations and debates in response to texts, as well as those lodged in the texts, as special evidence of cultural attitudes, biases, and worldviews. Taken together, the different ways in which messages work with the media to convey ideas, embody values, and persuade audiences are summarized as *discourse*. Often scholarly analysis of discourse hinges on the use of keywords and the formation of stylised rhetoric, both verbal and visual, and their performance. Moving beyond linguistics into cultural studies, scholars frequently point to the contexts of texts, defining them broadly to include events, images, objects, and landscapes (Edwards 2017). A prominent model evident in the study of media productions with Jewish themes identifies the signs by which Jews and non-Jews identify, or misidentify, Jewishness. In addition, people's responses to media—in conversation on the street, in the home, in published reviews, and more recently in digital social media—indicate the perceived meanings of texts and the framing of figurative words or images as meaningful or iconic. Ultimately, the analysis leads to social and cultural perspectives on identity and the way that heritage is enacted in everyday life and informs a sense of self and community (Machin and Mayr 2015; Strauss and Feiz 2013). According to cultural historian Alan Trachtenberg, such heritage discourses are significant because they can determine behaviour and affect social and political life, as well as economic issues of production and consumption. They are, in his words, 'vehicles of self-knowledge, of the concepts upon which people act. They are also, especially in the public domain, forces in their own right, often coloring perceptions in a certain way even against all evidence. At the same time, figurative representations occupy the same social world as other forces, material and political' (Trachtenberg 1982: 8). In the Jewish world, discourse analysis is complicated further by representations in different ethnic-regional dialects and cultural products with esoteric audiences in mind, as well as the use of languages and images known widely in the host society. Symbolic readings are also made of ethnic keywords and images that enter into the 'popular domain', often acquiring new or multiple meanings when they do, such as chutzpah, bagels and lox, 'delis', and red string bracelets (Balinska 2008; Bronner 2008: 4–10; Merwin 2015; Teman 2008).

To demonstrate the analytical approach of discourse in popular culture, one can consider how a media production such as *The Jazz Singer* lifted the ethnic-religious symbol of singing Kol Nidrei on Yom Kippur into public consciousness. The play *The Day of Atonement* by Samson Raphaelson, upon which the movie *The Jazz Singer* is based, had a successful run on Broadway in 1926, but film studios, probably leery of producing a movie perceived to be a 'Hebrew play', were not anxious to put the story on the screen (Hoberman 2003: 78). Indeed, the reviewer for the *New York Herald Tribune* worried that the play would be unintelligible to non-Jewish audiences, largely on the basis of the esoteric knowledge of the significance of Kol Nidrei. The writer, noting a predominantly Jewish audience in the theatre, thought the play required an unusual 'understanding of and sympathy with the Jew and his faith' (Hoberman 2003: 78).

The Warner Brothers studio, upon the advice of contract director Ernst Lubitsch, took a chance and bought the movie rights to the show. Lubitsch related to *The Jazz Singer* as a German-born son of a Russian Jewish tailor, expected to continue in his father's business, who had left his family and home for the theatre. The Warner (originally Wonsal) brothers consisted of Harry, Albert, Jack, and Sam, the Polish-born sons of a Jewish shoemaker. Sam was the first to venture into the film industry, after seeing Thomas Edison's *The Great Train Robbery* (1903), a short western. He was directly involved in the production of *The Jazz Singer*, although 25-year-old Daryl F. Zanuck, raised a Protestant in Wahoo, Nebraska, was given producer credits. Like the protagonist in *The Jazz Singer*, who has a love affair outside his faith after entering the entertainment industry, Sam married *Ziegfeld Follies* performer Lina Basquette, an American-born Catholic, much to the chagrin of the Warner family.

The background of the making of *The Jazz Singer* has often been covered by film historians, but the focus of Jewish cultural studies is the social and psychological processes by which cultural brokers and creative agents *encode* persuasive messages affecting public attitudes, patterns, and audiences, and communities *decode* the production of media with broader, often political, ramifications. On a technological and organizational level, global histories credit Warner Brothers' production of *The Jazz Singer* with changing the film industry and heightening the international impact of motion pictures. Although it opened in only two theatres in 1927, less than a year later it was showing in 235 theatres, resulting in the death of the silent film. According to film historian Ron Hutchinson, 'an entire industry had reinvented itself more completely . . . than any industry in the world' (Hutchinson 1996). Yet Jolson's next role for Warner Brothers, in *The Singing Fool* (1928), while commercially successful, did not dwell on his Jewish background. The Warners' first all-talking full-length feature *Lights of New York*, also produced in 1928, was an urban crime drama that, although set largely in New York, did not showcase Jewish content.

Working within a historical context, cultural critics usually point to Jolson's ethnic role as a breakthrough for Jews in the media. The film acknowledged a conflict between ethnic community and popular culture, threatening to displace centuries of tradition, but allowed that they could coexist. Did audiences view and hear it that way, especially since the 1920s ushered in a period of intolerance towards immigrants and minorities, as well as youthful post-war enthusiasm for technological advances (radio, phonograph, electrification) and modernization (Murphy 1964; Hing 2004: 62–70)? Cultural studies can illuminate the ethical and political message of *The Jazz Singer*, and the way audiences decoded it, in the midst of legislative measures to curb immigration and white Protestant efforts to establish a national culture in their image. The central conflicted figure in the movie is Jakie Rabinowitz, played by Al Jolson, a cantor's son growing up in an Orthodox Jewish household and traditional community. The popular stage lures him away from home and he loses evidence of his Jewishness in the process. Playwright Samson Raphaelson, who came from a New York Jewish family, cites a concert by Al Jolson which he thought sounded 'cantorial' as the inspiration in glitzy California for his writing *The Day of Atonement*, the basis of *The Jazz Singer* (Raphaelson 2003).

Al Jolson was born Asa Yoelson in Kovno, the son of a rabbi–cantor in present-day Lithuania. The children and mother immigrated to Washington, DC, in 1894 to join Rabbi Yoelson, who had found cantorial work there. Asa's mother died in 1895, and to help with the family's finances, Asa found work in the local circus and sang popular songs, before moving on to neighbourhood burlesque theatres. By the end of the first decade of the twentieth century, local theatres were being affected by the introduction of nickelodeons and, later, movies. Under the anglicized name Al Jolson, the cantor's son made the transition to Broadway theatre and movies, before embarking on *The Jazz Singer*. These roles did not invoke his Jewish background; in fact, Jolson became known for using blackface to frame southern plantation songs that involved melodramatic performances and would not have been appropriate in restrained popular songs. Cultural critic Jan Stratton interprets these performances as aligning Jolson with, rather than separating him from, dominant American and, more generally, English-speaking under-standings of race. By donning an African American costume, Jolson visualized himself as on the fringe of the white races and known for performance of the pop-ularized, de-ethnicized 'torch song', rather than as a racialized Jew singing in an accented English, reminding listeners of his or her othered status (Stratton 2009: 13; see also Musser 2011; Rogin 1996; Romeyn 2008: 187–212; Whitfield 2008). As a fixture of popular culture, lacking any association with ethnic identity, by the 1930s Jolson had issued 80 hit records and organized 16 national and interna-tional tours, making him the country's most famous and highest-paid enter-tainer.

In *The Jazz Singer*, Jolson as the popular entertainer Jack Robin returns after a five-year absence to visit his mother, who is still living in the traditional neigh-bourhood. She barely recognizes him in his posh attire after his five-year absence, and he in turn notices that his childhood portrait has been replaced with a generic landscape painting. In a scene that has synchronized sound, he shows her on the piano the difference between a mundane rendition of 'Blue Skies' (composed by Irving Berlin, 1926), and a jazzed, or modernized, version. It is a core scene, translated into a sentimentalized image on the main poster for the movie (Figure 1). The choice of the song is undoubtedly symbolic; the recording from 1927 by Ben Selvin's Orchestra (Columbia 860-D) topped record charts. Both Selvin and Irving Berlin came from Russian Jewish backgrounds and were well known in American popular culture. The singer cheerily repeats the chorus line of 'Blue skies smiling on me' to express his happiness at being in love, but in the context of the film appears to use it to point to the freedom, upward aspiration, and unlimited possibilities outside the dark, traditional home, in the modern world characterized by popular culture. The song's sunny lyrics contrast with the father's entrance and order to stop playing 'dirty music from the sidewalks' (Raphaelson 1935: 50). The cantor chides his son from turning away from his Jewish roots as Jakie, and as the anglicized Jack, the son retorts that he cannot live in this closed, sheltered world. To Jack's mind, inside the home is old and dark, while outside is new and bright. The father reminds his son that in the home he had meaning in his life, by learning to sing prayers and carry on the legacy of many generations.

However, after Jack's father falls ill, he takes the cantor's role in leading the Kol Nidrei prayer on the Day of Atonement. Besides signifying the sacredness of the holiday in Judaism and atoning for past sins, the particular chant of Kol Nidrei represents the folk community, because of its inclusion in the liturgy by com-munity custom rather than rabbinical authority (Deshen 1979; Gershon 1994). Jack's return to his religious–ethnic roots and community did not signal an abandonment of the outside popular world he had previously embraced, how-ever. One encoded message was that one could strategically situate one's identity privately, rather than treat Jewish culture as a total experience paraded publicly.

Figure 1 Poster for *The Jazz Singer (1927)*, showing Al Jolson, as Jack Robin, serenading his mother. *Everett Collection Inc.; Alamy stock photo*

In the course of everyday life, Jack integrated into a secularized mass society and navigated freely with the cultural capital he had attained. On special occasions, he could return to his community for an intensive dose of tradition. Arguably, this reassuring mass-mediated message was more for a nativist American audience who felt that national culture was threatened by physically and religiously alien Jewish immigrants, and worried particularly about the possibilities of romantic ties of Christians to Jews, as depicted in the film.

George Jessel, who had originally been asked to play the role of Jack Robin, rebuffed the appeasing meaning of the story by telling his Jewish fans in 1928, 'since I owe my success in great measure to the Jewish public, and the Jewish public expects me to be loyal to it, I could not sincerely do the picture' (Jessel 1928; Merwin 2006: 119). Yet he appeared in the original stage production, and, in films predating *The Jazz Singer*, played another Old World Jewish character— Isadore Goldberg, who becomes acculturated to an Irish neighbourhood and takes the name of Patrick Murphy, which helps him to prosper economically. When he develops an Irish romantic interest and his Jewishness is revealed, though, the Irish family objects (L. Friedman 1987: 106–8). Although the 'Izzy Murphy' series of movies sends out a message about problems stemming from inter-ethnic prejudices and stereotypes, it also values the Irish and Jewish immigrant communities as sharing nurturing qualities that will probably be lost within a modernizing society. The New York-born Jessel never let go of his Jewish persona in life or stage; he was associated throughout his life with Jewish characters in his stage and screen roles. He also recounted a father–son conflict regarding his life in the entertainment industry: his father opposed his work on the stage, and it was only after he died that Jessel began his show-business career.

In the Yiddish film *Dem khazns zundyl* (The Cantor's Son, 1937), Moishe Oysher plays Saul 'Shloimele' Reichman, who leaves his Polish shtetl for New York's bustling Lower East Side, and finds fame in the theatre. Like Jolson, Oysher was born to a cantorial family in the old Russian empire, and immigrated to the United States, but he was more connected with the Jewish community, as a practising cantor and Yiddish theatre actor, than Jolson, the popular star. In the movie, Oysher is drawn back by his parents' golden anniversary, and ultimately chooses to stay within the nourishing environment of his family and his childhood sweetheart. In answer to 'Blue Skies', Oysher, who in real life claimed to be the sixth generation in a line of cantors, sings 'Mayn Shtetele Belz' as he approaches the familiar village. In this song, composed by Alexander Olshanetsky and Jacob Jacobs specifically for the film, the 'we-ness' of the shtetl is fondly recalled: 'Belz, my little town! My little town where I had so many fine dreams!' The diminutive suffix -*leh*, added to the word shtetl, not only marks its size but acts as an endearment. Eleven words in three verses carry the diminutive tag. In the final verse, the singer couples *alt* ('old') with *shtibl* ('a little synagogue'), implying that by being small, it is more sociable and loving. The Jewish marker of the sabbath undergirds the specialness of the community. The song continues, 'Every *shabes* I would run to the river bank to play with other children under a little green tree, evoking the natural and idyllic life in the shtetl'. While the dank interior of the home in the *Jazz Singer* appeared stagnant and unchanging, in contrast to the futuristic 'blue skies', the image of the tree answers this charge with an organic life-cycle icon. Even if Jews decided to choose an assimilative path or not as a result of watching these films, it could be said that they became profoundly aware, beyond the plot lines of romance and father–son conflicts, of larger themes about the fragile role of the Jewish community, often set against the power of media to 'normalize' nationalist discourse.

Emanating from this example of popular culture and cultural brokers, that drew attention to the Jewish situation as both emblematic of wider ethnic dilemmas and particular to the Jewish urban experience, are questions about the impact of non-cinematic media at other periods and places in the modern era. In focusing on the effects of popular culture in connecting and uncoupling Jewish social networks, primarily in urban environments, we are not diminishing the dramas of identity for Jews in small town life, agricultural settlements, and Jewish 'frontiers', such as regions in the diaspora not usually associated with Jewish settlement. We caution against assuming that these locations have necessarily receded and are unaffected by popular culture. A number of scholars are concerned with their adaptation to media to enable Jewish lifestyles in new and changing areas for Jewish residence (see Gilman 2004; Libo and Howe 1984; Milligan 2016; Morawska 1996; Weissbach 2015). An example is the reliance on regional conventions and increasingly, social media, among international Jewish youth organizations devoted to 'community service' and 'identity development', such as the B'nai B'rith Youth Organization (BBYO) and United Synagogue Youth (USY), to give a sense of belonging to a coherent unit to youths from smaller communities (BBYO 2008). We query the kinds of relationships that arise through media in these and other Jewish community organizations and the way that outlooks on Jewish life are consequently affected.

We also enquire about the impact of media productions, not only in *reflecting* issues and narratives of the Jewish community and a mobile, multicultural society at large, but also as forces that *shape* actions and *project* anxieties, conflicts, and emotions. To set the background for the various perspectives on media productions, processes, and technologies presented in this volume, in the remainder of this introduction we offer guides to cultural processes that we find analytically important to the ongoing negotiation or mediation of, between, and within popular culture and Jewish community.

Technology and Mediation

Our example of films draws attention to the technology as well as content of media arising in the twentieth century and its contribution to the creation of a mass society on the one hand, and its effect on tradition-centred Jewish communities on the other. Writers often use the term 'mediation' beyond its literal meaning of arbitration to refer to the signal, even interventionist, role of media in the way that people receive and communicate ideas in a mass society (Bauman 2010; Bel et al. 2005; Kember and Zylinska 2015). It also refers to the push to advance media technology as a sign of progress and modernization. In this concept of technological mediation, emphasis is placed on devices that not only offer speed of communication, but also socially and psychologically emphasize novelty, privacy, and self-actualization for individuals navigating in a mass society of strangers. In a mass-mediated society, individuals gain status for possessing the latest device that promises wider and instantaneous communication (Kiran 2015; Morley 2005: 212; Verbeek 2005). The modernization of such devices is often exaggerated by a discourse in advertising and entertainment that ridicules the 'old-fashioned' ways of community groups. Early in commercial phonograph recording, for example, a string of records featured sketches such as 'Cohen on the Telephone', laughing at the difficulty experienced by Jews who spoke English with an accent when using popular technology such as the telephone (Bauman 2010; Merwin 2006: 24). It was first recorded by Joe Hayman in London for Regal Records, in July 1913, and released in the United States on Columbia. It reportedly sold hundreds of thousands of copies, and led to other performers, such as Monroe Silver, taking on the persona in various media. For cultural critic Ted Merwin, the character's technological difficulties symbolized the 'continuing perceptions of Jews as ethnic and racial outsiders', even as they became more visible outside their old enclaved communities (2006: 24).

To be sure, Jewish learning symbolically derives from a manual rather than mediated source—the Torah. A specially trained scribe (Hebrew: *sofer*) prepares Torah scrolls by hand. The scrolls are read aloud in the public religious spaces of the synagogue. The *sofer* prepares other documents of Jewish ritual practice, such as *mezuzot* (small parchment scrolls bearing biblical texts affixed to the doorposts), and *tefilin* (phylacteries), used in daily prayer. These objects thus connect Jews by the symbolism of the hand in personal, small-scale contact, 'handing down' or 'handing over' knowledge in oral tradition (and the 'Oral Law'), and by their manual means of production. Reverence is given to the oral recitation of the Torah, and festivals such as Passover involve storytelling that symbolically represents passing down traditions from elders to youngsters within small groups.

The synagogue has traditionally been a place to worship without media, especially on the sabbath, in keeping with the interpretation of the fifth commandment: 'Remember the sabbath day, to keep it holy' (Exod. 20: 8). In the nineteenth century rabbis drew a line in the sacred space of the sanctuary between prohibited mechanical media, such as magazines and photographs representative of work and potentially profane entertainment on the one hand, and acceptable printed books with religious material, on the other hand. With the growth of congregations, many synagogues added amplification systems in the mid-twentieth century, and a number of Reform and Conservative synagogues added screens to project prayer texts during services. In the twenty-first century, some synagogues went further by live-streaming services with the justification of reaching homebound and institutionalized congregants. Orthodox synagogue leaders have mostly prohibited the use of electronic devices on the sabbath, but a grassroots movement has arisen among some youth in the Modern Orthodox community, who keep what they call 'half-shabbos' by using personal devices to communicate through instant messaging and social media, because of their view that this constitutes communal socialization rather than *malakhah*, or work (Younger 2013). Indeed, a folklore has developed among Jewish youths with its own digital shorthand, such as 'gd Shbs' for 'good shabbos' (Lipman 2011). The Jewish press reports opposition to this trend, which has been characterized as an 'open secret in their schools and social circles'. Some rabbis, while insisting that electronics are off-limits on the sabbath, suggest that the problem is the dangerous addiction of youth to personal devices that makes it difficult to make the transition to the restrictions and spirit of the sabbath. Yet some pious teenagers argue that texting uses a low level of electricity, and avow that, just as religious books are allowed, so too using technology for religious purposes is not shameful (Lipman 2011).

Although ultra-Orthodox leaders have been known to denounce the use of smartphones and the Internet altogether, in recognition of their pervasiveness as a work tool they have accepted use of a 'kosher' smartphone, modified in a way that controls the content, in order to restrict mediation by popular culture. Such phones are often accompanied by a certificate issued by a rabbi, attesting to the modifications. For example, the Google search engine is deactivated, and (on some phones) even the ability to make and receive calls; secular news and recreational sites are blocked. Digital banking, satellite navigation, and religious reading are allowed. The *ḥaredim* have a Rabbinic Committee for Matters of Communications that issues guidelines on use of the media (Jeffay 2013; see also Y. Cohen 2011). One issue has been limitations on the popular mobile application WhatsApp, which allows transnational communication, appealing to many ultra-Orthodox families as well as to businessmen (Figure 2). Founder Jan Koum, a Jewish immigrant to the United States from the Ukraine, was influenced by government surveillance in the former Soviet Union to design a communication tool that does not collect personal information (Reuters 2014). One 'kosher' response has been to block transmission of images and disable group chats, in order to encourage community ties and privilege voice-to-voice connections.

Meanwhile, within the Reform and Conservative movements questions about

Figure 2 Avreimi Wingut, co-founder of Kama Tech start-up accelerator in Benei Berak, Israel, in 2016, displays his modified 'kosher' smartphone, pointing to its black WhatsApp icon (bottom right corner), which indicates that the app cannot transfer or display images or participate in group chats. *Photograph by Nir Alon; Alamy stock photo*

using e-readers in synagogue on the sabbath have arisen because of their similarity to books. Critics worry that the devices will tempt users to surf the Internet, and that they will perform a type of work in pushing buttons and turning pages, constituting a *toledat kotev* (a derivative form of writing, which is prohibited on the sabbath), in the spiritual sanctuary, or that these devices will simply distract congregants from worship (Boorstein 2013; U. Friedman 2010; Holzel 2013). Proponents answer with the need to use communication technology to attract youth, whose popular culture in the digital age of the twenty-first century is based upon the screen rather than the printed page (Holzel 2013). While many rabbis insist on keeping a wall of separation between the popular culture world and the pre-modern sanctuary of the synagogue, in the face of declining numbers of attendees at services some innovative rabbis have invited congregants to employ social media to interact as a religious community during worship. Rabbi Paul Kipnes of Los Angeles, for instance, received a Techie award from the Union of Reform Judaism for making sermons interactive by inviting congregants to respond to the sermon. A Facebook page, Twitter handle, and mobile phone number appear on an enormous screen near the *bimah,* or central platform (A. Lewis 2012). In Miami Beach's Temple Beth Sholom, a Reform synagogue surrounded by reminders of hedonistic pleasure in a popular vacation destination, Rabbi Amy Morrison provides an alternative worship service for Jews in their twenties, attracted, she observes, by the temptations of the popular culture world. In a nod to the participatory nature of digital communication, she announces from the *bimah* that 'texting will give you a voice in the service'; she was willing to diminish her rabbinical authority to have them socially as well as electronically 'connected' (Alvarez 2012). An example is during the 'Mi sheberakh', or healing, prayers, in which congregants, who previously had been hesitant to announce the names of their ailing loved ones, participated enthusiastically when the rabbi asked congregants to text names of those in need of prayer (Alvarez 2012).

In the same year that Morrison introduced the service, an audience of 42,000 *ḥaredi* Jewish men rallied in Citi Field Stadium in Queens, New York, to hear warnings from rabbis of the dangers of the Internet to their families and societies, and receive admonishments to remove it from their homes. Mediation was evident, however, as another 20,000 *ḥaredim* crowded into nearby Arthur Ashe Stadium to watch on closed-circuit television screens, and thousands more watched on satellite broadcasts in Jerusalem, Benei Berak, London, and Antwerp (Ettinger 2012).

While Satmar and Bobover hasidic leaders steadfastly resist use of social media to get their message out to their followers, Chabad-Lubavitch has a conspicuous Internet presence in emphasizing its global network (Shandler 2009: 230–74). Its website Chabad.org is also the title of its Facebook and Instagram accounts. It counters video entertainment with links to over 15,000 videos on Jewish.tv, including over 3,000 on the life and teachings of the Rebbe, Menachem Mendel Schneerson (1902–94). Answering the question 'Is the Internet evil?', Moshe Goldman on Chabad.org posts that 'the status of every object is determined by the way it is used' and notes that the Internet is 'peerless in its ability to disseminate Torah information and values' (Goldman 2017; on religious use of earlier media technology, see Poll 1969: 228–30). In keeping with the movement's emphasis on *sheluḥim* (emissaries who educate Jews about religious piety and Lubavitch worldwide), Goldman asserts that the Internet helps reach isolated Jews and youth on college campuses. Nevertheless, he requires the use of filters to restrict access to profane aspects of the Internet and ensure limited use of the medium for work. Chabad encourages unmediated social gatherings at their centres, such as the 'Hakhel' meetings in 2015–16, named after the biblically mandated practice of holding assemblies in the Temple in Jerusalem every seven years. Chabad leaders describe them as 'a true celebration of Jewish community', owing to their face-to-face reinforcement of camaraderie and unity (Posner 2016).

Analysts of mediation interpret the way that mechanical and electronic technologies shape the relations between human beings, their communities, and their world. Questions arise among researchers as to how interventionist, democratizing, or deluding this process is, in which information is curated and distributed widely by faceless brokers representing the behemoth figure of 'the media'. Many cultural and media studies scholars credit the concept of mediation to translations of German Jewish philosopher Walter Benjamin's essay 'The Work of Art in the Age of Mechanical Reproduction', originally published in German in 1935 (J. Lewis 2002: 92; Mitchell and Hansen 2010: 11). Benjamin addresses the social ramifications of industrially produced paintings on posters and prints, and undoubtedly had in mind the mass production of artful propaganda posters that often took images out of their original context and had them speak an overarching, master narrative. He wrote, 'in the churches and monasteries of the Middle Ages and at the princely courts up to the end of the eighteenth century, a collective reception of paintings did not occur simultaneously, but by graduated and hierarchized *mediation*. The change that has come about is an expression of the particular conflict in which painting was implicated by the mechanical reproducibility of paintings. Although paintings began to be publicly exhibited in galleries and salons, there was no way for the masses to organize and control themselves in their reception' (Benjamin 2007: 235; emphasis added). In the original German, Benjamin used the adjective *vermittelt* to describe art, and to point out that all art is mediated, but that changes in technological reproduction have altered the way in which art is encountered and deciphered.

Benjamin continues to compare this experience to film, which he writes has the dual significance of its technological advancement over the photograph and 'the manner in which, by means of this apparatus, man can represent his environment' (Benjamin 2007: 235). He identified a modern age characterized by media devoted to mechanical reproduction on a mass scale that obviates the need to view the original object or congregate together in localized community. In addition, he theorized that moderns live segregated lives in which they experience the world primarily through media, and that their worldviews are affected through narratives implied or explicitly broadcast in images.

These observations led to claims by cultural critics of the disturbing extent of individuals' alienation, and limitations on community resistance. Although Benjamin was concerned about the danger of authoritarian and nationalistic appropriations of media, the concept of mediation suggested that the interpretation of information for a consuming public was negotiated between public and private interests, rather than imposed on a society. A case in point is the popular mediation of Sholem Aleichem's *Tevye der Milkhiker* (Tevye the Dairyman, 1894) into *Fiddler on the Roof*, first as a Broadway play (1964) and then a movie (1971), in the midst of an ethnic revival during the 1960s and 1970s (Figure 3). Tevye, living in a shtetl in the Russian Empire, grudgingly accepts social changes as his daughters choose spouses, but draws the line when Chava wants to marry outside their faith and community. For American audiences during this tumultuous period, the struggles of the intermarried couple for acceptance implied the need for integration and tolerance as a break with traditional social divisions of the past. The American translation of 'tradition' on the stage was to be faithful to one's ethnic identity while joining in a diverse, progressive society. Whereas the Broadway play and film allow the interfaith couple to reconcile with Tevye and his family, the

Figure 3 Norman Jewison directs
Topol, playing Tevye, on the set of
a Russian shtetl in the film version
of *Fiddler on the Roof* (1971).
AF archive; Alamy stock photo

earlier Yiddish-language dramatic play *Tevye der Milkhiker* (1919) and the movie
Tevye (1939), viewed primarily in Jewish neighbourhoods, would have none of
that. The distraught Chava, abused by her husband's non-Jewish family, aban-
dons the unhappy union and begs forgiveness from her father.

Another difference between *Fiddler on the Roof* and the Yiddish production
on which it was based is the explanation for Tevye's departure from his home.
In the Yiddish movie, the non-Jewish town council invidiously orders him out.
In the play, the culprit is the state, represented by the police loyal to the tsar. To
the American producers of *Fiddler on the Roof*, the anti-authoritarian theme must
have appeared easier to swallow for post-Second World War audiences than representation of the inherent vindictiveness of Christian neighbours. In the Yiddish-
language play and movie, Tevye makes a choice in response to expulsion. Rather
than remain in place waiting for the messiah, he takes the initiative to go to the
Holy Land so that he can live a traditional life basic to his beliefs (Wolitz 1988).
But in *Fiddler on the Roof* his destination is America, and what he will face there
is uncertain and worrying because of the implicit break with tradition and community. It is an omen of further pressures from modernization on community

to be expected that his wife berates the children: 'Stop that! Behave yourself! We're not in America yet!' In the last line, Tevye, who has already capitulated to his children's pressures to accept change, turns to the younger generation and quietly commands, 'Come, children. Let's go', as if he knows that his Old World ties of the shtetl and its representation of community are lost forever (Bronner 1998: 35).

Applying the idea that popular culture is more likely to be mediated than folk or elite processes—that is, produced and channelled through media—cultural critics have noted that the romanticized images of the shtetl in the movie have come to represent Jewish Old World experience in the wake of the popularity of *Fiddler on the Roof*, as well as the roots of Western Jewish cultural values, even though many scholars have pointed out the limited, and often misrepresented, picture of diverse Jewish communities that these images present (Katz 2007; Polonsky 2004; Shandler 2014). The significance of this issue of representation relates to its social and psychological effects on individuals: do non-Jews view Jews differently as a result of this representation, and conversely, do Jews view themselves in a light they did not before? As a further result, do attitudes toward heritage shift—perhaps as some have claimed, from a focus on sustaining religion to a cultural connection to roots in the eastern European Jewish experience (Estraikh and Krutikov 2000; Miron 2000)?

Many approaches contrast representations in media with reality, but to get answers to these questions, several contributors to this volume also explore the way in which mediation is a process in which boundaries between imaginative simulations and social reality become blurred. Following the ideas of French philosopher Jean Baudrillard, cultural critics often interpret theme parks and futuristic urban environments as simulations of reality using popularized images (taken together as an 'imaginary') that have come to represent their own social world with a distinctive ideology, and form what Baudrillard called a 'simulacrum' (Baudrillard 1994; Berger 2016; Kline 2016; Smith 2001). Baudrillard was especially taken with the power of Disneyland in its confined space to produce a global popular culture that can be experienced outside as well as inside its space. Its 'Main Street', the primary gateway to its parks in Florida and California in the United States, in addition to Paris and Tokyo, is both a representation of an imagined pleasant past and a future devoid of ethnic communities; it projects a utopian mass reality based upon a unified racial and environmental profile (Baudrillard 1994: 12–14). Irus Braverman (2013) suggests this model of constructing mediated space is evident for Jewish nationalistic, if not communal, purposes in Jerusalem's Biblical Zoo (officially titled the Tisch Family Zoological Gardens). It began in 1940 as a small children's zoo in the middle of a *ḥaredi* neighbourhood, with a religious mission to re-enact animal scenes from the Bible. Relocating to larger sites, the zoo declared a conservationist purpose by invoking the symbolism of Noah's Ark. The zoo has evolved to become a top tourist destination in Israel with approximately a million visitors. It has been estimated that a third of its visitors come from *ḥaredi* and Palestinian communities in Israel, and zoo directors point to the site as a 'cosmopolitan' multicultural location for coexistence (Braverman 2013: 134–5). Ethnographers, however, have viewed it as an 'intrinsically Jewish space, continuously substantiating the land's own identity' by eternalizing the biblical past in an understanding of the need for a Jewish national home (Braverman 2013: 137–8; El-Haj 2001: 18; see also Zerubavel 1995).

Whether such environments result from the influence of the media (such as thrill rides based upon popular movies and television) or constitute media themselves, by immersing audiences in a sight and sound experience of an eternalized past, is an issue that has generated commentaries on differences in the processes of mediation with different technologies. In *Understanding Media* (1964), Marshall McLuhan famously labelled films a 'hot' medium because viewers did not exert effort to fill in the details of a movie image. He categorized television as 'cool' and potentially more capable of culture change because it requires more effort by the viewer to determine meaning. Critics have found this bifurcation simplistic, but have built on McLuhan's questioning of the medium by which texts and images are broadcast as a message in itself (Jacobs 2011). McLuhan theorized that television would displace community programming in the USA because of the national broadcasting networks, in contrast to the regional reach of radio and the emphasis on locality in print culture. Yet the availability of cable and satellite broadcasting has made possible channels devoted to ethnic-linguistic and special interest groups, including the Jewish Channel and Jewish Life Television. Nonetheless, advocates for media pluralism argue that these corporately owned channels force viewers into passive positions rather than encouraging them to be interactive and activist (Gray 2005). In the twenty-first century, many Jewish organizations have launched Jewish film festivals to draw attention to the use of media to convey ethnic-religious issues that are lost in mainstream commercial productions (Figure 4). The festivals, often aimed at Jewish audiences while being public events, also imply a non-religious identity of Jews, based on their shared cultural, rather than spiritual, interests, that arguably arose in the post-Second World War era with the rise of television and suburbanization (Rocker 2015). Many adherents to a Jewish cultural, rather than religious, identity claim it as a result of immersion in popular culture, with visual representations of expansive, flexible Jewishness in film, television, and art. The move to a cultural identity can be especially clearly discerned in the Internet, often hailed as a triumphant evolution from the 'ghetto mentality' of secluded enclaves, based upon oral tradition, to liberating image or visual culture (Bronner 2011: 398–450; Rosen 2005).

The Internet is often imagined as the ultimate global, socially equalizing, and potentially homogenizing, medium (Zukin 2005: 227–52). Developers hailed the

Figure 4 Carol Kane (*left*) in conversation with award-winning Jewish film-maker Aviva
Kempner at the Washington Jewish Film Festival, in Silver Spring, Maryland, following a 40th-
anniversary screening of *Hester Street* (1975), based on Abraham Cahan's novella *Yekl: A Tale
of the New York Ghetto* (1896). Kane received an Academy Award nomination for best actress,
playing the role of Gitl, a Jewish immigrant who has trouble assimilating to life in New York.
Photograph by Ron Sachs, dpa picture alliance; Alamy stock photo

Internet as vast and open, and ultimately democratizing, because it simultaneously allows users to produce and consume, and therefore accords them more
economic clout, as well social power to shape the medium (Ritzer and Jurgenson 2010). It also is perceived differently from other media needing professional
production, because of the assumption that communication is instantaneous,
participatory, and indeed placeless out in 'cyberspace'. With the medium being
portable and highly individualized, some critics worry that it portends the end of
public space for community gathering and communication (Karppinen 2013; Nie
and Erbring 2000; Sennett 2012). Although giving the primary impression that it
goes beyond the capabilities of print, radio, and television to reach a global audience, the Internet also has facilitated small-scale 'online communities' and simu-
lated 'chat-rooms' for many individuals who do not have access to 'real' ethnic
spaces (Foster 1996; Norris 2004). It is possible with social media to localize as
well as globalize these spaces by delimiting, and even mapping, online members

logged in within a geographical area. Within the Jewish world, Ari Kelman finds that 'The internet has given both younger and more marginal voices a platform for speaking, broadcasting, organizing, and creating their own communities while still participating in larger communal conversations' (Kelman 2010: 78; see also Golan 2015; Roth 2015: 204–6). The question is whether users shape the Internet as a pluralistic medium, or are swayed by either corporate forces or the nature of the technology to become part of a homogeneous, de-ethnicized society.

Radio and arguably newspapers have a more localized connotation, as is evident in the framing of 'Jewish media', such as the Yiddish-language *Jewish Daily Forward* newspaper and WEVD radio station in New York as community outlets. The two are related because the newspaper appropriated the radio station in 1932, after it had been launched in 1927 by the Socialist Party of America. Many accounts of listening to the radio station are filled with nostalgia for a sense of *yidishkeyt* coming through the airwaves to sets placed in cosy kitchens. With the slogan of 'the station that speaks *your* language', it identified itself as an ethnic station intending to spread progressive ideas to a Jewish audience. However, with a sharp decline in the number of Yiddish speakers and the rise of mass-market radio programming, in 1981 the Forward Association sold the station to Salem Media Group, a national corporation that changed the format to Christian content (Kelman 2009: 95–107). The *Jewish Daily Forward* survived by transforming into a Yiddish biweekly and English weekly print edition, and maintains an online presence (Manor 2009). With many Yiddish readers coming from tradition-centred hasidic communities, new Yiddish newspapers have arisen to represent local concerns. Nineteenth-century hasidic leaders usually frowned upon newspaper reading, but as the twentieth-century moral line prohibited the viewing of television and films, newspapers became more important as a medium of communication within hasidic neighbourhoods (Greenbaum 2010).

Analogue and Digital Culture

With the advent of computer-assisted communication in the 1990s, cultural studies scholars posited a division of media into analogue and digital technologies, with cultural ramifications (Maley 2011). It was possible to differentiate between analogue and digital computational devices: analogue technology relies on continuous representations that approximate the source. Promoters touted digital devices as providing perfect, discrete representations (Haugeland 1981). One noticeable difference between digital and analogue devices, however, was the tendency of digital devices to combine forms of transmission that had previously demanded separate gadgets. Smart phones, for instance, included capabilities for video, photographic, audio, and textual broadcasting in a process that media studies scholar Henry Jenkins called 'convergence culture' (2006). This portends not only a risk of information overload in need of curating by media-savvy agents flexing 'cultural capital', who can direct attention to a variety of online identities, including Jewish networks, but it also has the effect of blurring the lines between sender and receiver, documenter and subject, or in entertainment, performer and audience (Zukin 2005: 227–52). It can appear that the instantaneity of the Internet encapsulates, and documents, the world in 'real time'. News, as it is transmitted instantly to a global or local audience, calls for popular response, often in the form of comments arranged in 'threads' (Blank 2013; Frank 2011; Sagan and Leighton 2010).

Electronic transmission via the Internet raises questions about the kind of cultural practice on digital equipment that constitutes social engagement. The association of generations and periods with technology, such as the computer age and the iPod generation, implies that lives are structured by the technology that people own and use. These labels communicate that users harness tools for individualistic purposes; users are digital selectors, in that they can create multiple personas suited for different Web events. People materialize digital power in everyday life by hanging equipment on belts, reminiscent of empowering gun holsters, by opening laptop lids like lifting a treasure chest lid or using a secret spy code unit, and by being called with disruptive sound effects, like an attention-grabbing siren showing off their importance. Whereas going to the mailbox by one's house is an occasional, laboured activity, or what computer geeks derisively call going to get 'snail mail', the cyberculture's instantaneous experience of 'checking' and 'receiving' mail is constant and intrusive, especially when engaging in 'instant messaging', with a rhetoric suggesting instant gratification. Accumulating messages and correspondents is valued.

Being disembodied or immobilized allows for role playing, speech play, visual representation, bricolage, and sometimes anonymity that supports elaboration of the self—and connection to a group—through expressive material. The frame requires some boundaries to manage risks in communication, and although limitations are policed and legislated, a regulatory tradition of folk law has arisen governing transgressions, voiced in the vernacular terms of trolling, flaming, snarking, lurking, spamming, phishing, socking, and thread bumping (Millard 1997; Stivale 1997). In other words, the Internet opens up investigation not just of the texts it produces, but the behaviours it spawns that draw attention to themselves as repeatable *practice*, related to logging on and rhetorically become ingrained into culture as *praxis*—representations for generalizable action such as 'networking' and 'connecting' (Bernstein 1971; Bronner 1988, 2012; Johnson 1999; Lavazzi 2001).

One digital age practice that carries symbolic attributes of *praxis* is blogging, self-publishing texts known as 'posts' on a personal website, diary-style. It has been important in the Jewish world as providing testimonies by individuals of Judaism as a lived religion, and of feelings, or identities, of Jewishness in a mass society. Religious studies scholar Andrea Lieber (2010) noted the use of blogging by Orthodox Jewish women, often at the risk of censure by rabbis. She found that these women, who gained a wide audience for their prosaic accounts of apparently mundane activities, blogged 'to overcome feelings of isolation and frustration with their lives and their communities' (2010: 266). Rather than constituting a form of feminist rebellion, the blogs, with titles such as 'Fancy Schmancy Anxiety Maven', 'Chayyei Sarah', and 'AidelMaidel', Lieber observed, sought social connection for support, even if some followers decoded their self-expression as a call for liberation of women from their communities. Considering the psychology of digital communication in the context of their decidedly analogue, tradition-oriented society, Lieber suggests that the blogging Orthodox women were 'motivated by a therapeutic need through previously unavailable means to "talk through" their internal conflicts in their writing and seek support from sympathetic readers' (2010: 266). The women she interviewed constructed a virtual Jewish community of their own, a *vaybershul* (Yiddish: literally a married women's synagogue, and idiomatically a religious women's gathering space outside the home). Lieber credits the 'blogosphere' of the Internet for making this networking possible for isolated pious women. In their 'talk, without fear of judgement', according to Lieber, the everyday lives of the women are politicized, although politics is not consciously motivating them to blog (2010: 277; see also Grinspan 2005). Lieber suggests, however, that the traditionally observant women mask a political dimension in order to embrace, or even judaize, the digital medium.

Talk of an all-encompassing 'digital age' and 'digital culture' constructs a binary with analogue culture that merits closer scrutiny. In this binary, that privileges the advancement of digitization, a number of structural oppositions are implied between digital and analogue: large-small, new-old, artificial-natural, formal-informal, electronic-manual, and discontinuous-continuous. The implication of this rhetoric is that thinking, digital and analogue, has shifted as the technology and culture have changed. Emblematic of the digital-analogue difference is the clock. The analogue version is understood by the position of hands on a dial that makes reference to the natural occurrence of lines and shadows formed by the sun and read by relative positions. 'O'clock' thus signifies the position of an observer in the centre with 12 o'clock considered straight ahead. The digital clock takes the observer out of the equation. Time is represented in exact numbers or language and can be received anywhere and in any form. Its display is continuous, and does not represent position as much as a code. Analogue is considered more interpersonal and tactile because it can be equated with the process of sensation, which can be perceived directly (Gregory 1970: 162–6; Stewart and Bennett 1991: 24–9). Digital is conceived as artificial and visual, and usually is depicted in alphanumeric symbols or icons framed in mechanistic rectangles in contrast to analogue's naturalistic circles.

Digital comes from the Latin *digitus*, 'finger', suggesting discrete counting, converting real-world information into binary numeric form. Analogue contains reference to the Greek *logos*, 'philosophizing meaning' that comes from the related senses of the word as 'word' (or 'say') and 'reason'; an analogue is an item in relative position to another. Further, the definitional strategy of holding up the face-to-face group and environmental context as vital to community shows analogue thinking because it is relational, emphasizing the immediacy and fragmentation of the social event or performance, whereas use of automation in new technology, including the Internet, is digital because it refers to placeless, faceless, aggregate data (see Bronner 2011: 398–450, 2016; Dégh 1994; Drout 2006; Köstlin and Shrake 1997; Koven 2000). Analogue culture, often attributed to the touch-oriented world of tradition, especially in pre-modern society, derives its meaning from sensory aspects of perception (Stewart and Bennett 1991: 28–32; Bronner 2013). Cultural practices are circumscribed rather than delineated. People will derive significance from face-to-face encounters because people's appearance, what they do, and how they do it will convey an encircled, functional reality (Stewart and Bennett 1991: 29). Thus storytelling in analogue culture is an event defined not just by a text, but by a physical setting and the perceptions between tellers and audience (Georges 1969; Oring 2008).

Digital culture emphasizes the representations of reality, and the outcomes of 'messages'. Thus digital culture may seem to connect more people, but it derives meaning less from social relationships and appearances than from textual similarities. Arguably, in an analogue context, meaning is attached to immediately perceived events within a small group; it is more sensitive to the 'natural', immediate social context. It privileges the ground of turf while digital values the action of surf. Both analogue and digital culture are capable of producing tradition through expression, but they may perceive it differently. Analogue culture might be said to be relational and localized, with a high degree of sensitivity to experience, context, emotions, relationships, and status—within place. Digital culture relies on analytical, inductive thinking that takes observable events to form informational pieces linked in causal chains and categorized into universal criteria (Stewart and Bennett 1991: 41–2; R. A. Cohen 1969: 841–2; Jones 1971). The misplaced perception that the Internet is devoid of culture is a relational, evolutionary outlook, in which digital equals machinery that replaces the human capacity to emote and embody. Viewed operationally or analytically, however, digital culture, as represented by the Internet, is replete with 'construction' and 'assemblage' of multi-layered messages into virtual, rather than natural, reality. One of those constructions is the binary itself, with the presumption that digital is preferred because it is more efficient and more cerebral than physical, leading to a certain illusion that the digital world is culture-free.

Viewing the Internet as daily practice rather than special performance raises the question of whether it structures perceptions outside users' awareness. This line of enquiry includes positing folk belief systems about Internet usage and its supposed global reach, classlessness, democratization, and gender-neutrality (see Poster 2001; Wallace 1999). Expressed beliefs about the Internet are not always consistent. In the rhetoric of transmission, the Internet is frequently characterized in terms of its mass globalization and acquisitive individualism, as well as its freedom and collectivity, for instance, even by its most avid, or addicted, fans. One can look for cultural expectations when logging on that affect the kind of traditions created online. Often negotiating between the expansiveness suggested by being on a *world-wide* web and a desire for more intimate social connections, users operating as secluded individuals often acquire online personas on different sites that accord identities, or simulations of them.

A prominent example of mediated social connection for Jews is the utility, and 'spreadability', of JDate, an online Jewish dating service, within a massifying digital society (Jenkins, Ford, and Green 2013). Founded in 1997 by Jewish digital media entrepreneur Yoav Shapira as a niche dating site modelled on Match.com (Figure 5), JDate announced its service as 'the modern shidduch' (Yiddish: arranged marriage) intended 'to strengthen the Jewish community and ensure Jewish traditions are sustained for generations to come' (JDate 2017). The emphasis on community continues with CEO David Siminoff's claim that its success is due to the effect of 'word-of-mouth' in 'small [Jewish] communities' (OPW interview 2006). The founders imagined that the site would be appealing to Jews looking for mates outside their immediate social circles, or for those disconnected from Jewish networks (Hill 2013). As the site grew, however, non-Jews also could join, but needed to indicate whether they were willing to convert. Reportedly, they were attracted by stereotypes of Jews as wealthy, kind, and family-minded (Hill 2013). Members could also state whether they sought heterosexual or homosexual relationships. By 2014, JDate boasted a roster of 750,000 active users per year around the world, and estimated that 20 per cent of all single Jewish adults had used JDate in a given year (Glassenberg 2014). Jewish civic leaders who had concentrated their efforts on communal institutions such as Jewish summer camps and community centres lauded the site for reversing trends toward intermarriage and the loss of Jewish continuity (Glassenberg 2014).

A more localized approach to connecting Jewish singles in the spirit of the traditional *shadkhan* (Yiddish: matchmaker) is evident in YentaNet, created by a rabbinical student in New York in 2014. Clients meet with volunteer matchmakers who interview them about their backgrounds, rather than rely on online profiles (D. N. Cohen 2016). Even Chabad-Lubavitch operates ChabadMatch.com specifically for members of the group worldwide. Joining enables Chabad *shadkhanim* to access the member's profile and work on arranging *shidukhim* (Hebrew: matches). Acknowledging modern mobility and work environments that often limit opportunities for faith-based courtship, many dating websites have adapted the Internet to facilitate the maintenance of Jewish households, although leaders

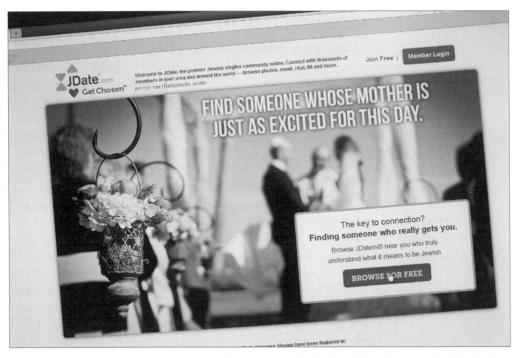

Figure 5 Screenshot of JDate.com (12 March 2014), which self-identifies as a 'Jewish singles community online'. The rhetoric referring to the image of apparently assimilated Jews under a *ḥupah* (wedding canopy) refers to the importance of Judaism passed down in the maternal line and the cultural representation of Jewish mothers pushing their children to marry within the faith. The trademarked phrase 'Get Chosen' has a double meaning of the biblical covenant of God with the Israelites (Deut. 7: 6) and the selection of potential mates online. *Contributed by Maurice Savage; Alamy stock photo*

nonetheless worry that these Internet-generated families will not coalesce in communities.

JDate and YentaNet strike at the heart of Jewish continuity because they address the way that the community will reproduce itself *ledor vador*. They indicate struggles within modern life to temper digital media as a tool for Jewish continuity, rather than a force undermining ethnic-religious identity. The idealization of the Internet as an untethered, unbureaucratized 'commons' suggests that, although it is certainly viewed as postmodern in its transcendence of space and time, it can also be constructed on the model of the premodern community, raising comparisons to McLuhan's 'global village', governed by tradition rather than the nationalistic rule of law. Its folk malleability is one of the Internet's culturally expected, spreadable, and addictive features, although modern folklore also casts a shadow over it because of popular conspiracy beliefs in secretive corporate hegemony and invasions of digital natives' privacy (Bronner 2011: 398–450; Etzioni 2015; Fenster 2008; Prensky 2012).

Massification and Domestication

Central to issues of the effects of media on society covered in this volume is the question whether the expansiveness of popular culture can work for or against maintaining Jewish communitarian ties. The rise of popular culture in the European Renaissance and early modern period resulted, in Nye's view, in 'the incorporation of the majority of the population into society', thus creating pressure to break the bonds of face-to-face community in favour of belonging to the mainstream on a large scale (Nye 1970: 1). The process of popularization at the expense of community accelerated, he reflected, with the mass industrialization and immigration of the late nineteenth century, particularly in North America. In Europe, urbanization and industrialization had increased dramatically, and migrations, often caused by wars, increased the need for transmission of information across borders. Nye thought that, in these social and historical contexts, the cultural standards of the mainstream over time increasingly shifted to the urban middle classes, who had a political as well as an economic interest in diminishing the hold of ethnic-linguistic communities on daily life and creating a commanding, de-ethnicized lingua franca of popular culture. Sociologists Richard A. Peterson and Paul Di Maggio articulated this outlook as a two-part 'massification hypothesis': first, that the forces of modernization had significantly reduced cultural diversity; and second, that an increasingly homogenous mass culture has emerged (1975: 498).

Analysts of massification frequently look to media as a driving force of modernization and gauge media's effects on diverse communities. These include assimilation into mass culture; adaptation of media for communitarian purposes, although possibly in a diminished or changed state; separation or unification of communities by tradition; and the 'domestication' of ethnic-religious groups by the dominant society. The movement of media as consumer entertainment into the home has informed the rise of the concept of domestication to account for changing social interactions associated with media. Domestication implies an attempt at nationalistic control, emasculation, or 'taming' of subcultural activities by external forces (as in the distinction between domestic and public space). It can have a physical connotation, of a private refuge organized around a 'media entertainment centre' (such as the 'TV' or 'family' room and home theatre in the dwelling, displacing the 'living room' or a hearth geared toward conversation), through arrangement and alteration to counter the effects of the boisterous outside world. These kinds of rooms and pastoral simulations of the lawn and backyard have been associated with the placidity, and disconnection, of suburbia (symbolized in the trope of the television-watching 'couch potato'), to which sociologists pointed as a magnet for urban Jews in the second half of the twentieth century, as a sign of socioeconomic success (Adler and Connolly 1960; J. S. Goldstein 2006; Gordon 1973; Rand 2001; Sklare 1979). Suburban enclaves often compensate for lack of public space and neighbourly connection by featuring extra media in the home, including the idea of a television and computer in private bedrooms that enable individualism (Bronner 1983). For cultural studies scholars, who often underscore the influence of social or intellectual construction, the domestic is literally imbued with symbolic messages built into the placement of walls, furniture, and objects. A connotation of domesticity is that it exudes harmony and serenity, and this state is imaginatively supported, or produced, by media believed to avoid conflict and encourage passive consumption. Cultural studies scholars often ask whether this is an illusion that reinforces social constraint.

The connection of domestication with identity borrows from cultural anthropologists, who refer to 'domesticated subjects' produced in the course of European colonial expansion, and some cultural studies scholars view media as a tool of colonialism or, following the Marxist critique of Antonio Gramsci, argue that ruling classes exert political control by convincing the masses to take on the values of popular culture (Lears 1985; Pratt 1992: 4–5; see also Cieraad 2006). In the anthropological view of colonial encounters with non-Western cultures, a master–subject relationship is created out of the contrast of wild natives close to nature—presumed to be backward, isolated, and exotic—with the artifice of modern civilization, which colonizers imagine will refine and tame indigenous people. A focus of cultural conflict is the colonial effort to change home life, because it is out of the public eye and difficult to police. Cultural forms, once taken for granted in an insular society, become forms of resistance as well as maintaining ethnic identity in the domestic sphere. The natives may indeed alter and invent traditions to serve the purposes of sustaining their culture, although they often need to change them from public displays to privatized practices. To enforce the majority view, according to this theory, media becomes a powerful instrument because it transcends the borders of the home and becomes part of daily routine. It creates a standard of modernity by which ethnic-religious groups, depicted as anti-modern or tradition-centred, appear subservient or inadequate.

Applied to Western ethnic groups, the issue becomes one of majority and minority social forces, especially when the exoticism of a minority group is viewed with ambivalence—both as enriching the diversity or spirituality of a society or polluting it and inhibiting progress. In his study of the Amish in American popular imagination, for example, David Weaver-Zercher advocates the use of domestication as an analytic concept because it 'holds promise for describing the ways in which twentieth-century mediators and consumers have "produced" the Amish. Less morally charged than the notion of exploitation, the concept of domestication nonetheless acknowledges the fact that, in the process of being mediated and consumed, the Old Order Amish have also been fashioned and refashioned to function toward particular ends' (Weaver-Zercher 2001: 12–13; see also Bronner 2017; Umble and Weaver-Zercher 2008).

In many countries of Europe and the Americas in which this popularization process emerged, Jews constituted a major subaltern, urbanized ethnic-religious group. Using various forms of Jewish community, therefore, as a prime example of a longstanding minority group, which in most societies is dominated by a majority media-controlling culture, contributors to this volume theorize the negotiation by Jews for access to media in order to become incorporated into national mainstream society, or even resist it, and at the same time intensify their localized community ties. With media becoming central to modern industrial economies as well as politics, questions arise about its role in othering and integrating Jews, and their relation to other minority groups (Cohen and Koch 2007; Goffman 2000; Stratton 2009). The contributors adopt a dual perspective on the way that Jews have been mediated by dominant society and how they have mediated themselves; the two often respond to one another, as evident in Caspar Battegay's enquiry into the influence of Jewish popular music in contemporary culture (Ch. 4) and Pavel Sládek's enquiry into Jewish makers of books in the Late Renaissance (Ch. 1). Some contributors, such as Amy K. Milligan (Ch. 2) and Simon J. Bronner (Ch. 7), analyse how the content and form of media, sometimes in the form of propaganda, racialize and embody Jews as swarthy, bearded primitives, suggesting a binary between 'dirty' or impure Jews and clean dominant whites. Such mediations historicize them as a survival from the ancient past who have not been able to progress, or exoticize them as uncontrolled, unscrupulous 'Orientals' amid more restrained and refined Occidental moderns (Brodkin 2010; Brunotte, Ludewig, and Stähler 2015; E. L. Goldstein 2008; Kalmar and Penslar 2005). Of significance is the way that media form and content generated by Jews speak simultaneously to Jews and to images of Jews created by the dominant society (Bartov 2005; Erdman 1997; Pearl and Pearl 1999; Shandler 2009).

This questioning raises an additional issue about the situation in Israel, in which Jews construct a national mainstream and create a discourse on the broadcasting of Jewish cultural values in a multicultural society. Or at the local level, how is the popularization process affected in urban enclaves such as the predominantly hasidic areas of New York, Israel, and Belgium, in which religious leaders place limits on their group's access to media and yet direct publishing houses to address intra-group divisions? Some of these communications reach a Yiddish-speaking population in outlets around the world and create a transnational identity. Varieties of communications also can mark, if not reinforce, cultural diversity within the broad movements of Judaism, including the role of women, non-whites, and homosexuals. And what about the role of converts, and claimants to their 'lost' Jewish heritage?

If the above thorny situations force examination of localized esoteric practices in which people engage with media in different situations every day, they also connote contextual consideration of a broad set of beliefs that people hold about media technology and its ethnic-religious ties that Jewish studies scholars need to consider. The main one in regard to Jewish culture is that Jews control national media, in an antisemitic innuendo of Jewish diabolical conspiracy (Dershowitz 2011). If we use psychoanalytic theory to analyse this phenomenon, are such accusations actually forms of projective inversion, in which Jews are accused of the very devious control to which they have been subjected (Dundes 2007)? Some historians claim that Jews were attracted to popular media because dominant groups considered the entertainment media industry unsavoury or unprofitable, and that Jews suppressed Jewish content in order to succeed (Benshoff and Griffin 2011: 65; see also Hoberman and Shandler 2003). Others note that the same democratizing process that allows for more Jewish connections, entrepreneurship, and expressions of Jewishness to be made in media also permits more antisemitic content to circulate, as Simon Bronner points out in his chapter on the Jewish joke online (Ch. 7). In any case, in the digital age Jews are not solely responsible for producing Jewish content. When the Jewish subject is 'cool', that is, popularized across groups, Jewish critics often worry that non-Jewish interpreters have domesticated Jews or stripped the texts of their Jewishness (Baskind 2007).

The Jewish editors of *Anne Frank Unbound: Media, Imagination, Memory* (Kirshenblatt-Gimblett and Shandler 2012a), for example, note that Anne Frank never participated in her renown, and yet, through innumerable films, radio and television broadcasts, and websites, she has become a global popular culture phenomenon, sometimes to the chagrin of Jewish critics, who find her Jewish experience muted at the expense of an optimistic coming-of-age story (Figure 6). The present volume shares the attention paid in *Anne Frank Unbound* 'to *mediation*— that is, to what happens when Anne's diary is translated, sung, dramatized, filmed, rendered as a graphic novel or museum exhibition. Her image has also become iconic and widely circulated as a meme, apparently with humorous intent, if not response. With textual labels superimposed over a smiling, carefree countenance, such as 'I am sick of these Jewish jokes, Anne Frankly, they need to stop', the memes have been variously received on the global Internet as offensive or creative references to her youthful idealism, or to her overwrought role in popular culture. Mediation does not simply reproduce or transfer its subject; instead, it produces something related to the source but also different—a new work (or practice or experience)' (Kirshenblatt-Gimblett and Shandler 2012b: 7). Our plan in this volume is to extend the issue of mediation to the effect on, and agency of, Jewish communities and the relationships within them. In presenting a variety of texts, practices, and contexts, we also variously bring into relief processes of popularization, modernization, massification, domestication, and digitization attendant on the ways that Jews engage media and thereby negotiate tradition and modernization; participate in the sweep of mass society; and through various devices and strategies connect to one another in community—face to face in place, in imagination, and in virtual reality.

Figure 6 The non-Jewish Millie Perkins (centre), who portrayed Anne Frank in the Hollywood production of *The Diary of Anne Frank* (1959), meets four Jewish Israeli actors who had portrayed Anne Frank, 20 May 1959. *Photograph by Fritz Cohen, Government Press Office, Israel, licensed under Creative Commons Attribution-Share Alike 3.0 unported licence*

We begin the volume with Pavel Sládek's study of the commercialization of printing in the late Renaissance and the role of Jewish printers in promoting the popularization of reading in the host society's languages, while also providing material to their ethnic-religious communities in Jewish languages. This negotiation of Jewish printers with their host societies and the ethnic-religious communities to which they belonged sets the stage for other media, as technology and its commercialization spread. We speed forward to the twentieth century, when the Jewish Home Beautiful campaign, a spinoff of the elite women's Home Beautiful movement that excluded Jews, mediated a leading role for Jewish women in their command of domestically oriented sabbath observance through books and photographs, as a function of their concern for the maintenance of tradition in a modernizing, massifying world. The first section of the volume, concerning the impact of texts on Jewish communities, closes with an analysis by Tsafi Sebba-Elran of study circles in Israel that shape ancient stories to express modern values. She considers whether these readings, mediated in different ways within Israeli society, form a cultural discourse to incorporate minority voices into an Israeli–Jewish consciousness.

The second section continues the questioning of discourse in broadcast media and oral performances in various locations. Caspar Battegay considers whether theories of a Black Atlantic cultural exchange can be adapted to the Jewish diasporic experience in popular music. He notices the popularity of Jewish subjects and singers within central European popular music, and asks whether this phenomenon suggests the localization or massification of a 'Jewish Atlantic'. Diana Popescu turns to the relationships in Israeli society mediated by the popular television series *Betipul* (Hebrew: In Therapy), about the personal and professional life of an Israeli psychologist. She analyses the appeal of the show in the personal anxieties of patients and doctors, presented weekly as representative of often unstated or underestimated national crises in the Jewish state. We move from Israeli communities, based upon Jewish ingathering, to Madagascar, where in May 2016 an Orthodox rabbinical court convened by a Moroccan rabbi from Canada answered the request of 121 islanders to convert to Judaism. In his essay on the group's discursive strategies to acquire a distinctive Jewish identity, Nathan Devir examines the role of various media, including radio and the Internet, on the converts' ability to gain knowledge about Judaism and form a community. The section closes with Simon J. Bronner's comparative historical and cultural analysis of self-mocking Jewish humour, traditionally performed by immigrant Jews and their descendants for other Jews. He contends that joke-telling at home and on stage often functioned to bond urban Jews navigating in a non-Jewish world; mediated within digital culture, the jokes and the praxis of their self-deprecatory delivery became available to, and even appropriated by, a wider public, with unforeseen consequences for Jewish communities.

The last section of the volume concentrates on digital texts and networks in the twenty-first century. Rachel Leah Jablon opens with a study of shtetls that no longer exist in reality but are reimagined through the Internet, attracting users who seek information about a specific place, and generating Jewish communities based on location. Instead of focusing on a Jewish way of life or Jewish lineage, these online communities, she argues, provide Jews who are searching for a homeland with a place to go, and are surrogates for the real thing. The complex relationship of online spaces with 'real life', especially for Jews who often bemoan a legacy of displacement, is analysed further by Julian Voloj and Anthony Bak Buccitelli in their study of the rise and fall of user-generated Jewish sites in the online virtual world of Second Life. They find significant the rise of Jewish users exploring their virtual worlds with avatars, and the cultural meanings of these representations. Placing Second Life in contemporary context, they analyse yet another Jewish migration from virtual Jewish worlds to the social media of Facebook and Twitter. The section closes within the national context of Hungary, home to the largest Jewish population in eastern central Europe. Anna Manchin credits social media with constructing new Jewish identities for a generation growing up in post-communist Hungary. She theorizes that social media have blurred public and private ways of talking about Jews and Jewishness, and in the process complicated post-communist notions of Hungarian Jews as network, ethnic group, and urban community.

From Budapest to Brooklyn, and from the Holy Land to Hollywood, Jews connect with one another through media, and the practices that produce solidarity and division demand enquiry into rapidly changing ideas of identity, agency, community, and reality. Once restricted to information within earshot, Jews can now instantly view events, and Jewish cultural continuities and differences, across the globe through constantly changing digital technology. For some Jews, this development has not been to the social advantage of community because of the lack of physically being 'in touch' and of real localized space in which to congregate publicly as a group. Despite the availability of mediated 'face time', they might even claim that media has disconnected Jews from what is important— their lived religion. To figure out the consequences and agency of media for Jewish culture, we maintain that our studies need to look at home as well as in the synagogue, and to explore the expansive mediated world for ways in which people and institutions harness, tolerate, or resist media to form their sense of ethnic-religious social belonging within mass society. In the pages, or screens, that follow, we demonstrate these approaches, and the cultural links they reveal that both connect and separate Jews.

References

ADLER, SELIG, and THOMAS E. CONNOLLY. 1960. *From Ararat to Suburbia: The History of the Jewish Community of Buffalo*. Philadelphia.

ALVAREZ, LIZETTE. 2012. 'Synagogue Uses Texting to Reach Young Members'. *Seattle Times* (17 Sept.) <http://www.seattletimes.com/nation-world/synagogue-uses-texting-to-reach-young-members/> (accessed 19 Sept. 2017).

BALINSKA, MARIA. 2008. *The Bagel: The Surprising History of a Modest Bread*. New Haven, Conn.

BARTH, GUNTHER. 1982. *City People: The Rise of Modern City Culture*. New York.

BARTOV, OMER. 2005. *The 'Jew' in Cinema: From* The Golem *to* Don't Touch My Holocaust. Bloomington, Ind.

BASKIND, SAMANTHA. 2007. 'The Fockerized Jew? Questioning Jewishness as Cool in American Popular Entertainment'. *Shofar*, 25: 3–17.

BAUDRILLARD, JEAN. 1994. *Simulacra and Simulation*, trans. Sheila Glaser. Ann Arbor, Mich.

BAUMAN, RICHARD. 2010. ' "It's Not a Telescope, It's a Telephone": Encounters with the Telephone on Early Commercial Sound Recordings'. In Sally Johnson and Thommaso M. Milani, eds., *Language, Ideologies, and Media Discourse: Texts, Practices, Politics*, 252–76. London.

BBYO. 2008. *The Jewish Community's Guide to Understanding Teens: A Compilation of Research on Teen Trends, Tween Trends and a Special Study on the Impact of BBYO on Alumni*. Washington, DC.

BEL, BERNARD, JAN BROUWER, BISWAJIT DAS, VIBODH PARTHASARAHTI, and GUY POITEVIN, eds. 2005. *Media and Mediation*, vol. 1. Thousand Oaks, Calif.

BENJAMIN, WALTER. 2007. 'The Work of Art in the Age of Mechanical Reproduction'. In Walter Benjamin, *Illuminations*, trans. Harry Zohn and ed. Hannah Arendt, 217–52. New York.

BENSHOFF, HARRY M., and SEAN GRIFFIN. 2011. *America on Film: Representing Race, Class, Gender, and Sexuality at the Movies*. 2nd edn. Hoboken, NJ.

BERGER, ARTHUR ASA. 2016. *Understanding American Icons: An Introduction to Semiotics*. New York.

BERNSTEIN, RICHARD. 1971. *Praxis and Action: Contemporary Philosophies of Human Activity*. Philadelphia.

BLANK, TREVOR J. 2013. *The Last Laugh: Folk Humor, Celebrity Culture, and Mass-Mediated Disasters*. Madison, Wisc.

BOORSTEIN, MICHELLE. 2013. 'Should Observing the Jewish Sabbath Mean Switching Off the Internet?' *Washington Post* (13 Sept.) <https://www.washingtonpost.com/local/2013/09/13/121e7118-1bd2-11e3-8685-5021e0c41964_story.html?utm_term=.adb0d8eeccad> (accessed 23 Oct. 2017).

BRAVERMAN, IRUS. 2013. 'Animal Frontiers: A Tale of Three Zoos in Israel/Palestine'. *Cultural Critique*, 85: 122–62.

BRODKIN, KAREN. 2010. *How Jews Became White Folks and What that Says about Race in America*. New Brunswick, NJ.

BRONNER, SIMON J. 1983. 'Suburban Houses and Manner Books: The Structure of Tradition and Aesthetics'. *Winterthur Portfolio*, 18: 61–8.

—— 1988. 'Art, Performance, and Praxis: The Rhetoric of Contemporary Folklore Studies'. *Western Folklore*, 47: 75–102.

—— 1998. *Following Tradition: Folklore in the Discourse of American Culture*. Logan, Utah.

—— 2008. 'The *Chutzpah* of Jewish Cultural Studies'. In Simon J. Bronner, ed., *Jewishness: Expression, Identity, and Representation*, Jewish Cultural Studies 1, 1–28. Oxford.

—— 2011. *Explaining Traditions: Folk Behavior in Modern Culture*. Lexington, Ky.

—— 2012. 'Practice Theory in Folklore and Folklife Studies'. *Folklore*, 123: 23–47.

—— 2013. 'The "Handiness" of Tradition'. In Trevor J. Blank and Robert Glenn Howard, eds., *Tradition in the Twenty-First Century: Locating the Role of the Past in the Present*, 186–218. Logan, Utah.

—— 2016. 'Toward a Definition of Folklore in Practice'. *Cultural Analysis*, 15: 6–27.

—— 2017. 'Popular Culture and Media'. In Simon J. Bronner and Joshua R. Brown, eds., *Pennsylvania Germans: An Interpretive Encyclopedia*, 441–68. Baltimore, Md.

BRUNOTTE, ULRIKE, ANNA-DOROTHEA LUDEWIG, and AXEL STÄHLER, eds. 2015. *Orientalism, Gender, and the Jews: Literary and Artistic Transformations of European National Discourses*. Berlin.

BUHLE, PAUL, and HARVEY PEKAR. 2007. 'Introduction'. In Paul Buhle, ed., *Jews and Popular Culture*, vol. 1: *Movies, Radio, and Television*, pp. ix–xiv. Westport, Conn.

CIERAAD, IRENE, ed. 2006. *At Home: An Anthropology of Domestic Space*. Syracuse, NY.

COHEN, DEBRA NUSSBAUM. 2016. 'Matchmakers Make Comeback in Age of Tinder and JDate'. *Forward* (14 Feb.) <http://forward.com/sisterhood/333501/matchmakers-make-comeback-in-age-of-tinder-and-jdate/> (accessed 23 Oct. 2017).

COHEN, ROSALIE A. 1969. 'Conceptual Styles, Cultural Conflict, and Nonverbal Tests of Intelligence'. *American Anthropologist*, 71: 828–56.

COHEN, SARAH BLACHER, and JOANNE BARBARA KOCH, eds. 2007. *Shared Stages: Ten American Dramas of Blacks and Jews*. Albany, NY.

COHEN, YOEL. 2011. 'Haredim and the Internet: A Hate-Love Affair', in Michael Bailey and Guy Redden (eds.), *Mediating Faiths: Religion and Socio-Cultural Change in the Twenty-First Century*, 63–74. London.

DÉGH, LINDA. 1994. *American Folklore and the Mass Media*. Bloomington, Ind.

DERSHOWITZ, ALAN. 2011. 'Do Jews Control the Media?' *HuffPost* (25 May). http://www.huffingtonpost.com/alan-dershowitz/do-jews-control-the-media_b_753227.html (accessed 24 Oct. 2017).

DESHEN, SHLOMO. 1979. 'The Kol Nidre Enigma: An Anthropological View of the Day of Atonement Liturgy'. *Ethnology*, 18: 121–33.

DINER, HASIA. 2000. *Lower East Side Memories: A Jewish Place in America*. Princeton, NJ.

DORCHAIN, CLAUDIA SIMONE, and FELICE NAOMI WONNENBERG, eds. 2013. *Contemporary Jewish Reality in Germany and its Reflection in Film*. Berlin.

DROUT, MICHAEL D.C. 2006. 'A Meme-Based Approach to Oral Traditional Theory'. *Oral Tradition*, 21: 269–94.

DUNDES, ALAN. 2007. 'The Ritual Murder or Blood Libel Legend: A Study of Anti-Semitic Victimization through Projective Inversion'. In Simon J. Bronner, ed., *The Meaning of Folklore: The Analytical Essays of Alan Dundes*, 382–409. Logan, Utah.

EDWARDS, JASON A. 2017. 'Rhetorical Criticism'. In Simon J. Bronner, ed., *Encyclopedia of American Studies* <http://eas-ref.press.jhu.edu/view?aid=806> (accessed 19 Sept. 2017).

EL-HAJ, NADIA. 2001. *Facts on the Ground: Archaeological Practice and Territorial Self-Fashioning in Israeli Society*. Chicago.

ERDMAN, HARLEY. 1997. *Staging the Jew: The Performance of an American Ethnicity, 1860–1920*. New Brunswick, NJ.

ESTRAIKH, GENNADY, and MIKHAIL KRUTIKOV, eds. 2000. *The Shtetl: Image and Reality. Papers of the 2nd Mendel Friedman International Conference on Yiddish*. Oxford.

ETTINGER, YAIR. 2012. 'Behind the Scenes of the Ultra-Orthodox Anti-Internet Rally'. *Haaretz* (22 May) <http://www.haaretz.com/jewish/news/behind-the-scenes-of-the-ultra-orthodox-anti-internet-rally.premium-1.431796> (accessed 24 Oct. 2017).

ETZIONI, AMITAI. 2015. *Privacy in a Cyber Age: Policy and Practice*. New York.

FENSTER, MARK. 2008. *Conspiracy Theories: Secrecy and Power in American Culture*. Minneapolis, Minn.

FIGEROTH, DANNY. 2007. *Disguised as Clark Kent: Jews, Comics, and the Creation of the Superhero*. New York.

FOSTER, DEREK. 1996. 'Community and Identity in the Electronic Village'. In David Porter, ed., *Internet Culture*, 23–38. New York.

FRANK, RUSSELL. 2011. *Newslore: Contemporary Folklore on the Internet*. Jackson, Miss.

FRIEDMAN, LESTER D. 1987. *The Jewish Image in American Film*. Secaucus, NJ.

FRIEDMAN, URI. 2010. 'People of the E-Book? Observant Jews Struggle with Sabbath in a Digital Age'. *Atlantic* (21 Dec.) <https://www.theatlantic.com/technology/archive/

2010/12/people-of-the-e-book-observant-jews-struggle-with-sabbath-in-a-digital-age/68289/> (accessed 23 Oct. 2017).

GABLER, NEAL. 1988. *An Empire of Their Own: How the Jews Invented Hollywood.* New York.

GEORGES, ROBERT A. 1969. 'Toward an Understanding of Storytelling Events'. *Journal of American Folklore*, 82: 313–28.

GERSHENSON, OLGA. 2008. 'Ambivalence and Identity in Russian Jewish Cinema'. In Simon J. Bronner, ed., *Jewishness: Expression, Identity, and Representation*, Jewish Cultural Studies 1, 175–94. Oxford.

GERSHON, STUART WEINBERG. 1994. *Kol Nidrei: Its Origin, Development and Significance.* Northvale, NJ.

GILMAN, SANDER L. 2004. *Jewish Frontiers: Essays on Bodies, Histories, and Identities.* New York.

GLASSENBERG, SAM Z. 2014. 'JDate Works for Profit—and the Continuity of the Jewish People'. *Forward* (10 Feb.) <http://forward.com/opinion/192429/jdate-works-for-profit-and-the-continuity-of-the/.UvpkOwBcc0o.facebook> (accessed 24 Oct. 2017).

GOFFMAN, ETHAN. 2000. *Imagining Each Other: Blacks and Jews in Contemporary American Literature.* Albany, NY.

GOLAN, OREN. 2015. 'Legitimation of New Media and Community Building among Jewish Denominations in the US'. In Heidi A. Campbell, ed., *Digital Judaism: Jewish Negotiations with Digital Media and Culture*, 125–44. New York.

GOLDMAN, MOSHE. 2017. 'Is the Internet Evil?' *Chabad.org* <http://www.chabad.org/library/article_cdo/aid/675087/jewish/Is-the-Internet-Evil.htm> (accessed 30 Dec. 2017).

GOLDSTEIN, ERIC L. 2008. *The Price of Whiteness: Jews, Race, and American Identity.* Princeton, NJ.

GOLDSTEIN, JUDITH S. 2006. *Inventing Great Neck: Jewish Identity and the American Dream.* New Brunswick, NJ.

GORDON, ALBERT ISAAC. 1973. *Jews in Suburbia.* Westport, Conn.

GRAY, HERMAN S. 2005. *Cultural Moves: African Americans and the Politics of Representation.* Berkeley, Calif.

GREENBAUM, AVRAHAM. 2010. 'Newspapers and Periodicals'. In Gershon David Hundert, ed., *YIVO Encyclopedia of Jews in Eastern Europe* <http://www.yivoencyclopedia.org/article.aspx> (accessed 24 Oct. 2017).

GREGORY, R. L. 1970. *The Intelligent Eye.* New York.

GRINSPAN, IZZY. 2005. 'Blogs Offer Glimpse into Hidden Corners of Orthodox Life'. *Forward* (26 Aug.) <http://forward.com/articles/2669/blogs-offer-glimpse-into-hidden-corners-of-orthodo/> (accessed 24 Oct. 2017).

HAUGELAND, JOHN. 1981. 'Analog and Analog'. *Philosophical Topics*, 12: 213–26.

HILL, LOGAN. 2013. 'At ChristianMingle and JDate, God's Your Wingman'. *Business Week* (25 Feb.): 1.

HING, BILL ONG. 2004. *Defining America through Immigration Policy.* Philadelphia.

HOBERMAN, J., 2003. 'On *The Jazz Singer*'. In J. Hoberman and Jeffrey Shandler, eds., *Entertaining America: Jews, Movies, and Broadcasting*, 77–81. Princeton, NJ.

HOBERMAN, J., and JEFFREY SHANDLER, eds. 2003. *Entertaining America: Jews, Movies, and Broadcasting*. Princeton, NJ.

HOLZEL, DAVID. 2013. 'E-readers to Join Prayer Books at Conservative Convention'. *Washington Jewish Week* (17 July) <http://washingtonjewishweek.com/3700/e-readers-to-join-prayer-books-at-conservative-convention/news/world-news/> (accessed 24 Oct. 2017).

HUTCHINSON, RON. 1996. 'The Jazz Singer'. National Film Preservation Board, *Library of Congress* <https://www.loc.gov/programs/national-film-preservation-board/film-registry/index-of-essays/> (accessed 24 Oct 2017).

JACOBOVICI, SIMCHA, dir. 1998. *Hollywoodism: Jews, Movies and the American Dream*. Waltham, Mass.

JACOBS, ALAN. 2011. 'Why Bother with Marshall McLuhan?' *New Atlantis*, 31: 123–35.

JDATE. 2017. 'About JDate'. *JDate* <https://www.jdate.com/help/about/> (accessed 24 Oct. 2017).

JEFFAY, NATHAN. 2013. 'Kosher Smart Phone Arrives as Ultra-Orthodox Tech Taboo Shifts'. *Forward* (18 Sept.) <http://forward.com/news/184099/kosher-smart-phone-arrives-as-ultra-orthodox-tech/> (accessed 24 Oct 2017).

JENKINS, HENRY. 2006. *Convergence Culture: Where Old and New Media Collide*. New York.

——SAM FORD, and JOSHUA GREEN. 2013. *Spreadable Media: Creating Value and Meaning in a Networked Culture*. New York.

JESSEL, GEORGE. 1928. 'Why I Alternate on Stage and Screen: A Player Who Frankly Avows that Only the Big Money Lured Him into Film Acting'. *Theatre Magazine*, 47, no. 323 (Feb.): 22.

JOHNSON, STEVEN. 1999. *Interface Culture: How New Technology Transforms the Way We Create and Communicate*. New York.

JONES, MICHAEL OWEN. 1971. '(PC + CB) SD (R + I + E) = Hero'. *New York Folklore Quarterly*, 27: 243–60.

KALMAR, IVAN DAVIDSON, and DEREK JONATHAN PENSLAR, eds., 2005. *Orientalism and the Jews*. Waltham, Mass.

KARPPINEN, KARI. 2013. *Rethinking Media Pluralism*. New York.

KATZ, STEVEN T. 2007. *The Shtetl: New Evaluations*. New York.

KELMAN, ARI Y. 2009. *Station Identification: A Cultural History of Yiddish Radio in the United States*. Berkeley, Calif.

——2010. *The Reality of the Virtual: Looking for Jewish Leadership Online*. AVI CHAI Foundation <http://www.bjpa.org/Publications/details.cfm?PublicationID=12881> (accessed 24 Oct. 2017).

KEMBER, SARAH, and JOANNA ZYLINSKA. 2015. *Life after New Media: Mediation as a Vital Process*. Cambridge, Mass.

KIRAN, ASLE H. 2015. 'Four Dimensions of Technological Mediation'. In Robert Rosenberger and Peter-Paul Verbeek, eds., *Postphenomenological Investigations: Essays on Human-Technology Relations*, 123–40. Lanham, Md.

KIRSHENBLATT-GIMBLETT, BARBARA, and JEFFREY SHANDLER, eds. 2012a. *Anne Frank Unbound: Media, Imagination, Memory*. Bloomington, Ind.

—— 2012b. 'Introduction: Anne Frank, the Phenomenon'. In Barbara Kirshenblatt-Gimblett and Jeffrey Shandler, eds. *Anne Frank Unbound: Media, Imagination, Memory*, 1–24. Bloomington, Ind.

KLINE, KIP. 2016. *Baudrillard, Youth, and American Film: Fatal Theory and Education*. Lanham, Md.

KÖSTLIN, KONRAD, and SCOTT M. SHRAKE. 1997. 'The Passion for the Whole: Interpreted Modernity or Modernity as Interpretation'. *Journal of American Folklore*, 110: 260–76.

KOVEN, MIKEL J. 2000. '"Have I Got a Monster for You!" Some Thoughts on the Golem, "The X-Files", and the Jewish Horror Movie'. *Folklore*, 111: 217–30.

LAVAZZI, TOM. 2001. 'Communication On(the)line'. *South Atlantic Review*, 66: 126–44.

LEARS, T. J. JACKSON. 1985. 'The Concept of Cultural Hegemony: Problems and Possibilities'. *American Historical Review*, 90: 567–93.

LEWIS, AMANDA. 2012. 'Texting During Yom Kippur Services? How One L.A. Rabbi is Bringing Social Media to His Synagogue'. *LA Weekly* (1 Oct.) <http://www.laweekly.com/arts/texting-during-yom-kippur-services-how-one-la-rabbi-is-bringing-social-media-to-his-synagogue-2374255> (accessed 24 Oct. 2017).

LEWIS, JEFF. 2002. *Cultural Studies: The Basics*. London.

LIBO, KENNETH, and IRVING HOWE. 1984. *We Lived There Too: In Their Own Words and Pictures: Pioneer Jews and the Westward Movement of America, 1630–1930*. New York.

LIEBER, ANDREA. 2010. 'Domesticity and the Home (Page): Blogging and the Blurring of Public and Private among Orthodox Jewish Women'. In Simon J. Bronner, ed., *Jews at Home: The Domestication of Identity*, Jewish Cultural Studies 2, 257–86. Oxford.

LIPMAN, STEVE. 2011. 'For Many Orthodox Teens, "Half-Shabbos" Is a Way of Life: Texting on Saturdays Seen as Increasingly Common "Addiction"'. *New York Jewish Week* (22 June) <http://jewishweek.timesofisrael.com/for-many-orthodox-teens-half-shabbos-is-a-way-of-life/> (accessed 24 Oct. 2017).

MACHIN, DAVID, and ANDREA MAYR. 2015. *How To Do Critical Discourse Analysis: A Multimodal Introduction*. Los Angeles.

MALEY, COREY J. 2011. 'Analog and Digital, Continuous and Discrete'. *Philosophical Studies*, 155: 117–31.

MANOR, EHUD. 2009. *Forward: The Jewish Daily Forward (Forverts) Newspaper: Immigrants, Socialism and Jewish Politics in New York, 1890–1917*. Brighton.

MASSA, MARK. 2004. '"As if in Prayer": A Response to "Catholicism as American Popular Culture"'. In Margaret O. Steinfels, ed., *American Catholics, American Culture: Tradition and Resistance*, 112–18. Lanham, Md.

MERWIN, TED. 2006. *In Their Own Image: New York Jews in Jazz Age Popular Culture*. New Brunswick, NJ.

—— 2015. *Pastrami on Rye: An Overstuffed History of the Jewish Deli*. New York.

MILLARD, WILLIAM B. 1997. 'I Flamed Freud: A Case Study in Teletextual Incendiarism'. In David Porter, ed. *Internet Culture*, 145–60. New York.

MILLIGAN, AMY K. 2016. *Hair, Headwear, and Orthodox Jewish Women*. Lanham, Md.

MIRON, DAN. 2000. *The Image of the Shtetl and Other Studies of Modern Jewish Literary Imagination*. Syracuse, NY.

MITCHELL, W. J. T., and MARK B. N. HANSEN. 2010. *Critical Terms for Media Studies*. Chicago.

MOORE, R. LAURENCE. 1994. *Selling God: American Religion in the Marketplace of Culture*. New York.

MORAWSKA, EWA T. 1996. *Insecure Prosperity: Small-Town Jews in Industrial America, 1890–1940*. Princeton, NJ.

MORLEY, DAVID. 2005. 'Media'. In Tony Bennett, Lawrence Grossberg, and Meaghan Morris, eds., *New Keywords: A Revised Vocabulary of Culture and Society*, 211–14. Malden, Mass.

MURPHY, PAUL L. 1964. 'Sources and Nature of Intolerance in the 1920s'. *Journal of American History*, 51: 60–76.

MUSSER, CHARLES. 2011. 'Why Did Negroes Love Al Jolson and *The Jazz Singer*? Melodrama, Blackface and Cosmopolitan Theatrical Culture'. *Film History*, 23: 196–222.

NIE, NORMAN H., and LUTZ ERBRING. 2000. *Internet and Society: A Preliminary Report*. Stanford Institute for the Quantitative Study of Society <http://www2.uca.es/HEURESIS/documentos/Preliminary_Report.pdf> (accessed 24 Oct. 2017).

NORRIS, PIPPA. 2004. 'The Bridging and Bonding Role of Online Communities'. In Philip N. Howard and Steve Jones, eds., *Society Online: The Internet in Context*, 31–42. Thousand Oaks, Calif.

NYE, RUSSEL. 1970. *The Unembarrassed Muse: The Popular Arts in America*. New York.

OPW Interview 2006. 'Spark Networks CEO, David Siminoff—OPW Interview'. *Internet Dating Investments* (20 Oct.) <http://www.onlinepersonalswatch.com/internet-datinginvestments/2006/10/spark-networks-ceo-david-siminoff-opw-interview.html> (accessed 26 Sept. 2017).

ORING, ELLIOTT. 2008. 'Legendry and the Rhetoric of Truth'. *Journal of American Folklore*, 121: 127–66.

PEARL, JONATHAN, and JUDITH PEARL. 1999. *The Chosen Image: Television's Portrayal of Jewish Themes and Characters*. Jefferson, NC.

PEARSE, HOLLY A. 2008. 'As *Goyish* as Lime Jell-O? Jack Benny and the American Construction of Jewishness'. In Simon J. Bronner, ed., *Jewishness: Expression, Identity, and Representation*, Jewish Cultural Studies 1, 272–90. Oxford.

——— 2014. 'Negative Interfaith Romances and the Reassertion of Jewish Difference in Popular Film'. In Simon J. Bronner, ed. *Framing Jewish Culture: Boundaries and Representations*, Jewish Cultural Studies 4, 217–40. Oxford.

PETERSON, RICHARD A. and PAUL DI MAGGIO. 1975. 'From Region to Class, the Changing Locus of Country Music: A Test of the Massification Hypothesis'. *Social Forces*, 53: 497–506.

POLL, SOLOMON. 1969. *The Hasidic Community of Williamsburg: A Study in the Sociology of Religion*. New York.

POLONSKY, ANTONY, ed. 2004. *The Shtetl: Myth and Reality*, Polin Studies in Polish Jewry, 17. Oxford.

POSNER, MENACHEM. 2016. 'Multifaceted Montreal Campaign Inspires Jewish Gatherings'. *Chabad.org* (25 Feb.) <http://www.chabad.org/news/article_cdo/aid/3240709/jewish/Multifaceted-Montreal-Campaign-Inspires-Jewish-Gatherings.htm> (accessed 19 Sept. 2017).

POSTER, MARK. 2001. 'Cyberdemocracy: The Internet and the Public Sphere'. In David Trend, ed., *Reading Digital Culture*, 259–71. Malden, Mass.

PRATT, MARY LOUISE. 1992. *Imperial Eyes: Travel Writing and Transculturation*. London.

PRAWER, S. S. 2007. *Between Two Worlds: The Jewish Presence in German and Austrian Film, 1910–1933*. New York.

PRENSKY, MARC. 2012. *From Digital Natives to Digital Wisdom: Hopeful Essays for 21st Century Learning*. Thousand Oaks, Calif.

RAND, ROBERT. 2001. *My Suburban Shtetl: A Novel About Life in a Twentieth-Century Jewish American Village*. Syracuse, NY.

RAPHAELSON, SAMSON. 1935. *The Jazz Singer*. New York.

—— 2003. 'How I Came to Write "The Jazz Singer"'. In J. Hoberman and Jeffrey Shandler, eds., *Entertaining America: Jews, Movies, and Broadcasting*, 82–3. Princeton, NJ.

REUTERS. 2014. 'WhatsApp Founder Jan Koum's Jewish Rags-to-Riches Tale'. *Forward* (20 Feb.) <http://forward.com/news/world/193103/whatsapp-founder-jan-koums-jewish-rags-to-riches-t/> (accessed 26 Sept. 2017).

RITZER, GEORGE, and NATHAN JURGENSON. 2010. 'Production, Consumption, Prosumption: The Nature of Capitalism in the Age of the Digital "Prosumer"'. *Journal of Consumer Culture*, 10: 13–236.

ROCKER, SIMON. 2015. 'So What Is "Cultural" Judaism?' *Jewish Chronicle* (16 July) <https://www.thejc.com/lifestyle/features/so-what-is-cultural-judaism-1.67699> (accessed 24 Oct. 20170.

ROGIN, MICHAEL. 1996. *Blackface/White Noise: Jewish Immigrants in the Hollywood Melting Pot*. Berkeley, Calif.

ROMEYN, ESTHER. 2008. *Street Scenes: Staging the Self in Immigrant New York, 1880–1924*. Minneapolis, Minn.

ROSEN, CHRISTINE. 2005. 'The Image Culture'. *New Atlantis*, 10: 27–46

ROTH, LAURENCE. 2015. 'Networks'. In Laurence Roth and Nadia Valman, eds., *The Routledge Handbook of Contemporary Jewish Cultures*, 195–210. London.

SAGAN, PAUL, and TOM LEIGHTON. 2010. 'The Internet and the Future of News'. *Daedalus*, 139: 119–25.

SCHLÖR, JOACHIM. 2014a. 'Robert Gilbert, Hermann Leopoldi and the Role of Languages Between Exile and Return'. *Prezladaniec: A Journal of Translation Studies*, 29: 157–78.

—— 2014b. 'Robert Gilbert (1899–1978): Songwriter and Translator of Musical Comedy'. *Transatlantic Perspectives* (1 Feb.) <http://www.transatlanticperspectives.org/entry.php?rec=149> (accessed 24 Oct. 2017).

—— 2016. 'Werner Richard Heymann in Hollywood: A Case Study of German–Jewish Emigration after 1933 as a Transnational Experience'. *Jewish Culture and History*, 17: 115–32.

SCHMALZBAUER, JOHN. 2010. 'Popular Culture'. In Philip Goff, ed., *The Blackwell Companion to Religion in America*, 254–75. Malden, Mass.

SENNETT, RICHARD. 2012. *Together: The Rituals, Pleasures, and Politics of Cooperation*. New Haven, Conn.

SHANDLER, JEFFREY. 2009. *Jews, God, and Videotape: Religion and Media in America*. New York.

SHANDLER, JEFFREY. 2014. *Shtetl: A Vernacular Intellectual History*. New Brunswick, NJ.

SKLARE, MARSHALL. 1979. *Jewish Identity on the Suburban Frontier: A Study of Group Survival in the Open Society*. 2nd edn. Chicago.

SMITH, M.W. 2001. *Reading Simulacra: Fatal Theories for Postmodernity*. Albany, NY.

STEWART, EDWARD C., and MILTON J. BENNETT. 1991. *American Cultural Patterns*, rev. edn. Yarmouth, Maine.

STIVALE, CHARLES J. 1997. 'Spam: Heteroglossia and Harassment in Cyberspace'. In David Porter, ed., *Internet Culture*, 133–44. New York.

STRADOMSKI, WIESŁAW. 1989. 'The Jewish Cinema in Inter-War Poland'. *Polish Art Studies*, 10: 167–77.

STRATTON, JON. 2009. *Jews, Race and Popular Music*. Farnham.

STRAUSS, SUSAN, and PARASTOU FEIZ. 2013. *Discourse Analysis: Putting Our Worlds into Words*. New York.

TEMAN, ELLY. 2008. 'The Red String: The Cultural History of a Jewish Folk Symbol'. In Simon J. Bronner, ed., *Jewishness: Expression, Identity, and Representation*, Jewish Cultural Studies 1, 29–57. Oxford.

TRACHTENBERG, ALAN. 1982. *The Incorporation of America: Culture and Society in the Gilded Age*. New York.

UMBLE, DIANE ZIMMERMAN, and DAVID WEAVER-ZERCHER, eds. 2008. *The Amish and the Media*. Baltimore, Md.

VERBEEK, PETER-PAUL. 2005. *What Things Do: Philosophical Reflections on Technology, Agency, and Design*. University Park, Penn.

WALLACE, PATRICIA. 1999. *The Psychology of the Internet*. Cambridge.

WEAVER-ZERCHER, DAVID. 2001. *The Amish in the American Imagination*. Baltimore, Md.

WEBER, DONALD. 2003. 'Accents of the Future: Jewish American Popular Culture'. In Hana Wirth-Nesher and Michael P. Kramer, eds., *The Cambridge Companion to Jewish American Literature*, 129–48. Cambridge.

WEISS, SHAYNA. 2016. '*Frum* with Benefits: Israeli Television, Globalization, and *Srugim*'s American Appeal'. *Jewish Film & New Media: An International Journal*, 4: 68–89.

WEISSBACH, LEE SHAI. 2015. *The Synagogues of Kentucky: Architecture and History*. Lexington, Ky.

WHITFIELD, STEPHEN J. 2008. 'Black Like Us'. *Jewish History*, 22: 353–71.

WOLITZ, SETH L. 1988. 'The Americanization of Tevye or Boarding the Jewish *Mayflower*'. *American Quarterly*, 40: 514–36.

YOUNGER, ARYEH. 2013. 'Texting and the Power of "Half Shabbat"'. *Forward* (20 June) <http://forward.com/opinion/178988/texting-and-the-power-of-half-shabbat/> (accessed 23 Oct. 2017).

ZERUBAVEL, YAEL. 1995. *Recovered Roots: Collective Memory and the Making of Israeli National Tradition*. Chicago.

ZUKIN, SHARON. 2005. *Point of Purchase: How Shopping Changed American Culture*, rev. edn. New York.

ZURAWIK, DAVID. 2003. *The Jews of Prime Time*. Lebanon, NH.

PART I

The Impact of Texts On, and In, Jewish Community

Sixteenth-Century Jewish Makers of Printed Books and the Shaping of Late Renaissance Jewish Literacy

PAVEL SLÁDEK

SOON AFTER ITS EMERGENCE in the mid-fifteenth century, the medium of printed books was introduced into Jewish culture. Around 200 Hebrew incunabula are known to exist, the oldest being dated to the 1460s (Freimann and Marx 1967–9; Offenberg 2004: p. xlv). Beginning in the 1480s with the emergence of presses run by different members of the Jewish Soncino family in Italy and elsewhere, a wide variety of genres appeared in print. The Soncino editions were distinguished among printers at the time by both the accuracy and beauty of their typefaces (Habermann 1978: 13–96). By 1500 the technology of hand-press printing had been perfected, and did not undergo any substantial changes until the beginning of the nineteenth century (Gaskell 1985: 2; McKerrow 1962: 7). The new medium became widespread among the Jews by the 1520s at the latest, with the emergence of the Venetian firm of Daniel Bomberg. During this period the printed book became an object of everyday life, not limited to the intellectual elite, as indicated by the rich production of locally marketable liturgical works in Prague (Sixtová 2012a: 33).

As a cultural phenomenon, the early printed book must be seen as a radical innovation in the age of complex cultural transformations both within and outside Jewish society (Eisenstein 2002). Indeed, the 'knowledge explosion' spurred by the rise of the printing press, according to historian David Ruderman (2010: 14–15), was a key factor in the formation of early modern Jewish cultural history, in addition to accelerated mobility, a heightened sense of communal cohesiveness, a crisis of rabbinical authority, and a blurring of religious identities. Speaking of the printing press, Ruderman builds on the seminal interpretation of Elizabeth Eisenstein, who described the printed book as a major agent of cultural change during this period (Eisenstein 1979).

In his synthetic study, Ruderman investigated the impact of the new medium. Building on the magisterial research of Elchanan Reiner (1997, 2000), he pointed especially to the break between the fluid oral and scribal tradition on the one hand and the hegemony of printed text on the other, to the relation between the printed book and the teacher's authoritative capacity, and to the emergence of a new textual corpus, merging Ashkenazi and Sephardi traditions (Ruderman 2010: 99–103). Important synthetic accounts usually serve in academic research as nodal points, inviting further elaboration. This study thus accepts Ruderman's résumé but follows a different trajectory. While Ruderman wrote about the impact of the 'printed book' (99) and 'presses' (102), this essay examines the people who operated the presses and contributed, by their effort or resources, to the making of the Jewish printed book. It outlines the inner dynamics of early printed book production, concentrating on books printed in Hebrew characters by both Jewish- and Christian-owned presses from their beginning until the 1620s, the second major period in the history of the printing of Hebrew books. The social and economic aspects of Hebrew book production in this period raise an important question, often omitted from historical surveys of books and printing: how did Hebrew printing sustain itself in spite of the extremely fragile economy that underlay it? From the outset, early Hebrew printed books functioned not only as material carriers of the text, but also as an important platform for expressing the personalities of those who were involved in the production of the text and the book in the form of title pages, colophons, and various notes: living authors, owners of the model manuscripts, editors, compositors, 'correctors' (a term used from the sixteenth to the nineteenth centuries for a printer's employee who marks corrections, comparable to a modern proofreader), publishers, sponsors, and authors of approbations. More often than not these roles overlapped, and the men and women involved in book production played several roles at once.[1]

In this essay, I highlight the optimism of a newly constituted, albeit loosely delimited, group within Jewish society—Jewish makers of the printed book. The paratextual evidence (Genette 1997) shows that this group functioned as a collaborative web or a community, determined 'to print many books without end and bring merit to many people', as many of the sixteenth-century printers declared in their books. I argue that their confessions should not be taken only as literary figures, but that they document the authentic enthusiasm of all those involved in the production of books. The driving force of their optimism was their awareness that they were giving direction to the cultural process and acting as agents of cultural change by reshaping the Jewish textual corpus.

Manuscript versus Printed Book: Some Economic Considerations

Hebrew manuscripts originated in two basic ways. Either a professional (or semi-professional) scribe was hired by an individual customer to produce a copy of an existing text, or individual scholars or students copied texts for themselves (an author writing down a new text being a variant of the latter). In both cases, the precondition was the availability of the model manuscript, based on the owner's consent to the reproduction of the material. In both cases the newly produced copy was designated for a specific customer—a reader who wished to own a copy and who either paid the scribe or invested his time and effort if he himself served as the copyist (cases when a scribe produced a copy intending to find a buyer later were rare). As codicologist Malachi Beit-Arié pointed out, in comparison to the Christian environment, in which monastic scriptoria, cathedral schools, or the universities and aristocratic and ecclesiastical collectors represented the institutionalized framework for production, dissemination, and preservation of books, 'medieval Hebrew books were not produced, preserved or disseminated by any establishment or upon its initiative . . . but were privately and individually produced and consumed' (Beit-Arié 1993: 81).

Although especially in the first half of the fifteenth century there is evidence of serial production of manuscript copies of some frequently used texts in the university scriptoria (Richardson 1999: 6–7) or commercial urban lay ateliers (Beit-Arié 1993: 81; Rouse and Rouse 1990), Hebrew manuscripts were only rarely connected with commercial speculation, while for the production of the printed book such speculation was essential. Both manuscripts and printed books were always regarded as valuable objects that could be resold, bequeathed, or used as pledges. However, unlike a manuscript, the serial production of a text in the form of a printed book presupposed a body of anonymous customers. From a slightly different perspective, historian Shlomo Berger speaks of the 'imaginary, anonymous, average reader', in his groundbreaking study of early modern Yiddish paratexts (Berger 2013: 4). While the manuscript typically originated only as a result of pre-existing demand, the printed book, being a subject of an intricate social game of supply and demand, was a typical modern commodity, associated with the necessity of initial commercial speculation, preliminary calculation, and subsequent marketing, including new advertising techniques.

The Title Page

The most significant new feature resulting from the character of the printed book as a commercial commodity was the emergence of a title page. Like manuscripts, early printed books did not have any title pages. Information about the book (or a section of it) concentrated on the circumstances of its origin rather than on the actual text, and appeared in the so-called colophon (literally a final stroke), often indicating the names of the scribe and those who commissioned the copy, the locality, the date, and other details (Beit-Arié 1993: 12). The colophon, which appeared inconsistently in manuscripts, regularly appeared in Jewish printed books until well into modernity. Title pages, in contrast, started to emerge in the early sixteenth century, assuming new functions compared to colophons. Primitive title pages consisted of a blank leaf with just a couple of lines recording the title and printer. The earliest extant Hebrew book with a title page (albeit a simple one) was *Sefer haroke'aḥ* by Elazar ben Yehudah of Worms (*c.*1176–1238), printed in Fano by Gershom Soncino in 1504/5 (Spiegel 2014: 6 and 98).

Besides indicating the year, the place of printing, and the name of the printer, which it shared with the colophon, the title page gradually assumed the function of informing the potential buyer about the contents of the book, attracting his or her attention and thus helping to sell the book. Intricate artistic frames and borders decorated the title page to make it visually appealing. The most common form of title page became the architectural motif of a gate, often with the self-referential quotation from Psalm 188: 20: 'This is the gate of the Lord, into which the righteous shall enter.'

Living authors in particular were often praised in the most flowery style. For example, Rabbi Yosef Caro was characterized on the title page of the Venetian *editio princeps* of his abbreviated legal code, the *Shulḥan arukh*, as 'a luminary, marvel of the generation, accomplished scholar . . . whose Torah shines like the light of the day in the city of Safed, the springs of his teachings are widely disseminated, his name is known in Judah and Israel' (Caro 1565: 1*a*).

The publishers would often emphasize (or even overstate) the usefulness of a book for the widest possible reading public, going far beyond the declared intention of the author. Thus, in his introduction, Caro presented his *Shulḥan arukh* as a tool intended to facilitate the orientation of the wider, non-scholarly Jewish public in halakhic issues, so that 'when anybody from the people of Israel asks a scholar about a law, he shall not stutter' (Caro 1565: 2*a*). However, the publishers of the Venetian *editio princeps* (perhaps the famous editor Me'ir Parenzo) promised on the title page that 'anybody seeking the Lord will find what he is looking for with ease—each and every law' (Caro 1565: 1*a*). In a note at the end of the first volume, the Italian physician and scholar Avraham Menahem Porto even described the *Shulḥan arukh* as 'an abbreviation of the halakhah . . . based on which all Jewish households, both unlearned and learned, shall issue judgements, restrictions, and permissions related to alimentary laws' (Caro 1565: 132*a*). Not surprisingly, the idea of taking decision-making in practical halakhah out of the hands of professional scholars caused a great stir and strong criticism of Caro's codification by central-eastern European rabbis, although other factors were also involved (Davis 2004: 122–6; Ruderman 2010: 99–101).

In other instances, the title page served as a space for advertising the book to the buyer in the same way as products were advertised in a marketplace. Thus the publisher of the 1491 edition of David Kimhi's Hebrew lexicon *Sefer hashorashim* (*Book of Roots*) calls on his customers on the title page:

This day is a day of joy, and we hurry towards you, O people! My voice calls to the experienced as well as to novices of wisdom, to old, young and venerable, to men and women: Take your silver, heap your gold! There is no end to the knowledge that you may find in these *Roots*, newly arranged, while all the books printed so far on the topic are bland and say nothing, like pottage of lentils [Gen. 25: 34]. (Kimhi 1491: 167*b*; cf. Spiegel 2014: 97)

The title page also featured the name of the publisher or the printing house, which were not often identical. Especially in Italy in the second half of the sixteenth century, publishers would work in workshops they rented from Christian owners. The marketing practices used by sixteenth-century printers were often truly modern. For example, they tried to create brand loyalty in the prospective customer by copying decorative elements. One such example is the symbol of the Jerusalem temple, used from 1545 as a printer's mark by the famous Giustiniani press in Venice. The firm closed in 1552 after having published over sixty titles, including the Babylonian Talmud. Its reputation was so high that numerous printers imitated the mark and used it for decades, apparently trying to make their own books resemble those from Guistiniani's press. Olga Sixtová found that two different printing blocks with the same motif were used in Prague. One was used by the Gersonides workshop between 1569 and the 1650s (cf. Isserles 1569; Ya'ari 1971: no. 40). The other was used at different times by the presses of Schedel, Heida, and Bak (e.g. Yafeh 1603; cf. Ya'ari 1971: nos. 40 and 50; Heller 2008: 44–53). The same motif also appeared in some of the Lublin prints until 1622, while Eli'ezer ben Yitshak Ashkenazi of Lublin used it in the books he published in Constantinople and Safed, carrying with him a block of Prague provenance.[2]

Shaping the Standard Text

A long-outdated bibliographical assumption is that, compared to manuscripts, the printed book offered a text that was identical in all copies of a specific edition. With better understanding of hand-press technology it has become clear that the process of book production, as practised in the early modern period, allowed for intentional differences between different copies of the same edition (McKitterick 2003: 102–11). Most often, the diversity among the individual copies resulted from the printers' reluctance to make last-minute corrections, since in order to avoid wasting time the corrector read the proofs while the workers were still printing (cf. Heller 2008: 267). By the time the forme was finally dismantled and the composition corrected, some of the sheets, including the original errors, had already been printed (Rivkind 1950) and later sold. At other times, the printer experimented with different versions of the layout. Thus, for example, it is possible to differentiate among the extant copies of the Prague edition of *Pane'ah raza* (by Yitshak ben Shimshon, 1607) two sets with slightly different title pages and featuring differences in the composition of the first quire.

The occasional variation among copies at the micro-level notwithstanding, the early prints manifested a hitherto unprecedented degree of uniformity. More importantly, early modern standardization must be seen as a multilayered process of give and take between the new medium and both its producers and users. Much has been written about the formation and acceptance of the talmudic page (e.g. Heller 2008: 92–105). However, the notion of standardization must be studied primarily as a cultural phenomenon, reflecting the changing attitude of the reader to the text. Speaking of the Talmud page, it is thus less important that ultimately all editions tend to have the same layout; the true measure of growing standardization is the fact that the post-Bomberg and Guistiniani editions started indicating the Bomberg edition's foliation in their margins, even if the layout was for some reason different and thus the foliation could not be identical (Heller 2008: 99). In addition, the foliation of this edition was used as a reference for isolated Talmud quotations in other texts, as is the case of one of the sermons of Judah Loew ben Betsalel of Prague, known as the Maharal (c.1525–1609) (Maharal 1593). The implicit idea of a reference edition had a far-reaching impact. Readers, especially those of scholarly texts, began to think about the text differently. For the first time, the modern technique of referencing became possible, because the author could presume that his reader had access to the identical edition of the text. Thus the Prague Jewish historian David Gans (1541–1613) often indicated a specific folio or page number of his printed Jewish and even non-Jewish sources in his chronicle *Tsemaḥ david* (Gans 1592).

Writing about Yehudah Moscato, Adam Shear (2012: 130) applied to the Jewish environment the notion of information overload, used by the historian Ann Blair with regard to the early modern period (Blair 2003). Adam Shear speaks of a sense on the part of contemporaries that there was too much to read, too much to learn. The rise of new encyclopedias, bibliographies, lexicons, and dictionaries seems designed in part to transmit all this new knowledge and in part to manage the flow of information (Shear 2012: 130).

To the newly emerging genres enumerated by Adam Shear must be added a number of literary and typographic tools enabling a quick search for information: tables of contents, surveys, marginal notes, and also the structured layout of the text. Some of these tools were located within the volume, both in the margins and before or after the main text. The early prints inherited their basic elements from late medieval manuscripts (McKitterick 2003: 33–4), but in the era of the hand-press they never became the norm, although after the mid-sixteenth century they appeared more often. Sometimes the reference tools appeared as independent volumes, but they were inseparably linked with not just a specific text but a specific edition, as in the case of *Mareh kohen* (Katz 1589), which is an index of biblical verses in the Zohar according to the Cremona edition of 1558 (Katz 1589: 2b, line 3) (Sládek 2016).

The presence of various reference tools was seen by the printers as an added value and was often advertised on the title page. Thus the editor of the responsa of Asher ben Yehi'el (c.1250–1327, Rosh) declared: 'a table of contents [*mareh makom*] was added to this print because I, Me'ir ben Ya'akov Parenzo, saw it as a great benefit to know each and every law and its source' (Asher ben Yehiel 1552: 1*a*).

All the reference tools were linked to the process of standardization and had a common function: to enable the user of the book to read in a way that was not consecutive but fragmentary, allowing him or her to search for information (cf. Berger 2013: 4 and n. 14). Such reading would necessarily be individualized, driven by the specific interest of each reader and thus excluding group study. At the same time, the early modern reader entered into virtual dialogue with many more authors than ever before and often communicated with a great number of living ones. The editors and publishers, who were responsible for including the reference tools within the composition or for appending them to the main text, fostered a new practice of reading. They equipped their reader with the typographic and textual devices that enabled him or her to consume a larger quantity of texts than before.

Towards a Description of Early Modern Jewish Literacies and Practices of Reading

The makers of the printed book thus helped to bring about new modes of reading and study. The impact of these innovations is corroborated by the fact that some prominent scholars opposed the printed book and blamed it for undermining traditional patterns of scholarship. Among the narrow class of professional rabbinic scholars, the ability to read and write was a commonplace for centuries. However, during the period under discussion, the emergence of large communities with developed administrations (Katz 2000), as well as the new professional opportunities offered by the printing press itself, generated another important group of people who were both recipients of printed books and their producers: communal leaders and scribes, various officials, and even independent intellectuals who often also served as editors, compositors, correctors, copyists, and providers of manuscripts for print, as well as many progressively educated householders (*ba'alei batim*), for whom Elchanan Reiner coined the term secondary elite (e.g. Reiner 1997, 2000).

No less important but more difficult to identify is yet another group of readers, whom I would define as those for whom reading and writing (contrary to the secondary elite) in no way represented part of their professional career—male Jews working in professions that did not necessitate book-keeping or business correspondence, women, whose access to formal education was still very limited (cf. Fram 2007: 135 and *passim*), and minors.

The new modes of reading, exemplified by the new readers, threatened religious authority and decision-making, hitherto monopolized by the rabbinic elites. The emphasis already placed by classical rabbinic Judaism on the mediating role of the sage (Jaffee 2001: 140–52), who ensured the correct appropriation of the material by the pupil at each stage of oral transfer from teacher to pupil, would be lost.

However, although the rabbis' concerns about these transformations were justified, we still need to determine the extent to which the new attitudes towards text actually displaced older ones, or whether the new trends, rather, enriched the existing spectrum of modes of handling the text. No matter how omnipresent the printed text suddenly seems to be for a bibliographer of Jewish books in the sixteenth century, attention should also be directed in the opposite direction. It would be misleading to surmise general literacy among early modern Jews. Although it is impossible to quantify, there was a large group of people who still could not read at all and others who could not read more complicated text fluently. Thus, for example, sixteenth- and seventeenth-century halakhic manuals still discussed how a man with limited literacy should participate in various public liturgical events. As emphasized by historian Edward Fram, the importance of oral instruction and aural learning remained very high in this period (Fram 2007: 135; cf. Caro, SA 'OḤ' 101: 2).[3] It seems that the very notion of literacy should be reconsidered with regard to early modern Jewish society. It might be more accurate to speak of different literacies and the corresponding practices of reading among different groups within Jewish society. By the means of their books, Jewish printers not only promoted the new fragmentary reading, adopted by the secondary elites and by many of the elite scholars, but also supplied material for those new readers who still struggled with written text. Paradoxically, the tiny booklets containing liturgical, ethical, educational, and entertaining texts that addressed these readers were typically devoid of any typographic tools structuring the layout of the page, of the type found in books designed for more erudite readers. While economic considerations certainly played their role, the less educated readers who were murmuring the text aloud probably did not need the new typographic features and reference tools, nor were they willing to pay the associated costs.

Against the Anarchy of Interpretation

Historian Elchanan Reiner has linked the transition from scribal to printed culture to the transformation of the notion of text. According to the older pattern, he maintains, any significance that a text has exists only by virtue of living, direct contact with its writer. Thus the text is a reflection of another, oral text; that oral text is the authoritative one, its source of authority being the fact that it is transmitted from teacher to pupil (Reiner 1997: 88). The printed text, circulating in multiple copies, precluded control of the meaning by an authoritative interpreter. Deprived of its oral component, the text is restricted to the letter, while from the point of view of the solitary recipient, it is open to anarchic interpretation. Understandably, some elite scholars intentionally avoided the medium of the printed book altogether, and, as in the case of Rabbi Hayim of Friedberg, emphatically opposed the new authorial position, which abandoned the collaborative and performative components of reading. While the interaction of teacher and pupil over the text used to allow for mutual interpretative negotiation of the meaning, those rabbinic authors who fully accepted the new culture of the printed book consciously wrote for anonymous readers. Speaking of his published books, Rabbi Mordekhai Yafeh (d. 1612) made a clear contrast between oral instruction and reaching a much wider audience by means of a printed book:

Therefore, when I saw that I was naked [Gen 3: 10], I trembled with fear lest I die in that state of nakedness. I said to myself, It would be beneficial for me to depart from the practices of a number of my contemporaries. Therefore I will diminish the amount of time I spend studying with my students. But let me build for myself a tranquil habitation wherein I can dwell alone, so that I might be able to clothe myself with a new garment to cover my nakedness. (Kaplan 1975: 369)

Many members of the rabbinic elite thus realized that ignoring the new medium would effectively silence their voices. Many rabbinic scholars either fully accepted the new medium and even supported the new trends, or at least wished to control them. Awareness of the power of the new medium is palpable, especially in polemical discourse. Thus, in the course of his attack on Azariah de' Rossi's *Me'or einayim* (Mantua 1574), the Maharal repeatedly emphasized that his error must be refuted only because his words were printed in the book (*nidpasim basefer*) (Maharal 1598: 38a, col. b). In another book, the Maharal tried to regulate what types of books and what areas of study are commendable, excluding rhetoric as a discipline, for example, and warning against the proliferation of scientific non-Jewish books that include theological issues (Maharal 1595–6: 17b–19a). Yosef Caro advocated a similar position, and explicitly indicted the printers:

Poems and fables with profane subjects, as well as immodest texts, such as the book of Immanuel [Haromi], and also books about wars, are forbidden to be read on the sabbath, and in fact they are forbidden on weekdays too, because they constitute the sin of non-Jewish entertainment [lit. 'company of scorners': *moshav letsim*, Ps. 1: 1], and one would trespass [the commandment of] turn not to idols [Lev. 19: 4]. . . . And one who composes such texts or copies them, and obviously one who prints them [*hamadpisan*]—they make many others sin. (*SA* 'OḤ' 307: 16)

The Maharal also criticized the contemporary proliferation of codes such as the *Shulḥan arukh*. But was not the apodictic formulation of halakhic norms one of the modes adopted by rabbinic Judaism from the very beginning, as exemplified by classics such as the Mishnah, Maimonides' *Mishneh torah*, or the *Arba'ah turim* by Ya'akov ben Asher? The Maharal answered that only in his days had the 'norms without explication', i.e. the apodictic norms formulated in codes such as the *Shulḥan arukh*, received such standing that people would ignore the Talmud, on the study of which halakhic decisions should always be based

(Maharal 1595–6: 21*a*). The Maharal argued that contemporary readers were using the apodictic codes to find out what the law is, without knowing the reasoning behind it in the Talmud. He asked rhetorically whether such practice was not in fact saving people from mistakes in orthopraxy, as the process of deriving norms from the Talmud is beyond the intellectual means of most people, while the codes offered decisions formulated by expert scholars. He answered the question in the negative, pointing to the intrinsic value of the employment of human reason in the process of the derivation of the law, which he considered the essential condition for fulfilling the obligation of Torah study. Together with religious practice, Torah study represented for the Maharal the only instrument for fully realizing the potential humanity of each individual. In other words, the Maharal complained that the easily available printed codes and similar manuals, used as reference tools and thus as externalized knowledge, were easy to peruse but did not allow men (the Maharal denied the capacity of learning the Torah to women) to accomplish the crucial goal of becoming as fully human as possible. Thus, for the Maharal, the printed book, without proper regulation of its use, was a dangerous invention, whose unregulated use could harm Jewish society.[4]

An Elite Scholar Writes for Passive Recipients of the Text

The Maharal's contemporary, Rabbi Yitshak ben Avraham Hayut (1538–c.1615), in his *Penei yitshak* (1591), a versified survey of the laws of ritual slaughter and related alimentary rules, enumerated older accounts of the material and concluded:

> Even the author of the *Shulḥan arukh* came before me. . . . Yet they certainly left empty space for me to enter because there are many uneducated people in our generation who pride themselves on knowing how to read the Scripture, to speculate about few lines from the *Shulḥan arukh*, and to make themselves look like a real rabbi . . . but would soon get tired of searching for the decision or its source, as they do not know where the light dwells. This is why I decided on both length and brevity: I dealt in detail with the explanation of the law based on *pilpul*, Talmud, and the halakhic decisors [*poskim*], while I also simply listed the abbreviated decisions from the *Shulḥan arukh*. (Hayut 1591: 2*a*)

The elite rabbinic scholar thus admitted that he had decided to cater to a very specific segment of readers: laymen who liked to peruse books for the momentary pleasure of feeling like real scholars and wished to get satisfaction from an easily obtainable result. Hayut's text thus confirms that the Maharal's assessment reflected reality. Still, unlike the Maharal, who tried to remedy the situation by establishing special study groups for adults (Davis 2004: 56, 69) and even endorsed printing special study editions of talmudic texts (Heller 2007: 298–314), Hayut tried to accommodate such lazy readers, while including more analytical material in his text, hoping to lead the reader from less demanding to more complicated and intellectually engaging reading. Hayut's solution did not attempt to bring adult lay readers to personalized oral study, and accepted the shift to either solitary or even group reading without a skilled mentor. Such an attitude should not be regarded as hypocritical, from the point of view of either the author or his readers. Scholarly books had only been made available to larger numbers of those who were not professional scholars with the emergence of printing, and they quickly turned into a status symbol, which they remain today. Libraries containing the socially certified classics are often owned by people who never read them. At the same time, it is clear that at least some rabbinic authors decided to take advantage of the new medium's popularity and used it to propagate more serious learning, especially in non-halakhic disciplines. Avraham Horowitz (c.1545–1615) declared in the introduction to his commentary on Maimonides' *Eight Chapters* that it was intended for

the group of yeshiva students [*baḥurim*] who do not have experience with analytical investigation, because the pride of such students and their forte is in the Mishnah, Gemara, *pilpul*, and halakhic speculation and not in the great and wonderful miracles of the philosophers. . . . Everybody will understand and be versed in the *Eight Chapters*. . . . From now, the yeshiva student will not have to learn the *Eight Chapters* from his master [during the period] between the terms, as has been done for many years, but he can learn it on his own. (Horowitz 1622: 1*b*)

Printed books assumed a subversive function here, disseminating the teachings of philosophers (the term used by Horowitz himself) and allowing yeshiva students to study philosophy on their own. As in the case of Caro's *Shulḥan arukh* quoted above, the printer went further than the author. On the title page, he promised the prospective customers that the commentary

shows to many their direction, so that the road is conquered for all yeshiva students to enter the [*Eight*] *Chapters* without the need to spend much time and to listen to others [i.e. to a teacher]. (Horowitz 1622: 1*a*)

To return to the case of *Penei yitsḥak*, Hayut underestimated the economic constraint felt by the publishers as well as their occasionally cavalier approach towards the text and patronizing attitude even to prominent authors (Hayut served as the chief rabbi of Prague). As so often occurs in modern publishing, the publisher thought he knew better than the author what the customers would buy, and thus the original text was drastically changed—deprived of exactly those analytical and explicatory parts that Hayut wanted to smuggle into the otherwise 'easy reading' book. It is almost grotesque that we learn about it from what the author himself said in the introduction to his expurgated work, complaining that 'to make the publication of my work easier and faster, the printers decided to publish for the moment only an abbreviated section of my book. . . . Indeed, the digest of the laws will be useful for the lay person.'

Popularization, Ethical Literature, and Women

While in the realm of halakhah such abridgements were sensitive issues, this was not the case with ethical texts. On the contrary, the ethical writer could feel safe when accommodating the content of his text to the specific needs of the group he (or she) wished to address. A multifaceted example is Avraham Horowitz's *Berit avraham*. The book was printed by Kalonymos ben Mordekhai Yafeh and his son Hayim in Lublin (Horowitz 1577). According to the colophon, the holy work (*melekhet hakodesh*) was completed on Monday 24 January 1577. It is interesting to note that the title page is decorated with beautiful Renaissance borders, with naked putti playing music and two mermaids carrying the coat of arms of the Old Town of Prague. The borders were identified by Petr Voit (2012: 150; 2013: 189) as originating in the Prague atelier of the Christian printer Pavel Severýn. They were produced for the Prague Jewish printer Gershom ben Shelomoh Kohen, who used them in the second part of his *Maḥzor* (Sixtová 2012b: 108, no. 15), completed on 27 October 1529, and in other books. The Lublin printing press was established by the members of the family of Hayim Shahor (Schwartz, d. *c.*1549), who came from Prague and brought some printing material with him to Poland. Kalonymus ben Mordekhai Yafeh married Hayim's granddaughter and also learnt the craft of printing in Prague. The reuse of printing material, often over many decades, was sometimes motivated by marketing, as in the case of the copying of the Giustiniani sign described above. More often than not, it was simply the result of lack of resources (Rivkind 1961; Heller 2008: 1–17, 168).

In the introduction, which follows a poem, written 'to remind you of the day of death and of the day of burial' (Horowitz 1577: 2*a*), the author added a warning: his name and the name of his father have been woven among the verses in an acrostic, 'so that nobody can come and say "I composed it"'. Horowitz feels compelled to define his text in contrast to other ethical writings, and his formulation is typical of the new post-medieval age. Novelty becomes a positive feature, while the author prides himself on making the material more digestible for non-expert readers:

I saw many books on the topic of how to serve God, like the *Book of the Duties of the Heart* [*Ḥovot halevavot*] by Rabenu Bahyah ben Pakudah, the *Book of the Straightforward* [*Sefer hayashar*] by Rabenu Tam [wrongly attributed], the *Gates of Penitence* [*Sha'arei teshuvah*] and the *Book of Reverence* [*Sefer hayirah*] by Rabenu Jonah [Gerondi], and many other eminent books that speak about penitence. However, not a few of their topics are [too] esoteric and lengthy, while the non-specialist reader [*ba'al habayit*] is worn out by his labour. In spite of iniquities he fulfils his duties. He succeeds in his activities [1 Sam. 18: 15], wanders after his business, and has no leisure to enter holiness and to progress, to occupy himself with complicated and difficult secrets. And furthermore, not everybody owns those books, to be able to peruse them day and night and thus to bring redemption closer to his soul. Lest his hands become negligent and he interrupt his penitence, for this reason I decided to select a short admonishment in clear and simple language, which is not complicated. I have arranged for it to be printed so that everybody can hold it in his hand. (Horowitz 1577: 5*a*)

Horowitz explains that the reader should not be astounded if the book contains material presented elsewhere. According to the author, the reader, who is not really a scholar (*eino kol kakh ba'al hatorah*), will appreciate that the rules of penitence, scattered in many different books, are systematized here in one place (Horowitz 1577: 5*a–b*). Once again, abbreviation and systematization are presented as a benefit of the new book, together with its wide dissemination thanks to print.

The voice of early modern Jewish society was still predominantly masculine, and men looked down on women. Yet the respective evaluation of both sexes started to change, even though slowly and imperfectly. While some scholars such as Maharal denied women full humanity (Sládek 2009: 23–8), others accorded them only inferior intellect. Speaking of the halakhic work *Kol bo*, David Conforte (*c*.1618–*c*.1685) rejected the opinion that a scholarly book could have been authored by a woman (Conforte 1846: 25*b*).

The printed book was one of the driving forces behind the intellectual emancipation of Jewish women. In his spiritual testimony, Rabbi Sheftel ben Shabetai Horowitz, son of the famous author of *Shenei luḥot haberit* (Amsterdam, 1649) called upon the women in his family to read Torah (*Ḥumash*) in Yiddish regularly and also the book *Lev tov* (Horowitz 1894: 29*a*). Printing books in Yiddish (or in Ladino, for that matter), both translations and original texts, enabled sixteenth-century printers to address a segment of the population which could not read Hebrew but was eager to read (or to listen to others reading to them). Yiddish versions of the *Ḥumash*, usually printed with a commentary, represented an important part of early modern Jewish book production, together with liturgy, household halakhic manuals, custom literature, entertaining, and ethical works. For example, *Sefer lev tov* (*Book of the Good Heart*) by Yitshak ben Elyakim of Poznań (1620), recommended by Sheftel Horowitz, was one of the most influential original ethical treatises in Yiddish (Rubin and Turniansky 2010; Berger 2013: 36) and it is not by chance that the text of the title page begins 'to you, all men and women' (Yitshak ben Elyakim 1620: 1*a*).

The sixteenth century is thus the moment when women started to read and to be addressed as a specific group by male authors, as exemplified by a Yiddish manual on women's religious duties by Binyamin Aharon ben Avraham Slonik, printed several times under the title *Seyder mitsves noshim: ayn sheyn frauen bikhlen* (*The Set of Commandments for Women: A Nice Little Book for Women*) and even translated into Italian in 1616 (Fram 2007: p. xviii). Towards the end of the century, readers encountered the first published Jewish female author, Rivke bas Me'ir of Tikotin (d. 1605) (Rivke bas Me'ir 2007). Rivke's ethical work *Meynekes rivke* (*Rebecca's Wetnurse*) was published in Prague in 1609 and obviously became popular; another edition appeared in Kraków in 1618, though, as was so often the case with popular and smaller books, almost no copies survive. The Prague *editio princeps* was considered lost until a *unicum* copy was discovered by Frauke von Rohden (Rivke bas Me'ir 2007; Heller 2013: 253; cf. Fram 2007: 151).

While many of the Yiddish books, usually printed in special typefaces called *vaybertaytsh* (German: '[letters] for women'), were labelled as literature for women and those men who are like women (cf. Fram 2007: p. xv, n. 12), such condescending formulations were clearly hypocritical, ignoring the fact that many sixteenth-century women reached such high levels of education that they were active in many spheres of Jewish economic life (Fram 1997: 76–81), including the printing business. Women worked as managers, typesetters, and correctors (Habermann 1933; Ya'ari 1958: 256–302).[5] The one example of a public anti-misogynist stand, cited by Edward Fram as a contrast to the predominant view, is a lament by the Kraków printer Yitshak Prostitz in the preface to his 1589 edition of a Yiddish translation of the Scroll of Esther: 'it is the way of the world that women especially are considered nothing at all and are regarded as good for nothing, and whether young or old, they are done much injustice and violence' (Fram 2007: 43). Even with regard to gender, the printed book as a cultural phenomenon retained its two-way dynamic: the availability of books fostered the education of Jewish women. At the same time, women, together with non-elite male readers, were not only passive recipients of the simplified or abridged texts produced by male members of scholarly elites, but their own reading preferences encouraged a specific new type of book production, while both male and female members of this group acted as authors and publishers of this literature.

'To Print Many Books Without End and to Give Merit to Many People'

Although in its material aspects the early modern book did not substantially differ from the book as we know it today, its functions and the cultural context it reflected were strikingly different. The paratextual approach not only improves our understanding of the specifics of early modern Jewish book production and its dynamics, but also testifies to the emergence of a self-aware functional group, formed by those who participated in the production of printed books for Jewish use. The makers of early modern Jewish books shared the desire to leave a durable imprint in the books they helped to print. Their pride and enthusiasm are revealed time and again in the paratexts as a collective signature.

The fascination of Jewish printers with the new technology, as well as the ways in which this fascination was expressed, were analogous to those of non-Jewish printers. When the makers of Jewish books called their job *melekhet hakodesh* ('holy work'), it was equivalent to expressions such as *art divin*, *divina ars*, or *sacra ars* used by their non-Jewish counterparts. The title pages, as well as many colophons and various notes, provide ample evidence of the pride felt by all those involved in the editing, printing, proof-correcting, and financing of printed books. The master printer Yitshak ben Aharon Prostitz proudly called himself the man appointed over the work of printing (*gever hukam al melekhet hadefus*) (Ibn Gabbai 1576–7: 1a). Rabbi Mordekhai ben Moshe Halevi of Prague explained on the title page of Efrayim Shelomoh Luntschitz's *Ir giborim* (1580), and again in a special note at the end of the volume, that after he received the manuscript from Lviv and failed to publish it in Prague (for reasons unknown to us), he decided to travel to Basle after hearing of 'the famous printer Mr Yisra'el Zifroni . . . who was in charge of printing the Talmud and whose repute is heard of in all the lands, and the fruit of his labour is good because he is an expert in printing' (Luntschitz 1580: 137b).

The self-awareness of this group is also demonstrated by their use of the names of their professions as their cognomens. The colophons and other paratexts often preserved for posterity the complete cast involved in the making of a book. To give just one example, the colophon of Yehudah Leib ben Ovadiah Eilenburg's *Minḥat yehudah* (Eilenburg 1639) says:

> The weekly order 'And this is the blessing' (Deut. 33: 1–34: 12)
> has been finished in the name of the God of the orderly array
> and the explanations of Rashi on the Torah have been completed
> with the help of the great God, the mighty and awesome.
> Being the prayer to God the Creator of the world,
> [the printing of this book] has been finished
> on Wednesday, 27th day of the month of Sivan, in year of THE GOOD HOUR [i.e. 1639].
> By the female compositor [*Setzerin*] Mrs Tcherna, daughter of Mr Menahem Printer,
> by the compositor [*Setzer*] in the heavenly art Ze'ev called Wolf, son of Mordekhai,
> by the compositor Uri Shragah called Seibt, son of Shelomoh,
> by the compositor Ze'ev called Wolf, son of Avram the Compositor,
> by the printer [*Pressenzieher*] Avigdor ben Yisra'el Yosef,
> by the printer Ze'ev called Wolf, son of Yitshak Yozels,
> by the printer Yitshak ben Menahem Tsoref,
> by the compositor in the heavenly art Katri'el son of Tsevi from Apta.

Verbose and florid as the colophons and other paratexts can be, they attest to the wish of the Jewish makers of early modern books to be inseparably linked to their work and to be regarded as conferring religious merit on all other Jews by 'printing many books without end' (see Greenblatt 2014). The paratexts also reveal the high mobility of Jewish 'workers in sacred art'. To give just a random example, Shabetai Bass, who was from Poland but identified himself as originally from

Prague, learned the craft in Amsterdam and started his printing-shop in Silesian Dyhernfurt. For printing *Sefer amudei hashivah* he employed two compositors from Prague and a printer from the great city of Venice (Betsalel Darshan 1692: 72*b*).

Mobility was indeed facilitated by the technological uniformity of the hand-press in the period between 1500 and 1800, but it was triggered by the instability of the industry. The insecure situation of Jewish printers resulted not only from occasional external restrictive measures, such as bans on Jewish printing, confiscations of Jewish books, and censorship (Raz-Krakotzkin 2007), but especially from the fact that the production of books in Hebrew, and even in Jewish vernaculars such as Yiddish, represented a narrow and thus fragile branch, susceptible to even minor economic, political, or simply personal swings, which more often than not cannot be assessed by modern historians. For example, why was Luntschitz's *Ir giborim* (1580) not printed in Prague if the Maharal's *Gur aryeh* (Maharal 1578), comparable in size, was printed there two years earlier? While a temporary decline is obvious (Sixtová 2012a: 47), its reasons were too diffuse to leave an imprint in the surviving documents. Similarly, why could Rabbi Natan Spira's son not complete the printing of his father's supercommentary on Rashi in Kraków? Why did he have to wait several years until managing to print the last three parts in Lublin (Natan Spira 1597: 1*a*), while the Kraków press was operating throughout the 1590s?

Shared language as well as shared professional self-awareness point to the fact that the hand-press as a new technology allowed increased social interaction between Jews and Christians during the fifteenth and sixteenth centuries: Jewish and non-Jewish printers shared or traded their printing material, Christian entrepreneurs employed Jewish editors and correctors, Jewish printers employed Christian typesetters (Ya'ari 1958: 245–55), Christian publishers printed books in Hebrew characters for both Jews and non-Jews (Daniel Bomberg in Venice or Ambrosio Froben in Basle), while at times (though less often) Jewish printers did not shy away from printing in Latin characters for a non-Jewish public, Gershom Soncino's edition of Petrarch's *Sonnets* being the most famous example (1503).

In his Latin and Italian dedication to Cesare Borgia, this printer, signing himself as Hieronymus Soncino, boasted that he employed the most notable and efficient typesetters and used the new cursive types, cut by Francesco Griffo da Bologna, *nobilissimo sculptore de litere latine/graece/et hebraice* (Petrarch 1503: [407]). Griffo joined Soncino in Fano after he had quarrelled with the famous Aldus Manutius for whom he had previously worked (Richardson 2002: 57). To add to the curiosity, only two years earlier Aldus used for his introduction to a Hebrew grammar (Manutius 1501) types so similar to those employed by Soncino in 1492 that it is likely that Griffo had worked for Soncino previously (Amram 1909: 94–101). While the sixteenth century witnessed the rise of segregation between Jews and Christians in many respects, manifested especially by the emergence of the ghettos (Ravid 2008), in the same period the printing press fostered the creation of an enclave of a shared social and cultural space, mirrored in printed books as a shared knowledge.

For both Jewish and non-Jewish printers, the attractive appearance of the books they produced, as well as the correctness of the text, were not only a value *per se* and an important marketing device, but also reflected their self-awareness as a specific group, bound by mutual collaboration and competition. Thus the Christian printer Giovanni (Zuan) di Gara proudly designated himself as the heir of Bomberg (Amram 1909: 351), and many of his books advertise on their title pages that they were printed by Zoan di Gara with Bomberg's letters (e.g. Uçeda 1579: 1*a*). In turn, Polish printers copied di Gara's characteristic title page, featuring a Roman arch with pillars garlanded with flowers and fruits (Amram 1909: 352).[6]

The makers of Hebrew and Yiddish prints were well aware of the difference between manuscript and printed book in that the latter, being mechanically reproduced in large quantities, could reach many more people. In the paratexts, the publishers and editors often speak of manuscript copies as if their scarcity equalled non-existence, as if forgetting in their ardour that manuscripts had served as the carriers of texts for centuries. In reality, such expressions reveal the breach between pre-print manuscript culture and print culture, notwithstanding the continued use of manuscripts. The makers of printed books consciously assumed the role of those who work to 'benefit others with religious merit [*lezakot harabim*]' by disseminating texts hitherto available only to a few in manuscript form by 'printing books without end [*lidpos sefarim ein kets*]'. This is for example how the editor Ya'akov ben Yosefo Shorzina of Castile spoke of preparing the text of the *editio princeps* of *Tana devei eliyahu* in Daniel Zanetti's workshop in 1598:

The *Tana devei eliyahu* has never been printed before with pen of iron and lead, as to our best knowledge nobody has seen it printed, excluding our edition. Therefore this day means a merit for us and for our sons. . . . Now I am the one who edited it. Anointed by the oil of my minuscule understanding, I extracted the deficient <text> from an antique manuscript, written as well as concealed by the hand of its writer in the year 4946 [i.e. 1185/6]. If some words are missing or some letters are erroneous, it is because the editing was complicated and I had to resort to inferring the meaning. . . . It is possible that some parts I did not understand <correctly> because of the limitations of my intellect. (*Tana devei eliyahu* 1598: 69*b*)

The self-awareness of this group enabled and also further enhanced their view of publishing as a cumulative process of shaping Jewish culture, taking place in diachronic perspective. Editions of books serve as reference points in the global perspective, structuring the spatial and temporal continuum. This is most markedly manifested by the fact that publishers often felt obliged to justify the need for repeated editions. Thus the editors of a *Maḥzor* (1568) explain that, unlike the older edition, the new one features the vowels and thus is especially suitable for 'old men, students, and girls [*zekenim, bahurim uvetulot*]'. The publisher of the second edition of Efrayim Shelomoh Luntschitz's *Olelot efrayim* (1619) wrote on the title page that the book was 'printed for the second time . . . by Avraham Heida here in the holy community of Prague . . . and it has been edited with the necessary care by the printer himself from a copy belonging to the author himself, which he refined many times, added many corrections and [supplied] many additions'.

Mordekhai ben Gershom Kohen, who identifies himself as 'the printer [*mehokek*] and later on as the head of artisans [*rosh umanim*]', says on the verso of the title page of his edition of a *Mahzor* (1585: 1b) that 'the commentary on the *Mahzor* printed in the Lublin edition of that book is approved of by all . . . and thus I will retain it. . . . Yet I also added explications, sweet as honey, which I found in old *mahzorim*'. In a lengthy note Mordekhai ben Gershom or his editor, Moshe ben Avraham Schedel, in his name (Sixtová 2012a: 47) speaks of his professional determination, but also refers to other printers' work as inferior:

Said the printer: According to our sages the verse 'He has made every thing beautiful in his time' [Eccles. 3: 11] teaches that each and every person should perform his craft beautifully. Thus I set to my work today, the heavenly art. . . . I desired the work of God . . . to print the *Mahzor for the whole year* with pen of iron and lead, to benefit many with the excellency of dignity, and the excellency of power [Gen. 49: 3] by many advantages . . . over other *mahzorim* printed since olden days, and especially over the *Mahzor* newly printed in the holy community of Kraków. (*Mahzor* 1585: 2a)

Mordekhai ben Gershom's note is the paean of a master printer to his shop's produce that enables us to learn what sixteenth-century professionals, and also their customers, appreciated: he did not spare money but purchased extraordinarily large sheets of high-quality paper so that there was a wide margin on all sides of the text ('two fingers wide'); the liturgical poems were composed stichographically and the acrostics were typographically highlighted; and the incipits were decorated with decorative initial woodblocks 'to embellish the work in the manner of the sophisticated and most accomplished artisans'. Other important features include the quality of the editorial work and various glosses, and useful additional texts such as the readings from Prophets (*haftarot*) and commentaries ('as for commentaries, I added at least a third on top of what has been printed in the holy communities of Lublin and Kraków').

Examples of the professional pride and self-awareness of fifteenth- and sixteenth-century makers of Jewish books could be multiplied without end. So could the examples of competition, as well as of many difficulties and obstacles, only some of which the Jewish makers shared with their non-Jewish counterparts. The indefatigable enthusiasm of the Jewish printers, editors, correctors, and financiers was driven by optimism, stemming from the overall conviction that by means of the new technology of reproduction of texts they could make books available to the widest Jewish public, not only consisting of professional scholars but also including educated laymen (*ba'alei batim*), their wives, and children. In the words of the Prague Jewish polymath David Gans:

> The invention of book printing occurred in the city of Mainz by the means of a Christian gentleman named Johannes Gutenberg. . . . Craftsmen, labourers, goldsmiths, builders, stonemasons, and others will reveal and disseminate by means of print countless useful things and inventions, as many books without end will be printed for workers in all professions! (Gans 1592: ii, 95*b*)

Their triumphant tone was simultaneously motivated not only by the awareness that each newly published book would shape the new Jewish textual corpus, but also by the fragile state of their business. On one hand, Jewish printers could see the impact of their work, but on the other, the printing of Jewish books could never be taken for granted. It comes as no surprise that when a Prague printer's daughter set the types of a manual of Hebrew grammar, *Siaḥ yitsḥak* by R. Yitshak ben Shemuel, in 1628, she signed her name in the colophon with evident pride: 'And I also work in the heavenly art . . . Gittel, daughter of Leib the Compositor Katz from Prague' (Ya'ari 1958: 260).

Notes

Work for this chapter was supported by the European Regional Development Fund Project, 'Creativity and Adaptability as Conditions of the Success of Europe in an Interrelated World' (No. CZ.02.1.01/0.0/0.0/16_019/0000734).

1   The examples used in this study are generic and should be understood as typical samples of what the makers of Jewish books tell their public about their work. If the words of the northern printers of Prague, Kraków, or Lublin sound more spontaneous, personal, and diverse when communicating various obstacles than the paratexts of their Italian colleagues (and thus appear more frequently in this essay), it is mainly because the latter faced political rather than economic strictures, unable to work independently and usually under the auspices of Christian entrepreneurs and in the context of Church censorship. While the respective situations of northern and Italian Jewish printers were thus not identical and a comparative study is necessary, I believe that in their overall attitude to their mission they can be treated as a single group.

2   The analysis of the history and changing use of the decorative elements used by Prague Jewish printers of the 16th and 17th centuries forms part of Olga Sixtová's doctoral dissertation (Charles University, 2018). I am grateful to her for permission to use it here.

3   The diachronic analysis of Jewish teaching and learning methods from this perspective would be highly desirable, especially with regard to non-elite groups. To give a glimpse into this problem, for example, Caro's *Shulḥan arukh* ('OḤ' 101: 4) implies that there were people who could follow the fixed communal prayer but could not formulate their personal wishes in the Holy Tongue and had to resort to the vernacular. The paragraph of the same legal code referred to before ('OḤ' 101: 2) regulates the way in which private prayer

should be recited. It should be neither recited in one's mind (*belibo*) nor out loud, but rather murmured by the lips. However, if one cannot concentrate while murmuring, he is permitted to raise his voice. The same is permitted in one's house if he wants to instruct his sons (Moshe Isserles quoting the *Tur*). Cf. also *Shulḥan arukh* 'OḤ' 128: 33, disqualifying a *kohen* who makes mistakes in pronunciation of Hebrew letters from reciting the priestly benediction, or 'OḤ' 135: 4, implying the existence of a *kohen* who cannot read the Torah. 'OḤ' 139: 2 instructs a person who cannot read from the scroll to wave his arm to indicate that fact if he should be called to read. The same paragraph speaks of a person who cannot really read from the scroll but can still recite the text if somebody else would prompt him word by word, so that he can link the sound to the written text. The *Shulḥan arukh* also deals with the situation when there is nobody in the synagogue who can read properly from the Torah ('OḤ' 142: 2 and 143: 5). Caro's code also deals with the problem of the legal position and responsibilities of an illiterate Jew (e.g. 'EH' 66: 13 or 130: 16).

4   The classical study on Maharal's pedagogic thought is Kleinberger 1962. On his attitude to the sciences and non-Jewish learning, the classical statement is Ruderman 1995: 76–85.

5   Habermann listed 59 women who were involved in book-production. Twenty-five years later, Ya'ari lists over 100 before the mid-18th cent. The first was Estellina, wife of Avraham ben Shelomoh Conat, who started printing Hebrew books in Mantua after 1476. At the end of *Beḥinat olam* by Yedayah Hapenini (*c.*1477) she wrote: I, Estellina, the wife of my esteemed husband Mr Avraham Conat . . . wrote (i.e. printed) this epistle *Beḥinat olam* with the help of an apprentice, Ya'akov Levi from Tarrascon in Provence (quoted in Ya'ari 1958: 259).

6   A close comparison reveals that they are not imprints of the same block but manifest slight differences, and were thus simply modelled after the original, to make the Kraków and Lublin prints look like the highly valued Venetian prints. Compare for example Uçeda 1579: 1*a*, from Venice, and Ibn Gabai 1581: 1*a*, from Kraków. The actual sharing and purchasing of typographic material among printing-shops (even between Christian and Jewish ones) was also common; see Voit 2012 for examples from Prague.

References

Primary Sources

ASHER BEN YEHI'EL (ROSH). 1517. *She'elot uteshuvot*. Constantinople.

—— 1552. *She'elot uteshuvot*. Venice.

BERGER, SHLOMO. 2013. *Producing Redemption in Amsterdam: Early Modern Yiddish Book in Paratextual Perspective*. Leiden.

BETSALEL DARSHAN. 1692. *Sefer amudei hashivah*. Dyhernfurt.

CARO, YOSEF BEN EFRAYIM. 1565. *Shulḥan arukh*. Venice.

CONFORTE, DAVID. 1846. *Kore dorot*. Ed. David Cassel. Berlin.

DE' ROSSI, AZARIAH. 1573–5. *Me'or einayim*. Mantua.

—— 1619. *Olelot efrayim*. Prague.

EILENBURG, YEHUDAH LEIB BEN OVADIAH. 1639. *Minḥat yehudah*. Kraków.

ELAZAR BEN YEHUDAH OF WORMS. 1504/5. *Sefer haroke'aḥ*. Fano.

GANS, DAVID. 1592. *Tsemaḥ david*. Prague.

HAYUT, YITSHAK BEN ABRAHAM. 1591. *Penei yitsḥak*. Kraków.

HOROWITZ, AVRAHAM. 1577. *Berit avraham*. Lublin.

—— 1622. *Ḥesed avraham*. Lublin.

HOROWITZ, SHEFTEL BEN SHABETAI. 1894. 'Tsava'at shel hagaon heḥasid moharar sheftel ben hagaon hagadol moharar yeshayah zts´'l'. In Avraham Horowitz, *Berit avraham*, 24b–32b. Munkács.

IBN GABBAI, ME'IR. 1576–7. *Avodat hakodesh*. Kraków.

—— 1581. *Tola'at ya'akov*. Kraków.

ISSERLES, MOSHE. 1559. *Meḥir yayin*. Cremona.

KATZ, ISSAKHAR BERMAN BEN NAFTALI. 1589. *Mareh kohen*. Kraków.

KIMHI, DAVID. 1491. *Sefer hashorashim*. Naples.

LUNTSCHITZ, EFRAYIM SHELOMOH. 1580. *Ir giborim*. Basle.

MAHARAL (JUDAH LOEW BEN BETSALEL). 1578. *Gur aryeh*. Prague.

—— 1593. *Derush al hatorah*. Prague.

—— 1595–6. *Netivot olam*. Prague.

—— 1598. *Be'er hagoleh*. Prague.

Maḥzor. 1529. Prague (Gershom ben Shelomoh Kohen).

Maḥzor. 1568. Venice (Giorgio Cavalli).

Maḥzor. 1585. Prague (Mordekhai ben Gershom Katz).

MANUTIUS, ALDUS. 1501. 'Introductio per brevis ad hebraicam linguam'. In Aldus Manutius, *Aldi Manutii romani rudimenta grammatices latinae linguae . . .* (no pagination). Venice.

PETRARCH, FRANCESCO. 1503. *Opere volgari di messer Francesco Petrarcha*. Fano.

RIVKE BAS ME'IR OF TIKOTIN. 1609. *Meynekes rivke*. Prague.

—— 1618. *Meynekes rivke*. Kraków.

—— 2007. *Meneket Rivkah: A Manual of Wisdom and Piety for Jewish Women* (ed. Frauke von Rohden). Philadelphia.

SPIRA, NATAN. 1597. *Imrei shefer*. Kraków–Lublin.

Tana devei eliyahu. 1598. Venice.

UÇEDA, SHEMUEL. 1579. *Midrash shemuel*. Venice.

YAFEH, MORDEKHAI BEN AVRAHAM. 1603. *Levush ha'orah*. Prague.

—— 1609. *Levush pinat yikrat*. Prague.

YITSHAK BEN ELYAKIM OF POZNAŃ. 1620. *Lev tov*. Prague.

—— 1714. *Lev tov*. Wilhelmsdorf.

YITSHAK BEN SHIMSHON KATZ HALEVI. 1607. *Pane'aḥ raza*. Prague.

Zohar. 1558. Cremona.

Other Sources

AMRAM, DAVID WERNER. 1909. *The Makers of Hebrew Books in Italy: Being Chapters in the History of the Hebrew Printing Press*. Philadelphia.

BEIT-ARIÉ, MALACHI. 1993. *The Panizzi Lectures 1992, viii: Hebrew Manuscripts of East and West: Towards a Comparative Codicology*. London.

BERGER, SHLOMO. 2013. *Producing Redemption in Amsterdam: Early Modern Yiddish Books in Paratextual Perspective.* Leiden.

BLAIR, ANN. 2003. 'Reading Strategies for Coping with Information Overload, ca. 1550–1700'. *Journal of the History of Ideas*, 64: 11–28.

DAVIS, JOSEPH M. 2004. *Yom-Tov Lipmann Heller: Portrait of a Seventeenth-Century Rabbi.* Oxford.

EISENSTEIN, ELIZABETH. 1979. *The Printing Press as an Agent of Change.* Cambridge.

——2002. 'An Unacknowledged Revolution Revisited'. *American Historical Review*, 107: 87–105.

FRAM, EDWARD. 1997. *Ideals Face Reality: Jewish Law and Life in Poland 1550–1655.* Cincinnati, Ohio.

——2007. *My Dear Daughter: Rabbi Benjamin Slonik and the Education of Jewish Women in Sixteenth-Century Poland.* Cincinnati, Ohio.

FREIMANN, ARON, and MOSES MARX. 1967–9 [1934–31]. *Thesaurus Typographiae Hebraicae Saeculi XV.* Jerusalem.

GASKELL, PHILIP. 1985 [1972]. *A New Introduction to Bibliography.* Oxford.

GENETTE, GÉRARD. 1997. *Paratexts: Thresholds of Interpretation.* Cambridge.

GREENBLATT, RACHEL L. 2014. *To Tell Their Children: Jewish Communal Memory in Early Modern Prague.* Stanford, Calif.

——2015. '"And He Wrote Many Books": Print, Remembrance, Autobiographical Writing and the Maharal of Prague'. In Elchanan Reiner, ed., *Maharal, Overtures: Biography, Doctrine, Influence*, 75–99 (Heb.) Jerusalem.

HABERMANN, AVRAHAM ME'IR. 1933. *Jewish Women as Printers, Typesetters, Publishers, and Patrons of Authors* [Nashim ivriyot betor madpisot, mesadrot, motsiot le'or vetomkhot bimeḥaberim]. Berlin.

——1978. *Studies on Hebrew Printers and their Books* [Perakim betoldot hamadpisim ha'ivriyim ve'inyenei sefarim]. Jerusalem.

HELLER, MARVIN J. 2008. *Studies in the Making of the Early Hebrew Book.* Leiden.

——2013. *Further Studies in the Making of the Early Hebrew Book.* Leiden.

JAFFEE, MARTIN S. 2001. *Torah in the Mouth: Writing and Oral Tradition in Palestinian Judaism, 200 BCE–400 CE.* New York.

KAPLAN, LAWRENCE JAY. 1975. 'Rationalism and Rabbinic Culture in Sixteenth Century Eastern Europe: Rabbi Mordekhai Jaffe's *Levush Pinat Yikrat*'. Ph.D. diss., Harvard University, Cambridge, Mass.

KATZ, JACOB. 2000. *Tradition and Crisis: Jewish Society at the End of the Middle Ages.* Syracuse, NY.

KLEINBERGER, AHARON FRITZ. 1962. *The Pedagogical Thought of the Maharal of Prague* [Hamaḥshavah hapedagogit shel hamaharal miprag]. Jerusalem.

MCKERROW, RONALD B. 1962 [1927]. *An Introduction to Bibliography for Literary Students.* Oxford.

MCKITTERICK, DAVID. 2003. *Print, Manuscript, and the Search for Order 1450–1830.* Cambridge.

OFFENBERG, A. K. 2004 [1908]. *Catalogue of Books Printed in the XVth Century Now in the British Library (BMC), Part XIII: Hebraica.* 't Goy-Houten.

RAVID, BENJAMIN. 2008. 'All Ghettos Were Jewish Quarters, But Not All Jewish Quarters Were Ghettos'. *Jewish Culture and History*, 10: 5–24.

RAZ-KRAKOTZKIN, AMNON. 2007. *The Censor, the Editor, and the Text*. Philadelphia.

REINER, ELCHANAN. 1997. 'The Ashkenazi Elite at the Beginning of the Modern Era: Manuscript versus Printed Book'. *Polin*, 10: 85–98.

—— 2000. 'A Biography of an Agent of Culture: Eleazar Altschul of Prague and his Literary Activity'. In M. Graetz, ed., *Schöpferische Momente des europäischen Judentums in der frühen Neuzeit*, 229–247. Heidelberg.

RICHARDSON, BRIAN. 1999. *Printing, Writers, and Readers in Renaissance Italy*. Cambridge.

—— 2002. *Print Culture in Renaissance Italy: The Editor and the Vernacular Text 1470–1600*. Cambridge.

RIVKIND, ISAAC. 1950. 'Variants in Old Books' (Heb.). *Alexander Marx Jubilee Volume*, vol. 2, 401–32.

—— 1961. 'The Migration of Frames' (Heb.). *Studies in Bibliography and Booklore*, 5: 1–11.

ROUSE, RICHARD H., and MARY A. ROUSE. 1990. 'The Commercial Production of Manuscript Books in Late-Thirteenth-Century and Early-Fourteenth-Century Paris'. In L. L. Brownrigg, ed., *Medieval Book Production: Assessing the Evidence. Proceedings of the Second Conference of the Seminar in the History of the Book to 1500, Oxford, July 1988*, 103–15. Los Altos Hills, Calif.

RUBIN, NOGA, and CHAVA TURNIANSKY. 2010. 'Lev Tov, Seyfer'. *YIVO Encyclopedia of Jews in Eastern Europe*. <http://www.yivoencyclopedia.org/article.aspx/Lev_Tov_Seyfer>

RUDERMAN, DAVID B. 1995. *Jewish Thought and Scientific Discovery in Early Modern Europe*. New Haven, Conn.

—— 2010. *Early Modern Jewry. A New Cultural History*. Princeton, NJ.

SHEAR, ADAM. 2012. 'Judah Moscato's Sources and Hebrew Printing in the Sixteenth Century: A Preliminary Survey'. In Giuseppe Veltri and Gianfranco Miletto, eds., *Rabbi Judah Moscato and the Jewish Intellectual World of Mantua in the 16th–17th Centuries*, 121–42. Leiden.

SIXTOVÁ, OLGA. 2012a. 'Jewish Printers and Printing Presses in Prague 1512–1670 (1672)'. In Olga Sixtová, ed., *Hebrew Printing in Bohemia and Moravia*, 33–74. Prague.

—— 2012b. 'The Beginnings of Prague Hebrew Typography 1512–1669'. In Olga Sixtová, ed., *Hebrew Printing in Bohemia and Moravia*, 75–121. Prague.

SLÁDEK, PAVEL. 2009. 'Maharal's Anthropology: Toward Defining the Limits of his Humanism'. *Judaica Bohemiae*, 44: 5–40.

—— 2016. 'Typography and Practices of Reading: The Lesson of *Tzemah David*', *Judaica Bohemiae*, 51/1: 5–24.

SPIEGEL, YA'AKOV SHMUEL. 2014. *Pages in the History of the Hebrew Book: The Beginning of Printing* [Amudim betoledot hasefer ha'ivri: besha'arei hadefus]. Jerusalem.

VOIT, PETR. 2012. 'Ornamentation of Prague Hebrew Books during the First Half of the 16th Century as a Part of Bohemian Book Design'. In Olga Sixtová, ed., *Hebrew Printing in Bohemia and Moravia*, 123–51. Prague.

—— 2013. *Český knihtisk mezi pozdní gotikou a renesancí I*. Prague.

YA'ARI, AVRAHAM. 1958. *Book Studies: Chapters in the History of the Hebrew Book* [Meḥkarei sefer: Perakim betoldot hasefer ha'ivri]. Jerusalem.

—— 1971 [1943]. *Hebrew Printers' Marks from the Beginning of Printing to the End of the Nineteenth Century* [Diglei hamadpisim ha'ivriyim mereshit hadefus ve'ad sof hame'ah ha-19]. Farnborough.

TWO

Settings of Silver: The Feminization of the Jewish Sabbath, 1920–1945

AMY K. MILLIGAN

The table is set for dinner for six people; damask tablecloth and napkins, fine china, silver and glassware. Two handsome, tall old silver candlesticks with white candles and a low bowl of flowers on either side, keeping the candlesticks together in the center, make the centerpiece for the Shabbat[1] table. At the head of the table are two hallot covered with a beautiful embroidered hallah cover, a Shabbat knife and a salt shaker, a wine bottle and a silver Kiddush cup. At the foot of the table is a soup tureen with noodle soup and a ladle nearby. A large platter of gefilte fish, a container of horse radish, a platter of eierkichel and a round noodle or potato kugel, partly cut, are also on the table.

(Greenberg and Silverman 1941: 73)

THE SCENE is set in the 1941 guide-book *The Jewish Home Beautiful*: the sabbath is about to commence. A publishing sensation, *The Jewish Home Beautiful*, initiated by synagogue sisterhoods, eschewed describing tradition and instead decided to create it. It aestheticized the sacred ritual much as guides to interior decoration aestheticized middle-class homes. But would families follow this advice? And why should they? In this essay, I answer these key questions by addressing the emergence of Jewish homemaking guidebooks, with particular attention to their description of sabbath preparation, culminating with an analysis of the feminization of the American Jewish sabbath. I argue that through a contextualized understanding of the changes in sabbath observance—including the agency of Jewish Sisterhoods in promoting a female-driven synagogue life, as demonstrated through their self-published guidebooks—the feminization of the sabbath was seen as necessary to ensure the survival of Judaism in America. This essay concentrates on the period between 1920 and 1945, as east European Jews negotiated with German American Jews, together facing the diasporic problem of maintaining cultural continuity within a dominant society that held conflicting values and norms, and mediating tradition that both connected and divided Jews as an American community.

The American Concept of Judaism

Although the United States provided greater opportunities and significantly less persecution than eastern Europe, the life of early Jewish American immigrants was not easy. In addition to the Immigration Act of 1924, also known as the Johnson–Reed Act, which restricted the number of immigrants (particularly from eastern Europe and East Asia), there were other domestic concerns for the new immigrants. Having traded the enforced ghettoization of eastern Europe for the ghettos of New York City, most Jewish immigrants struggled both socially and economically. Within the United States, the diverse east European Jewish community self-subdivided into cultural and linguistic neighbourhoods where Russian, Lithuanian, Polish, Romanian, and Galician Jews settled with others from the 'old country'. Within these communities, tensions also arose in terms of religious observance. More pious Jews attempted to transplant their rituals and practices in their entirety. In an attempt to defy assimilation, they strove to live separately and distinctly, abjuring American culture in favour of 'old world' traditions. For these pious Jews, their American dream was the ability to remain religiously observant, freedom from persecution, and the possibility of achieving modest financial security. They were willing to take lower-paying employment in order to ensure their ability to participate fully in observant Jewish life. Yet even these communities did not escape the pressing threat of assimilation, a message that spread quickly back to eastern Europe.

Largely, though, Jewish immigrants at this time were willing to give up religious observance in favour of assimilation, financial stability, and the dream of creating promising futures for their children. These immigrants did not eschew their Jewishness, but believed that they could retain a sense of Jewish identity while still living as fully assimilated Americans. This merging of identities highlighted several cultural tensions: first, religious dress became unpopular as it marked the wearer as unassimilated. Second, ethnic-identified language, most often Yiddish, was moved into the home and fell into disuse as it also served as a marker of 'otherness'. Finally, men struggled to negotiate competing employment expectations, as it was difficult to observe religious holidays and the Jewish sabbath alongside American Christian-centric job expectations (Sarna 2004: 159). Likewise, many women and children found themselves in factory work as families struggled financially.

Because of these assimilation pressures, Jewish spirituality (both as individual Jews and as a larger Jewish religious community) saw a drastic shift between 1920 and 1945. With American laws protecting freedom of religion, Jews were no longer forced by law to identify themselves as Jewish, meaning that, for the first time, they could decide whether or not they wished to affiliate themselves with Judaism. As individuals grappled with their own understandings of *yidishkeyt*, the larger American Jewish community had few trained rabbis to lead them,[2] which increased the schism between Jewish communal life and the Jewish home. That is to say, there were two types of American Judaism emerging: one, where Jews attended synagogue, remained publicly religiously observant, and were largely isolated from American culture; and another, embraced by the majority of American Jews, where active participation in Jewish communal life was replaced by American cultural assimilation and Jewish affiliation was privatized into the home. Using 1906 census data, Jonathan Sarna (2004) calculates that synagogues at the time could only have seated 26 per cent of American Jews, in contrast to churches, which had seating for 70 per cent of American Christians. This data is paralleled in the 1900 *American Jewish Yearbook*, which estimates that 80 per cent of American Jews were no longer participating in public Jewish life (Adler 1900: 500). Sarna estimates that by 1916 only 12 per cent of Jews held synagogue membership (2004: 161), which does not account for whether members were participants in the religious community or simply held synagogue membership. Indeed, observant Judaism, as it had been known, appeared to be faltering in America.

This decline in synagogue participation and attendance marks two significant shifts in American Judaism. As Judaism became progressively privatized and moved away from the communal synagogue-based approach, it became increasingly feminized. Centred on the family and the home, Jewish mothers were responsible for creating a Jewish refuge or 'little temple' in the home, in which to instil children with Jewish values. At the same time, observance of the sabbath was changing radically, which only served to move Judaism increasingly into the home and away from the synagogue. Coupled with the increased secularization of Judaism, this era marked a significant reconceptualization of Jewish life (Bronner 2010: 6–21).

In the shtetls of eastern Europe, Jews had upheld strict sabbath laws. Forced to function as an independent class, they did not encounter the same social pressure to violate sabbath observance and there was communal pressure to adhere to these religious commandments (Heller and Glazer 1994). However, in the United States, Jews were almost always forced to work on Saturdays, often as part of their employment contracts. Those who owned their own businesses felt pressured to stay open on Saturdays in order to remain economically viable. With most Jewish men working on the sabbath, many women found themselves alone at the head of the sabbath table on Friday night. Encouraged in *Shas teḥinah ḥadashah*, a 1916 Yiddish prayer-book, to pray about the new lack of sabbath observance, women were entreated to add a prayer to their sabbath candle-lighting which lamented 'that in this diaspora land where the burden of making a living is so great, resting on sabbath and holidays [has] become impossible'. The prayer pleads for divine compassion, asking, 'Grant a bountiful living to all Jewish children . . . that they should not . . . have to desecrate your holy day.'[3]

Figure 1 Synagogue Sisterhoods hosted demonstrations of holiday celebrations. In this cultivated table display from Harrisburg, Pennsylvania, a woman portrays a family Hanukah celebration. In addition to the traditional menorah, her tablescape features items indicating the commodification of Hanukah, including a tinsel Star of David, mass-produced dreidels, gifts wrapped in Hanukah paper, and children's holiday books. *Photograph by Arnold Zuckerman. Historical Society of Dauphin County*

Despite some women adding this ardent prayer, the majority of American Jewish women and their families did not observe the sabbath. At this time, Jewish women served a curious role as both guardians of Judaism and agents of assimilation. Although they were responsible for maintaining a Jewish home and for the Jewish education of their children, female immigrants were also highly motivated to become involved in American culture. Most of the women faced a significant language barrier, and one of the easiest ways for them to Americanize themselves and their families was through consumer culture. By changing their dress, abandoning their hair coverings, and modelling their residences on American homes with parlours and pianos, these women created an American facade around an increasingly private Jewish affiliation (Sarna 2004: 164). It was at this time that the barmitzvah experienced revitalization and became what some continue to criticize as a consumption-centred lifecycle event. Other ritual occasions, like Passover (with its proximity to Easter) and Hanukah (with its propinquity to Christmas), became increasingly important as religious holidays (Figure 1). Even non-observant Jews hosted Passover Seder meals and exchanged Hanukah gifts, despite having abandoned central tenets of Jewish religious observance such as keeping kosher, celebrating the High Holy Days, and observing the sabbath (Pleck 2000: 95).

The focus of the barmitzvah celebration, Hanukah, and Passover all centred on the family. These celebrations—save for the public Torah reading of the bar-mitzvah, which was, more often than not, eclipsed by the parties and celebrations afterwards—took place in the home within the family unit, running parallel to the privatization of Jewish life away from the synagogue. Public religious cele-brations, like the building of booths for Sukkot or dancing as a community on Simhat Torah, were only celebrated by the most pious American Jews. Domestic Judaism flourished. As Rabbi Joseph Blau explained, 'The Jewish God is a House-hold God' (Blau 1910: 8).

Americanized Jewish Women and Their Guides

Women were instructed by both rabbis and guidebooks that if they wished to ensure the survival of Judaism, they had to create a domestic sanctuary for their Jewish family. As a result, the importance of private family-based celebrations flourished. Both Passover and Hanukah evolved into consumer-driven holidays, where women were enticed to purchase various accoutrements to create a more attractive table for their family and guests, and women became the driving force and motivation behind celebrating these holidays. Just as American women of the same period were experiencing a new consumerism that centred on men as financial providers and women as family spenders, Jewish women focused their economic energy on creating a Jewish table for holiday celebrations. Unable to decorate for the 'American' holidays in the ways that ladies' magazines urged, Jewish women reappropriated these ideas to fashion their own distinctively Jew-ish application of homemaking. This new Jewish homemaking brought together consumerism and religion in a domestic celebration, often concentrated on table decoration and the display of Jewish art, objects, or novelty items (Pleck 2000: 103–4). That is to say, they brought together secular consumerism and religious identity and blended them in a way that allowed Jewish women to fashion 'appro-priate' American homes that still retained Jewish characteristics.

By the time that east European Jews arrived on the American scene, early Ger-man American Jewish immigrants had already largely assimilated into American culture. They took it upon themselves to educate the 'old world' Jews on the finer points of American homemaking. German Jews often felt that east European Jews were lacking in style, hygiene, and homemaking skills, fearing that their 'un-American' ways would cause others to assume that all Jews were as unedu-cated, unhygienic, and inept as German Jews supposed their sisters to be. In an effort to help 'educate' new immigrants, several publications emerged, including

Mabel Hyde Kittredge's 1911 publication, *Housekeeping Notes: How to Furnish and Keep Home in a Tenement Flat*. In 1905 the Council of Jewish Women unveiled their 'Home-Making Center and Model Flat' in Brownsville, New York. Over 1,500 young women visited it in the first six months. The Model Flat was intended as an education centre to teach young women proper hygiene for both themselves and their children. They were taught to 'see the benefits that come from fresh air and a clean home', as well as 'the dangers that lurk in neglected plumbing'. Beyond cleanliness, the Model Flat also offered lessons in childrearing, teaching about 'the proper feeding of children and the time for feeding and the absolute necessity of system in every life and most of all the baby's' (Charity Organization of the City of New York 1905: 181).

Americanized Jewish women were particularly critical of the lack of contemporary commercialized Judaica and decorative items on display in the homes of east European immigrants. Failing to take into account the crushing poverty from which they had fled, the relatively few items they had been able to bring with them, and the limited purchasing power they possessed, German women found the few old world items—generally *yahrzeit* memorials, kiddush cups, and sabbath candlesticks—that east European women possessed to be unsuitable. Assimilated American Jews considered such items 'ancient relics' and, if not completely abandoned, they remained boxed up or tucked out of eyesight. As a 1931 survey suggests, these 'manifestations of Jewishness' were found in fewer than 20 per cent of Jewish homes (Joselit 1994: 148).

Although they were secure in their role as guardians of Judaism in the home, which was in part demonstrated through the display of Judaica, including items such as table accoutrements, decorative art, and stylized novelty items, between the First and Second World Wars German American Jewish women began to question their role in synagogue life. The first Jewish Sisterhood of Personal Service was established in 1888 by Rabbi Gustav Gottheil (Goldman 2006: 535). The prototype spread, but it was not until the Sisterhoods began focusing their energy on aiding east European immigrants that they truly flourished. Much as Christian women championed missionary work and the temperance movement, Sisterhoods quickly expanded beyond improving the hygiene of their 'old world' sisters and focused increasingly on social action and justice. Perhaps most illuminating is the story of Hannah G. Solomon, the founder of the National Council of Jewish Women (NCJW). After organizing a group of Jewish women to participate in the 1893 Chicago World's Fair and being relegated to serving coffee and snacks, Solomon, followed by her team, walked out of the event. Discouraged that volunteer work was not viewed as a serious enterprise, Solomon founded NCJW, which remains an active organization.

After the First World War, NCJW not only worked for universal female suffrage and sent aid worldwide to other Jews, but also concentrated on helping those within the United States through such efforts as the foundation of the Jewish Braille Institute in 1931 (Goldman 2006: 538) and by working to spread medical care through the Farm and Rural Work Program. American feminized domestic Judaism began to move outside the home and found its manifestation and voice in social action. One way in which this collective voice of justice manifested was through the publication of resources specifically tailored to the needs of Jewish women engaged in this type of work, creating a form of self and collective agency, as well as fostering connections between Sisterhoods and organizations.

Although some women questioned the female role in synagogue life—indeed, it was in 1920 that Martha Neumark 'asked' to serve in the pulpit at Hebrew Union College's High Holy Day services—most were still content to remain in the home. Like their Christian counterparts, these women identified themselves first as wives and mothers. However, unlike Christian women, they were not actively attending religious services in addition to completing their charitable aid work. Without any halakhic (Jewish legal) imperative to attend religious services, women had historically been largely absent from the synagogue. This served only to increase the exclusionary language barrier that most of these women encountered when they entered the synagogue. Since they were unschooled in Hebrew, the liturgical language, most of the literature targeting Jewish women was, therefore, written in Yiddish or English.

Facing increasingly empty synagogues, Jewish leaders realized that it was through women that Judaism could be revived. Rose Goldstein explained in 1938, 'The future of American Jewry is directly conditioned on the education of its womanhood' (Goldstein 1938: 13; Sarna 2004: 268–9). With the gradual shift, particularly within the Reform movement, towards English and Yiddish services, women trickled in to fill the pews. As noted in Leah Morton's popular 1926 novel *I Am a Woman—And a Jew*, 'The men pay their dues to the synagogue and feel it's enough. You can't get them to come to services . . . The women come and they bring the children. But the men stay home' (Joselit 1994: 255).[4] Many synagogues shifted services from Saturday mornings to Friday nights, with the hope that more men could be persuaded to attend.[5] Some Reform congregations even dared to shift services to Sunday mornings, although that idea yielded little result and has exhibited no lasting power.

Feminizing and Aestheticizing Shabbat

Jenna Weissman Joselit identifies lack of interest in sabbath observance as an extension of home-centred religion in America. That is to say, it was not that American Jews were entirely uninterested in the sabbath. Rather, they were uninterested in communal worship and preferred to celebrate the sabbath in an individualized way that echoed the flavour of their family life. Women were told in a 1941 publication that, 'The observance and rites of the Sabbath, as well as those of all Jewish holidays, are centered in the home. Except for attendance at synagogue services, the ritual of the Sabbath calls for the home environment and aims at fostering family loyalty in the harmonious spirit of Sabbath joy' (Isaacs and Rosmarin 1941: 34).

Working hand in hand with Sisterhoods, many congregations began to honour women during special sabbath services called 'Sisterhood sabbaths'. These events, beginning with a directive from the National Federation of Temple Sisterhoods in 1922, served as a way of recognizing the accomplishments of Jewish women in the local community. Not only did they recognize the significant contributions of Jewish women, but they also encouraged women to attend sabbath services. Coupled with attendance, many Conservative and Reform Sisterhoods used this as a time to allow women to lead sabbath services, preach, and engage in public religious expression (Goldman 2006: 539).

As an extension of this increasingly female interest in sabbath and Jewish observance, Sisterhoods penned Jewish homemaking guides that challenged the idea that Judaism was an antiquated religion. The Temple Women's Association in the East released a statement in 1939 that encouraged women to help their families avoid the distractions of entertainment and parties during the sabbath, and noted that it is both 'unnecessary and undesirable for Jewish people to permit any interference with the hours of public worship on Sabbath and Holy Days'. It went on to urge all women 'to aid in preserving the sanctity of our Sabbaths and Holy Days and through an active and enlightened Jewish consciousness to guarantee the preservation of Judaism as our most precious heritage to coming generations of Jews'.[6]

The sabbath was not as easy to sell to Jewish women as Passover and Hanukah had been. Rather, it required some creative repackaging (Figure 2). The Union of American Hebrew Congregations in their 1942 publication, *Leading a Jewish Life in the Modern World*, suggested that 'the only way we can produce the Sabbath and start changing the pattern of behavior on that day is to sell it to a group of young intelligent mothers and their children and make them feel good about it, [because] they are setting a new fashion for the Sabbath Day, giving it a "new look" so to speak' (Markowitz 1942: 141). In keeping with the American trend of turning to guidebooks for homemaking and childrearing—Dr Benjamin Spock's pivotal *Baby and Childcare* was published first in 1946—Jewish women sought out books specifically targeted to their needs. Esther Levy's *Jewish Cookery Book on Principles of Economy Adapted for Jewish Housekeepers with Medicinal Recipes and Other Valuable Information Relative to Housekeeping and Domestic Management* (1871) was the first widely distributed publication for Jewish women, incorporating both recipes and homemaking guidelines. Focusing on important points of etiquette and direction of housekeepers, the publication reflects a very bourgeois approach to homemaking typical of German Jewish communities of the time. Likewise, Bertha F. Kramer's *Aunt Babette's Cook Book, Foreign and Domestic*

Figure 2 Guidebooks especially encouraged women to celebrate the sabbath and High Holy Days. At this Sisterhood event in Harrisburg, Pennsylvania, a woman sits at a Rosh Hashanah table she has curated. The table is largely modernized, without traditional 'Old World' candlesticks, but with a kiddush cup paired with a modern wine decanter and wineglasses. The prominently displayed pineapple symbolizes hospitality. *Photograph by Arnold Zuckerman. Historical Society of Dauphin County*

Resipst [sic] *for the Household* (1889) also focused on more formal applications of Jewish homemaking.

The arrival of east European Jewish immigrants challenged American Jewish cultural assumptions, and new guidebooks emerged to 'educate' immigrant women. These new books included practical advice—like not eating banana peel—as well as American-style cookery and homemaking tips. The early forerunner was Deborah Melamed's *The Three Pillars: Thought, Practice and Worship for Jewish Women* (Melamed 1902), which was followed by the popular editions of Betty Greenberg and Althea Silverman's *The Jewish Home Beautiful* (Greenberg and Silverman 1941), Hyman Elias Goldin's *The Jewish Woman and Her Home* (Goldin 1941), and Miriam Isaacs and Trude Weiss Rosmarin's *What Every Jewish Woman Should Know: A Guide for Jewish Women* (Isaacs and Rosmarin 1941: 34). These books offered a combination of practical advice mixed with compelling arguments for greater religious observance that appealed to both the Jewish wife and consumer.

The emergence of these books is linked to the experience of Jewish immigrant adjustment to America. By the 1930s, east European immigrant women had transcended the well-intentioned guidance offered by German American Jews. They were largely assimilated, gradually moving out of ghetto tenements and into single-family apartments and homes, and beginning to experience a sense of economic security. As their husbands achieved greater economic success through job development and promotion, Jewish women were relocated from the work force back into the home. Like other American women of the time, they turned their attention to maintaining the social status of their family through the cultivation of a sophisticated home and personal style. Their conception of the Jewish home, however, differed from that of the typical American home. As Elizabeth Pleck describes it, 'the Gentile home was to be a refuge against corruption and evil, [but] the Jewish home was supposed to function as a bulwark against assimilation'. In line with the popular behavioural psychology trends of the time, Jews were encouraged to create a home with a 'truly Jewish atmosphere' to help form a child's character within the first four years of his/her life (Pleck 2000: 104).

Although the Jewish homemaking guides were similar to other non-Jewish feminine guidebooks of the era in terms of childrearing advice, they differed in other content. The creation of these guidebooks, even the title of *The Jewish Home Beautiful*, were influenced by other popular homemaking guides of the same era, including J. R. Miller's *The Home Beautiful* (1912), Hester Reisinger's *The Home Beautiful* (1925), and Mattie Shannon's *The Home Beautiful* (1939). These guides to homemaking concentrated on thriftiness, housekeeping, and cultivating a sense of (Christian) moral virtue in the home. Other non-Jewish guides, like the *Household Searchlight Homemaking Guide* (Migliario, Titus, and Nunemaker 1937) or features in *Ladies' Home Journal* and *Good Housekeeping*, focused on organized kitchens, Christian holiday celebrations, and recipes (Walker 1998: 145–92). Jewish guidebooks, on the other hand, focused on three general themes: sabbath observance, creating a Jewish atmosphere in the home, and how the celebration of Jewish holidays could be just as fulfilling and full of material culture as Christian holidays.

Lest Jewish women be afraid that having a Jewish home seem un-American, they are reminded that there is no shame in beautifying their homes with Judaica, which could be easily purchased at synagogue Judaica shops (Zollman 2010). Indeed, it is their duty to enrich 'the American scene with beautiful and significant values, which only *she* and the members of her minority can contribute'. Seen as a hallmark of democracy, 'The Jewish woman should therefore proudly display the markers of Jewishness in her home. There is no reason for her to hide her Jewishness or keep from observing it in order not to be "different"' (Isaacs and Rosmarin 1941: 6).

The Women's League of the United Synagogue, affiliated with the Conservative movement, established a series of pageants beginning in 1932. This series was eventually photographed and published in the first edition of *The Jewish Home Beautiful* in 1941. Jewish homemaking pageants were popular and quickly spread beyond Conservative Sisterhoods to reach other Jewish women. In fact, the movement became so popular that it was featured as part of the Joint Sisterhood Assembly in the Temple of Religion at the 1940 World's Fair. The subsequent publication of the guidebook created an illustrated and informative text on the basis of which Jewish American women could model their homes. The book, published for over two decades in fourteen editions, is filled with photographs of various table settings, as well as narrative text for those wishing to create their own pageant. It also included a healthy dose of advice and guidance, generally centred on encouraging women to become more religiously observant through their homemaking preparations. Women were told, 'The Jewish woman today, guided by the memories and traditions of yesterday, must create new glory and new beauty for the Jewish home of today' (Greenberg and Silverman 1941: 13). It goes on to tell women that 'every mother in Israel [should] assume her role as artist, and on every festival, Sabbath and holiday [strive] to make her home and her family table a thing of beauty as precious and as elevating as anything painted on canvas or chiseled in stone' (Greenberg and Silverman 1941: 13–14). Apparently, judging from photographs of displays and contests for decorated holiday tables in many synagogues during the 1950s and 1960s, the guide was essential for materializing and mediating a Jewish modernism (Figures 3 and 4).

Although most of these guidebooks assumed that women had the purchasing power and initiative to create beautiful table-scapes filled with settings of silver, fresh and luxurious table linens, china, crystal, and other luxuries, the writers of *The Jewish Home Beautiful* recognized that not all women possessed the same socioeconomic privileges. In an effort to encourage even those with lesser means to become involved in religious homemaking, they reminded their readers, 'A little skill and love and understanding can transform the humblest surroundings into a sanctuary more holy and beautiful than the house decorated elaborately, but without love and intelligence and religious warmth' (Greenberg and Silverman 1941: 14). Likewise, the guide asserted, 'Whether that home be a crude hut or a rich mansion, it is within the power of the Jewish woman to beautify it with the beauty of holiness' (Greenberg and Silverman 1941: 17; see Figure 4).

In addition to avoiding the lure of Christian holidays and celebrations[7] and working to create and maintain a more Jewish home atmosphere, the power of these guidebooks is in their repackaging of the Jewish sabbath. It is not surprising that Jewish women were interested in reconceptualizing Jewish holidays and rituals—they felt excluded from participation in Christian festivities, and this gave them an entry point into American consumer-based celebration. Likewise, in an era when women were turning increasingly to guidebooks, homemaking and childrearing manuals, and cookbooks, it can be expected that Jewish women would desire and purchase materials that catered to their needs. What is startling,

Figure 3 Two women display an elaborate tablescape for Sukkot in Harrisburg, Pennsylvania. Their tableau includes the traditional lulav and etrog, as well as a miniature sukkah, complete with a table, candlesticks, and small dolls. The pineapple symbolizes hospitality. *Photograph by Arnold Zuckerman. Historical Society of Dauphin County*

however, is how sabbath observance crept into these guidebooks. Its presence permeates the text—both subtly and, at times, overtly.

These guidebooks, for the most part, consider the laws of *kashrut* (kosher dietary laws) outdated and unnecessary. Their only lasting shadow remains in recipe sections, which do not explicitly separate meat and milk, but offer no recipes in which they are combined. Likewise, these recipes also exclude forbidden foods like pig and shellfish. The laws of *nidah* (sexual purity) are similarly absent and are rarely mentioned or even hinted at.[8] Why, then, is the sabbath included as one of the ways in which a Jewish woman can create her own Jewish Home Beautiful?

This question has all too often been glossed over. The easy answer is that for most Jews, the sabbath is considered the most important and holiest holiday of the year. Despite its weekly occurrence, it is treated as a celebration. However, that answer ignores the contextualized nuances of the era in which the works were written. It seems more likely that the sabbath was included for two complementary reasons. First, in terms of creating an aesthetically pleasing table setting, sabbath meals lent themselves particularly well to the task. Unlike Yom Kippur, a

Figure 4 A woman from Harrisburg, Pennsylvania, shows how some ingenuity can create a captivating Purim tablescape. Her table features handmade masks, money from children's board games, a small floral centrepiece, and homemade *hamentashen*, all interspersed with more everyday Judaica, such as an embroidered challah cover. *Photograph by Arnold Zuckerman. Historical Society of Dauphin County*

solemn holiday of fasting, the sabbath was joyous. It appealed to the female Jewish consumer: items could be purchased to help enhance the sabbath ambiance.

Second, the sabbath appealed to Jewish women in terms of female ritual observance. Just as the Sisterhoods had been heavily involved in the suffrage movement, American Jewish women were known for being both liberal and forward-thinking. Decades before their Jewish sister Betty Friedan would pen *The Feminine Mystique* (1963), American Jewish women were gently beginning to probe issues of gender. Many felt that Judaism had long been a patriarchal religion that largely excluded women. As non-Orthodox synagogues became more female-friendly through the elimination of the *meḥitsah* (the partition between the sexes), thus allowing mixed and family seating, as well as through the shift to English-language services and the increase of female Jewish education, women began to seek their place within Jewish practice.

Much Jewish legal discourse is centred on the commandments that men are required to uphold. There are, however, three *mitsvot* (commandments) traditionally associated with women (Weissler 1998: 29). Although women are included in other *mitsvot*, such as keeping kosher, that target Jews at large, the three *mitsvot* particularly associated with women are *nerot* (lighting candles), *ḥalah* (separating a portion of dough), and *nidah* (sexual purity laws that require men and women to be separate during the menstrual cycle and require a female to immerse herself in a *mikveh* (ritual bath) afterwards in order to cleanse herself). Sexual purity laws were, unsurprisingly, considered outdated and vestiges of 'old world Judaism'. Candle-lighting and *ḥalah*-baking, both integral parts of sabbath observance, were easy to reinstate as central female practices. They were not only an entry point into Judaism for women, but they were uniquely feminine and, to be quite honest, not difficult to implement. Unlike keeping a kosher kitchen or observing sexual purity laws, which would have required significant lifestyle changes, sabbath celebration could occur at various levels of observance.

The Jewish sabbath also reasserted the Jewish woman's role in the home. This occurs on two levels: Judaic and domestic, through association with the *Eshet ḥayil* ('woman of valour') ushering in the sabbath and her role in cultivating a Jewish home sanctuary. With Jewish men participating in synagogue life in staggeringly low numbers, the perpetuation of Judaism fell on the shoulders of women. Guidebooks reminded them that '[the sabbath] has preserved the dignity and self-respect of the Jew through centuries of oppression and darkness' (Greenberg and Silverman 1941: 35) and that 'the woman is privileged to be the first to usher in the Shabbat' (ibid.: 35). Although she was not considered the head of the household, nor could serve in a prominent role in the synagogue, at the head of the sabbath table, the woman stood in a position of domestic and religious power. Even though few of these women would adhere to all of the sabbath laws and mainly concentrated on the family meal on Friday night, it was through their action that women were made guardians 'of light, which is symbolic of happiness, joy, and the good life, [and] is the most beautiful tribute and privilege which Judaism bestows upon her'. Indeed, it is through the lighting of candles that women are able to 'actively participate in the sharing of the religious life of the home and the community' (Isaacs and Rosmarin 1941: 71).

It was not, however, enough for the home to be beautiful. It needed to be *Jewishly* beautiful in order to ensure Judaism's survival. Jewish women were told, 'the Jewish home is still the strongest citadel of Judaism. It is the source of Jewish loyalty and inspiration, the bedrock of Jewish observance and of the Jewish way of life. The Jewish home is the living plasma that gives rise to the Jewish community, and its character and pattern determine and condition Jewish group life as no other agency or factor' (Isaacs and Rosmarin 1941: 5). The creation of the Jewish home rested squarely on women. They alone could ensure the continuation of the Jewish people: 'The Jewish fate, the Jewish present, and the Jewish future are in [your] keeping' (ibid.: 5). One of the clearest and easiest ways to do this was through 'the festive Sabbath meal . . . [which] offers the Jewish woman a singular opportunity for creating "Jewish atmosphere" and engendering admiration and enthusiasm for the Jewish way of life in the family' (ibid.: 5). The sabbath, then, 'should inspire Jewish children with pride and happiness in their Jewishness' (ibid.: 10–11).This certainly was no small task for Jewish mothers.

When considering the general domestic role of women in the home, the sabbath dinner stage played out much like a meal in any other American home in the era. Women, in general, were experiencing a shift in which their role as wife and mother was rendered an occupation, causing a reconception and revaluation of the domestic role. Similarly, the emphasis of the father or husband as family provider gained prominence. This was particularly true for east European immigrants. After years of working in textile factories, most had achieved sufficient economic success to move out of the tenements (Braunstein and Joselit 1990: 48). Sensitive to this shift, *The Jewish Home Beautiful* offers the following affirmation of female domestic roles:

So long as there are homes to which men turn
At the close of day;
So long as there are homes where children are,
Where women stay;
If love and loyalty and faith be found
Across those sills—
A stricken nation can recover from
Its gravest ills.

(Greenberg and Silverman 1941: 36)

With women and children now out of the factory and transplanted into the home, the father achieved the role of overall family provider, modelling the assimilated American family structure. Removed from the family in many ways, he sought to demonstrate his love by making gifts or gestures towards his wife and children. In the context of the Jewish home, this played out in a particular way: through the recitation of *Eshet ḥayil*.

The Return of the Sabbath Queen

Sixteenth-century kabbalists (Jewish mystics) would go into the fields, dressed in their sabbath finery, and chant, 'Come, let us welcome the sabbath queen!' (Kolatch 2005). For them, welcoming the Sabbath Queen did not mean the literal anticipation of angelic arrival. Rather, she represented a divinely given bride (BT *Shabat* 119a) for which one waits with eager anticipation. She is welcomed by chanting *Eshet ḥayil*, a 22-verse passage from Proverbs 31 commonly referred to as 'The Woman of Valour'.

Jewish commentators have long considered this biblical passage to be an allegory for the Sabbath Queen or the Shekhinah (the divine presence). It became customary to recite this text before sitting down to eat the sabbath evening meal.

Some communities even left literal space for the Sabbath Queen at their sabbath tables. Beginning with 'An accomplished woman, who can find? Her value is far beyond pearls. Her husband's heart relies on her, and he shall lack no fortune. She does him good and not evil, all the days of her life', the verses go on to laud the woman's wisdom, kindness, charity, and her household management.

East European Jews had largely abandoned the idea of the Sabbath Queen, replacing her with the popular belief that the sabbath represented a foretaste of the afterlife (Cardozo 1982: 8). However, her presence continued to be subtly felt in two ways: through the recitation of *Eshet ḥayil* and in the preparation of the food and table as a festive welcoming. The sabbath was one of the few times of the week when meat was served, and Andrew Heinze notes that through the 'delicious meals, fine garments, and choice tableware' eighteenth- and nineteenth-century east European Jews were able to transform their households (Heinze 1990: 55).

A renewed interest in the Sabbath Queen emerged between 1920 and 1945. Joselit describes American Jews as seeking 'spiritual nourishment' in homes that were considered 'touched by the presence of the proverbial Sabbath Queen and her angels' (Joselit 1994: 259). The idea of the Sabbath Queen embodied much of what the newly repackaged sabbath observance represented. Tables were to be set for royalty, with the finest place settings and decorations. Women were encouraged to place fresh flowers on the table and to create an atmosphere suitable for entertaining an important guest—as the guidebooks asked, 'What more distinguished guest could be entertained in the Jewish home than the "Princess Sabbath"?' (Isaacs and Rosmarin 1941: 36).

There is a significant development of phrases used to describe how a woman ought to prepare for the sabbath. Before this period, the Sabbath Queen had been the allegorical *Eshet ḥayil*. A rhetorical shift occurred that associates the Jewish mother with the *Eshet ḥayil*. She was told, in speech that sounds quite similar to Proverbs 31, that 'Praiseworthy are those women who wash themselves, dress their hair, pare and polish their nails, and put on their best Sabbath apparel before lighting the Sabbath candles' (Goldin 1941: 125). Likewise, women are instructed that it is 'because the Jewish woman is the spirit and the life of the home [that] our sages decreed that the husband, on Friday evening, should recite Proverbs, Chapter xxxi, verses 10–30. In these beautiful poetic verses, King Solomon sings the praises of the valiant God-fearing Jewish woman whom the husband must love, cherish, and admire above all earthly treasures' (ibid.: 130–1).

It is no great wonder that Jewish women identified with the *Eshet ḥayil*. It is she who 'arises while it is still night and gives food to her household' and who engages in both charitable work and household labour. The recitation of the text had earlier been done by the father and directed at the entire family. However, as it was reinterpreted, the father, often arriving home with fresh flowers as his contribution to the sabbath preparations, now turned towards his wife and recited this laudatory hymn. In front of both children and guests, the wife was thanked for her hard work during the week and in sabbath preparations. Her contributions to the family were formally recognized and praised. This served to re-emphasize the importance of her female domestic role as separate and unique. In praising her for her feminine work, the association of the wife and mother with the *Eshet ḥayil* undergirded the general American cultural reaffirmation of separate family gender roles.

Although the idea of the wife as a woman of valour would soon fade due to its patriarchal implications, its impact continues to be felt even at modern sabbath tables.[9] In Orthodox homes, men still recite the verses to praise their wives. Other modern homes eliminate the text, replacing it with a psalm or sections from Song of Songs (Hoffman 2004: 84), or use it to once again refer to the welcoming of the Sabbath Queen. Despite the feminist interest in creating more equitable gender roles within Judaism, the reality is that even in the most liberal of homes, most of the sabbath dinner preparation continues to fall on the mother. With most contemporary women working outside the home, it is more difficult to find time for such elaborate food and table preparation. However, contemporary guides urge that tables continue to be set with 'clean, fresh cloth, the best china, crystal, silver, and flowers', with the caveat that, 'if you happen to be a paper plate user, then get special paper plates for Shabbat, just as you would for a party' (Greenberg 1983: 34). Even if the family must eat takeout or prepackaged food, contemporary mothers are told that 'any menu can be made special with a tablecloth and flowers on the dining room table' (Diamant 1991: 33).

Perhaps even more significant than the reintroduction of Judaica into the home is the revitalization of Judaism that stemmed from Jewish women turning to these guidebooks. Through their bonding as Jewish women, they in turn acted socially to construct a new Jewish family practice that they deemed appropriate for America (Boyarin 2013). Having been raised by immigrant parents who had largely abandoned traditional practices, this new generation of women used these books to establish the foundation upon which they re-Judaized their families. Through their commitment, creative repackaging of the Jewish sabbath, and imaginative new approaches to religious ritual, Judaism was revived and preserved for present generations. The new Judaism that emerged was one that was much more female-friendly, affirming the roles of Jewish women both in the home and in the synagogue. Jewish women were empowered to act as agents of social change in the community and were equally equipped to act as instruments of change within their homes. Through their conscious choices to reimagine Jewish ritual and reinstitute family sabbath observance, they brought Judaism to a whole new generation of believers and helped define an American Jewish identity and practice.

Notes

1   *Shabat* (Hebrew) and *shabes* (Yiddish) are direct cognates of the English word 'sabbath'. For the purposes of this paper, 'sabbath' has been used throughout, except for direct quotations.

2   Indeed, it would be laity who would pen the guidebooks, not rabbis or other trained Jewish educators.

3   Translated and quoted by Sarna (2004: 164).

4   Leah Morton was the pen name of Elizabeth Stern, also known for writing for the *Philadelphia Sunday Record*, the *New York Times*, and the *Philadelphia Public Leader*. Stern published several autobiographical pieces addressing the roles of Jewish women and the tensions they encountered during the early 1900s.

5   Indeed, this continues to be the practice among most Reform and Conservative congregations. Orthodox synagogues, on the other hand, generally adhere to Saturday morning sabbath services as well as Friday night ones.

6   This resolution is quoted in its entirety in Bookstaber 1939: 210–11. This book may also be of particular local interest, as Rabbi Bookstaber served as the head rabbi at the Reform Synagogue Ohev Sholom in Harrisburg, Pennsylvania, while writing it.

7   Greenberg and Silverman remind their readers on p. 14 that, 'The attractive settings offered by our large department stores and women's magazines for Valentine's Day, Hallowe'en, Christmas and other non-Jewish festive days have won the hearts of many of our women who either through lack of knowledge or of imagination have failed to explore the possibilities of our own traditions.' Isaacs also notes on p. 35 that 'the intelligent Jewish woman will carefully plan the program, for each and every Sabbath of the year and vary the spiritual fare and home entertainment, so that her family will not even think of envying their Christian or Jewish friends who spend Saturday afternoon at the movies or in another diversion incompatible with the Sabbath law and the Sabbath spirit'.

8   The exception for both the laws of *kashrut* and *nidah* is Isaacs' book. She offers roughly four paragraphs on *nidah* and nine pages as an introduction to keeping a kosher kitchen.

9   For an example, see Hoffman 2004. On p. 84, the *Eshet ḥayil* is critiqued by Ellen Frankel: 'It praises only the wife, not her partner; it reflects an ancient reality, not our own; it extols workaholism as a virtue, not a neurosis; it fails to consider that partners might share tasks in a marriage; it obviously excludes the possibility of same sex partnerships.'

References

ADLER, CYRUS. 1900. *American Jewish Yearbook: September 25, 1900 to September 13, 1901*. Philadelphia.

BLAU, RABBI JOSEPH. 1910. 'Who Will Question?', *Hebrew Standard* (6 May): 8.

BOOKSTABER, PHILLIP DAVID. 1939. *Judaism and the American Mind in Theory and Practice*, New York.

BOYARIN, JONATHAN. 2013. *Jewish Families*. New Brunswick, NJ.

BRAUNSTEIN SUSAN L., and JENNA WEISSMAN JOSELIT. 1990. *Getting Comfortable in New York: The American Jewish Home, 1880–1950*. New York.

BRONNER, SIMON J. 2010. 'The Dualities of House and Home in Jewish Culture'. In Simon J. Bronner, ed., *Jews at Home: The Domestication of Identity*, Jewish Cultural Studies 2, 1–42. Oxford.

CARDOZO, ARLENE. 1982. *Jewish Family Celebrations: The Sabbath, Festivals, and Ceremonies*. New York.

Charity Organization of the City of New York. 1905. *The Survey*. New York.

DIAMANT, ANITA. 1991. *Living a Jewish Life: Jewish Traditions, Customs, and Values for Today's Families*. New York.

FRIEDAN, BETTY. 1963. *The Feminine Mystique*. New York.

GOLDIN, HYMAN ELIAS. 1941. *The Jewish Woman and Her Home*. New York.

GOLDMAN, KARLA. 2006. 'Reform Judaism'. In Rosemary Skinner Keller and Rosemary Radford Ruether, eds., *Encyclopedia of Women and Religion in North America*. Bloomington, Ind.

GOLDSTEIN, ROSE B. 1938. 'Women's Share of Responsibilities for the Future of Judaism'. *Women's League Outlook*, 8 (May): 13.

GREENBERG, BETTY D., and ALTHEA O. SILVERMAN. 1941. *The Jewish Home Beautiful*. New York.

GREENBERG, BLU. 1983. *How to Run a Traditional Jewish Household*. New York.

HEINZE, ANDREW. 1990. *Adapting to Abundance: Jewish Immigrants, Mass Consumption, and the Search for American Identity*. New York.

HELLER, CELIA S., and NATHAN GLAZER. 1994. *On the Edge of Destruction: Jews of Poland between the Two World Wars*. Detroit, Mich.

HOFFMAN, LAWRENCE (ed.). 2004. *My People's Prayer Book: 7: Shabbat at Home*. New York.

ISAACS, MIRIAM, and TRUDE WEISS ROSMARIN. 1941. *What Every Jewish Woman Should Know: A Guide for Jewish Women*. New York.

JOSELIT, JENNA WEISSMAN. 1994. *The Wonders of America: Reinventing Jewish Culture, 1880–1950*. New York.

KITTREDGE, MABEL HYDE. 1911. *Housekeeping Notes: How to Furnish and Keep Home in a Tenement Flat*. New York.

KOLATCH, ALFRED J. 2005. *A Handbook for the Jewish Home*. New York.

KRAMER, BERTHA F. 1889. *Aunt Babette's Cook Book, Foreign and Domestic Resipst [sic] for the Household*. New York.

LEVY, ESTHER. 1871. *Jewish Cookery Book on Principles of Economy Adapted for Jewish Housekeepers with Medicinal Recipes and Other Valuable Information Relative to Housekeeping and Domestic Management*. New York.

MARKOWITZ, SAMUEL HARRISON. 1942. *Leading a Jewish Life in the Modern World*. New York.

MELAMED, DEBORAH M. 1902. *The Three Pillars: Thought, Worship, and Practice for the Jewish Woman*. New York.

MIGLIARIO, IDA RIGNEY, ZORADA Z. TITUS, and IRENE NUNEMAKER, eds. 1937. *The Household Searchlight Homemaking Guide*. Topeka, Kans.

MILLER, J. R. 1912. *The Home Beautiful*. New York.

PLECK, ELIZABETH H. 2000. *Celebrating the Family: Ethnicity, Consumer Culture, and Family Rituals*. Cambridge, Mass.

REISINGER, HESTER. 1925. *The Home Beautiful*. New York.

SARNA, JONATHAN D. 2004. *American Judaism: A History*. New Haven, Conn.

SHANNON, MATTIE. 1939. *The Home Beautiful*. New York.

WALKER, NANCY A. 1998. *Women's Magazines: 1940–1960, Gender Roles and the Popular Press*. Cambridge, Mass.

WEISSLER, CHAVA. 1998. *Voices of the Matriarchs: Listening to the Prayers of Early Modern Jewish Women*. Boston, Mass.

ZOLLMAN, JOELLYN WALLEN. 2010. 'Every Wise Woman Shoppeth for Her House: The Sisterhood Gift Shop and the American Jewish Home in the Mid-Twentieth Century'. In Simon J. Bronner, ed., *Jews at Home: The Domestication of Identity*, Jewish Cultural Studies 2, 5–106. Oxford.

THREE

Social Tensions and Cultural Encounters in Contemporary Israeli *Midrash*

TSAFI SEBBA-ELRAN

A NEW JEWISH–ISRAELI DISCOURSE has evolved on multiple fronts since the last decades of the twentieth century. The establishment of pluralistic *batei midrash* (houses of study) in Israel, dedicated to the study of Jewish literature, to the practice of Jewish rituals, and to the formation of local communities, has been part and parcel of this development (see Sheleg 2010; Katz 2011: 195–264; Werczberger 2011: 203–25; Jacobson 2017). Another aspect of this discursive landscape has been the renewal of the 'Jewish bookshelf' as a modern term, referring not merely to traditional Jewish writings but also to modern works echoing earlier ones.[1] This renewal is reflected first and foremost in the resurgence of particular ancient stories, turning up as popular legends in different Jewish study groups.

One example of such a modern rereading involves Rabbi Hiya bar Ashi and his struggle with the *yetser hara*, the evil inclination (BT *Kid.* 81b). This story, probably set down in writing around the fifth century CE, has recently sprung to new life as part of an emerging discussion on the relationship between femininity, sexuality, Jewishness, and Zionism. In what follows I will try to account for its growing popularity among contemporary Israeli readers, and elaborate on its adaptation in and contribution to a modern Jewish discourse.[2] I will show that contemporary readings of this story both infused it with new substance (mainly involving feminist interpretations) and set it within modern genres such as poetry, popular music, and emails. From a functional point of view, contemporary commentators on the Rabbi Hiya bar Ashi story not only created new ideological (feminist) horizons for the newly read text, but also used it to establish a 'challenging' local discourse, to use Bruner and Gorfain's words (1984). This discourse or narration act resists, as a whole, a single definitive interpretation (Bruner and Gorfain 1984: 60), both by employing different genres from various cultural contexts, and by metaphorically marking the conflict between competing groups within Israeli society.

The renewed textual traditions under discussion are usually called by their authors 'readings', 'interpretations' or 'exegeses' (in Hebrew, *keriah, peirush, midrash*, or *derashah*). Like the midrash of the early sages, and unlike the scientific, academic study of such texts, these readings are usually rooted in the life of their writers, reflecting a patent, conscious effort to express modern values and even personal experience using ancient stories, and thus reinfuse them into the lifeblood of the community. In another similarity to classical midrash, contemporary readings clothe ancient texts in fresh literary and conceptual garb, and appeal to their readership by underlining the artistic and experiential dimensions of the narratives. Such creative readings are thus founded on literary and rhetorical devices, of which I shall highlight and expound on the following two: first, the fashioning of binary contrasts in modern texts; and second, intertextual readings, juxtaposing texts from different historical and literary contexts. Importantly, though these readings are not religiously motivated, writers tend to empathize with the world of the sages, and reflect their cultural commitment to it.[3]

Moreover, while the new Israeli midrash should be considered a part of Israeli print culture, both its roots and horizons exceed it. First, most of the readings discussed below were written by teachers and participants in pluralistic *batei midrash* in Israel, and were developed in the course and for the benefit of study sessions and communal gatherings. Second, many of the writers encouraged the participation of reading and writing collaborators—deviating from conventional norms of individualistic writing. These were usually partners from different genders, religious backgrounds, or professional occupations, presumably in an effort to assert the dialogic nature of the modern midrash. Finally, not all readings went to print: two were published on the Internet, becoming part of the world of digital media and reaching new audiences.

From Rabbi Hiya to Haruta: Jewish 'Mothers' as Role Models

The story discussed here first appeared as one of five traditions set forth as part of the *yiḥud* (physical intimacy) issue in Jewish law, regarding sages who have confronted the *yetser hara* (BT *Kid.* 81a–b). It is quoted, with some modifications, from the Soncino translation, with additions from other printed editions in parentheses:

Whenever Rabbi Hiya b. Ashi fell upon his face [in prayer] he would say, 'Let the Merciful save us from the evil inclination.' One day his wife overheard him. 'Let us see', she reflected, 'for so many years he has held aloof from me: why then should he pray thus?' One day, while he was studying in his garden, she adorned herself and walked up and down before him. 'Who are you?' he demanded. 'I am Haruta [a famous whore, according to Rashi], and I have returned today', she replied. He desired her. Said she to him, 'Bring me that pomegranate from the uppermost bough.' He jumped up, went, and brought it to her. When he re-entered his house, his wife was firing the oven, whereupon he ascended and sat in it. 'What does this mean?' she demanded. He told her what had befallen. 'It was I', she assured him; [but he paid no heed to her until she gave him proof]. 'Nevertheless', said he, 'my intention was evil.' [For the rest of his life the righteous man fasted until he died on that account.]

This story is open to a wide range of possible interpretations, for it leaves many questions unanswered: why was Rabbi Hiya fighting his urges in the first place? Was it on account of past failures, or rather in order to persist in his abstinence? Was his wife happy or dismayed when she found out about it, and what was it that she wanted to accomplish by assuming the identity of Haruta—was she trying to thwart his efforts or rather to save him from temptation, and bring him closer to her? Furthermore, does the story end in success or in failure? In other words, does Rabbi Hiya b. Ashi atone for his forbidden thoughts, reflecting a rabbinic ideal, or is this purported ideal (i.e. abstinence and self-torment) proved to be untenable by the end of the story?[4]

The questions that the story raises, and the fact that it deals with issues pertinent to our own times—such as liberty and permissiveness, desire and sexuality, relationships and communication, masculinity and femininity—make it a fertile ground not just for academic study but also for midrashic readings. And as mentioned earlier, such readings do not merely reflect but also create a novel Jewish consciousness, pregnant with its own answers to and questions for the story.

The roots of the midrashic effort to revive the story of Rabbi Hiya bar Ashi can be traced back to a feminist desire to elicit repressed voices and insights about gender from ancient texts. Ruth Calderon, one of the first contemporary Israeli rejuvenators of rabbinic tales, goes on a literary voyage whose aim is 'to present my daughters with positive role models instead of oppressed ones' (Calderon 2001: 11). Ruchama Weiss confesses that 'I'm looking for mothers.' She explains: 'I don't have a single example for a woman who has "made it": who has managed to effortlessly combine professional self-realization with the traditional roles of women—ones that I want for myself as well' (Weiss and HaCohen 2012: 12, 16). These seemingly personal purposes of Calderon and Weiss evidently echo ideological ones. Inbar Raveh shares in this search for women guides:

I hope we can create more equal social relationships between men and women, as well as give them Jewish legitimization. . . . It is my hope that by getting to the bottom of tacit, sophisticated cultural mechanisms of oppression, silencing, and exclusion, we might draw closer to neutralizing and dismantling them (Raveh 2012: 19).[5]

This ideological purpose shared by Raveh and other contemporary writers goes hand in hand with a search for a 'feminine language' or a 'mother tongue', as Nehama Weingarten-Mintz (2009: 18) calls the quest for a 'different' Jewish-feminine expression, one that might inspire a new Jewish midrash.

It is Haruta, then, rather than Rabbi Hiya, who is called upon here to portray a new kind of femininity—to teach us about the workings of oppressive social mechanisms in order to dismantle them, to serve as spiritual mother and leader. Can she realize these expectations, and if so, how?

Between Eve and Lilith: Feminism in Quest and Crisis

One of the first renewed readings in the story of Rabbi Hiya and Haruta was proposed by Ruth Calderon. She starts off with the narrative itself, continues with a 'midrash', which in this case is, essentially, a creative rewrite of the story, and closes with 'thoughts on the story'. Calderon calls the new midrash in her book a 'barefoot reading', that is, a free, unmediated reading of the rabbinic text, intended to bring both her readers and herself closer to the distant and unfamiliar world of the sages. But the midrash that she offers in her book bears no similarity to the rabbinic story in terms of structure or language, and most certainly not in terms of world-view. The centrepiece of this new narrative in Calderon's book is the character of the woman, and her chapter is titled, accordingly, 'Haruta'. Rabbi Hiya's wife disguises herself as a prostitute in order to attain a freedom of action—and perhaps of thought as well—usually unavailable for women in her society. As a prostitute she is free to discover her sensual body, her sexuality, and even to celebrate them briefly. Calderon points out, as do other writers, the connection between the heroine's name, Haruta, and the Hebrew word for freedom, ḥerut. She uses this link to characterize the woman in the story:

On the next market day she went out as usual . . . chose a dress, jewellery, sandals and a belt . . . then in a secluded corner put on her revealing dress, tied the belt around her waist, untied her headscarf to let her hair down, put a bell bracelet on her wrist and an anklet on her ankle. . . . The bundle of myrrh she tied in a string round her neck, so that it dangled between her breasts. . . . As she approached the well in the yard, a new woman was reflected in the clear waters: the face of Haruta, terror of matrons. 'I am Haruta', she whispered, 'The Great Woman of Babylon. Let the Merciful save you.' (Calderon 2001: 51–2)

Apart from the accented sexuality of the feminine body, the location of the story is given a central role in Calderon's characterization of her protagonist. First she highlights the gender inequality of space: 'the whole world is open to him [Rabbi Hiya]', while his wife 'is cooped up in her corner'. But whereas he chooses to stay at home in order to keep himself away from 'alien [unwelcome] thoughts', she goes out to the market and enjoys adorning herself. Her symbolic going out to the garden is a crucial moment in the story—it can develop in either of two ways: turn into a lovers' union or else end tragically. Haruta 'enjoys the game', but Rabbi Hiya is depicted in his nakedness, 'his body exposed like a dog's'. So she seems to be at peace with the act, while he cannot rid himself of the sense of sin. It is a 'flat paradise', adds Calderon in her 'thoughts on the story'—a paradise that the woman seeks to escape, leaving the man behind.

When the woman and the man go back inside (turning 'from one role-playing to another'), she fires the oven and he gets inside it; she pulls him out with her two strong hands but he 'looks away'. Space again serves the narrator to reinforce the dramatic opposition between a man fighting his desires, pursuing abstinence, and a woman longing for her body (and for her man), seeking human reconciliation. She looks straight at him while he evades her; she is strong and he is weak.

To an extent, similar tensions characterize the rabbinic narrative as well; but while in its talmudic context Rabbi Hiya's struggle with the *yetser hara* may be interpreted as a moral example, Calderon clearly finds fault with his efforts: 'the man's existential condition . . . is pathetic and infuriating . . . vacillating between his wish to be saintly and his desire for a prostitute exhausts him and humiliates his lonely wife' (Calderon 2001: 56). Calderon highlights the woman's superiority, her practical wisdom, her energy, her physical and mental health, and perhaps even her sense of humour. But as it is the man's point of view which defines the essence of woman in the story, Calderon's midrash ends in failure: the woman's solicitations are rejected and she is destined to move back and forth between house and market, her own needs unanswered. So to previous oppositions there is added another: the mythical conflict between Eve and Lilith, the dangerous temptress-demon of Jewish lore versus the perfect mother:

The story of Rabbi Hiya bar Ashi is yet another link in a cultural chain that splits Woman into Eve, the good wife and mother, and Lilith, the Other Woman, attractive and threatening. (Calderon 2001: 56)

In other words, the woman's character in this reading is ready to break out, but is prevented from doing so. She is imprisoned by a cultural point of view (either masculine or feminine) that allows her to choose either of two narrowly defined, extreme roles: dedicated mother and faithful wife, on the one hand (Eve), or temptress-whore whose liberality is taken as promiscuity (Lilith).

In her talk show, *Haḥeder* (2001, Channel 2), Calderon hosted Israeli poetess Agi Mishol and poet and professor of Talmud Admiel Kosman, in order to talk about the story of Rabbi Hiya and Haruta, in keeping with the model of traditional study in partnership (*ḥevruta*). Naming the programme *Haḥeder*, after the traditional elementary Jewish school, goes hand in hand with calling modern readings of ancient Jewish sources 'midrash'. The new *ḥeder* does not attempt to simulate the arrangements of the old Jewish *ḥeder*, but rather draws some authority and inspiration from it. Moreover, it alludes to the chambers of the heart, also called *ḥeder* in Hebrew. The name of the show thus reflects a neo-hasidic ideal, already hinted at in the title of Calderon's first book (*The Market, the Home, the Heart*), tracing Jewish religiosity primarily to a universal spiritual need or human emotion.

Calderon's decision to invite both a man and a woman to her show for a dialogic reading of the story is replicated in other Israeli midrashim, recognizing the interdependence between the sexes. But this specific televised encounter ended, much like the story itself, in disagreement and conflict: while Calderon and Mishol pointed out the Eros revealed in the heroine's character, an Eros that found no partner, Kosman (in an interpretation which I shall elaborate on later) discerned some change in the male figure, as well as some communication between them. To end the show, the two guests read excerpts from their poetry, thus creating the typical Israeli-midrashic link between the ancient and the modern, and between the objective nature of study and the subjective nature of personal lyric.

Two other modern readings of our story, both pointing out the paralysing split in each of the protagonists' characters, and indicating their evasion of an honest, intimate meeting, are offered by Ezrahi and Gafni (2005: 15–29) and by Inbar (2013: 57–82). Much like Calderon's, these two readings recreate the rabbinic tradition in hopes that it might manifest a fuller, richer feminine experience than what the Israeli public is usually presented with in the context of traditional texts. Ezrahi and Gafni's reading is directed by such contrasts as stasis and dynamism, dark and light, beast and human, and, correspondingly, Lilith and Eve. They mostly criticize Rabbi Hiya for being static, estranged from himself and from his body, and constantly fighting his urges—themes highlighted in Calderon's reading as well. But they also suggest something else: the possibility that the human tragedy unites the sexes, trapped as they both are in unspoken, restrictive cultural definitions and concealed behind masks and costumes. These protagonists are subject to paralysing conceptions of 'fathers' and 'mothers', which do not allow them to give free rein to their bodies and spirits.

Ezrahi and Gafni themselves co-operated in hopes of realizing the potential for a dialogical reading. But shortly after publication, when Gafni was accused of sexually exploiting women in his congregation, Ezrahi renounced their partnership and claimed that the book was his own, exclusive creation.[6] Even in this belated statement Ezrahi admits to Gafni's influence and to the inclusion of some of his ideas in the book. So notwithstanding the particular biographical context of this new reading, one can still identify here too an effort to break the boundaries of print culture and to integrate into new interpretations fresh voices which influence and shape the Israeli sphere of public discourse.

Another landmark in constructing the new Israeli midrash is Ruchama Weiss's readings in rabbinic literature. Weiss has co-written with Avner Ha-Cohen the book 'Mothers in Therapy' (*Imahot betipul*), in which they construct an intertextual reading of Rabbi Hiya bar Ashi's story, combining email correspondence that highlights the different voice of each contributor. Weiss argues that women's liberation cannot advance any further without enlisting men to the joint cause of subverting gender essentialism:

This meeting held several small scenes which challenged our talk about strict divisions between 'feminine' and 'masculine'. Neri [HaCohen] is feeding and I am eating . . . At one point Neri's eyes welled up, and at another it was I who wanted to cry but did not have the courage. Can we really typify feminine and masculine responses? Or is it, perhaps, the very need to typify which is the root cause of our error? (Weiss and Ha-Cohen 2012: 111, see also 16–18)

Weiss thus warns that the journey whose aim is the crowning of culture heroines is itself an all too human endeavour—subject to the effects of personal weaknesses, communication issues, and above all, an elusive, unfathomable essence. Her reading thus reflects the significant developments made by feminist interpretations of the Talmud, which started out by trying to identify female role models and later progressed to eliciting local gender insights, while spotlighting the multiple facets of rabbinical texts (see Fonrobert 2006: 79–80; Hauptman 1994; Ilan 2007; Israeli and Fisher 2013: 6–7).

The man whom Weiss invites for a joint reading is not an artist or author or an academic who regularly deals with rabbinical texts; he is a psychologist, whose calling is healing and saving those very 'exemplary mothers' from their tragic fate. Weiss thus inserts into the interpretative discourse not merely an ideological, feminist purpose but also rhetoric taken from a modern discursive field, that of psychoanalysis. She exposes her own emotional involvement in the text, and the personal meaning she finds therein. The dialogue between HaCohen as a psychologist and friend and Weiss as a scholar and author is reflected in the book, both in their email exchanges and in the conclusions of their study meetings. The multiplicity of roles and perspectives that they express, and the multiplicity of genres and rhetorical patterns directed by their respective professional fields, echo tensions built into the modern Jewish–Israeli identity as a whole.

Like Calderon and her partners, Weiss too finds hidden strengths in Haruta's character, and points out the importance of both the sensual experience of the body and the couple's meeting place for the success of their connection, or at least for its understanding. But Weiss and HaCohen do not celebrate the resultant superiority of Woman; rather, they discern fear in Haruta's character, or alternatively aggression, blindness, and impulsiveness:

I actually think that to a certain extent, she [Haruta] is to blame and should take responsibility. Her mistake being that she ran too quickly and by herself. From a complete lack of any intimacy with her husband she advances directly to the scene in the garden—why did she not try something more gradual? . . . She never asked why he would not touch her—what was the point of always guessing? (Weiss and HaCohen 2012: 114)

This reading clears Rabbi Hiya from blame for the failure of the attempted reconnection—a charge directed at him by Calderon, Ezrahi, and Gafni. In addition, it makes Rabbi Hiya into 'a success story, generally speaking'. Weiss argues that Haruta 'appears ridiculous, while he appears as a pious man' (Weiss and Ha-Cohen 2012: 115). It is not only society that is to blame, despite its rigidity and occasional hostility towards women; Haruta too should be faulted, for not seizing the opportunity to save the relationship.

Compared with previous readings, that offered by Weiss and HaCohen is guided by a completely different set of oppositions. Weiss and HaCohen do not pit woman against man, but rather outline an internal, psychological drama taking place primarily in a feminine consciousness shared by narrator, heroine, and reader. It is a consciousness wrought by tensions: loneliness versus recognition, cold versus heat, outside versus inside, passivity versus movement, silence versus talk, and fear versus faith or hope. Weiss examines herself by way of Haruta: would she be able break the walls of loneliness and reach out to a man, despite the threat of disappointment? Would she stop avoiding the meeting with a partner? The meeting with herself?

Weiss concludes on a personal note, saying that though there may have been expressions of freedom, leadership, and creativity in Haruta's attempt to seduce her husband, these 'did not pay off'. Haruta keeps losing—intimacy, sex, and her freedom as well—as a result of the disparity between her own personal needs and the readiness of her surroundings to acknowledge them:

So ultimately—as is the case with my other mothers, the bold, the creative, the leaders—independence does not pay off. She gained nothing from her choice to go out all adorned. She keeps losing her sexuality, and now with added guilt and social criticism. Her husband becomes more tormented, and she becomes more of a whore. . . . I am starting to think that only women who do not wish to be written into history gain life, which is, in a way, a choice between two types of death. (Weiss and HaCohen 2012: 117)

The path that started out in seeking female role models and by trying to save the mothers of old from marginality and inferiority ended up here with a feeling of crisis—whether as a result of Rabbi Hiya's lack of co-operation and the narrow, limiting range of roles allotted to women throughout history, or as a result of certain personal weaknesses. Woman's hope, according to this perspective, lies in giving up the fantasy of Haruta—the fantasy of the supposedly liberated and desirable woman. This concession would allow women to go beyond internalized social expectations and essentialist definitions of femininity. And it would also allow women to keep their supposedly contrasting ties to both home and career, to seemingly competing roles like wife, mother, and lover, or the roles of patient and narrator-researcher.

The contemporary midrash allows the author to bridge the various forces (personal, feminine, Jewish, Israeli) competing for her identity, for it skips back and forth between academic writing intended for study, writing on the Internet for social purposes, writing fiction, and confessions rooted in the singular subjective experiences of the interpreter. The hybrid language seems essential for the success of such a narrative, meant to reflect and perhaps solve the complexity of modern Israeli experience.

Between the Synagogue and the Rock Club:
Faith vs Freedom

In his book *A New Song: Essays on Israeli Rock Songs* (*Shir ḥadash*), Roni Shweka's reading of the Rabbi Hiya and Haruta story is meant to act as a bridge between the temptations of knowledge and sexual conquest (both termed *lada'at* in Hebrew), on the one hand, and practical commitment to Judaism, on the other. Shweka is trying to connect study with experience, freedom with reverence, and rock 'n' roll with the Jewish canon.

Our story is featured in a chapter called 'The Big City', right after Shweka discusses the song 'My Freedom' (*Ḥeruti*) written by Israeli singer–songwriter Dana Berger. The woman in Berger's song 'goes away, returns, sleeps with whomever she likes', portraying the transient magic of temptation (Shweka 2011: 37). But it is Rabbi Hiya bar Ashi rather than Haruta who is at the centre of Shweka's *derashah* (interpretation). The sage in this case (as in others in the book) is held captive by his 'beastly soul', caught in a tragic loop of sin and punishment. His desire to know burns inside him daily, as Shweka puts it, surrounding him with a band of censuring hounds. According to Shweka, it is only a matter of time before the hungry, aggressive hunter in him turns into victim and prey: because desire, represented in this case by sexual temptation, woman, and fire, tends to conquer the mind and dominate the self.

Like the other commentators discussed above, Shweka responds to the sensual experience of the characters—to the sounds and sights they meet and to the role of space in shaping the meaning of the story. He locates Rabbi Hiya in the forest that served as place of exile for the deposed prince in Rabbi Nahman of Bratslav's story ('The Exchanged Children', *Ma'aseh miben melekh uben shifḥah shenithalfu*), turning day into night in order to draw attention to the dead end confronting the sinning soul. As is the case with the prince in the hasidic tale, Rabbi Hiya lets his body dominate his soul, bringing exile and debauchery upon himself. But in his rendering of the story Shweka also steers Rabbi Hiya out of there, towards the path and the light, guided by laughter, weeping, and melody. Like desire, these sounds are the product of natural, healthy needs; but in the darkness of the night, they too are foreign and uncanny. Shweka thus ascribes special significance to the role of performers rather than songwriters, and to the experience of listening to them in a typically dark rock club, where texts can infiltrate a listener's consciousness directly through the senses.[7] However, according to Shweka, only in the light of faith is it possible and worthwhile to experience, enjoy, and be inspired by the sounds of laughter, weeping, and melody:

When the world is taken as arbitrary and chaotic, lacking purpose and plan, its sounds are perceived as a discordant cacophony of roars and growls: a pride of lions clamouring for prey. But when one believes in the Creator of the universe, who made it according to His divine wisdom and plan, then the sounds of creation can be perceived as a most wonderful melody. (Shweka 2011: 59)

Shweka argues that repairing the exilic godly soul (whether the prince's or Rabbi Hiya's) cannot be done by renouncing the beastly soul and through religious repentance, but rather by seeking out a balance between body and soul, between faith and the temptations of knowledge, between tradition and novelty, and between ancient Jewish canons and marginal contemporary rock songs: 'At some point one must come out of the woods and into the glaring sun, to find that faith alone will not do. . . . One must, then, replace faith with knowledge' (Shweka 2011: 64).

Rabbi Nahman's challenge is also Shweka's: maintaining a religious consciousness in a more 'knowledgeable' world. For Rabbi Hiya, this means dominating the desiring body, using Jewish law and tradition, but not suppressing the body. On the contrary: now, when he resides within the boundaries of the permitted, lying in the bosom of his lawful wife, the 'big city' man can safely express his desires, and liberate his urges. Shweka addresses Rabbi Hiya in the words of Israeli singer–songwriter Ehud Banai, 'Know that pure gold sparkles in your home / And that a better woman you will not find anywhere / But you must see her differently with each passing day / Like a new sun shining again and again / You must see her sanctified each night / Like the new moon.'

Having 'shared' with Rabbi Hiya the teachings of both Rabbi Nahman and Ehud Banai, Shweka embraces the Jewish ritual of *kidush levanah* (sanctification of the moon) as an exemplar of balance. Just as Jews celebrate the reappearance of the moon every month, by prayers and a special blessing, so does the Jewish woman celebrate the end of her menstrual cycle, by breaking her daily routine and bathing in the *mikveh*, in ritual preparation for marital union. The light of the sun, representing knowledge throughout this chapter in Shweka's book, is replaced with the softer illumination of the moon, suggesting 'renewal by periodicity'. Shweka uses the word *levanah*, the grammatically feminine term for 'moon' in Hebrew, in order to emphasize the feminine nature of the ritual. The woman covers herself like the moon (and like Haruta) in order to reveal herself later, affording renewed opportunities not just for the man but for them both. In other words, traditional ritual strengthens marital intimacy, conjoining faith with knowledge.

The multiplicity of sources from different times and cultural contexts employed in Shweka's *derashah*, his constant transitions 'between the synagogue and the rock club'—between the canonic and the marginal, the familiar and the new, and between the supposedly bright world of the devoted believer and the dark realm of the free rock artist—might also reflect the endless search of the modern interpreter for sources of authority. As much as this search is thrilling and fruitful, it is also interminable. The modern *darshan* (interpreter) serves his

God with 'two hearts', as Shweka states in another *derashah*: with a pure heart and with an impure one (2011: 93–140).

The problem of freedom and its boundaries comes up again in a reading offered by members of Nigun Nashim, a women's institute for Jewish studies. In this reading, Haruta once again represents women's liberation. This time, however, freedom is taken as a virtue. Freedom and movement do not necessarily mean promiscuity, a coupling which only results from a masculine point of view, itself bound by desire and an instrumental conceptualization of women (see also Zivan 2008). But as in Shweka's reading, freedom does not constitute an absolute value, and should only serve to control desire rather than provide an outlet for it. It is an instrument of relationship and intimacy, replacing objectification and manipulation. The 'masculine point of view', commonly applied in reading this story, does not prevent the liberation of the woman in the story, say the interpreters of Nigun Nashim; it does, however, preclude the success of their relationship, putting a damper on the future of their family unit. 'I am Freedom returned', writes Elisabeth Goldwyn under the title *davar aḥer* (another explanation), a trope borrowed from Rashi's interpretations: 'I and the wife of Rav Rahumi. I and Penelope. . . / and today I have returned, and shall wait no more. For it is said: "If I am not for myself, who will be for me?"' (Israeli and Fisher 2013: 56).

In this reading, it is not just the woman protagonist (whether Haruta or Penelope) who is called on to set herself free from the man who has forsaken her; it is also the female interpreter, breaking the structure of halakhic discourse in modern midrash with a personal poem. This poem bridges not merely Greek mythology and talmudic narratives, women and other women, or women and men (coiners of the saying 'If I am not for myself, who will be for me?' (Mishnah, *Pirkei avot* 1: 14)); it also links—as in other readings—the collective and the personal. Thus, a story which started in yearning for interpersonal dialogue establishes an intertextual discourse, juxtaposing and contrasting the multiple voices defining Jewish identity today.

Communication and the Political Horizon of Contemporary Israeli *Midrash*

The folk tale 'wants' to return to balance, and balance usually means a victory for communal norms, a restoration of social order. The rabbinic story does this by reinforcing the notion that every act of *yiḥud* between man and woman is a hazardous trial, and that forbidden thoughts result in forbidden acts and should therefore be punished as sinful. Contemporary midrash, rooted as it is in a modern, liberal, and feminist context, cannot accept this sort of demonization of desire and of women. So its conceptual horizons are different: not anti-establishment but pro-women. These features characterize every one of the

readings I have discussed, applauding, as they do, Haruta's initiative and supporting the renewal of intimacy between Rabbi Hiya bar Ashi and his wife. But
while most readings end tragically, that offered by Admiel Kosman points directly
to the possibility of reparation (*tikun*), arguing that Rabbi Hiya handles his trial
successfully (see Kosman 2007: 83–93).

As with the previous readers, the gendered point of view serves Kosman as a
fertile point of departure for a contemporary re-examination of the text and for
working out its cultural significance. As in Ezrahi and Gafni's interpretation,
Kosman's woman adapts herself to the reality of her life and accepts it with practical simplicity—unlike her husband, who is rapt in a narcissistic pursuit of
religious achievements. Kosman reads into the narrative yet more tensions, contrasting arrogance and humility, which manifest materially in the elements of fire
and wood, and find cultural–historical expression in the clash between Pauline
Christianity and rabbinic Judaism. In his reading, then, Haruta depicts a better
nature. But are her efforts 'worthwhile', as Weiss put it? Kosman thinks that they
definitely are. He believes there is no tragic ending, because the closing scene
is set in the common space of the kitchen, after both she and he have unmasked
and disarmed themselves, and have decided, for the first time, to look each other
in the eye and talk:

Something *shattered*, finally, in that emotional bulwark. The terrible emotional state that
he [Rabbi Hiya] found himself in caused him to open up, and for the first time he
approaches her as his wife, of his own initiative, talking to her honestly about what had
happened in the garden, about his painful failure . . . this desperate honesty calls for self
murder, but it also evokes an honest dialogue—without those 'masks'—whether 'religious' (prayers to God) or 'secular' (masquerading as a prostitute), which up until that
moment had served as the only means of communication between the couple. (Kosman
2007: 91)

The new context for the modern interpretation is neither sexuality generally nor
feminine sexuality in particular, but rather human dialogue and communication.
God is revealed, in this Buberian reading, in an honest and non-manipulative
(though not necessarily happy) meeting between husband and wife:

Man's purpose must be much more modest: to make room for the 'other' and then natu-
rally, for the Divine Presence, which always reveals itself to us down *here*, on the face of
this earthly world, in the meeting *of the two*, when the dialogue between them takes
place honestly, simply, directly. (Kosman 2007: 92)

Dialogue rather than dichotomy is therefore Kosman's religious and moral solution; a dialogue that needs mutual recognition by the two sexes—a fruitful result
of the feminist revolution—but no less so, warmth and intimacy, typical of the
kitchen both in the story itself and in its various readings. Freedom, therefore, is a
necessary condition (though not a sufficient one) for a successful meeting. No
less important is the (occasionally limiting) acknowledgement of the 'other', that

is, the male partner, and the place—home or kitchen—which puts the dialogue in context.

In conclusion, Calderon's reading, as well as the reading proposed by Ezrahi and Gafni, reflects a critical stance towards the narrative as a gender-oppressive story, and therefore a tragic one. Weiss and HaCohen chose to write their essay together, thereby renewing the dialogue between the sexes in the story. The kitchen, which was an arena of woe for Haruta and Rabbi Hiya bar Ashi, becomes for Weiss and HaCohen a space of reparation, where social conditions are broken and a renewed meeting between the sexes is 'cooked'. Shweka's suggestion of a 'renewal by periodicity' could also be explained as a belated return 'home'—to a traditional ritual, which would anchor the couple's meeting in a sacred time. The members of Nigun Nashim similarly end their own reading with a call for 'neither objectification nor manipulation; it is peace that I seek, and control over desire' (Israeli and Fisher 2013: 57)—an obvious call for dialogue, then, issued to members of the other sex.

Is the Israeli context for these readings an active one, affecting the construction of a new Israeli–Jewish discourse? The repertoire of stories discussed alongside our story, as well as the interpretations that I have presented at length, point to a potentially allegorical reading, one which might bear great cultural significance for the Israeli public.

A great many stories that have (re)entered the Israeli 'bloodstream' over the past decades (e.g. 'the oven of Akhnai', or 'Rabbi Yohanan and Resh Lakish') illustrate the results of a tragic conflict between a (mostly masculine) devotion to spiritual ideals and a (mostly feminine) compromise with a social reality more earthly and impulsive in nature. In Israeli midrash Rabbi Hiya bar Ashi and Haruta too reflect the tension between the supposedly idealist asceticism of the man and the liberated sexuality of his wife—the asceticism actually leading to an enslavement to desire, while liberality provides release from it. David Biale (1992) and Daniel Boyarin (1997), as well as other cultural commentators, view this tension as a foundational one in the early days of Zionism as well, arguing that for a long time it expressed the relation between 'Zionism' (masculine, secular, restrained) and 'Judaism' (feminine, religious, and sexual). On this view, the first had adopted the constrictive ideals of the bourgeois ethos, while the second had turned into the 'internal other' (see also Aschkenasy 2009: 221–3; Mayer 2000; Plaskow 1991: 107–20). Gluzman argues that the paradox of Zionist ideology, in this respect, lies in the fact that the same movement that embraced a strategy of realpolitik based on physical power, had rejected (or turned its back on) the feminine, sexual, and bodily aspects of Jewish tradition (Gluzman 2007: 11–33).

Modern Israeli midrash developed in the late twentieth century out of a new sensibility to the rift that grew between 'Zionism' and 'Judaism'. It sought a common, Jewish–Israeli horizon for religious, secular, and traditional (*masorti*) groups in Israeli society (see Jacobson 2017; Yadgar and Liebman 2003; Katz

2011: 195–264; Werczberger 2011: 203–25). This sort of midrash was meant to bridge imagery that would otherwise enhance the dichotomy between Zionism and Judaism, by interpreting and adapting Jewish traditions for contemporary Israeli reality. As a part of this spiritual renewal, Rabbi Hiya and Haruta might therefore be taken to demonstrate the consequences of coupling Zionism (Rabbi Hiya) and Judaism (Haruta), as constructs simultaneously linked with each other and alienated from one another. If any line of communication might be set up between them (a controversial issue, to be sure), then a national *shalom bayit*—marital reconciliation—might be achievable between different Jewish groups in Israel today.

On this understanding, Israeli midrash does not content itself with promoting feminist or liberal principles, but rather seeks something far larger: to construct a language and a nomenclature able to express and incorporate the experience of multiple 'others'—women, 'diasporic' Jews, and minorities in Israel or abroad—previously rejected and relegated to the far reaches of Israeli–Zionist consciousness. This new language, as we have seen, is fundamentally dialogic. It shuns individualistic writing norms by inviting stimulating partners to a shared study of texts and into a collaborative process of writing about them. It can be said to be taking inspiration not merely from the relatively new feminist discourse but also from post-colonial theories; from ancient texts and interpretations as well as from contemporary poems and rock songs, emails, and various other kinds of creative writing. The local dialogic discourse thus penetrates Israeli society through contemporary midrash about rabbinic texts. It articulates the multiplicity of voices competing in the Israeli public arena without necessarily judging them, challenging both religious and national authorities without a claim for an alternative exclusive position, but rather with an invitation to a further, intertextual, reading.

Acknowledgements

I am grateful to Dina Stein, Eli Yassif, and Idit Pintel-Ginsberg for their valuable comments on drafts of this essay. For an earlier version of this study in Hebrew see Sebba-Elran 2015.

Notes

1   The term 'Jewish bookshelf' (*aron sefarim yehudi*) evolved in reference to H. N. Bialik's poem 'Before the Bookshelf' (1911) and to his ingathering project (*kinus*) that aimed to establish a new national library of Jewish books in Hebrew. In its current use it was first coined by Professor Avraham Shapira and the Israeli novelist Haim Be'er in the early 1990s, as a name for a book series they started and that Shapira edited for the Am Oved publishing house. The term was adopted from Gershom Scholem's essay on Berl Katznelson (Scholem 1975: 487), and was further developed according to Shapira's vision. In a telephone interview (19 Aug. 2016), Shapira said that the book series aimed to reveal the

multiple facets of Judaism, and to connect an academic, historical enquiry with a wider cultural discourse concerning the future horizons of Jewish society. The term 'Jewish bookshelf' has since spread to multiple contemporary contexts and has come to represent not merely concrete collections of Jewish writing, but also the very notion of Jewish written culture.

2   My search yielded ten interpretative readings of the story: Calderon 2001: 49–57; Calderon 2014: 96–7; Ezrahi and Gafni 2005: 15–29; Inbar 2013: 57–82; Israeli and Fisher 2013: 47–57; Kosman 2007: 83–93; Shweka 2011: 35–67; Weiss and HaCohen 2012: 83–131; Zivan 2008; and one more that was downloaded by *Matah* ([CET, (Israeli) Centre for Educational Technology] from the television show: *Haheder* 2001), with Ruth Calderon, Agi Mishol, and Admiel Kosman.

3   The evolution of contemporary 'midrashic' readings of rabbinic texts falls outside the scope of this essay. It should be noted, though, that modern interpretations both influenced and were influenced by recent developments in academic discourse. See especially the contribution of Yona Fraenkel to the perception of the rabbinic text as literature (Levinson 2006; Levinson 2007; Newman 2006; Rubenstein 1999: 1–33; Rubenstein 2006), and Jacobson's (2017) pioneering study on this hermeneutic discourse.

4   The vast popularity of this story is demonstrated not merely by midrashic readings but also by multiple academic studies of it. For a survey of the latter, see Sebba-Elran 2015: 271–5.

5   See also Biala 2009; Hauptman 1998; Israeli and Fisher 2013: 6–8; Plaskow 1991: p. xvii; and the critical reflections on this notion in Baskin 1997 and Weisberg 2009.

6   See <http://kabalove.org/articles/misc/gafni-lilith>.

7   See his 2011 interview with Amichai Hason in *Makor rishon* and in <https://amichaich. wordpress.com/2011/09/16>.

References

ASCHKENASY, NEHAMA. 2009. 'Text, Nation, and Gender in Israeli Women's Fiction'. In Frederick E. Greenspahn, ed., *Women and Judaism*, 221–44. New York.

BASKIN, JUDITH R. 1997. 'Rabbinic Judaism and the Creation of Woman'. In Miriam Peskowitz and Laura Levitt, eds., *Judaism Since Gender*, 125–30. New York.

BIALA, TAMAR. 2009. 'Epilogue' (Heb.). In Nehama Weingarten and Tamar Biala, eds., *Dirshuni: Women's Midrashim* [Dirshuni: midreshei nashim], 199–201. Tel Aviv.

BIALE, DAVID. 1992. *Eros and the Jews: From Biblical Israel to Contemporary America*. New York.

BOYARIN, DANIEL. 1997. *Unheroic Conduct: The Rise of Heterosexuality and the Invention of the Jewish Man*. Los Angeles, Calif.

BRUNER, EDWARD M., and PHYLLIS GORFAIN. 1984. 'Dialogic Narration and the Paradoxes of Masada'. In Edward M. Bruner, ed., *Text, Play, and Story: The Construction and Reconstruction of Self and Society*, 56–79. Washington, DC.

CALDERON, RUTH. 2001. *The Market, the Home, the Heart: Talmudic Legends* [Hashuk, habayit, halev: agudot talmudiyot]. Jerusalem.

—— 2014. *A Talmudic Alphabet: Private Collection* [Alfa beta talmudi: osef perati]. Tel Aviv.

EZRAHI, OHAD, and MORDECAI GAFNI. 2005. *Who's Afraid of Lilith?* [Mi mefaḥed mililit?]. Ben Shemen.

FONROBERT, CHARLOTTE E. 2006. 'The Semiotics of the Sexed Body in Early Halakhic Discourse'. In Matthew Kraus, ed., *How Should Rabbinic Literature Be Read in the Modern World?*, 79–104. Piscataway, NJ.

GLUZMAN, MICHAEL. 2007. *The Zionist Body: Nationalism, Gender and Sexuality in Modern Hebrew Literature* [Haguf hatsiyoni: le'umiyut, migdar veminiyut basifrut ha'ivrit haḥadashah]. Tel Aviv.

Haḥeder. 2001. 'The Story of Rabbi Hiya bar Ashi and Heruta' [*Sipur r. ḥiya bar ashi veḥeruta*] <http://tarbut.cet.ac.il/showitem.aspx?itemid=1b1c7648-1d2c-47b0-850d-f426a8f94ef5&lang=heb> (accessed 1 Oct. 2017).

HAUPTMAN, JUDITH. 1994. 'Feminist Perspectives on Rabbinic Texts'. In Lynn Davidman and Shelly Tenenbaum, eds., *Feminist Perspectives on Jewish Studies*, 40–61. New Haven, Conn.

——1998. *Rereading the Rabbis: A Woman's Voice*. Boulder, Colo.

ILAN, TAL. 2007. 'A Feminist Commentary on the Babylonian Talmud: Introduction'. In Tal Ilan, Tamara Or, Dorothea M. Salzer, Christiane Steuer, and Irina Wandrey, eds., *A Feminist Commentary on the Babylonian Talmud*, 1–23. Tübingen.

INBAR, YA'ARA. 2013. *A Dream at Twilight* [Ḥalom shel bein hashemashot: iyun uderishah besipurim talmudiyim]. Tel Aviv.

ISRAELI, ANAT, and ESTHER FISHER, eds. 2013. *Collective and Feminist Interpretation on the Prohibitions of* Yiḥchud [Dorshot tov: perush kevutsati feministi lesugiyat isurei yiḥud]. Kiryat Tivon.

JACOBSON, DAVID C. 2017. *The Charm of Wise Hesitancy: Talmudic Stories in Contemporary Israeli Culture*. Boston, Mass.

KATZ, GIDEON. 2011. *To The Core of Secularism: A Philosophical Analysis of Secularism within the Israeli Context* [Le'etsem haḥiloniyut: nituaḥ filosofi shel haḥiloniyut beheksher yisra'eli]. Jerusalem.

KOSMAN, ADMIEL. 2007. *The Women's Tractate: Wisdom, Love, Faithfulness, Passion, Beauty, Sex, Holiness* [Masekhet nashim: ḥokhmah, ahavah, ne'emanut, teshukah, yofi, min, kedushah. Keriah besipurim talmudiyim verabaniyim veshenei midrashei shir]. Jerusalem.

LEVINSON, JOSHUA. 2006. 'Literary Approaches to Midrash'. In Carol Bakhos, ed., *Current Trends in the Study of Midrash*, 189–226. Leiden.

——2007. 'From Parable to Fiction: The Rise of Fiction as a Cultural Category' (Heb.). In Joshua Levinson, Jacob Elbaum, and Galit Hasan-Rokem, eds., *Higayon Leyonah: New Aspects in the Study of Midrash, Aggadah, and Piyut in Honour of Professor Yona Fraenkel* [Higayon leyonah: hebetim ḥadashim beḥeker sifrut hamidrash, ha'agadah, vehapiyut. Kovets meḥkarim likhvodo shel profesor yonah frenkel], 1–32. Jerusalem.

MAYER, TAMAR. 2000. 'From Zero to Hero: Masculinity in Jewish Nationalism'. In Tamar Mayer, ed., *Gender Ironies of Nationalism: Sexing the Nation*, 283–307. London and New York.

NEWMAN, HILLEL, I. 2006. 'Closing the Circle: Yonah Fraenkel, the Talmudic Story, and Rabbinic History'. In Matthew Kraus, ed., *How Should Rabbinic Literature Be Read in the Modern World?*, 105–35. Piscataway, NJ.

PLASKOW, JUDITH. 1991. *Standing Again at Sinai: Judaism from a Feminist Perspective.* San Francisco, Calif.

RAVEH, INBAR. 2012. *On Their Own: Feminist Readings in Rabbinic Literature* [Bifnei atsman: keriot feministiyot besifrut ḥazal]. Tel Aviv.

RUBENSTEIN, JEFFREY L. 1999. *Talmudic Stories: Narrative Art, Composition, and Culture.* Baltimore, Md.

——2006. 'Context and Genre: Elements of a Literary Approach to the Rabbinic Narrative'. In Matthew Kraus, ed., *How Should Rabbinic Literature Be Read in the Modern World?*, 137–65. Piscataway, N.J.

SCHOLEM, GERSHOM. 1975. *Explications and Implications: Writing on Jewish Heritage and Renaissance* [Devarim bego: pirkei morashah veteḥiyah]. Compiled by Avraham Shapira. Tel Aviv.

SEBBA-ELRAN, TSAFI. 2015. '"I am Haruta": A Rabbinic Legend and the Portrait of a Local Judaism' (Heb.). In Avihu Zakai, Paul Mendes-Flohr, and Zeev Gries, eds., *Fields in the Wind: A Tribute to Avraham Shapira* [Shedemot veruaḥ: minḥat hokarah veyedidut le'avraham shapira], 270–84. Jerusalem.

SHELEG, YA'IR. 2010. *The Jewish Renaissance in Israeli Society: The Emergence of a New Jew* [Mi'ivri yashan leyehudi ḥadash: renesans hayahadut baḥevrah hayisra'elit]. Jerusalem.

SHWEKA, RONI. 2011. *A New Song: Essays on Israeli Rock Songs* [Shir ḥadash: derashot al yetsirot rok yisra'eliyot]. Jerusalem.

WEINGARTEN-MINTZ, NEHAMA. 2009. 'Forward' [Petaḥ davar]. In Nehama Weingarten and Tamar Biala, eds., *Dirshuni: Women's Midrashim* [Dirshuni: midreshei nashim], 13–21. Tel Aviv.

WEISBERG, DVORA E. 2009. 'Women and Torah Study in Aggadah'. In Frederick E. Greenspahn, ed., *Women and Judaism: New Insights and Scholarship*, 41–63. New York.

WEISS, RUCHAMA, and AVNER HACOHEN. 2012. *Mothers in Therapy: A Psychological Look at Four Talmudic Women* [Imahot betipul: masa pesikhologi-sifruti im giborot hatalmud]. Tel Aviv.

WERCZBERGER, RACHEL. 2011. 'New Age of Judaism: Jewish Spiritual Renewal in Israel' [Kesheha'idan haḥadash nikhnas le'aron hasefarim hayehudi: hitḥadshut ruḥanit yehudit beyisra'el]. Ph.D. diss., Hebrew University of Jerusalem.

YADGAR, YAACOV, and CHARLES C. LIEBMAN. 2003. 'Jewish Traditionalism and Popular Culture in Israel' (Heb.), *Iyunim bitekumat yisra'el* 13: 163–80.

ZIVAN, GILI. 2008. 'The Modesty Discourse Trap' [Milkod siaḥ hatseniyut]. *The Yaacov Herzog Centre for Jewish Studies* <http://www.merkazherzog.org.il/article/58> (accessed 19 Sept. 2017).

PART II

Media, Performance, and Popular Discourse in the Formation of Jewish Community

The Jewish Atlantic: Diaspora and Pop Music

CASPAR BATTEGAY

TO MANY LISTENERS, no ethnic significance can be found in the emergence of 'pop music'—a distinctive musical genre that is, according to cultural historian Timothy Berg, 'non-classical, very mainstream, intended for very wide audiences, and often controlled by the giants of the music business' (Berg 2000: 83). In many ways, however, pop is characterized by the specific conditions of religious and cultural minorities: historically, jazz, blues, rock 'n' roll, reggae, disco music, soul, and hip hop are closely linked to African American history (Frith 1981).

To this day, these genres work with a phantasm of being black: that is, with the mythical idea of an African origin of the music that can now be found in the diaspora. In an influential work, the British scholar of cultural studies Paul Gilroy, for example, defined the production conditions of hip hop as 'transnational structures of circulation and intercultural exchange' (Gilroy 1993: 87). According to Gilroy, an imaginary Africa is at the centre of these processes that is almost completely disconnected from the real Africa with all its problems. While this relationship between the hip hop world and the real world might have changed since Gilroy's observations in the 1990s, his insistence on the diasporic context of the 'Black Atlantic' and its kinship with Jewish modernity remains pivotal to any pursuit of the diaspora in popular culture. As Gilroy notes, it is precisely the dual awareness of the Jewish exile—to sense, as a community, a commitment towards the Land of Israel and towards the temporary residence, each in a different manner—that also constitutes a paradigm for the ambivalent experiences of the slaves deported from Africa and their descendants (Gilroy 1993: 205–12).

The idea and the definition of diaspora vary greatly. However, all diasporic communities keep a collective or individual connection to a real or imagined homeland. This link can be expressed in language, religion, custom, or folklore. According to Robin Cohen, the consciousness of a common migration history and a sense of co-ethnicity with other members of the community demonstrate this inescapable link to the 'old country' (Cohen 1997: p. xi). This wide definition of diaspora informed the 'turn to diaspora', as Lily Cho put it, in cultural studies. In her view, diaspora is 'first and foremost a subjective condition marked by the contingencies of long histories of displacements and genealogies of dispossession' (Cho 2007: 14).

In this essay I will analyse representative examples from different eras of pop music in conjunction with their motifs or narratives of displacement, and I will discuss the sense of Jewishness as a link to dispossessed ethnic and religious communities. In this regard, the term 'diaspora' loses the specific religious, or at least traditional, meaning it has had in Jewish history, and becomes something like a 'diaspora of the mind', as Bryan Cheyette called the metaphorical adoptions and transformations of the notion of diaspora in cultural studies (Cheyette 2013). Scholars of music and musicology, such as Sarah Daynes, have pointed out the 'construction of the African diasporas as a multidimensional space of memory made of many places' in reggae music and Rastafari culture (Daynes 2005: 25), and in regard to Jewish music, Jeff Janeczko advocated for the study of 'Jewish music *through/as* diaspora' in the United States (Janeczko 2009: 10). In contrast to the latter, I do not focus on the notion of 'Jewish music' and its aesthetic potential, but rather want to unfold and specify the concept of diaspora in order to understand how Jewishness is negotiated, constructed, and perceived in pop music by artists and audiences. The term 'diaspora' and its theoretical impact help me to analyse the role of pop music in connecting Jewish communities on both sides of the Atlantic, but it will also show how pop music can lead to a universalization of Jewish identity in a global context that transcends the boundaries of traditional Jewish communities.

Post-colonial and Jewish Diaspora

The ambivalent consciousness of many European Jewish authors in the late nineteenth and twentieth centuries towards their own Jewishness (and their acceptance or refusal of the diasporic condition) is often seen as a model for other ethnic and religious identities (see Cohen 1997; Safran 1991). To get a grasp of modern and post-colonial African identity, Gilroy keeps referring to European Jewish intellectuals and their complex deconstructions of essential identities. Scholars of post-colonial conditions constantly refer to the Jewish model. For example in an analysis of the literature of the Indian diaspora, Vijai Mishra states that, despite the different structures of diasporic communities, 'the Jewish diaspora is the fundamental ethnic model for diaspora theory and all serious study of diasporas will have to begin with it' (2007: 6).

Yet by the same token, the reflection of post-colonial diaspora theory has also become a source of inspiration for contemplating Jewry in the twenty-first century. Jonathan and Daniel Boyarin have prominently declared how the specific 'powers of diaspora' are produced precisely as a result of the ongoing substitution of Zion with ever new Zions and the formation of ever new exiles (Boyarin and Boyarin 2002: 1–33): Babylon, Alexandria, Speyer, Cordoba, or Vilna have turned, as Jerusalem before them, into melancholically remembered and symbolically over-determined places of origin within a continuum of exile that, as a whole, can be called diaspora. In the process, Jewish identity was constituted in the absence of any real geographical connection to these places, and mostly with reference to holy and literary texts. The two Boyarins emphatically call to mind that the interpretative and commentary practices of Judaism have evolved in exile, pivotally by way of the Babylonian Talmud. In Judaism, diaspora means an awareness of the exile, and it may refer to the voluntary dispersion of the Jewish people in the Hellenistic period or to the forced dispersion (*galut*) after the destruction of the Second Temple in 70 CE and after the Bar Kochba revolt ended in 135 CE. The use of the term diaspora in today's discourse on Jewish identity refers to both voluntary and forced types of exile.

The consciousness of diaspora may be one of the central elements of Judaism. That and the actual effects of the Jewish history of wandering led to the Jews often being perceived as 'oriental' others during their long European history (Kalmar and Penslar 2004), but likewise they were also subjects in the European discourse on the exotic and essential other, which Edward Said called Orientalism. This dual position as subjects *and* objects of Orientalism demonstrates that Jews as a group elude the European dichotomy of West and East, Occident and Orient, colonial power and the colonized, an ambivalent position which seems paradigmatic for diasporic groups (Goetschel and Quayson 2016). Gilroy shows an analogous movement of diasporization for the descendants of African slaves. The catchphrase 'Black Atlantic', which was coined in this context, refers to an exile culture that is articulated and formed in and through pop music. 'Black Atlantic' is Gilroy's term for a political and cultural formation that was born from the transatlantic slave trade and the violent displacement of millions of people to America and the European colonies between the seventeenth and nineteenth centuries. The community that originated from this dispersion has no centre and is only mediated through a common consciousness of a catastrophic history. Gilroy analyses the writings of black and Caribbean intellectuals, mostly from the early twentieth century, in detail. In these writings he actually sees the wish to transcend the structures of the Western national state and the national particularity, however, not only directed towards hybridity or openness but towards an ideology of African unity and autonomy, as for example in Pan-Africanism. The perception of the black experience 'inside and outside modernity' (Gilroy 1993: 206) is, according to Gilroy, modelled in some ways by the Jewish experience. This is the reason why African American and Caribbean intellectuals adopted the notion of diaspora in the 1950s and 1960s.

Since the 1960s there has been a broad influx of Jews into the sphere of pop music, though it started earlier. Here, only the different meanings of exile and home in various constellations of pop music will be addressed. In what follows, the understanding of Jewishness and Jewish tradition as well as the ways pop music refers to it will be discussed in a transatlantic setting: North America, eastern Europe, and Germany (and in some ways also Israel) constitute the (real and imagined) geographical boundaries of the examples below. These examples are meant to illuminate the motif, consciousness, and narratives of the diaspora. However, they do not provide a complete history of diaspora in pop culture. In their geographical arrangement between Europe, the Land of Israel, and the Americas, they outline a transient cartography of the 'Jewish Atlantic'. This title refers to Gilroy and indicates the consciousness of a multinational and mobile community that has been a largely transatlantic diaspora culture, at least since the end of the nineteenth century, that is, since the onset of emigration of east European Jews to North America (and the occasional re-immigration to Europe).

In the Jewish imagination the shtetls of Poland, Lithuania, the Ukraine, Romania, or Russia seem to be comparable to the coasts of West Africa in the conception of the 'Black Atlantic'. The difference is, of course, that the State of Israel represents a third place within this spiritual and real geography. In Zionist ideology Israel is not just a place to emigrate, but is meant to be the home of the Jewish people and the end of the diaspora. In reality, however, it is also the beginning of an even more complex situation, for since the foundation of the State of Israel there has also evolved an Israeli (and not just a Jewish) diaspora in cities like New York, Los Angeles, and Berlin. In this regard, the historian Michael Brenner has spoken of a 'global Israel' (Brenner 2016: 194–230).

In this transatlantic Jewish context of constant deterritorialization, pop culture has played and still plays a critical role in negotiating interpretations of diaspora. Throughout the history of modernity, pop music has been formed by different technologies—from the early gramophone records to digital music streaming—and it has always mediated dispersed Jews from both sides of the Atlantic *and* Jewish acculturation to the mainstream. In other words, the analysis of the negotiations of Jewishness in popular music always oscillates between two poles: the Jewish dimension and the popularity of the music. Both poles are responsible for a sense of identity created by the music. In his classic analysis of the connection of music and identity, Simon Frith pointed out that the question we should be asking is not what popular music reveals about the people who play and use it, but how it creates them as a people and as 'a web of identities'. According to Frith, popular music is popular not because it authentically articulates some sort of popular taste or experience, but because it generates our understanding of what 'popularity' is, and because popular music places us in the social world in a particular way (Frith 1996: 121).

The Double Representation of the Jews

For centuries the Torah, the Talmud, and their rabbinical exegesis formed a canonical body of texts, which served as the 'mobile homeland of the Jews', as the German poet Heinrich Heine famously called the Bible. With the advent of modernity, however, these classical means of creating a 'web of identities' and placing the Jews in their particular social world were supplemented and sometimes even substituted with other forms of communication, expression, and representation, culminating in the postmodern pop culture of today. Joshua Neuman, the former editor of the magazine *Heeb*, for example, wrote in 2011 on the Jewishness of popular culture:

Among many Jews in North America, but particularly the younger generations, a new way of life exists, which treats pop culture like a Jewish text and the act of 'reading it' as quasi religious activity. This curious form of religious expression is engaged with the ideas, perspectives, attitudes, memes and visual language that permeate everyday life. Its Pentateuch consists of television, film, music, art, and literature, its community centers are websites, and its sacred language is humor. (Neuman 2011)

If this somewhat ironic statement is taken completely seriously, it means two things. First, Jewish tradition as it has been commercially disseminated in records, radio, film, and digital media can constitute an alternative body of tradition and distributes models for Jewish communities which are more and more secular. In this perspective, popular culture is inflected with a symbolic ethnic component. Second, it can give Jews a subcultural connection, which at the same time gives them some claim to be a part of the mainstream.

Jewish influence on popular music and the way it has been effective in transcending or transforming the Jewish tradition has been a topic since the first half of the twentieth century, as in the example of the 1927 film classic *The Jazz Singer*, which is based on Samson Raphaelson's short story and his stage play *The Day of Atonement*. Yankel/Jakie Rabinowitz (played by Al Jolson, who, by the way, appears featuring a so-called 'blackface', which anticipates the interweaving of African American and Jewish history) refuses to continue the family tradition and, instead of a cantor, becomes a musical star on Broadway. From the angle of media history, this film is of great significance as the first sound film; for Jewish media history, the brief appearance of the star cantor Yossele Rosenblatt, who intones Kaddish at the start of the film, is also significant. Rosenblatt enjoyed great fame, which was enhanced by numerous records of him performing liturgical music and folksongs. Yossele Rosenblatt's recordings stand at the inception of a Jewish popular culture, and show that Judaism as a religion is characterized by technical reproducibility.

Yet the main plot of *The Jazz Singer* is precisely about a Jewish artist who does not move through popular culture as a Jew. Instead, he transcends his Judaism to reach an existence in the majority culture. In the course of a dispute, Jakie tells his father, the fictional cantor: 'My songs mean as much to my audience as yours to your congregation.' However, Jakie does not finally break the bounds of tradition and does not leave his Jewish community for good, as he replaces his terminally ill father in the synagogue at the Yom Kippur service and intones Kol Nidrei, instead of performing on Broadway. Thus, on the one hand, the movie shows the

Figure 1 Molly Picon (*right of centre*) as Molly Brown in a scene from *Mizrekh un Mayrev* or *Ost und West* (East and West, 1923) produced in Vienna. The silent film, directed by Sidney M. Goldin, had English and Yiddish intertitles. *American Jewish Historical Society, Center for Jewish History Digital Collections, New York*

Jewish star transcending the boundaries between the public and his ethnic/religious community; but, on the other hand, his double performance also confirms these boundaries. This twofold function of the Jewish singer is even more apparent in the 1980 remake starring Neil Diamond. In this otherwise tedious story, two things are noteworthy: first, the elaborate connection of the Jewish singer to his African American friends and band members—which shows an overlapping of different minority histories in the American context; second, Neil Diamond's patriotic song 'America'—which was a part of the movie's soundtrack and became one of the greatest hits of all of pop history. The song's opening lines articulate a vague diasporic consciousness, omitting any explicit Jewish identity and thus potentially including many immigrant groups: 'Far, we've been traveling far. Without a home, but not without a star.' Most likely it is precisely the vagueness of the diasporic image that created the song's immense popularity.

In the early days of modern popular culture, Jews were active in using the new technical possibilities such as film and gramophone recordings, and this use often reflected the Jewish history of migration. It is noteworthy that the phonograph record was invented by Emile Berliner, a German Jew who emigrated from his birthplace of Hanover to the United States in 1870 (Loewy 2014). The first two generations of Jewish immigrants, and the thriving cultural scene they created in

Figure 2 Publicity photograph for the CBS television programme *Gomer Pyle U.S.M.C.*, showing guest star Molly Picon as Molly Gordon, with Jim Nabors as Gomer Pyle, in an episode titled 'A Little Chicken Soup Wouldn't Hurt', broadcast 6 December 1968. *Photograph by CBS Television Network, Creative Clearance Publicity*

America, generated innumerable shellac and vinyl recordings in Yiddish, including religious and popular music, as well as comedy recordings. Singers, songwriters, comedians, and actors, such as Molly Picon (born Malka Opiekun in New York in 1898; died 1992 in Lancaster, Pennsylvania), were performing for an exclusively Jewish audience at the beginning of their careers, but eventually changed their language to English and had a tremendous influence on Broadway and Hollywood (Gottlieb 2004). In this respect, and in the context of the 'Jewish Atlantic', Picon's biography and work is especially revealing (Figures 1 and 2).

Molly Picon was born on the Lower East Side of Manhattan, where she also had her first shows in different cabarets and theatres. Yet her career as a movie star started on the other side of the Atlantic, in Yiddish and German productions for a non-Jewish audience. Her later American films were produced for a general audience. In 1929's *Little Girl with Big Ideas*, her talkie debut, Picon acted in English with a heavy Yiddish accent (Green 2009). This artificial linguistic marker of difference and 'Jewish' identity is typical of the representation of Jews in the early twentieth century and gives rise to the 'Comic Image of the Jew', as Sig Altman titled a study on Jewish humour (Altman 1971) in North America. To understand Jews as a community in diaspora also means to grasp the double representation of modern Jewish artists as Jews inside their natal community *and* as members of a globalized pop cultural industry who transcend this community.

Records and film were used from their inception to bind Jews across geographical and social borders. One of the paradoxes in this process of modern media history is that the very media that displaced traditions and folk culture to some extent also forged cultural identities and folklore. In technically mediated diaspora culture, though, the sense of place becomes a nostalgic identity which is no longer bound to a specific geographical place, but to a mythical or imaginary 'Jewish' landscape. In popular music in general, not only in the Jewish context, the reality of the location is transformed into the mere sound of names (Connell and Gibson 2003: 71–89). In the next part of this essay I will consider some examples of this sound of Jewishness and Jewish places in popular music.

Show Me the Place

Representations of Jews, Judaism, or Jewishness in popular culture and the complex interactions of self- and external perceptions regarding the image of popular musicians have frequently been the subject of scientific study (see Koven 2007; Stratton 2009). These works mostly deal with categories such as 'race', 'religion', or 'stereotypes' and do not include an examination of cultural narratives such as the concept of diaspora, although it is hard to overlook the motifs and the rhetoric of diaspora in popular music. This becomes obvious if one looks, for example, at the work of the Canadian superstar Leonard Cohen, a master of explicit Jewish identity enactment (Figure 3). Time and again, Cohen integrates into his musical oeuvre paraphrases of biblical stories ('The Story of Isaac', *Songs from a Room*, 1969), references to Jewish liturgy ('Who by Fire', *New Skin for the Old Ceremony*, 1974), and various allusions to kabbalistic ideas ('Hallelujah', *Various Positions*, 1984) or to deliberate Jewish stereotypes. Cohen's literary work, too, consisting of two novels and various volumes of poetry, is shaped in various ways—be it through sociohistorical descriptions or religious references—by his Judaism. In the epic song 'The Future' (*The Future*, 1992), the lyrical 'I' is the 'little Jew who

Figure 3 Leonard Cohen during a concert in Geneva, 27 October 2008. *Photograph by Rama. Wikimedia, Creative Commons licence*

wrote the Bible', which endows the song's historic-pessimistic perspective with a specific religious–cultural position: the 'little Jew who wrote the Bible' is a figure who displays a fundamental scepticism towards progress that also remains intact at the epochal rupture in world history of the early 1990s; and through its horrific diasporic history, this figure is particularly apt at recognizing and evoking the apocalyptic dimension inherent in any messianism.

The lyrical 'I' in the more recent song 'By the Rivers Dark' (*Ten New Songs*, 2001) is akin to this figure, although it omits explaining itself in greater detail. The song's lyrics are an intertextual play on Psalm 137, the central poem for contemplating the diaspora in Jewish history.

By the rivers dark
I wandered on.
I lived my life
In Babylon.

And I did forget
My holy song:
And I had no strength
In Babylon.

Initially, the situation seems analogous to that of the psalmist in exile by the rivers of Babylon; Cohen's song even presents itself as a modern adaptation. But in another stanza, one realizes that this is, in fact, rather an inversion.

Be the truth unsaid
And the blessing gone,
If I forget
My Babylon.

This genuinely modern 'I' recalls only Babylon, presented here as the topos of yearning. Jerusalem or Zion remain unmentioned; they do not even exist in the topology that Cohen evokes. Ultimately, it remains unclear whether the 'I' in the song represents an individual or a collective entity, and whether the song is to be understood psychologically or theologically. This ambiguity is reflected in the musical form: Cohen's at times almost whispered, sombre *Sprechgesang* is contrasted with female voices that accompany and repeat, but also answer, him. This duplicated song articulates itself above a seemingly kitschy synthesizer soundscape and a simple pop rhythm. Cohen appears as priest of a cryptic private religion, which, on the one hand, decontextualizes the theological content of the Jewish diaspora, but, on the other hand, bestows sacrality upon popular culture.

This ambiguity is carried to extremes on Cohen's penultimate album, *Old Ideas*, which was released in 2012 and self-reflectively toys with the pop star's own mortality ('Going home without the costume that I wore'). In the song 'Show Me the Place' (track 3 on *Old Ideas*), the singer's function as a medium becomes the dominating theme with respect to another place, and Cohen's figure is depicted as a disciple or prophet. 'Show me the place, where you want your slave to go. Show me the place, I've forgotten, I don't know. Show me the place, where my head is bending, oh show me the place, where you want your slave to go.' The forgotten—maybe holy—place demonstrates the insecurity of a diasporic 'I' that no longer knows where it belongs, where it must go. This forgotten place has a Christological or messianic meaning. The final lyrics contain considerable pathos: 'Show me the place, where the word became a man. Show me the place, where the suffering began.' It could be implied that, with the discovery or indication of this privileged place, some sort of redemption and, hence, the end of the diaspora might occur, although no such hope is expressed. Indeed, throughout the song it is difficult to discern whether the 'place' mentioned signifies Zion or Babylon, or perhaps somewhere else. Moreover, in this song, the religious difference between these two geographical designations has become obsolete. Cohen's later work transcended the Jewish aspect, whose representation definitely constituted the starting point in his early work, to become the universal topography of a hidden home that could be anywhere.

In most Western contexts Leonard Cohen is not especially regarded as a Jewish singer. This is the case in Germany, where Cohen's Jewish identity and the Jewish aspects of his works are all but ignored. For example, after the publication of the translation of his *Book of Longing* (2006) in 2008, the generally positive reviews in German newspapers made no mention of the highly visible Jewish themes, motifs, and symbols in the book. Instead, reviewers celebrated Cohen as an alternative American idol and a poet of ironic romanticism. On the other hand, an event in Israel made it clear that the Jewish perception of Cohen is different. When Cohen performed in Ramat Gan in September 2009, in front of 50,000 people, at the end of the concert he recited the traditional priestly blessing in Hebrew—and the crowd answered with a loud 'Amen'. This incident (recorded on YouTube and circulated widely in Jewish circles) primarily shows that in Leonard Cohen's perspective a pop concert and a religious service are not definitely separated. But it also shows that his performance, *as a pop star*, creates a community that understands itself as Jewish.

Mayn Heymele

Notions of community, tradition, and Jewishness also are involved in the popular genre of klezmer, classified as a branch of 'world music'. It is often meant by its producers and the audience alike to connect to a lost authenticity of (eastern) European Jewry. In Europe, klezmer has the reputation of being played by non-Jewish musicians, but the genre has undoubtedly evolved into an equally problematic and interesting field of experimentation and into a 'contact zone' between

Jews and non-Jews, as Magdalena Waligórska writes, referring to a concept introduced by Marie Louise Pratt (Waligórska 2013: 12). The historical genre is transferred to new contexts and thus updated. In doing so, however, klezmer has acquired a new appeal to Jewish artists as well. Klezmer 'inspires alternative ways of living Jewish identities. . . . klezmer, allowing negotiation and contestation of cultural boundaries, has become a realm of shifting categories and risky identity quests, where the very borders of Jewish culture are being constantly defined, questioned and redrawn' (Waligórska 2013: 12). In the following, I describe shifting boundaries that burst the genre of klezmer with the song 'Mayn Shtetele Belz' by drawing on a classic notion of exile and trying to deconstruct it.

It is often forgotten that klezmer, as it is known today, was shaped by the blossoming music industry of the early twentieth century (Slobin 2002). The song 'Mayn Shtetele Belz', a Jewish classic, was written in 1932 in New York by Alexander Olshanetzky (1892–1946), to lyrics by Jacob Jacobs (1892–1972) for the Jewish play *Ghetto Song*, as a tribute to the singer Isa Kremer who was born in Bălți (today in the Republic of Moldova) (Yad Vashem 2015). However, it is also often linked to the small Ukrainian (east Polish) town of Belz. It was also sung in 1930s Poland as an American import in Polish translation. Related recording 'hits' that continued to appeal to ethnic Jewish communities included 'My Yiddishe Momme' and 'Bay Mir Bistu Sheyn', which together with 'Mayn Shtetele Belz' formed a canon of songs performed by innumerable Jewish and non-Jewish artists, from Sophie Tucker to the Barry Sisters and Tom Jones. These recordings have endowed the memory of east European origins with a kitschy quality. Although 'Mayn Shtetele Belz' is less popular than 'My Yiddishe Momme', it can be understood as a quintessential Jewish song about a homeland: the geographical designation is less important than the accompanying sense that the singer is no longer in that place of origin. It is a song of transatlantic yearning, of exile, and thus of diaspora. The 'I' envisions the lost place of childhood, the riverbank and the green trees where one used to sit on Shabat. Belz is a place of dreams in two senses: a place of the child's past dreams of the future and of the ageing 'I's' dreams of return. The nostalgia that comes with the song has nothing intrinsically unsettling about it, but rather can be enjoyed by the audience since it suggests an inviolable identity, a lost place, to which one could actually belong, and for which the song and its performance provide a substitute.

In recent years, this nostalgic identification has been ironically refracted from various perspectives by popular music (Popescu 2013). An example of such deconstruction and of an innovative treatment of klezmer is the work of the Canadian musician, rapper, composer, producer, and puppet-theatre maker Socalled, an alias for Josh Dolgin (Figure 4). The artist, born in 1976 in Montreal, has appeared with such jazz and klezmer luminaries as the clarinet player David Krakauer, but also with renowned hip hop artists. His albums and album titles refer in various ways to Jewish tradition and to klezmer as the music of exile

Figure 4 Canadian Jewish producer and artist Socalled with accordion (*right*), with klezmer band Nayechovichi, during a concert at the Bilingua Club in Moscow, April 2010. *Photograph by Alaexis. Wikimedia, Creative Commons licence*

(*HiphopKhasene*, 2003; *The So Called Seder: A Hip Hop Haggadah*, 2005; *Ghetto-blaster*, 2007; *SleepOver*, 2011).

'(Rock the) Belz', track 6 on the album *Ghettoblaster*, can be interpreted as the explicit deconstruction of an authentic klezmer culture defined as Jewish. The track starts with 'Mayn Shtetele Belz', performed in a classical manner by Theodore Bikel, the legendary folk singer, actor, and one of the founders of the Cameri Theatre in Tel Aviv. Socalled backs the singing with beats and a melodic sequence of various samples; to this, he performs together with the Québécois rapper Sans Pression. This mix is accompanied by a virtuosic fabric of various levels of speech, sound, and rhythm, which, if nothing else, also point to the various levels of time that blend within the mediated space of these songs and point to each other. The Jewish universe of eastern Europe, where Yiddish, Russian, Polish, and Romanian were spoken, as well as the Canadian present that is also characterized by various languages—English, French, and immigrants' languages from around the world—are not presented in a historical sequence, but as parallel universes that exist side by side and inside each other.

The nostalgic, backward movement of the Yiddish classic with its memories of childhood is counteracted by the rap lyrics. While 'Mayn Shtetele Belz' brings a childhood landscape to mind ('Oy, eyden Shabes fleg ikh loyfn / Mit ale inglekh tsuglaykh / Tsu zitsn unter dem grinem beymele / Leynen bay dem taykh': 'Oy, every Shabes I used to run / together with the other boys / to sit under the little green tree / and read by the river'), Socalled sings of the Friday evenings of his youth in the 'spoiled middle class', when he would party and hang out with his crowd. Here he criticizes the nostalgic impulse that sustains not only folklore but also popular music: 'I think today if I could I would run back, but it's never the same if you try to come back.'

As recognized here, the place that exists in memory is never the same as the real place that actually existed. As to the Jewish dimension of music, this can never be about an alleged authenticity and, in view of the dislocated, catastrophic history of the Jews, never about an imagined single thread of tradition, but rather about rendering the metaphorical dissonance or discontinuities of a fragmented Jewish heritage. This rendering is evident in disrupting perceived audible as well visible conventions, and thus drawing the listener–viewer's attention to paradoxical symbols. Consider, for example, the song's music video and the apparently Jewish issues it raises. The video depicts the musicians as string puppets, creating images as well as sounds of conflict between being muted and outspoken. The Afro-French rapper, the urban Jewish musician Socalled, and the folk singer Theodore Bikel seem to be impersonating themselves. As their own doppelgängers, they are imaginary figures in a collective landscape of memories. The video opens with a Chagall-like setting. Suddenly, one notices how the puppet Socalled is riding across this scenery in an American car, parodying the usual hip hop videos. Here, the motif of turning back, going back, remains ever present since all of a sudden the car is driving backwards, yet the surroundings are no longer the same, they lose their attribution. The interior of an underground train, a dense fir forest that is illuminated or set on fire by sabbath candles, desert, and artificial snow that might be ashes, alternate with one another. The shtetl turns into another ghetto, the post-colonial space of slaves deported from Africa and their descendants. The viewers look into a psychedelic dream, which can no longer be the nostalgically self-assuring 'khulem' (dream) mentioned in the song, but a nightmare that captures—in merging images of great intensity—the past seventy years of Jewish history and North America's history of immigration.

In Socalled's video, exile becomes the matrix of the song and of popular music itself: the sound of east European Jewry, as well as rap, as a genuine expression of African American consciousness, 'Jewish Atlantic' as well as 'Black Atlantic', intertwine without any of these elements serving as a guarantor of authenticity. On the contrary: at one point, Theodore Bikel's puppet strays around in a dark corner as if unable to find his shtetl anymore. It is no longer even shown on the map, as Bikel says, in English, and perhaps it never was. Here, traditionally clad

Jews, who as cardboard puppets wave at the start of the video, are not figures of authenticity that might represent a better past and a homeland. They are characters of a mad simultaneity that has been shaping the globalized world for quite some time. These are walking anachronisms in a world that no longer has a time of its own and a place of its own, but consists solely of anachronisms and cross-cultural dynamics. In Socalled's '(Rock the) Belz' the diaspora is not evoked in order to construct a homeland. Instead of representing nostalgia, the diaspora signifies acceptance of the fact that places cannot vouch for a stable identity.

'You Can Be the Ewiger Jew'

Another important co-ordinate of the 'Jewish Atlantic' is Berlin, the former and new capital of Germany, which is a central site of Holocaust remembrance, besides serving many political and mnemonic functions. However, from the 1990s onwards it has also assumed an increasingly significant role as a metropolis of Israeli and Jewish artists. The latter 'discover in the streets of Berlin and in its real or metaphorical basements the treasures of Israel's intellectual origins —from language to architecture, from law to ideology' (Oz-Salzberger 2009: 167). In the face of such a traumatic history, however, these discoveries inevitably lead to ambivalence.

The song 'Görlitzer Park' by the American Jewish musician Daniel Kahn, born in Detroit in 1978 and living in Berlin since 2005, can be understood as evoking this ambivalence, as a wistful and desperate song about Berlin as a place of Jewish diaspora history. German culture includes the popular genre of *Heimatlied*, literally a 'song of home', which is often an unofficial hymn to a certain town or region. Among the most famous of these tunes are 'Wien, Wien nur Du allein' ('Vienna, Vienna, Only You') or 'Berliner Luft' ('The Air of Berlin'). In American folk and country music too, the nostalgic nexus between a certain place and identity is frequently evoked. As I will show, this nexus is deconstructed by 'Görlitzer Park'.

Kahn has created a furore with his combination of klezmer, vaudeville, punk, Yiddish working-class songs, songs in the style of Weill/Brecht, and songs following Bob Dylan or Leonard Cohen (Figure 5). In his 2012 album *Bad Old Songs*, Kahn has covered 'The Story of Isaac'—possibly Leonard Cohen's most Jewish song. When Kahn celebrates a certain nostalgia, he stages himself unbashfully as a hipster; hence, it is only logical that *Bad Old Songs* has also appeared as an LP, the material fetish par excellence of pop nostalgia. Besides making music, Kahn has also performed as an actor at the 'alternative theatre' Ballhaus Naunynstraße in Berlin; he is active as a musician in productions of the Maxim Gorki Theatre. Between 2006 and 2012, he and his band, The Painted Bird, released four albums. (*The Broken Tongue*, 2006; *Partisans & Parasites*, 2009; *Lost Causes*, 2010; *Bad Old Songs*, 2012).

Figure 5 Daniel Kahn, in a concert with the band The Painted Bird in Luxembourg, 23 January 2013. *Photograph by MMFE. Wikimedia, Creative Commons licence*

Kahn and his band include numerous references to the Holocaust. The band's name, for example, alludes to the Holocaust novel *The Painted Bird* (1965) by Polish Jewish writer Jerzy Kosiński. His sarcastic song 'Six Million Germans' (track 6 on *Partisans & Parasites*) must be emphasized; it is based on the plan of the Lithuanian Jewish partisan and poet Abba Kovner to kill six million Germans in revenge. 'Görlitzer Park' (track 10 on *Lost Causes*) refrains from using simple slogans. The song is an example of the American singer-songwriter tradition, a quiet folk ballad, which is sparingly accompanied with ukulele, harmonica, percussion, double bass, and violin; with its rattling circus sound and grotesque elements, it is clearly reminiscent of the work of the American singer-songwriter Tom Waits. This song enacts the exile linguistically, since the lyrics are both in English and German, thereby drawing on multilingualism and language mixture as elements of numerous migratory experiences. To construe this song as a genuine expression of the 'Jewish Atlantic', consider the complete set of lyrics.

Görlitzer Park
Die Ruinen vom Görlitzer Park [the ruins of Görlitzer Park]
were cold as a stone in the ground
aber Steine sind eben so stark [but stones are as strong]
as the rubble hid under the mound

& your hair was as red as the glow
of the fire that fell from the sky
& the ruins are covered with snow
just as white as the white of your eye

& the trains of Berlin
they run her und hin [back and forth]
through tunnels below in the dark

but the station is gone,
so I'll wait for you on
the ruins of Görlitzer Park

in the garden of frozen desire
on the derelict couch we sat down
wie die Stadt hier wir brauchten ein Feuer [like the city we needed a fire]
um uns aufzuwecken vom Traum [to wake us up from the dream]
und du mit den blutigen Haaren [and you with bloody hair]
ich seh' deine Augen sind zu [I see your eyes are closed]
so I'll be the Wilhelmine Baron & you
can be the ewiger Jew [the Eternal Jew]

from the ivy at Grünewald station
to the Treptower Soviet blade
you built your triumphant narration out of stones
from the Mendelssohn grave
where the sun is as gold as the names on the ground
& the walls grow up over the trees
& the tower antenna is haunting the town
& the past is a quiet disease

where the air is filled up with sparrows
when once it was clouded with crows
& the Sleepwalker shot his last arrow
then he buried himself with his bow
oh my lover, my murderer's daughter
accomplice to all of my sins
our city of love & of slaughter
wird immer noch heißen Berlin. . . . [will still be called Berlin]

This is a love song, initially sung by a Jewish singer to his German (non-Jewish) lover ('oh my lover, my murderer's daughter'); then it becomes a love song to Berlin itself, the 'city of love & of slaughter'. Lover and city cannot be clearly distinguished here: the 'you' in the lyrics moves from a woman with red hair to Berlin with its 'triumphant narration'.

The point is not simply that Berlin is the subject of the *Heimatlied*. Rather, the lyrics are about Kreuzberg, a hip quarter, which until 1989 led an exposed existence by the Berlin Wall, and was home to a large Turkish diaspora and other immigrants. Here, the ruins in Görlitzer Park (today a focal point of social grievances, drug dealing, and refugees), and the remains of the former train station are melancholic images of a place at the edge of history, a place that is not envisaged by the triumphant historical narrative. The trains run through tunnels without any specific direction ('they run her und hin'). In Görlitzer Park itself, however, there is no movement, only waiting. The 'I' is in a place where memory and future, past and expectation, dream and reality, individual history and world history blend.

Kahn's text contains various signals that refer to Berlin's Jewish history and the Holocaust as a breach in this history: the Grünewald railroad station, from which deportation trains left for the extermination camps, Moses Mendelssohn's grave, and the shiny Stolpersteine (literally 'stumbling blocks'), which, set into the pavement, commemorate individual victims of National Socialist terror. Against this perception of the city, the past appears to be 'a quiet disease' and the present to be haunted by ghosts. The line 'so I'll be the Wilhelmine Baron & you can be the ewiger Jew' perhaps points to such ghosts: the 'Wilhelmine Baron' and the 'ewiger Jude' (the Wandering Jew is called the 'Eternal Jew' in German) are two figures that emblematically capture this infection from the past. But this line also indicates an inversion of classical identification patterns. This might be a hint pointing to the strange role of the culture that in Germany is perceived as 'Jewish' such as, for instance, klezmer—'representing Jewishness as dreamed by others' (Waligórska 2013: 278). By contrast, this line could also suggest a new self-confident attitude in dealing with stereotypical attributions. Accordingly, Berlin Kreuzberg becomes the place where the Jewish 'I' is able to slip into the role of the Prussian Junker—and the German female descendant of the Nazis is identified as the 'ewiger Jude'. This signifies a dreamlike inversion of the historical roles of perpetrator and victim; the power of the historical traumas is finally suspended.

The Wandering Jew is a paradigmatic image of the Jewish diaspora. Originally derived from anti-Jewish folk tales and legends, the Wandering Jew is the embodiment of the Jewish people—which from a Christian point of view is going collectively astray—and is thus a coded reference to their own doubts regarding the Christian promise of redemption. In the nineteenth century, however, the figure was adapted by Jews themselves (Hasam-Rokem and Dundes 1986). The Wandering Jew becomes an image of the 'awareness of heteronomy' (Bodenheimer 2002: 21) for many Jewish intellectuals. In the post-Zionist context, where Daniel Kahn is located as well, this figure of the perpetual exile is positively reframed as a genuine expression of the 'powers of diaspora'.

Thus, in 'Görlitzer Park', Berlin is precisely the place that does not permit seamless identification with the place, the immediate appropriation of the place. Rather, Kreuzberg, in Berlin, is the place that enables an ironical play with the figures of identity and with nostalgia. After all, the nostalgia of 'Görlitzer Park' is a reflected nostalgia: it does not construct Berlin ex post facto as the lost place of origin, which it could never have been. Rather, the song is about Berlin as a diasporic place. On the one hand, this means that Berlin has a specific history as one of the sites of the Jewish diaspora, but, on the other hand, precisely because of this history, it represents something that can be pointedly described as a placeless place—a place that is neither homeland nor exile, but maybe just a domicile for a while.

Even if the majority of Kahn's audience can be located in large German cities, with their urban and diverse (though mostly non-Jewish) crowds, he also plays concerts in Europe, Israel, and North America. The community that his music creates is in many ways a diasporic community and cannot be reduced to one specific place or group. In an interview on the occasion of a show at the twenty-fourth Jewish Music Festival in San Francisco in 2009, Kahn spoke about the idea of diaspora and its conditions in the twenty-first century: 'I believe in diasporism, in some ways. . . . the diaspora is much more bound up, connected now. All diasporas are. To be spread out is normal. We're all living in the diaspora, because we spend half our time talking to someone who's on the other side of the planet, or the other side of the country' (Minkin 2009). By the statement that 'we're all living in the diaspora' Kahn obviously does not only mean the Jewish diaspora, but the world population under the conditions of globalization and digital revolution. Yet this universal and metaphorical understanding of diaspora resonates with Joshua Neuman's statement, cited above, that the new 'community centers are websites' and that the holy tradition of a new generation of Jews is also formed by popular cultural artefacts, and not solely by canonical texts.

Conclusion: The 'Jewish Atlantic'

The 'Jewish Atlantic' can be described as a constellation of Jewish experiences and notions of diaspora in pop music, which is simultaneously symbolic *and* real, imaginative *and* geographic. A general function of music, as described by Frith, is its potential to 'enable us to place ourselves in imaginative cultural narratives' (Frith 1996: 124). In this perspective, pop music offers many artists the option to return to the traditional narratives of exile in Judaism, and even to synthesize Judaism and Jewishness as a diaspora culture with pop culture. Regarding the *Jewish* dimension, the function of pop music is thus to connect the dispersed Jewish people and to create new communities, as other media used to do in earlier times in other ways; but the *popularity* of pop music also offers a powerful model of transcending Jewish identity to reach a general and metaphorical image of a diaspora.

While Leonard Cohen deals with Jewishness in poetic and overdetermined language that frequently works with biblical or traditional references (sometimes inverting them), younger musicians build on Jewish folklore, on a secular Yiddish musical tradition, and the history of Jewish migration, in an innovative and subversive manner. Being Jewish is no longer an exclusive and defensive identity, but appears as an important strand of a global and diverse music culture. In this context, diaspora means mainly the global and multicultural conditions of music in a society shaped by immigration and globalization, as it does, for instance, for the Canadian artist Socalled. Ultimately, however, the 'Jewish Atlantic' should not be romanticized, but must be understood as a consequence of the Holocaust as well. The return to Europe and especially Germany constitutes a specific form of exposing oneself to the diaspora and its traumatic history. But, as I showed in the example of Daniel Kahn, Berlin represents exactly the place that permits a certain weightlessness—in the face of trauma and fixed identity ascriptions. Thus Berlin has a paradoxical status: based on Kahn's song 'Görlitzer Park', it can be noted that diaspora is becoming a state that equally abolishes and strengthens the sense of Jewish community. In this sense, the 'Jewish Atlantic' opens up a space for negotiating Jewishness in pop music *and* for acting out its popularity. This space is mediated: over the course of the twentieth century, the Jewish people morph from the People of the Book into the People of the Record (e.g. Del Negro 2010, which demonstrates the significance of records for Jewish identity in the 1950s). In the first decades of the twenty-first century the children of Israel are suddenly reborn as digital natives. This technological shift in media history, which generates and accompanies pop music, also leads to new understandings of being Jewish in modern times and being a part of the 'Jewish Atlantic'. It can mean to feel connected as a community through the new media and to be represented as Jews in popular culture. But it can also mean to express a metaphorical state of dispersion, which resonates in the global dimension of pop music.

References

ALTMAN, SIG. 1971. *The Comic Image of the Jew: Explorations of a Pop Culture Phenomenon.* Rutherford, NJ.

BERG, TIMOTHY. 2000. 'Pop Music'. In *St James Encyclopedia of Popular Culture* <http://www.encyclopedia.com/media/encyclopedias-almanacs-transcripts-and-maps/pop-music> (accessed 26 Oct. 2017).

BODENHEIMER, ALFRED. 2002. *Wandernde Schatten: Ahasver, Moses und die Authentizität der jüdischen Moderne.* Göttingen.

BOYARIN, DANIEL, and JONATHAN BOYARIN. 2001. *Powers of Diaspora: Two Essays on the Relevance of Jewish Culture.* Minneapolis, Minn.

BRENNER, MICHAEL. 2016. *Israel: Traum und Wirklichkeit des jüdischen Staates. Von Theodor Herzl bis heute.* Munich.

CHEYETTE, BRYAN. 2013. *Diasporas of the Mind: Jewish and Postcolonial Writing and the Nightmare of History.* New Haven, Conn.

CHO, LILY M. 2007. 'The Turn to Diaspora'. *Topia*, 17: 11–30.

COHEN, ROBIN. 1997. *Global Diasporas: An Introduction.* London.

CONNELL, JOHN, and CHRIS GIBSON. 2003. *Sound Tracks: Popular Music, Identity and Place*. London.

DAYNES, SARAH. 2005. 'The Musical Construction of the Diaspora: The Case of Reggae and Rastafari'. In Sheila Whiteley, Andy Bennett, and Stan Hawkings, eds., *Music, Space and Place: Popular Music and Cultural Identity*, 25–41. London.

DEL NEGRO, GIOVANNA P. 2010. 'From the Nightclub to the Living Room: Gender, Ethnicity, and Upward Mobility in the 1950s: Party Records of Three Jewish Woman Comics'. In Simon J. Bronner, ed., *Jews at Home: The Domestication of Identity*, Jewish Cultural Studies 2, 188–216. Oxford.

FRITH, SIMON. 1981. *Sound Effects: Youth, Leisure, and the Politics of Rock 'n' Roll*. New York.

—— 1996. 'Music and Identity'. In Stuart Hall and Paul du Gay, eds., *Questions of Cultural Identity*, 108–27. London.

GILROY, PAUL. 1993. *The Black Atlantic: Modernity and Double Consciousness*. London.

GOETSCHEL, WILLI, and ATO QUAYSON. 2016. 'Introduction: Jewish Studies and Postcolonialism'. *Cambridge Journal of Postcolonial Literary Inquiry*, 3: 1–10.

GOTTLIEB, JACK. 2004. *Funny, It Doesn't Sound Jewish: How Yiddish Songs and Synagogue Melodies Influenced Tin Pan Alley, Broadway, and Hollywood*. New York.

GREEN, JOANN. 2009. 'Molly Picon'. *Jewish Women: A Comprehensive Historical Encyclopedia, Jewish Women's Archive* <http://jwa.org/encyclopedia/article/picon-molly> (accessed 17 July 2017).

HASAM-ROKEM, GALIT, and ALAN DUNDES. 1986. *The Wandering Jew: Essays in the Interpretation of a Christian Legend*. Bloomington, Ind.

JANECZKO, JEFF. 2009. 'A Tale of Four Diasporas: Case Studies on the Relevance of "Diaspora" in Contemporary American Jewish Music'. In Jonathan L. Friedman, ed., *Perspectives on Jewish Music*, 9–40. Lanham, Md.

KALMAR, IVAN DAVIDSON, and DEREK PENSLAR, eds. 2005. *Orientalism and the Jews*. Waltham, Mass.

KOVEN, MIKEL J. 2007. 'Cool Jewz: Contemporary Jewish Identity in Popular Culture— An Introduction'. *Shofar: An Interdisciplinary Journal of Jewish Studies*, 25: 1–2.

LOEWY, HANNO. 2014. *Jukebox, Jewkbox! A Jewish Century on Shellac and Vinyl*. Hohenems. [Catalogue accompanying the exhibition in the Jewish Museum Hohenems from 19 Oct. 2014 to 8 Mar. 2015].

MINKIN, SARAH ANNE. 2009. 'Daniel Kahn on a Tradition of Subversion and a Subversive Tradition'. *Jvoices*, 27 Mar. 2009 <http://jvoices.com/2009/03/27/daniel-kahn-on-a-tradition-of-subversion-and-a-subversive-tradition> (accessed 29 Aug. 2017).

MISHRA, VIJAI. 2007. *The Literature of the Diaspora: Theorizing the Diasporic Imaginary*. London.

NEUMAN, JOSHUA. 2011. 'The Religion of Jewish Popular Culture'. *JMB Journal* [*Journal of the Jewish Museum Berlin*], 4: 60–1.

OZ-SALZBERGER, FANIA. 2009. 'Israelis in Berlin. Ein neues Bücherregal'. In Anat Feinberg, ed., *Rück-Blick auf Deutschland. Ansicht hebräischsprachiger Autoren*, 151–70. Munich.

POPESCU, DIANA I. 2013. 'The Persistence of Nostalgia? When Poles Miss Their Jews and Israelis Yearn for Europe'. *Jewish Culture and History*, 14(2–3): 140–52 <http://

www.tandfonline.com/doi/pdf/10.1080/1462169X.2013.805897> (accessed 29 Aug. 2017).

SAFRAN, WILLIAM. 1991. 'Diasporas in Modern Societies: Myths of Homeland and Return'. *Diaspora: A Journal of Transnational Studies*, 1: 83–99.

SLOBIN, MARK. 2002. *American Klezmer: Its Roots and Offshoots*. Oakland, Calif.

STRATTON, JON. 2009. *Jews, Race, and Popular Music*. Farnham.

WALIGÓRSKA, MAGDALENA. 2013. *Klezmer's Afterlife: An Ethnography of the Jewish Music Revival in Poland and Germany*. Oxford.

Yad Vashem. 2015. 'The Story of the Jewish Community of Bălţi'. The Holocaust Martyrs' and Heroes' Remembrance Authority <http://www.yadvashem.org/yv/en/exhibitions/communities/balti/mein_shtetle_belz.asp> (accessed 29 Aug. 2017).

FIVE

The Hidden Legacies of Jewish Traditions and the Global Allure of Psychotherapy: A Case Study of the Israeli TV series *Betipul*

DIANA I. POPESCU

More often than not, cinema's interest in psychotherapy seems to revolve around representations of the analyst. Given the Jewish origins of psychoanalysis, the preferred ethnicity of the psychoanalyst character for many filmmakers is Jewish. Freud's creation of the therapeutic setting, its framework, and basic rules laid the foundations for many of the psychotherapeutic practices that we presently see. The Israeli TV series *Betipul* is a prime example of an outstanding attempt to enter the reality of the psychotherapy practice. Given its wide popularity at home, I explore the symbolic significance of *Betipul* as an atypical mediation of a Jewish Israeli identity in crisis, and the function of and responses to this mediation among Israeli audiences. The popularity of the show abroad is also of unprecedented scale in the history of Israeli television. The many remakes of the original TV series in Europe and in the United States reveal significant cultural differences in the approach to psychotherapy. Nonetheless, underlying these differences is a global consensus on the representation of the therapist. I will argue that references to the Jewishness of the therapist, while subtle, are critical to the cinematic portrayals of the Israeli therapist abroad. In addition to considering responses of Jewish audiences to this character, I discuss its appeal to a non-Jewish and global viewer. In view of this goal I ask what *Betipul* adds to the representation of the Jewish psychotherapist in popular culture and how the Jewish aspects of this representation function when they leave Jewish contexts.

A Production for Israeli Jews that Goes Global

The TV series *Betipul* focuses on the professional and private personae of the Israeli psychologist Reuven Dagan, who is played by Assi Dayan, a beloved figure of Israeli cinema. Its formula is simple: we meet Dagan and his clients during the week, and at the end of each week we encounter him again, this time as a patient consulting with his supervisor, played by Gila Almagor. In each of the two seasons, consisting of 45 and 35 episodes, Dagan and his many patients come together in the same setting—the consultation room, which is in his own home. Each episode is dedicated to one patient, whom the therapist sees once a week. The patients come from all walks of life, led to therapy by various existential troubles: Na'ama is a young paramedic struggling to deal with her difficulties in committing to a relationship; Orna and Michael are a couple contemplating an abortion as their own relationship deteriorates; teenager Ayala is a talented gymnast whose accident appears more and more like a suicide attempt; Yadin is an Israel Defence Forces (IDF) fighter pilot who rejects any feelings of guilt after his mission of bombing a Palestinian apartment building which led to the death of children. At the end of the week, Reuven Dagan meets with his ex-mentor Gila to talk about his anger and confusion over his failing marriage and his concerns that his professional skills are also failing.

The series, created by Hagai Levi in collaboration with Ori Sivan and Nir Bergman, ran over a period of three years, from 2005 to 2008. The storylines of each patient are written by four screenwriters. The TV series' ambition to portray psychotherapy as it is in real life is made apparent by the decision to invite Israeli psychotherapists Roni Baht, specializing in relational therapy, Irit Kleiner Paz, an expert in couple therapy, and Amir Shneider, a child psychotherapist, to act as consultants, to advise and shape the characters and give authenticity to the cinematic therapy sessions. Even though initially the proposal for the series did not raise interest among the Israeli TV producers, channel Hot3 was in the end persuaded to buy the production and broadcast it in the late evenings. The programme quickly gained national popularity and won Israeli academy awards for the best drama series, best script, and directing. The title of best actor was granted to Assi Dayan and that of best actress awarded to Ayelet Zurer.

Unlike the majority of representations of psychotherapists in films, *Betipul* presents a portrait of the psychotherapist that has been embraced by the Israeli therapeutic community. After the show was broadcast, psychoanalysts reported an increase in referrals to therapy and a return to therapy by those who had left it in the past. Roni Baht noted that 'the influence of the show on the Israeli public was shown to create more positive views of psychological treatment and the view that psychotherapy could be more effective than previously believed' (Baht 2010: 244). Compared to earlier periods, these responses point to a notable shift in Israeli collective perceptions of psychoanalysis. In the early 1980s, for example, psychologist Emanuel Berman remarked on the general unwillingness to integrate psychotherapy within Israeli culture, since at that time it was viewed as weakening national ideals such as 'strength, control, and manliness'. 'An exploration of fantasy, dreams, and memories' offered by psychoanalysis was perceived as working against this mentality (Berman 1981: 169–70). Since the 1980s, the rise of individualism as a collective psychological mind-set led to an increased Jewish interest in therapy. Consequently, the benefits of psychotherapy were better understood and integrated in IDF culture. In the past few decades, argued Edna Lomsky-Feder and Eyal Ben-Ari, 'Israel has witnessed a change in how violent conflict is understood, interpreted and acted upon. What we have called the therapeutic discourse has emerged during this period as a result of global changes, such as the stress on suffering and victimhood, and more Israeli-based patterns entailing the spread of popular psychological models among the population at large' (Lomsky-Feder and Ben-Ari 2007: 126). Popular media have recognized the growing importance of psychological and therapeutic models in dealing with individual responses to pressure and crisis. *Betipul* is at the forefront of this popular therapeutic discourse. The series initiated an unprecedented phenomenon in the history of Israeli television culture, having rapidly gained international acclaim.

At first glance it seems surprising that American television production companies looking for high-quality international television series to suit the tastes of American audiences have turned to Israeli popular culture. A closer inspection shows, however, that Israeli television has been positively regarded by American producers, who perceive Israeli audiences as more refined, selective, and critical. This leads Israeli producers to create higher-quality programmes to meet these higher expectations (Chozick and Mitnick 2011). Furthermore, the Israeli television community has developed good marketing strategies. Israeli television is presented as 'providing an antidote to American television, which is usually more commercial', and as proposing 'a different way of making a show. Hollywood is much more of an industry, but in Israel our shows are slowly, carefully and originally tailor made', explained Avi Nir, chief executive of Keshet Broadcasting (Bettridge 2012).

Betipul was the first Israeli series to be remade for American television. HBO, the American television network, produced *In Treatment* (2008–10), which then paved the way for American adaptations of other Israeli dramas such as *Ḥatufim* ('Prisoners of War', 2009–12), recast as *Homeland* (2011–). Fox Channel also launched *Traffic Light* (2011), a sitcom based on the Israeli series *Ramzor* (2008–14). Following the success of the series in the United States, HBO Europe and HBO International created new adaptations. Hagai Levi was invited to serve as executive producer for local versions of the series in countries in eastern and central Europe, as well as in Russia, Brazil, Argentina, Canada, and Japan. To date, there are seventeen adaptations of the Israeli product, with the number increasing each year, as new countries develop their own versions of *Betipul*.

This international acclaim points to the growth of what has been termed 'the therapy culture', a culture of global dimensions which views affect and emotions as central aspects of individuals' social and public identities. The focus on emotions within the public sphere is greater than ever before, claims sociologist Frank Furedi, who calls this phenomenon the 'therapeutic turn' in

British–American culture. This phenomenon has polarized scholarly opinion. While Furedi warns that the growth of 'therapy culture' leads to a form of emotional governance, where the wish for public self-expression of emotions becomes the 'opiate of the people' (Furedi 2004; Yates 2011: 60–1), others regard this turn in positive terms. The emergence of a 'therapeutic ethos' signals a positive development, where new spaces can emerge to facilitate self-understanding to help us live with the shifts and uncertainties of late modernity, explains Yates (Richards 2007; Yates 2011: 61). Despite these concerns with regard to the social and personal effects of this turn, there is common agreement that the therapeutic style permeates many fields of social life. This emphasis on affect creates as, Eva Illouz explains, an 'emotional style' of relating to one's environment and to the other defined as: 'the combination of the ways a culture becomes "preoccupied" with certain emotions and devises specific "techniques"—linguistic, scientific, ritual—to apprehend them. An emotional style is established when a new "interpersonal imagination" is formulated, that is, a new way of thinking about the relationship of self to others, imagining its potentialities and implementing them in practice' (Illouz 2008: 14). The 'emotional style' is made apparent in popular culture, including 'professional treaties', popular culture, 'talk shows', and 'self-help books', as well as in 'the body of claims proffered by certified psychologists and the body of texts in which psychologists and/or therapy appear and play a role; e.g. *The Sopranos*, the Oprah Winfrey talk show, Woody Allen's movies' (Illouz 2008: 15). The 'emotional style', understood here as a heightened sense of self-awareness, is not uncommon in Jewish experience where, both in the diaspora and in Israel, Jews have been aware and have been made aware of their difference. This culture has provided a space for the emotional baggage of being different to be articulated and validated in the public sphere.

Betipul, too, can be defined as pertaining to such an emotional culture, because of its concrete focus on the process of therapy as a place where emotions are indeed validated, as well as its more symbolic function as a catalyst for difficult emotions with which the Israeli public struggles. Hence, the series serves as a cogent example of 'the therapeuticization of social experience', as argued by Alejandro and Alberto Martínez (Martínez and Martínez 2012: 116–17). This is made apparent in *Betipul*'s ambition to provide a safe space to explore at a distance one's own emotional problems, through witnessing the emotional difficulties encountered by others. It is fair to state that access to the intimate struggles of the therapist and his clients may also encourage a voyeuristic attitude. While the voyeuristic drive may partly explain the show's unparalleled popularity, we should not underestimate the viewers' ability to empathize, to learn about emotions, and to become more aware of how psychotherapy can help them in their own lives. The therapist invites the patient to enter an unthreatening zone where one can reflect on problems while being accompanied and sustained psychologically. One aspect which distinguishes this series from others is its detailed and intimate portrayal of the psychotherapist. In this essay, I will argue that despite cultural variations, the representation of the therapist includes, albeit discreetly, cultural aspects associated with Jewish traditions. I further suggest that these Jewish traditions may have made the series more appealing to an Israeli Jewish audience. To a non-Jewish audience, these discreet references to Jewish traditions have contributed to the construction of a humanistic and charismatic and therefore relatable persona of the therapist. In what follows I will take a closer look at psychotherapy and the therapist's persona as it is shaped in the Israeli cultural context.

Psychotherapy in Israeli Culture

Counselling in Israeli culture, though partly acknowledged by Israeli authorities through the therapy service available in the IDF, has gained a higher degree of importance, as this TV series brought therapy more urgently into current public consciousness. What has changed in Israeli society's relationship with this profession?

From its earliest years, Israeli society has been aware of the insights and benefits that Freud's talking cure could offer for the young state. The first pioneers in the Land of Israel were well-educated men and women who brought with them works such as Karl Marx's *Capital* and Sigmund Freud's *Interpretation of Dreams*. Kibbutz members also showed an interest in psychology, in particular in child-rearing and developing good parental behaviours (Yovell 2009). Israel's early interest in psychology is shown by the foundation of the Israel Psychoanalytic Society. Established in 1933 by Max Eitingon, a student and follower of Sigmund Freud, the Society came to play a role in times of national distress. During the Six Day War in 1967 psychoanalysts organized and offered psychological services, particularly in civil defence. Similarly, during the Yom Kippur War, psychoanalysts played a major role within the Israel Defence Forces, a role that has been continued and strengthened till today.

The distress resulting from the heightened state of anxiety caused by the unpredictability of war, and the effects of exposure to war and death faced by soldiers, have been acknowledged by the state, and indeed psychological and counselling services are readily available to those in need. Hence, one may argue that healing through talk is historically well recognized by Israeli society and embedded within its wider culture (Bar-On 1992: 289–301). While it is accessible, it is questionable to what extent this therapeutic service is in fact popular among Israelis. Opinion is divided in this regard. Some members of the therapeutic community observe that Israeli patients usually resist the therapeutic process. While this may be too broad a statement, and may not reflect the majority of Israeli views on this subject, in the absence of survey data it is useful to quote one

Israeli therapist's experiences of working with Israeli patients in the 1980s, embodied in an article written in 1981 by Emanuel Berman, an Israeli psychotherapist who returned to practise in Israel after a lengthy period in the United States.

Berman, arguably influenced by his experiences in the USA, a country with greater social openness to therapy culture, claimed that the tradition of therapy was missing from Israel until the 1970s. The lack of interest might have been related, he claimed, to the perception of therapy as an admission of deficiency and dysfunctionality. Admitting the need for treatment would be equal to deviating from the conventional norm of behaviour, which implied a show of toughness and resilience in the face of adversity, independence, and strength. Appeal to the services of therapy thus implied a form of helplessness and inability to handle problems on one's own. Reliance on external help implied vulnerability, or exposure to being seen as vulnerable. Given this, the author claimed that the historical attitude towards therapy in Israel was one of hostility. Berman argued: 'In fact the aim of psychotherapy which focuses on individual needs and self-realisation conflicted with the national ideals that one must sacrifice, in the most intimate and personal sense, individual needs and aspirations' (Berman 1981: 169).

Therapy was also marginalized because of the perception of the talking cure as something that has no immediate consequences. The engagement it needed, since therapy is a process that develops over a long period of time with no fixed end point, could have been perceived as frustrating for an individual raised in a culture where prolonged periods of reflection may equal hesitation and vulnerability.

Berman further argued that 'strength, control and manliness' are crucial to the Israeli national ego ideal, and are understood as requiring 'a task-oriented, action-focused, matter of fact style'. In contrast, 'an exploration of fantasy, dreams, and memories' went against this mentality. External reality was favoured over the recognition of inner reality. States of emotional turmoil were covered up. From his experience of working as a therapist in Israel, Berman concluded: 'It can be safely stated that denial and isolation of affect are central defence mechanisms among many Israelis seen in psychotherapy' (Berman 1981: 170).

Since the 1980s, however, the loosening of the ethos of the culture of collectivism implied the rise of individualism and the recognition of the centrality of individual needs for the larger good of society. As part of the self-liberation movement, an increased interest in therapy developed. On a national level, the benefits of psychotherapy are better understood and integrated within the fabric of the IDF culture. With the increased awareness of psychotherapy comes a higher level of ability to recognize emotional stress and admit to one's own vulnerabilities.

Displays of Vulnerability and Empowerment

Betipul reflects upon the meaning of being vulnerable and offers a safe space where, through the witnessing of therapy on the screen, Israeli audiences connect with their own vulnerabilities. The paradigm of *sabra* (native Israeli) culture, with its apparent neglect of emotional life, is debunked by *Betipul*. The patients who enter treatment, while undergoing personal crisis, are not defeated by it, but, in the spirit of *sabra* culture, they act upon it and seek help. Hence, *Betipul* provides an interesting commentary on the meaning of *sabra* culture by highlighting a previously overlooked aspect. The patients present stereotypical traits of the *sabra*: they display strong defence mechanisms and behave as if they are in full control of their emotions. They do not show any apparent signs of weakness or distress, even though their presence in the analyst's room denotes their recognition of emotional distress and their inability to deal with distress on their own.

Betipul makes apparent the interplay between the display of strength and of vulnerability. Through its portrayal of therapeutic work *Betipul* proposes that empowerment does not come from denial of emotional distress but from its recognition and endurance at some time. The role of the therapist is gradually and at the patients' own pace to bring them to a position of safety from which they can face problems and develop strategies to cope with them. *Betipul* may also have gained unprecedented popularity among the Israeli public because it has challenged the notion that weakness and vulnerability are to be kept hidden. The series' exploration of vulnerabilities, and indirectly, of perceptions of toughness, reflects the gradual changes in collective perceptions of vulnerability and emotionalism within Israeli culture. The series argues that showing vulnerability within a psychotherapeutic setting is acceptable. Dagan is portrayed as conflicted and vulnerable, not unlike his patients. The notion that strength is a lack of vulnerability is challenged, and above all, reflects broader Israeli preoccupations with this topic. Traditionally, *sabra* culture implies that vulnerability is a sign of weakness and is not and cannot be expressed directly. The TV series, however, deals with patients' vulnerabilities openly and publicly. Emotions are not to be condemned but listened to, accepted, and understood.

Talking Cure and Talking *Dugri*

In the Israeli depiction, the Jewish analyst and his patients can or are willing to engage in direct conversation. *Dugri* (Hebrew slang, from Arabic: 'straight talk') as an Israeli conversational style presents similarities to the desired communication style of psychotherapy. Known for its conciseness and brevity but also for its frankness and directness, *dugri* is based on the principle that one speaks truthfully what one thinks and feels. In therapy, one may argue, being direct and truthful (and here one thinks of the directness of free association recommended by

Freud) is an essential condition for progress in therapeutic work with the patient. Furthermore, telling one's immediate thoughts through unrestricted talk about one's inner reality is a condition that any therapeutic work strives for. The *dugri* style is strengthened by army culture, and becomes part of an Israeli conversational discourse, unique in its promotion of directness (Katriel 1986). Being direct also represents a condition for building intimate relationships. Within the sphere of psychoanalytic practice, it leads to the creation of the so-called therapeutic bond developed between the patient and the therapist.

'Something is bothering me, I have to talk to you *dugri*' means to be willing to engage in a dialogue based on the pursuit of authenticity and truthfulness. Talking straight is a symbol of Israeli *sabra* culture (Katriel 1986), as it means to engage and acknowledge both the external and internal reality of things. Within everyday speech, *dugri*, as a language code specific to Israeli *sabra* identity, leaves no room for social barriers and promotes solidarity and social togetherness. This aim, too, is central to therapeutic work. Talking *dugri* as a collective conversational style is similar to talking within the frame of the therapy session. While the need to talk is well recognized, the creators of *Betipul* claim that talking therapy, while having a long history in Israel, used not to be publicly acknowledged to the extent it is today. Hagai Levi, for example, claims that being in therapy remained a secret, hidden in the closet, and that only since the 1980s has therapy infiltrated the wider social and cultural scene (Levi 2009). The growing awareness of the benefits of therapy and the perception of talking as leading to action and change, alongside the increased visibility of the profession within the public media, explains the positive reception of *Betipul*. The TV series further contributed to the mediatization of therapy as a form of crisis management. It offered a brand of therapy that is specific to Israeli culture.

An Israeli Approach to Psychotherapy

When comparing the American adaptation to the Israeli original, one notes significant differences in the portrayal of the psychotherapist and the development of his therapeutic bond with his patients. In particular, one notices how cultural and social norms infiltrate the therapy room.

The therapeutic relation established between Dagan and his patients is more flexible than in Western therapeutic practices. For example, Dagan considers attending the wedding of his patient, he accepts a coffee-maker as a gift from a patient, and comes close to breaking an essential therapeutic boundary, being tempted into entering a romantic relationship with his patient. Dagan is also more willing to share his emotional responses when asked by his patient, the IDF pilot, how the doctor feels about his having checked his personal records and his personal contacts. While in other practices the therapist may deflect this question by focusing on the patient's need to break the therapeutic boundary, Dagan engages fully in this confrontation, admitting his discomfort. The use of language also makes the loosening of boundaries apparent. Dagan's patients, unlike their American counterparts, avoid polite expressions or an indirect style of communication.

In the Israeli original, the therapist and the patient face one another, and the physical space between them is significantly less than in the American series. This physical closeness suggests an appreciation for and seeking of contact, and reveals a different manner of understanding and relating to the other's boundaries. The therapist and his patients are more comfortable with initiating and sustaining direct confrontation to resolve conflicts, or to clarify misunderstandings. This confrontational and intimate style of communication is a feature of *dugri* style and of *sabra* culture.

In *Betipul*, the private act of undertaking psychotherapy becomes public, as the audience is made a witness to this experience. The privacy of the therapeutic session and the pact of confidentiality between the therapist and the patient are broken and exposed to the Israeli public. The problems an individual deals with become known to the collective, thereby turning the process of therapy into a national preoccupation.

While Israeli culture cherishes the individual, the communal spirit has dominated in times of national crisis and war. Army culture also contains the message that in times of crisis, the individual can be sacrificed for the sake of the community's well-being, and promotes a national feeling of solidarity and togetherness. What prevails is communal well-being, which includes the well-being of individuals. *Betipul* deals solely with the individual's needs, emotions, and traumas. The focus on the private lives of the patients excludes the national problems of Israeli society as a whole. Hence, *Betipul* temporarily suspends the constraints of the group and the demands of the nation, and allows the Israeli individual to detach from national responsibilities, by focusing solely on individual problems. There are, however, many overlaps between national and personal concerns: a national crisis can easily become a private crisis (as in the case of the IDF pilot in *Betipul*), and insecurity as an external reality can easily turn into a mental reality. Consequently, there can be no clear-cut boundaries between the personal and the national.

The Cinematic Psychotherapist and the Hidden Legacies of Jewish Traditions

Cinema has offered a profusion of negative portrayals of therapists, psychiatrists, and psychoanalysts. Depictions of therapists in American film are generally not flattering (Gharaibeh 2005: 316–19; Young 2012). Almost half the figures examined by Gharaibeh are portrayed as incompetent or as violating boundaries, and approximately one quarter of the cinematic therapists break sexual boundaries, or are depicted as insane or perverse (for example in Brian de Palma's 1980 *Dressed to Kill*, or Jonathan Demme's 1991 *Silence of the Lambs*). It is also fair to say that there have been some sympathetic portrayals of therapists, such as in Robert Redford's 1980 *Ordinary People*, Norman Jewison's 1985 *Agnes of God*, and Craig Gillespie's 2007 *Lars and the Real Girl* (Celenza 2013: 216). In Hollywood especially, the psychotherapist is a favoured cinematic character. American film is replete with both sympathetic and less favourable representations of therapists.

Typically, the therapists in American films are predominantly Jewish. While the Jewish aspect may at times be downplayed, psychotherapy as a profession remains closely linked to being Jewish. American popular culture's use of the trope of the Jewish therapist, understandably originating in the history of psychoanalysis, has not changed over the years. The therapist, Jewish or gentile, has been portrayed in very sketchy terms in American cinema by default. He or she is more often than not a mere dramatic prop meant to sustain the film's narrative force and engage the audience more deeply with the main characters. The therapists lack depth of character, and in most cases play secondary roles. They remain veiled in an aura of mystery, yet marginal and unimportant. At times they become comic figures and are employed to shed light upon the absurdness, meaninglessness, irony, or comedy of the protagonists' lives (see depictions by Woody Allen in *Bananas* (1971), *Annie Hall* (1977), and *Husbands and Wives* (1992)).

The Jewish analyst remains a marginal figure, a caricature whose purpose is to prop up the plot and reflect the leading characters' inner turmoil. When portrayed positively, the therapist maintains an unassuming authoritative role. In the 1991 film *Prince of Tides*, Barbra Streisand plays Susan Lowenstein, a stereotypical psychologist who breaks the rules of psychotherapeutic practice by having an intimate relationship with her patient's brother. Dr Sobel, played by Robert de Niro in *Analyze This* (1999), is a prop meant to enhance the comic character of the film, which focuses on the figure of a Mafia gangster suffering from panic attacks. Dr Lisa Metzger, played by Meryl Streep in *Prime* (2005), albeit a central figure, serves merely to reinforce the romance and amuse the audience. The Jewish therapist, as an American cinematic figure, is in most cases a secondary figure employed to create or sustain dramatic effect. In the best-case scenario, he or she is a significant secondary character who helps audiences understand the main characters' inner conflicts and complexity better. While American, primarily Christian, audiences may get a sense of how the therapist lives outside the therapy room, his or her character remains ill-shaped and lacks narrative force.

Betipul and its many remakes have put an end to this tradition of cinematic representation. Dr Dagan does not fall into any of the stereotypical representations presented above. Furthermore, he is neither Dr Evil, the mad or psychopathic and manipulative scientist who abuses the patients, nor Dr Wonderful, the doctor completely dedicated to his profession and to his patients, always available to assist his patients outside normal consultation hours. Rather, he borrows some traits specific to the wounded healer, a therapist whose psychological issues interfere with his practice (Gabbard and Gabbard 1999; Greenberg 2011). In addition, Dagan comes close to what has been dubbed Dr Line-Crosser, someone who engages in sexual relationships with their patients (Gabbard and Gabbard 1999; Young 2012). Even though Dagan does not break the boundaries imposed by his profession, the creators of the TV series seem to imply that his flaws may interfere with his work. His desire to help his patients goes beyond the boundaries set up by therapeutic practice. In the course of his therapy, we find out that Dagan's motivation to help and heal his patients originates in real struggles to resolve or bypass his inner conflicts. His doubts as to whether he is a good therapist surface frequently in his therapy sessions with Gila. Weakness is admitted and discussed, and his failures and mistakes are discussed.

Audiences' perception of Dagan changes as the series progresses. His position of authority as a doctor is shifted to that of a vulnerable patient whose conflicts are visible, and whose defence mechanisms can be observed by viewers. As such, he too needs support, attention, and understanding, though this display of vulnerability does not detract from his role as a good practitioner. Dagan's abilities as a therapist are presented convincingly, as he shows flexibility and insight as an attentive listener and observer, and a translator of emotions that cannot be fully articulated by his patients. Dagan becomes a professional who 'knows something of the way in which repudiated wishes, thoughts, feelings and memories can translate themselves into symptoms, gestures and dreams, and who knows, as it were, the grammar and syntax of such translations and is therefore in a position to interpret them back again into the communal languages of consciousness' (Rycroft 1966: 18).

Dagan's conversations with Gila give some insight into the reality of psychotherapy as a healing practice. The therapist is described as someone who may not go further than 'participant observation, no further than illuminating the occulted causes of suffering. The therapist must strive to remove the blocks that nurture and nature, character and constitution, have put in the way of our patients becoming whatever they were meant to be' (Greenberg 2011). Dagan's portrayal, while slightly exaggerated at times, maintains a high degree of credibility. He is not the mysterious figure, nor the all-knowing healer, nor is he selflessly dedicated to all his patients. Though applauded by the therapeutic community, this representation of the therapist remains a cinematic representation. The Israeli psychotherapists who served as consultants pointed out that the character of the therapist emerges from balancing the rigour of fictional conventions with the desire to render the reality of psychotherapy on film (Baht 2010). Even though Dagan borrows some traits typical of traditional portrayals of therapists as breaking professional boundaries by falling in love with their patients, the creators of *Betipul* succeed in presenting a cinematic figure whose complexity and multifacetedness exceed any previous cinematic representation.

While this portrayal remains consistent, there are aspects of the doctor's personality and interaction with patients that are more prominent in the American adaptation. A closer comparative look at the American and Israeli portrayals of the therapist reveal small but significant cultural differences in the construction and understanding of privacy and of personal boundaries, as well as differences in the use of language registers to describe intimacy, distance, or social connection. In the American version, the therapist, Dr Paul Weston (played by Gabriel Byrne), avoids direct answers and is more likely to respect his patients' private space. This distance is most evidently present in the arrangement of the doctor's consultation rooms. Weston sits at a considerable distance from his patients, while Dagan is physically closer to his patients; he faces them directly, and not at an angle as in Weston's case (Szekely 2012). The Israeli analyst does not avoid difficult questions. When the combat fighter Yadin asks Dagan if it bothers him that he ran some checks, and spoke with some of the doctor's former patients and relatives, who confirmed his good reputation, Dagan does not avoid the question but answers directly that it does make him feel a bit uncomfortable. In the same situation, Weston replies with a question, 'Does it matter to you that I am the best?', avoiding disclosure of his own emotional responses. Dagan is less likely to impose strict personal boundaries, as he considers attending the weddings or funerals of his patients. The therapeutic relation established between Dagan and his patients allows room for more direct personal contact.

The use of language demonstrates the loosening of boundaries. The Israeli patients, unlike their American counterparts, avoid polite expressions or an indirect style of communication. This directness or closeness reveals a different manner of understanding and relating to the other's boundaries. The Israeli therapist is more comfortable with initiating and sustaining direct confrontation to resolve conflicts and clarify misunderstandings. Despite these minor variations, the core attributes of the therapist, namely his listening skills, understanding and empathy, goodwill, and warm engagement with all his patients, and his consistent professional behaviour, do not vary much in the American or the east European versions of the show, except in one case.

The most striking deviation from the original portrayal of the therapist appears in the Russian adaptation, where the male therapist is replaced with a woman. Levi explains that this decision was made to meet the expectations of a general audience which sees women as more likely to have this profession in Russia than men. The need to create a credible character for local audiences convinced Levi to agree to this alteration (Levi 2012). Cultural differences related to understandings of trust are also apparent in the Russian remake: the patients are relatives, friends, or acquaintances of the therapist. This change was accepted as reflecting the expectations of the public, who would not share intimate stories with a stranger.

Other adaptations worked to change local mentalities about the role and meaning of psychotherapy. In Romania and Poland in particular, the adaptations introduced audiences to a subject rarely discussed in the media or popular culture. Before the fall of communism, many countries in eastern Europe did not have a therapeutic culture. In Romania under Nicolae Ceaușescu's regime, the study of psychology and sociology was banned, and the expression of emotions in public was severely discouraged. Any personal sign of dissatisfaction with one's own life was regarded as a direct attack on the regime. In Poland, it was the Catholic Church which undertook the role of therapy, and the priest that of confessor. Religion stood in the place of therapy and offered comfort and guidance to the emotionally troubled. In these countries in particular, the adaptations created a space for emotional problems to be dealt with in the public sphere, showing that those who enter therapy should not be stigmatised as mentally ill. In these contexts, the interest displayed in the programme points to a cultural revival of individualism, seen as a collective cultural approach where emotions are symbolic of the uniqueness of individuals and for whom expressing emotions in public is no longer taboo. The therapists in these adaptations closely follow the example offered by Dr Weston, as they are represented as middle-class intellectuals in a bourgeois environment, with their consultation rooms richly decorated with shelves full of books and objects, and dimly lit to create an atmosphere of intimacy.

The Jewish Context and Connection of *Betipul*

The Israeli drama and the worldwide adaptions construct a cinematic character defined by humanistic values rather than ethnic or cultural affiliation. They add a depth of character to the figure of the psychotherapist and mark a clear departure from previous cinematic renditions. Still, adding to this complex portrayal, there are certain values in the Israeli drama that have been traditionally associated with Jewish ethics. In particular, the doctor's compassion, consistent counselling, and psychological support to those in need is reminiscent of the concept of *ḥesed*, 'loving-kindness', and of man's duty to make the world a better place. Dagan's propensity to help his patients understand and resolve their inner conflicts corroborates his portrayal as a wounded healer, driven by the wish to cure the wounds of others. This drive reminds Israeli audiences of the Jewish traditional belief in the role of man in repairing the world through good deeds, and hence, of the concept of *tikun ha'olam* (in Hebrew, 'world repair', signifying acts of kindness conducted in pursuit of social action and justice). While some of the doctor's attributes may find a correspondence in Jewish ethics, in the context of the TV series and the adaptations these characteristics are meant to throw the analyst's identity as a humanist psychotherapist into sharp relief. This portrayal is further complicated by seemingly irreconcilable character traits that have been historically associated with the Jewish experience. The figure of the Jew, commonly perceived as both an insider and outsider to another's culture (Biale, Galchinsky, and Heschel 1998), is further explored in the context of the therapeutic setting. Positions that can lead to irreconcilable dilemmas outside the therapeutic frame become very advantageous in the practice of psychotherapy. The binary opposites 'outsider'/'insider', 'power'/'vulnerability' are deconstructed at the level of characterization of both the doctor and his patients.

While deeply concerned with his patients' problems, the analyst in the Israeli drama maintains a constant level of resolute detachedness in his interactions with them. The status of 'outsider' commonly associated with the Jewish experience in diaspora and regarded as a position of weakness becomes a position of strength in the world of psychotherapy. In *Betipul*, the Jewish psychoanalyst derives insight from this position, as it allows him to come to a more objective understanding of his patients' dilemmas. *Betipul* further complicates this strictly 'outsider' position, as the therapist is in fact both an insider and outsider in relation to himself and to his clients. He is separated from the world outside his office and completely immersed in the world of his patients, whose dilemmas, crises, and struggles he attentively observes. He is trained to observe both the patient's and his own reactions simultaneously, and should be able to rise above the dynamics of transference and counter-transference resulting from this interaction. This condition of duality, with which Jews in the diaspora have had to struggle, has benefits in the therapeutic setting. The Jewish analyst's insider/outsider status is further reinforced when Israeli audiences are made privy to the therapist's sessions with his mentor. This exchange of roles allows viewers to relate to the therapist differently, through their witnessing of the therapist's dual or multiple roles. This ambivalent positioning further ensures the dramatic force and our fascination with the figure of the therapist.

The dynamics of this duality are also made apparent in changing perceptions of vulnerability and/or strength of the characters. While vulnerable as they go through a personal crisis, the patients are not defeated by their problems but act upon them and seek help. In the Israeli original in particular, some patients display strong defence mechanisms, or behave as if they are in full control of their emotions. Yet their very presence in the analyst's room is an admission of emotional distress and their inability to deal with it on their own. *Betipul* proposes that empowerment does not come from the denial of emotional distress but from the recognition and acceptance of this condition. The series gained an unprecedented level of popularity in Israeli society because it gives centrality to a space where weakness and vulnerability need not be hidden. Its exploration of vulnerabilities and, indirectly, of perceptions of toughness, reflects the gradual changes in collective perceptions of vulnerability. The notion that strength is a lack of vulnerability is challenged. The message that *Betipul* transmits is that it is fine to let one's guard down within the secure environment of the therapy room. Emotions are not to be condemned but listened to, accepted, and understood, and seen as a source of empowerment rather than weakness. The psychoanalyst is the catalyst of these dynamics as well as their interpreter.

Dagan's role as interpreter is worth discussing at greater length for the purposes of reaching a more complex portrayal of the humanist psychotherapist rooted in Jewish traditions. It is notable that *Betipul* relies on an extensive script produced by guest screenwriters in consultation with Israeli psychotherapists. The wordiness of the script is one of the most remarkable features of the show. The reliance on the 'text' can be associated with the centrality of the biblical text in Jewish tradition. Levi himself suggests that the propensity to give priority to the script and to reflection rather than to action is inspired by his practising Judaism in earlier life (Levi 2009).

There are parallels between the work of the psychotherapist and that of the practising Jew that are worth noting. For the therapist words have an all-encompassing power. The therapist's central duty is to reflect upon and interpret how language is used by individuals to narrate life events and construct memory and identity narratives. We see the analyst time and again as someone deeply engaged in interpretation. The dialogue between the doctor and his patients relies on an intimate understanding and observation of the patient's choice of words, facial expressions, and body movements. The patient presents the therapist, trained in listening skills, with the challenge of interpretation. He or she is a symbolic text that needs to be questioned and deconstructed in order to reach a deeper explanation of who the patient is and may become. Unravelling these layers of meaning and experience is a practice similar to that of interpreting the biblical text, proceeding from the literal to the enigmatic, the simple to the complex. Just as every letter of the Torah scroll possesses significance and interpretative potential, so every word or gesture expressed by the client has meaning to be unravelled in the therapeutic process. Words or the lack of them are highly significant. It is through language that problems or traumas are articulated, and through reformulations of existing narratives that new narratives emerge. Through its focus on self-reflection and the interpretation of actions and interactions, *Betipul* reminds Israeli Jewish viewers of central aspects of a Jewish tradition of textual interpretation.

In the secular context of psychotherapy, it is the patient, and not the text, who is the source for close interpretation. The psychotherapist, like the rabbi, is revered as a guide in the search for emotional and spiritual meaning. Furthermore, in the secular world, in times of crisis which call for professional intervention, individuals can reach out to counselling. In contrast to religion, psychotherapy offers humanism, by turning Jewish practices of interrogating the scriptures into secular practices of interrogating the human mind. It thus shares with Judaism a whole set of hermeneutic and interpretative methods. Similar comparisons also appear in recent studies about Sigmund Freud's relationship with Judaism (Berke 2015). Stephen Frosh convincingly argues that, for Freud, 'Jewish connections of psychoanalysis were a source of very mixed feelings, ranging from pride in the idea that psychoanalysis might be an extension of Jewish intellectualism through anxiety over what this might mean for the safety of his creation, to discomfort due to the belief that psychoanalysis could not belong to any one people or share any ideology other than that of science itself, meaning, in his mind, the disinterested pursuit of truth' (Frosh 2005: 9). What seemed to prevail in Freud's relation to both Judaism and psychoanalysis was, to quote Frosh again, 'Freud's inclination towards universalism and a mode of ethical humanism imbued with secularism and non-sectarianism' (Frosh 2008: 171). The portrayal of a humanist therapist originating in the Freudian beginnings of psychoanalysis, I argue, is also preferred by the creators of *Betipul*.

Conclusion: Representations and Meanings of the Jewish Analyst

What does *Betipul* add to the representation of Israeli identities in popular culture? If the figure of the Jewish analyst has hitherto been stereotyped and caricatured, *Betipul* radically challenges these depictions. If the Jewish psychoanalyst has hitherto been regarded as a product of the diaspora experience, since previous cinematic representations were produced in Hollywood and had no intention of putting the psychotherapist centre stage, *Betipul* breaks away from these conventions. The figure of the therapist is taken seriously, and concomitantly the understanding of psychotherapy in popular culture gains further depth and nuance.

Betipul is meaningful for Israeli audiences because it presents a local representation of a Jewish analyst who appeals to a society where personal crisis is often underestimated or overshadowed by national crisis. It challenges the idea that there is no space for individual problems when faced with life-threatening national problems. Instead, *Betipul* reinforces the message that this personal space can and should exist in Israeli society. Television, argues Caroline Bainbridge, can become 'a transitional object of the inner world, an object through which we can explore our identities and one that produces fantasies that open up spaces for all the projections, both bearable and unbearable, that such spaces may entail' (Bainbridge 2012: 166). In a sense, the figure of the Israeli analyst deepens the importance of self-reflection, the need to validate and encourage the creation of a safe space for individuals, and for handling individual crises. In order for therapy to work, the relationship of trust established with the therapist is crucial. The therapist represents safety and security, and invites the patient to enter an unthreatening zone where one can reflect on problems while being accompanied and sustained psychologically. The therapy room, as depicted in *Betipul*, is the place of cinematic drama but also, metaphorically, represents a safe haven where the patient is held securely and affectionately. Perhaps the reassurance that a place of safety does exist, or can be cultivated in therapy, explains the popularity of the programme in Israel. Every week, the viewer connects with characters on TV whose personal difficulties are brought into discussion within an environment that remains safe and unchanging. This frame is missing from contemporary Israel, where safety and security are frequently under attack.

References

BAINBRIDGE, CAROLINE. 2012. 'Psychotherapy on the Couch: Exploring the Fantasies of *In Treatment*'. *Psychoanalysis, Culture, and Society*, 17: 153–68.

BAHT, RONI. 2010. 'A Psychologist across the Lines'. *Contemporary Psychoanalysis*, 46: 235–49.

BAR-ON, DAN. 1992. 'A Testimony on the Moment before the (Possible) Occurrence of a Massacre: On a Possible Contradiction between the Ability to Adjust which Means Mental Health and the Maintaining of Human Moral Values', *Journal of Traumatic Stress*, 5: 289–301.

BERMAN, EMANUEL. 1981. 'Dilemmas of Psychotherapy in Israel'. *American Journal of Psychoanalysis*, 41: 169–72.

BERKE, JOSEPH. 2015. *The Hidden Freud: His Hassidic Roots*. London.

BETTRIDGE, DANIEL. 2012. 'Homeland's Debt to Israeli TV'. *The Guardian*, 24 Feb. <https://www.theguardian.com/tv-and-radio/tvandradioblog/2012/feb/24/homeland-israeli-tv> (accessed 30 Sept. 2017).

BIALE, DAVID, MICHAEL GALCHINSKY, and SUSANNAH HESCHEL. 1998. *Insider/Outsider: American Jews and Multiculturalism*. Berkeley, Calif.

CELENZA, ANDREA. 2013. 'Mutual Influence in Contemporary Film'. *Contemporary Psychoanalysis*, 46: 215–23.

CHOZICK, AMY, and JOSHUA MITNICK. 2011. 'Coming to America'. *The Wall Street Journal*, 11 Mar. <https://www.wsj.com/articles/SB10001424052748704758904576188740968759616> (accessed 24 Apr. 2018).

FROSH, STEPHEN. 2005. *Hate and the 'Jewish Science': Anti-Semitism, Nazism and Psychoanalysis*. London.

—— 2008. 'Freud and Jewish Identity'. *Theory and Psychology*, 18: 167–78.

FUREDI, FRANK. 2004. *Therapy Culture: Cultivating Vulnerability in an Uncertain Age*. London.

GABBARD, GLEN O., and KRIN GABBARD. 1999. *Psychiatry and the Cinema*. Washington, DC.

GHARAIBEH, N. M. 2005. 'The Psychiatrist's Image in Commercially Available American Movies'. *Acta Psychiatrica Scandinavica*, 111: 316–19.

GREENBERG, HARVEY ROY. 2011. 'In Treatment: Doctor Paul Weston—Psychotherapist or Cinetherapist?'. *Psychoanalytic Review*, 98: 121–34 <http://internationalpsychoanalysis.net/wp-content/uploads/2010/04/InTreatmentGreengerWeston.pdf> (accessed 30 Aug. 2017).

ILLOUZ, EVA. 2008. *Saving the Modern Soul: Therapy, Emotions, and the Culture of Self-Help*. Berkeley, Calif.

KATRIEL, TAMAR. 1986. *Dugri Speech in Israeli Sabra Culture*. Cambridge.

LEVI, HAGAI. 2009. 'Be-Tipul and its Significance for Israeli TV and Society' (interview, 3 Apr. 2009) <http://www.international.ucla.edu/israel/article/114965> (accessed 30 Aug. 2017).

——2012. 'Is Television Series the New Psychological Treatment?' *Youtube* (14 June). <https://www.youtube.com/watch?v=l_EzaysXkJ8> (accessed 30 Sept. 2017).

LOMSKY-FEDER, EDNA, and EYAL BEN-ARI. 2007. 'Trauma, Therapy and Responsibility: Psychology and War in Contemporary Israel'. In Aparna Rao, Michael Bollig, and Monika Böck, eds., *The Practice of War: Production, Reproduction and Communication of Armed Violence*, 111–33. Oxford.

MARTÍNEZ, ALEJANDRO N. GARCÍA, and ALBERTO N. GARCÍA MARTÍNEZ, 2012. 'Fractured Identity: *In Treatment* as a Symptom and Reflection of Contemporary Emotional Culture'. In Ana Marta González, ed., *The Emotions and Cultural Analysis*, 115–32. London.

RICHARDS, BERNARD. 2007. *Emotional Governance: Politics, Media, and Terror*. London.

RYCROFT, CHARLES, ed. 1966. *Psychoanalysis Observed*. Harmondsworth.

SZEKELY, GAL. 2012. 'HBO's *In Treatment* versus *Be-tipul*: Cultural Differences and Psychotherapy'. *Youtube* (28 July) <https://www.youtube.com/watch?v=EMqcsKwfgvQ> (accessed 30 Aug. 2017).

YATES, CANDIDA. 2011. 'Charismatic Therapy Culture and the Seductions of Emotional Well-Being'. *Free Associations: Psychoanalysis and Culture, Media, Groups, Politics*, 62: 59–84.

YOUNG, SKIP DINE. 2012. *Psychology at the Movies*. Chichester.

YOVELL, YORAM. 2009. 'Be-Tipul and its Significance for Israeli TV and Society' (interview, 3 Apr. 2009) <http://www.international.ucla.edu/israel/article/114965> (accessed 30 Aug. 2017).

Propagating Modern Jewish Identity in Madagascar: A Contextual Analysis of One Community's Discursive Strategies

NATHAN P. DEVIR

IN MID-MAY 2016, a group of 121 women, men, and children on the island of Madagascar formally converted to Judaism.[1] The members of the North American Orthodox rabbinical court who conducted the conversions, as well as the organizers of the occasion—leaders of the New York City-based Jewish outreach group Kulanu—had never met any of the individuals scheduled to undergo conversion in person.[2] Before the conversions, the Westerners had only vague and secondhand notions about the proselytes' difficulties in maintaining a religiously observant lifestyle in a country that has been plagued with endemic corruption and barely functioning infrastructure for decades. What is more, only one of the three rabbis on the rabbinical court and several volunteers who accompanied the Kulanu delegation spoke French, Madagascar's second official language; none spoke Malagasy, the converts' native tongue.

Given these ostensibly dire barriers in communication, which might have easily set the proselytes up for a post-conversion descent into mayhem, confusion, and backsliding, how could all parties involved be reasonably certain that this life-altering event had any chance of coming to a successful fruition? The answer is a twenty-first-century one: their reliance upon and faith in the efficacy of the culture of digital communications, which they had harnessed in myriad ways since 2013 in order to prepare for the conversions. Their exploitation of globalized digital mechanisms towards this spiritual end included Google Translate, YouTube, Facebook, Skype, WhatsApp, Google Chat, online encyclopedias, and even that veritable dinosaur of store-and-forward technology, email. In retrospect, it seems fitting that the Malagasies' eventual inclusion into *kelal yisra'el*, the worldwide Jewish community, was facilitated by the same kind of medium—the globalized matrix of mass communication—that had initially enabled them to come together to learn about post-exilic Judaism in the first place.

As individuals who have only recently come to know about normative Judaism through mainly online means, the Malagasies are in good company. Other such groups of contemporary 'Internet Jews' from the developing world, especially the sub-Saharan African regions, include the Igbo of Nigeria, the Beth Yeshourun (House of the Righteous) community of Cameroon, and the Communauté juive du Gabon neutraliste (Neutralist Jewish Community of Gabon), all of which, in Heidi Campbell's categorization, belong to the 'increasingly flexible, transitional, and transnational' world of 'networked religion', in which the modes of tradition- ally transmitted spiritual propriety are usurped in favour of decentralized com- municative strategies (Campbell 2012: 85).[3] The aforementioned groups are all part of the ever-increasing phenomenon of 'Judaizing', 'emergent', or 'neo- Jewish' communities, i.e. communities whose adherents lack any previously known discursive or historical ties to established centres of Jewish life elsewhere in the world, but who have nonetheless expressed a desire for formal inclusion and/or recognition. Although a rich body of scholarship has developed on this subject, and growing awareness of such groups has been more or less a constant in recent popular news media dealing with subjects of Jewish interest, most com- munities of this kind have been heretofore ignored by or are still unknown to more conventional streams of Jewry in Israel, Europe, and the Americas.[4] It is difficult to quantify how many such people around the world self-identify as Jews, but the number is possibly as high as several million.[5]

While most of these groups claim a genealogical connection with the Jewish people based on a supposed Hebraic or Israelite ancestry (frequently associated with local ideas about 'lost races' that were originally implanted by colonial or missionary sources and subsequently imparted to the native peoples), some com- munities have also chosen to approach Judaism through a purely spiritual per- spective. In the African context, especially, Judaism is seen as a religion with no ideological 'baggage' connected to it. Unlike Islam (which conjures up images of the slave trade) or Christianity (which is seen as part and parcel of European colo- nialism's imperialist project), Judaism in sub-Saharan Africa is more or less an untainted option, insofar as traditional Western antisemitism largely failed to take hold in that region. In fact, in many cases, the parallels between alimentary, kinship, or hygienic practices outlined in the Hebrew Scriptures and precolonial customs suppressed by European powers—not to mention the psychological identification with the sufferings of the Jewish people and the desire to be seen as 'chosen'—have prompted marginalized individuals in developing post- colonial nations to see Judaism as the most fitting religious code for their desired lifestyles. As we shall see, the motivations of the Judaizing community from Madagascar profiled in this chapter stem from more or less all of the above com- ponents, but the genealogical one in particular.[6]

As a case study of the formation of one specific neo-Jewish community in the Global South, this essay explores the ways in which the members of the dominant

Communauté juive de Madagascar (Jewish Community of Madagascar) have interpreted and (re)presented Jewish history in the context of the aforementioned widespread notions surrounding precolonial heritage and the psychological identification with instances of historical trauma. In particular, it analyses how such notions of heritage and identification have been inspired either by foreign visitors, anecdotal (local) impressions of belonging, or new digital media; how such notions are then articulated among members of the community; and, finally, how Jewish identity as a hereditary signifier is then disseminated and promulgated to others in different settings, both inside and outside Madagascar. All the analyses are based on qualitative ethnographic fieldwork conducted on the island in May and June 2013 and on subsequent telephone, Skype, email, and social media exchanges.[7]

The settings examined in this chapter of the communicative and discursive interactions relevant to the circulation of Jewish signifiers in Madagascar include an open-house 'Israel–Madagascar' celebration that I attended, which coincided with Israel's sixty-fifth Independence Day; broadcasts from the weekly radio show of the community's leader; and filmed public debates between this normative group and other Old Testament-oriented rival movements, such as Messianic Jews, Seventh Day Adventists, and hard-line practitioners of Malagasy traditional religion. It should be emphasized that nowhere does this essay deal with or provide a judgement regarding any empirical dimension of the bio-racial 'authenticity' of these self-defining Malagasy Jews, as the primary concern is to explore discursive methods of transmission and propagation.

Madagascar in Social and Geographical Context

The island country of Madagascar lies in the south-western region of the Indian Ocean, some 390 kilometres off the African mainland. The nearest neighbouring countries are the Comoros Islands and Mozambique, to the west, and Mauritius, to the east. The original inhabitants of the island were Malayo-Indonesians, who arrived via canoe between the sixth and third centuries BCE; they were later joined by Bantu peoples from the African mainland after 1000 CE (Diagram Group 2000: 138).[8] From the sixteenth century onwards, Madagascar had relatively constant contact with Portuguese, British, French, and Dutch trade missions, all of whom competed for commercial dominance on the island. That competition was finally won by the French, who vanquished the last of the native resistance in 1897 and subsequently ruled the territory as a French colony until Madagascar's political independence in 1960.

Independence, however, was achieved only in theory. Madagascar's early state institutions were essentially renamed vestiges of the colonialist French enterprise, and the country relied heavily on French aid. Philibert Tsiranana, the country's first president, adopted a pro-Western policy until 1972, the year in which he resigned. In contrast, his self-proclaimed socialist successors aligned themselves with the Soviet Union, expelled the French, and wreaked havoc on the national economy. The latter part of the 1980s saw a rapprochement with the West, and the first multiparty democratic elections were held in 1993. Opposition parties became increasingly powerful in the late 1990s, and their activities, often violent, destabilized the budding democratic political process in the country. A series of coups and near-coups in the first decade of the new millennium scared away investors, cut off aid from the European Union, and isolated Madagascar internationally. In recent years, political instability has taken its toll on the well-being of the nation's inhabitants, who are estimated at almost 25 million people (Worldometers n.d.).

Hery Rajaonarimampianina, the current president of Madagascar, was elected in relatively undisputed voting in 2013. He has the formidable task of attempting to reassemble a country whose economy and infrastructure are in tatters. According to the World Bank, 70 per cent of Madagascar's population is defined as 'poor', while 59 per cent are 'extremely poor' (World Bank n.d.). In 2011, *Forbes* ranked Madagascar as the 'World's Worst Economy' (see Fisher 2011). The black market remains the only functioning commercial outlet for the majority of the island's inhabitants. Madagascar frequently makes headlines for the unsavoury ease with which human trafficking, in particular child prostitution, is conducted on the island. Although tourism, fishing, mineral mining, and forestry are all potentially lucrative investment sectors, the country has yet to translate the exploitation of these sectors into improved living standards for its population. It also must tackle the problem of state corruption, which is all-encompassing.

The religious composition of the country's inhabitants reflects the lasting impact of nineteenth-century British missions and the French colonial legacy, not to mention twenty-first-century evangelistic efforts. Approximately half of the population identifies as Christian, increasingly of the Protestant persuasion (Diagram Group 2000: 140). It is difficult to provide precise figures for the followers of traditional religion, though it appears that approximately 40 per cent of the population practises some form of this vestige of precolonial life, which often involves ancestor worship, divination, and dietary proscriptions.[9] Many syncretistic forms of worship combine such practices with elements of Christianity. Around 5 per cent of the population identifies as Muslim, but this cohort is made up mostly of foreign residents (Diagram Group 2000: 140).

Although there was no formalized Jewish congregation on the island until the official state recognition of the Jewish Community of Madagascar in 2012, legends surrounding the Malagasies' supposed Hebraic or Israelite provenance have circulated for centuries. First propagated by Arab explorers and later by missionaries and colonial functionaries, Madagascar's inhabitants have been described as 'Hebrews', 'Hamites', 'Israelites', 'Jews', and 'Semites', among other qualifiers.[10] Customs such as circumcision and menstrual seclusion, linguistic similarities between the Malagasy and Hebrew languages, and prohibitions on the eating of pork and eel were among many of the 'proof phenomena' singled out by visitors to the island (and later by Malagasies themselves) as evidence of the inhabitants' connection to the Children of Israel. By the mid-twentieth century, when much of the island's peoples had already been Christianized, the notion of Hebrew or Israelite origin was so familiar that to dwell on it would be considered trite (see Bruder 2008: 178–85).

Preaching to the Choir

The pervasiveness of Madagascar's Jewish origin narrative was brought home to me at an event that I attended in Soavimbahoaka, a township near Antananarivo, the capital city of Madagascar. The event, filmed for national television and organized jointly by the Jewish Community of Madagascar and the Club Shalom Madagascar (a non-religious association made up primarily of governmental employees who have spent time in Israel), had been advertised heavily in print, digital, television, and radio coverage under the banner of a 'Journée Israël–Madagascar' (Israel–Madagascar Day), which, as mentioned, coincided approximately with the date of Israel's sixty-fifth Independence Day (Figures 1, 2, and 3). However, the focus of the activities was on far more than geopolitics or on the purely diplomatic relations between the two countries. In fact, at the time (and at the time of this writing), Israel and Madagascar had no official state ties. Instead, the reference to 'Israel' was mainly to the Hebrew patriarchs, the Ten Lost Tribes, the two kingdoms of ancient Israel, and the Jewish people in general, in both their pre- and post-exilic iterations. Of course, this reference also encompassed the history and character of the modern State of Israel, although that aspect of the event was hardly the focal point of the activities.

The open-house event attracted a religiously diverse audience. For example, among the people whom I met and interacted with personally, there were Christians from a wide range of denominations. The Protestants included Pentecostals, Baptists, Presbyterians, Lutherans, and, of course, people from the national church, the Reformed Fiangonan'i Jesoa Kristy eto Madagasikara (Church of Jesus Christ in Madagascar). Also present were many Roman Catholics, Latter Day Saints, and Messianic Jews. Outside the Christian mould were followers of traditional religion from most of the island's major ethnic groups, such as the Antaimoro, Antalaotra, Antambahoaka, Antandroy, Bara, Betsileo, Betsimisaraka, Mahafaly, Merina, Sakalava, and Tanala peoples. There were also several famous syncretistic prophets, soothsayers, and faith healers, with wide-eyed devotees in tow. No less significant was a small number of Sunni Muslims. Last but not least were the members of the self-defining Jewish Community of Madagascar, the only group of people in the country who have expressed the desire to follow normative Jewish religious practice, as opposed to simply acknowledging a shared genealogical provenance.

The professional and class-based composition of the crowd was equally as diverse. On the modest side of the socio-economic divide, there were taxi drivers, plumbers, policemen, and farmers from all parts of the island, some of whom had travelled for days to attend the event. At the other end of the spectrum were some of the most well-heeled political and business elite of the country. These included the former Malagasy ambassador to the United Nations; several government ministers and parliamentarians; senior professors from the University of Antananarivo; members of the Malagasy royal family; and leading entrepreneurial figures in national industry and commerce. The only conspicuous no-show was then-president Andry Rajoelina, a devout Catholic, whose high-profile visit to Jerusalem earlier in the year had only served to reinforce the public perceptions surrounding his Judaeophilia.

The location of the event was the courtyard of the compound that was used at the time as the synagogue for the Jewish Community of Madagascar, and it was bursting at the seams. An estimated 400 people were in attendance, all of them Malagasy except for me. Local television and radio crews pushed their way through the thick mass of people, jockeying for positions near the podium where Ashrey Dayves Andrianarisoa, the 40-something *moreh* (spiritual leader) of the community and the host of the day's events, was to be the first of the day's speakers.

On ascending the podium, Andrianarisoa welcomed those assembled, said a few words about the lineup of speakers and exhibits, and informed the group that the events of the day would be geared toward informing the attendees about various aspects of the 'Hebrew blood' that, he said, all Malagasies share. After these introductory remarks, he led the audience in the singing of Israel's national anthem, *Hatikvah* (The Hope), the Hebrew words of which had been transliterated on pamphlets distributed to the crowd. Only after the Israeli anthem did he lead the crowd in singing *Ry Tanindrazanay malala o!* (O Beloved Land of Our Ancestors!), the Malagasy national anthem. He then recited the benediction of the *birkat hakohanim* (the Priestly Blessing), in nearly flawless Hebrew, treating the entire assembly of people as if they were his own congregation. He followed the blessing with a translation, and an explanation as to why he had chosen that particular prayer to showcase during the opening ceremony. Since, he said, most residents of the island are the direct descendants of Aaron the Levite, brother of Moses (one of the common origin legends among the dominant Merina people), it was fitting to start the day off with a benediction that was allowed only to the privileged priestly inheritors of that line.

In the speeches that followed, the genealogical trope remained the occasion's dominant theme. Historians noted the 'linguistic similarities' between the Malagasy and Hebrew languages.[11] They also made reference to supposed patterns of migration from the Holy Land to the island, and indicated that both peoples share the same customs surrounding animal slaughter, hygiene taboos, and life-cycle events. Two famous Protestant ministers—opponents of the current regime whose names shall remain anonymous—declared themselves 'more Jewish than the Pope is Catholic', simply by virtue of 'blood', even though they had no plans to join the organized Jewish community. Representatives from the formal community later chided them, maintaining that it was no longer acceptable to simply acknowledge in an informal fashion, as Malagasies had done for far too many years, one's shared history. Instead, each Malagasy seeking the truth about his heritage had the responsibility to *participate actively* in Jewish religious life in order to appreciate it fully. This was not just a public relations stunt to increase the number of formal Jewish community members, they stressed. Rather, it represented the community's genuine belief that the adherence to prescribed Jewish religious practice is the most effective way of reconstituting a pristine, precolonial past.

Anti- and Neocolonial Rhetoric

How had it come to pass that Malagasies had not yet fully embraced their Hebraic identity? Many at this event insisted that the French knew very well about the inhabitants' provenance from such a majestic lineage, and had purposefully hidden this fact in order to subjugate the people of their former colony. In the meantime, Christianity had taken hold, and it simply became more convenient for the ruling class to preserve the status quo.

But enforced ignorance would not last. Each of the subsequent speakers agreed that the current political turmoil in Madagascar was connected to the burgeoning recognition of the people's Jewish roots. And this was but a prelude to a much greater upheaval, which had been prophesied long ago: the return of all the descendants of Israel to their rightful ancestral homeland. Even the icing on the giant cake that was served at the beginning of the lunch break called attention to this point, as it proclaimed, in the words of Jeremiah 31: 9: 'He that scattered Israel doth gather him, and keep him, as a shepherd doth his flock.' Again and again, the speakers stressed that Malagasies needed to know about their lost heritage in order to be ready for an eventual return to the ancestral homeland.

During the entire series of lectures, only one person in the audience questioned the legitimacy of the speakers' claims. Community members later told me that they suspected the man of having been sent by the government's internal state security apparatus. Why? He spoke French better than the local Malagasy dialect, and he took copious photographs of the people in attendance. He also photographed every portion of the walk-through historical exhibit, which was decorated with maps and pictures taken primarily from French Wikipedia pages on the history of the Jews. The exhibit also featured a list of the various ruling kingdoms of Madagascar, printed from online media fora, which ostensibly was

Figure 1 Leaders of the Jewish community of Madagascar (*left*) and Club Shalom Madagascar (*right*) sign an accord of co-operation, 26 May 2013, Soavimbahoaka, Madagascar. *Photograph by Nathan P. Devir*

Figure 2 Leaders of the Jewish community with members of the Malagasy diplomatic corps and the royal family. Photograph by Nathan P. Devir

Figure 3 A Jewish community member guides visitors round sections of the historical walk-through exhibition dealing with purported migration routes from ancient Israel to Madagascar. *Photograph by Nathan P. Devir*

meant to be an addendum to the portion of the exhibit on Jewish history. My hosts did not seem overly concerned by the man's presence, since, according to them, the people in the upper corridors of power were clearly philosemitic. Sending him to monitor the situation was just standard procedure.

One particular section of the exhibit, which offered a fairly graphic pictorial history of the Holocaust, became a locus of weeping and wailing. One woman, crying uncontrollably, pointed to the pictures of emaciated Jewish corpses in a mass grave and asked Andrianarisoa, 'How could they do that to *us?*' Interestingly, there was no mention of the Nazis' 'Madagascar Plan'—the short-lived idea to use the island as a kind of large concentration camp to which the world's Jews would be deported.[12] Most of the people who came that day, and nearly all the people whom I met during my entire research trip, had no idea about the magnitude of the Holocaust. It was only mentioned briefly in schools as one of many 'side effects' of the Second World War, they claimed, so how could they have known? They felt duped, but were sure that the French colonizers were somehow to blame, both for masking the truth of these horrors as well as for their surrender to the force of the Nazi death machine. The raucous scene at the exhibit was captured by the supposed security man as he stood soberly before us with his camera.

Another reason the man became suspect was because his remarks were taken to be indicative of someone implying sedition. For example, when one parliamentarian extolled the virtues of the Israeli 'start-up nation' and lamented the fact that the Israeli ambassador to Madagascar was a non-resident diplomat whose office remained in Jerusalem, the suspected plant asked: 'Isn't there a potential security problem with dual loyalty here? What happens when a person comes to love another nation more than the nation in which he was born? And why should we support a state that has the same kind of apartheid practices as South Africa did?'

The parliamentarian, clearly frustrated, shot back. 'What are you, stupid?' he said. 'The Jews are a people who have been *chosen by God*! When all is said and done, whose side do you want to be on?' He then added, paraphrasing Genesis 12: 2–3, 'Everyone knows that those who help Israel are blessed, and those who don't are cursed.'[13] The audience erupted in applause. Some people shouted 'Hallelujah!' and 'Amen!', while the security man, embarrassed, did not offer a rebuttal. The speaker then mentioned the then-recent purchase by Madagascar of attack helicopters from Israel, a deal purportedly negotiated by famed General André Ndriarijaona. 'Why would our top military brass purchase things from a vendor whom they didn't trust?' he asked.

I mention this exchange regarding the themes of the day because the government man's reaction was the only dissenting voice that I encountered. In a crowd of around 400 people from exceedingly varied religious and socio-economic backgrounds, the presence of a lone dissenter would seem rather odd—unless, that is, the majority of the individuals present at the event already had subscribed to the fundamentals of the day's message. Granted, those who attended had obviously self-selected in their status as attendees. And yet, they represented a cross-section of Malagasy society that I was to encounter again and again. In light of these deeply entrenched notions of belonging, it may seem curious that only in the past several years has an organized Jewish community sprung up on the island of Madagascar. In retrospect, however, it is now apparent that it took the advent of globalized media culture to begin the process that culminated in the conversions of the previously mentioned individuals to Orthodox Judaism in May 2016.

From Israelites to Jews

The rapidity with which a group of former Christians decided to make the shift from lost Israelite believers in Jesus to followers of rabbinic Judaism is striking, and in many ways functions as a microcosm of the overarching, only-a-click-away paradigm of information access that typifies the Internet age. Although the initially labelled 'Judaist association' of charismatic Christians and Messianic Jews, who wanted to explore more deeply the parallels between traditional (especially ethnic Merina) Malagasy religion and that of the Hebrew Scriptures had existed for several years before they began to download relevant information from the Internet, it was knowledge gathered from online digital media that ultimately gave them the 'push' they needed to break with their previous church-initiated ideologies.

One recurring story about the formation of the community tells of a signifi-cant encounter with an individual from overseas who encouraged the eventual members of the Jewish community to give up the belief in Jesus and adopt nor-mative-style Judaism. This individual was a Dutch Messianic Jew who happened to attend a prayer meeting of one of the burgeoning Jewish cells. To help them along, the Dutchman gave them numerous photocopies of articles on Jewish practice. On a subsequent visit, the foreigner procured a copy of a French prayer book and directed them to useful websites on Jewish learning. One of the mem-bers who had reliable Internet access and who had already begun to download and print material to distribute to the congregation added information from these new websites to their study folders. The Dutchman also counselled them to adopt a Sephardi-style liturgy, since, he surmised, they were definitely not of European stock. (They now refer to their Jewish ethnic category as Sephardi, and the congre-gation's primary Facebook profile page is called 'Sefarad Madagascar'.) It should not escape notice that, whether or not the story is true, this focal point in their journey was, ironically, the direct result of European involvement and validation.

As early as 2011, the community had gained knowledge about current Jewish practices by randomly Googling their questions in the French version of the search engine. Quickly they perceived the authoritative nature of sites such as www.torabox.com, www.aish.com, and those run by the ultra-Orthodox Jewish renewal movement Chabad. They did not, however, realize that such informa-tional sites are meant to draw secular Jews back into the religious fold, not to absorb new members. (Significantly, they had no idea about major Jewish out-reach organizations such as Be'chol Lashon, Kulanu, or Shavei Israel, as none of these organizations maintain French versions of their websites.[14]) They also gained adherents—sidestepping the formal Jewish prohibition against prosely-tizing—by informing fellow Malagasies of their new movement on community leader Andrianarisoa's Radio Antsiva FM 97.6 weekly broadcast. Once a Chris-tian programme (on a mainly Muslim-oriented station), Andrianarisoa's show now began to deal with questions of proper Jewish observance, in order to help Malagasies fill in the blanks regarding their lost ancestral heritage.

A few words should be dedicated here to radio as a particularly useful outreach medium for this burgeoning Jewish community. This choice of medium is very significant, because, in a country where most people cannot afford to buy news-papers, radio has proven to be a powerful force. Indeed, much has been written about the important social role played by radio (both in its broadcast and later Internet formats) in Madagascar, especially concerning this medium's capacity to 'reinforce freedom of expression' and its role in 'constructing (or renewing) a con-sciousness of citizenship' among the island's inhabitants (Razafimbelo-Harisoa 2005: 36, 43). For instance, many scholars have noted that, since 1991, when the radio station called *Forces Vives* ('Lifeblood', a pirate radio station that challenged the political complacency of the state-owned national station) used its influence to bolster popular sentiment for democratic reforms, private radio outlets have been considered highly regarded sources of influence and interaction (Poindexter 2001; Andriantsoa et al. 2005).Even the former president, Andry Rajoelina, began his career as a disc jockey. In fact, throughout Rajoelina's political ascent, he deftly used the medium of radio to enhance his interests all the way to the walls of the Ambohitsorohitra, the presidential palace. A similar argument can be made regarding the power of private television stations in Madagascar, albeit beginning from the first decade of the millennium, when their accessibility among the population increased. Like radio, television in Madagascar has the potential for an extremely wide reach, given that there is only one native language among all of the country's indigenous ethnic groups.

In addition to his previous stint as the host of a Christian programme on Radio Antsiva FM 97.6, community leader Andrianarisoa had served as director of publicity at RDA Radio in 2001. As part of his occasional work as a professional pastry chef, he also had experience hosting culinary talk shows on Space Radio, Radio Télévision Analamanga, and Télévision Nationale Malagasy, the government-run television station. After persuading the producers of his culinary programmes that Malagasies were just as likely to tune in to Jewish television shows as they were to Muslim, Roman Catholic, or Protestant ones, Andrianarisoa began recording Jewish-oriented programming on these stations. When a drop in accessory prices made wireless Internet more readily available around 2012, many viewers and listeners discovered him via such recordings that had been uploaded to YouTube. Today, other members of the community have taken to filming themselves discussing issues of Jewish religious and cultural interest and then sharing them on various forms of social media.

Starting in 2013, members of the community began to correspond by email with volunteer rabbis in the United States, who helped (using Google Translate, as the Americans spoke no French, and the Malagasies spoke no English) to answer their questions about correct methods of observing ritual obligations. (The introductions were made by a Francophone Jewish tourist who visited the group that year.) At that point, the majority of community members still used the homemade binders made up of printed material downloaded from how-to Francophone Jewish websites. When reading the weekly Torah portion, members relied on French Bibles from their previous lives as Christians, since Hebrew-language Bibles in Madagascar are a closely guarded commodity. Only one bookstore in the country sells them (the Biblia Hebraica Stuttgartensia edition), and those who wish to purchase copies must first demonstrate their status as registered students in an accredited theological seminary. Photocopies provided by the community's leadership allowed congregants to follow the Hebrew prayers with transliterations and translations/explanations of the texts in question.

By the time I arrived in Madagascar in May 2013 (I had discovered their congregation on social media a year and a half earlier by using the sophisticated research method of Googling the terms 'juifs' [Jews] and 'Madagascar' together), their services looked very much like any Orthodox-oriented Sephardi services in established Jewish communities abroad, save that many stumbled over Hebrew prayers or mispronounced certain terms, and that the order of the elements in the services was sometimes atypical. Indigenous ceremonial customs were not incorporated into the ritual practice, and so no practical syncretism existed, despite the pervasive belief that both methods of worship were once one and the same. YouTube, Facebook, Vimeo, and the chapter-by-chapter mp3 file recordings of the Hebrew Bible (used especially for practice in reading and chanting Hebrew) posted on the website of Mechon Mamre (the Mamre Institute—an organization dedicated to the free diffusion of Jewish source texts) were all to thank for this advanced level of ceremonial mimicry, as were the organizational skills of most of the leadership in arranging religious services, with which they had had previous general experience during their former lives as Christian clergy.

Mimicry in the context of less-than-obvious 'worship materials' also manifested itself in other forms. For instance, I was shocked to discover that most of the congregants knew dozens of popular songs from the Israeli *muzikah mizraḥit* (Middle Eastern music) genre, which combines Arabic and Mediterranean instrumentation with lyrics copied from or evoking the style of popular Middle Eastern tunes from countries outside Israel. (Pirated copies of this form of Israeli pop music, downloaded using illegal file-sharing programmes, were frequently broadcast on Andrianarisoa's radio show and subsequently internalized by the congregants.) The genre also is known for decrying, symbolically if not literally, the marginalization by the Israeli Ashkenazi mainstream of Jews hailing from Islamic countries.[15] The Malagasies who heard such songs played on the weekly radio programme used the memorization of the Hebrew lyrics as a kind of lesson in what they saw to be a way of practising liturgy. Obviously, the irony of their internalization of the genre escaped them, since almost no one understood more than a handful of words in biblical Hebrew. This minor confusion over the place of Israeli pop music in normative Jewish life was but one small misstep in the members' growing familiarity with the intricacies of modern Jewish life outside their island.

Modes of Ritual Observation

What level of practice does the organized Jewish community in Madagascar observe? At the time of my visit, a rough estimation would have been something akin to the level of the kind of Conservative Judaism practised in North America. I offer this estimation of the community's level of religious practice primarily because they endeavour to follow Jewish law as much as possible, given the lack of adequate community infrastructure. This, however, is not by choice. Their preference, like the preference of the rabbinical court that recently converted them, is that they live as Orthodox (or even ultra-Orthodox) Jews. But they do not have the capacity or the infrastructure to do this. When I was asked to explain the differences between Reconstructionist, Reform, Conservative, and Orthodox Jewish movements, only one person openly admitted to being attracted to a non-Orthodox lifestyle. Later, in a private conversation, he asked if I could help facilitate the 'conversion of all the community to Conservative Judaism'. I had to make clear that I was not interested in encouraging anyone to follow a specific spiritual path, but that I could definitely give further details about the differences between denominational options and the varying perspectives surrounding them in the larger Jewish world.

When asked exactly how they follow Jewish law, community members frequently cited the following elements of standard ritual practice. They ensure that all sons are circumcised, although the procedure is usually done in a hospital, and the ceremony surrounding the event is often conducted in an impromptu fashion. They also observe 'all of the feasts and holidays mentioned in Leviticus 23'. Because, before the conversions, no one had been formally trained in methods of kosher slaughter, they took care to buy meat that is certified as *halal* (ritually slaughtered under the tenets of Islamic law), both because the slaughtering process resembles that of the Jewish analogue, and because they suspect that Christian butchers 'mix pork and beef' without telling anyone in order to turn a profit. In the future, they would like to remedy this shortcoming by opening a kosher butcher shop and restaurant. Women practise menstrual seclusion. No one works on the sabbath, but some must use mechanized transportation in order to attend synagogue. This unpleasant reality often goes undiscussed, simply because there is nothing to be done about it, given the capital's sprawling urban landscape and the dangers of walking in most areas after dark.

As far as dress is concerned, men who can afford to often wear skullcaps and ritual fringes (*tsitsit*), which they have purchased from local Messianic Jewish retailers. Not everyone has a prayer shawl (*talit*) for the synagogue, but the men who do possess them wear them casually by day, as well as in the synagogue, as one would a regular scarf. Before the conversions, only one person owned a set of phylacteries (*tefilin*), since these are prohibitively expensive. Women cover their hair with scarves similar to the Muslim *hijab* (headscarf), and wear modest clothing. Community members report that most neighbours and coworkers infer from the style of dress that they are Muslims, and that, therefore, they do not run the risk of standing out too much in the crowd. People who do learn about their religious observance almost universally respond favourably to the idea of a Jewish religious identity, but assume that Judaism is just one more denomination of Protestant Christianity, combined with elements of island folk religion.

Marriage is one critical area in which people are unable to observe normative

Jewish custom. Most accept the fact that many spouses of Jews will not wish to join, and so mixed marriages, or intermarriages, are the norm. As might be expected, most of the people who choose to go against the wishes of their families are men. Some couples are able to live with the differences between them, but, more often than not, the divergence in belief and practice presents a problem. Divorce, and threats of divorce, are common. While many Malagasies are proud of their so-called 'Hebrew blood', normative Jewish religious practice is completely new on the island. How does normative Judaism look to them? Externally, it seems a lot like Islam, but makes demands of its adherents that some equate with the dynamics of a cult. Several members reported that, in the eyes of their families, they are seen as 'sect crazies'. That following Judaism means to give up on Jesus and thereby abandon potential salvation does not help to make spouses and their families any more comfortable with this choice.

Despite these difficulties, a handful of members report finding arrangements in the interim period that are satisfactory to all parties involved. For instance, one man commented to me that, since his wife belongs to a Restorationist church similar to the Jehovah's Witnesses, there is no religious problem with their marriage. She does not accept the doctrine of the Trinity, and is, in his words, 'still a monotheist'. He declares that they are raising the children in the 'Judeo-Christian' religion. Other members who know of this and other comparable arrangements do not approve, but acknowledge the difficulty of navigating this very sensitive issue.

When asked if there is any kind of ceremony conducted for the vetting of new members, one person, perplexed, said to me, 'Why do we need a ceremony?' In the congregants' view, all Malagasies—at least, those who are not clearly the offspring of recent immigrants to the island—are eligible to join. Even those whose physiognomy clearly testifies to a more Bantu origin have still had enough time on the island to intermingle with the others and be considered part of the accepted 'mixed multitude'. Of course, being of the Merina ethnic group means that Jewishness goes without saying, since that group has been the most closely associated with Jews throughout the ages. According to Andrianarisoa, when he is asked to weigh in on the pedigree of a potential community member, God's spirit 'comes down and indicates if the person is a Jew or not'. During Andrianarisoa's frequent trips to the provinces for his culinary workshops, he comes into contact with many non-Merina individuals who express a desire to be recognized as Jews. How the community will welcome new members and deal with marriage issues post-conversion has not yet been decided.

Regarding the awareness about Jewish life in other countries, no one seemed to have much information, in part because no one whom I met had ever encountered an 'outside Jew' before. (I was the first normative Jew from the West to visit the community.) On this point, one man told me that he knows there are Jews in most places, but admitted that the details of where escape him. He complained that Jews are not mentioned at all on the local news channels, although there are frequent mentions of Christians from other nations. When asked how he might go about obtaining information about Jews in other lands, he told me, 'I'm waiting for the prophet Elijah to explain it to me.'

The idea that Elijah is a link in the chain of significant Jewish events seems to be a commonly held conception in the community, perhaps due to a combination of the prophet's place in Judaism as the harbinger of the messiah, and his role in Christianity as a figure contemporaneous with the End Times. In that vein, Elijah's arrival is often mentioned in tandem with the eventual appearance of 'Gog and Magog' as Madagascar's political crisis deepens. In other words, the prophet will make his entry in tandem with other prophesied entities (as per Ezekiel 38) at the time of the final battle before redemption.

Disambiguating: One, Two . . .

Part of obtaining recognition from established Jewish groups overseas rests upon the ability to exhibit sufficient knowledge of historical, ceremonial, and theological Jewish topics. No one in the West will take seriously a community that is not demonstrably learned in those areas. In other words, neo-Jewish communities such as the Malagasy one need to fill in the missing pieces of the Jewish puzzle in order for such a dialogue to take place. With that in mind, community members are constantly attempting to plug the existing gaps in their Jewish knowledge (which, in line with their previous knowledge of biblical history, only extended as far as the period of the destruction of the Second Temple) with information on the Talmud, the *midrashim*, and other exegetical sources. During my fieldwork, I was often peppered with questions about post-exilic Judaism. At some point, it was suggested that I hold an open question-and-answer session, selections of which would later be broadcast on the weekly Radio Antsiva FM 97.6 show.

As with the Journée Israël–Madagascar event that I had attended at Soavimbahoaka, many people were present in the audience for the taping of this open-house radio broadcast. Attendees included Christians from different denominations, but especially Seventh Day Adventists; hard-line practitioners of Malagasy traditional religion (Figures 4 and 5); and, of course, members of the official Jewish community. As a Westerner and an academic, I at first attempted —somewhat naively, in retrospect—to emphasize the importance of context as the decisive factor in the formation and therefore the perspectives of varied Jewish communities around the world. But my words largely fell on deaf ears. What people really wanted to know about was what constituted proper ritual procedure according to the word of God.

Some of the questions asked included: How many times should one say the

Figure 4 Musicians from the community of Loharanom-Pitahiana (the Source of the Blessing), a traditional Malagasy religious congregation in the farming commune of Ambohimiadana, perform for their rabbinically oriented urban guests in 2013. Members of this community, who also call themselves Aaronites, trace their lineage directly to the Jewish priestly class.
Photograph by Nathan P. Devir

Shema (the central invocation and the cornerstone of Jewish prayer services) on the sabbath? Is tithing really required? What is the mystical symbolism of the *sho-far* (the ceremonial ram's horn)? Is one obligated to take medications for healing if there is a suspicion that they have been made with gelatin derived from pork? Can one have sexual relations on days such as Yom Kippur? Is anal sex within marriage permitted, as long as it is consensual? What is the precise authority of hermeneutic interpretations of the Torah, given that they are not part of the Written or Oral Laws? And how could they protect themselves against a Muslim invasion, which they were sure would one day come? For every question save the last, I answered as best as I could, often directing them to the appropriate Web-based sources.

Questions frequently involved issues of purification. One such query from the congregation began with a background explanation. A male congregant, a 'vile and uncircumcised brother', had allegedly raped his stepdaughter. (I could not tell whether the qualifier 'uncircumcised' was literal or metaphorical.) Should both the wife and the daughter be purified, and if so, how should it be done? Was

Figure 5 In a demonstration in 2013 of indigenous practices for the rabbinic Jews in Antananarivo, Aaronite women of Ambohimiadana line up behind a prayer leader to receive benedictions. The cultural exchange occurred as a result of shared interest in their connection to Israel, but the Aaronites do not adhere to rabbinic standards or call themselves Jews as do the Antananarivo group. *Photograph by Nathan P. Devir*

it possible to carry out a purification ceremony without the guilty man being punished? Did the entire congregation need purification, since the man had stepped into the synagogue after the alleged act?

One person suggested that they hold what he referred to as a 'local *beit din*' (a Jewish religious court). Another member dismissed the need for such a body, establishing that, according to Deuteronomy 22: 22–5, the man should be stoned to death. But what to do when such a law cannot be applied in Madagascar without inflicting criminal punishment on the ones obligated to carry out the sentence? I advised them that no Jews with whom I was personally acquainted followed such protocol in the modern world, and suggested that they go to the police with the evidence. Finally, I pointed out that God would know best how to judge and punish the guilty party. When another community member insisted that it might be prudent to wring off the heads of doves as sin offerings, as indicated in Leviticus 1: 5, one of the more learned members answered for me, correctly stating that, according to normative Jewish law, animal sacrifices would not be allowed until the Temple was rebuilt.

That comment sparked an intense discussion about the construction of the Third Temple. One person had heard about the movement called the 'Temple Mount Faithful', which, according to its website, seeks to reconstruct the Temple 'in our lifetime in accordance with the Word of G-d and all the Hebrew prophets, and the liberation of the Temple Mount from Arab/Islamic occupation so that it may be consecrated to the Name of G-d' (Temple Mount and Land of Israel Faithful Movement n.d.). When I confirmed the existence of the group, several people indicated that, should Israel need them, they would be ready to fight alongside their kin to destroy the Dome of the Rock and make way for the Third Temple. A loud round of applause followed. I audibly gulped. One member, however, expressed his reservations about the need for overseas military volunteers, noting that, 'The modern state of Israel already has a lot of strength and power. I see it in the papers.'

Someone then asked if Ariel Sharon, who had been in a coma since 2006, was still alive. I assumed that the person must have heard about Sharon's provocative walk across the Temple Mount in 2001, often cited by the international media as the act that ignited the Second Intifada (2000–5). I informed them of Sharon's still vegetative condition, and the atmosphere at once became sombre. People knew about Sharon's military record, and considered him and 'the one-eyed general' (Moshe Dayan) most responsible for Israel's military prowess.

During my visit, and since that time via Skype and email, I have been privy to ample discussion about secular expressions of Jewishness. Often, I have been asked to disambiguate certain things about modern Jewish lifestyles that are not clear. For instance, in this particular open-house meeting, many questions revolved around why I did not look like a 'real' Jew. Why did I not have a beard or side-curls, or wear ritual fringes or a skullcap? When I explained my secular approach to Jewishness, the people in attendance understood the rationale behind my personal decision. They also understood my explanation of the historical events from the time of the Enlightenment that had led many Jews away from Orthodoxy. But almost none seemed to want to internalize the possibility that, for a majority of the world's Jews today, a largely secular lifestyle, together with non-specific ideas about Jewish identity, constitute notions of Jewishness. One of the senior leaders of the association exasperatedly protested that the Jews 'have always been people of faith', which is one of the obvious parallels with their Malagasy brothers.

To offer an illustration of the serious considerations with which one is faced when attempting to live according to tradition, I announced that I would be leaving Madagascar on a Saturday. Several people openly shuddered. Murmurs of disapproval spread throughout the crowd, and the clicking of tongues followed. I explained that I had a limited budget from my university to make the trip, and that the ticket would have been almost a thousand dollars more if I were to travel the following day. I made clear that, in my own personal outlook, ensuring the stability of my family by conserving the resources allocated to me was just as worthy a task as observing a day of rest. No one openly reproached me, but the tension in the room was palpable.

I learned some time later that the information absorbed in this session represented a major turning point in sowing the seeds of discord between members of the congregation who wished to vigorously pursue connections with the outside Jewish world and those who thought that further contact would sully their efforts. Of the 1,000 original members of the group, over half would leave within a year of this event; the vast majority of them would return to their Messianic synagogues. The remainder of the individuals divided up into three camps: one, composed of those who wished to maintain a close connection to overseas Jews and go in the direction of normative Judaism; another, composed of the former cantor and his followers, who temporarily cut off all contact with overseas Jews and even considered electronic communications as contaminants; and the third, composed of a former kabbalah teacher and his followers, who wished to pursue overseas connections while ensuring that their practice retained a mystical component not usually present in services conducted by normative Jewish groups overseas.

Several years later, back at home in Salt Lake City, I mentioned to a friend who remained in the official community in an email that my wife had recently been ill. He was distressed to hear the news and responded to me with sincere wishes for her continued health. However, he told me that, 'Le premier remède et la première condition d'obtention de la guérison de la part d'Hashem est notre obéissance des Mitsvots contenus dans la Torah' ('The first remedy and the first condition for obtaining Hashem's [God's] healing is our observance of the *mitsvot* [commandments] found in the Torah'). I was touched by his words, which I knew were given in complete sincerity. Still, I could not help but be amused at the slightly admonitory tone, and imagined him wagging his finger at me through cyberspace. He also must have been aware of his somewhat scolding manner, as he ended the message with the innocuous postscript, 'Ce n'est qu'un petit rappel' ('It's just a little reminder').

Public Debates with Rival Interest Groups

A number of Malagasies who have expressed an interest in the efforts of the Jewish Community of Madagascar have nonetheless resisted joining their ranks. I met many such individuals during my time in the country, and have maintained email correspondence with several of them since my return. Despite their enthusiasm for the steps undertaken to resurrect the lost Malagasy heritage, these dissenters have their reasons for not wanting to join the community formally. Since they espouse similar opinions regarding the colonial suppression of Madagascar's 'true' history, they represent a like-minded constituency whose perspectives should be taken into account when examining neo-Jewish phenomena on the island. Although I acknowledge that theoretical categories are always somewhat arbitrary, I have divided the interaction with interested onlookers in this last section into two principal parts: the first, with a cohort of mystics, prophets, and charismatics; and the second, with Messianic Jews.

The first group is by far the most diverse. The uniting thread among these onlookers is that they all value the mystical, astrological, or occult aspects of Jewishness as those most worthy of interest. Many claim to know the secrets of the kabbalah and often employ Hebrew terminology as a kind of magical metalanguage to describe supposed paranormal events. Their followers boast of the leaders' miracle-working, and proclaim their readiness to follow them through fire. However, from my experience with these individuals, their knowledge of Judaism is superficial. They call themselves Jewish and attend major holiday celebrations and events at the Jewish community's headquarters, but otherwise remain aloof from normative practice.

One such person is the self-declared *kohen* (Jewish priest) Rivo Lala. Prophet and leader of the Église du Judaïsme Hébraïque (Church of Hebraic Judaism), Lala has been arrested by the Malagasy authorities on several occasions, on charges ranging from fraud to rape. In one notable exchange with the press in 2012, he claimed:

Je peux faire revenir Marc Ravalomanana au pays et faire en sorte qu'on ne le voit qu'une fois au Magro s'il m'accepte en tant que Rabbin, et qu'il accepte de suivre la religion du judaïsme hébreux. (*Tana News* 2013)

[I can return Marc Ravalomanana [the former president, then in exile in South Africa] to the country and arrange it so that people only see him once at Magro [a popular shopping mall in Antananarivo] if he accepts me as [his] rabbi and agrees to follow the religion of Hebrew Judaism.]

Lala's 'Judaism' seems to be a mélange of spiritualism, Catholicism, and theosophy with a smattering of Aaronite-descent propaganda, complete with a cult-like emphasis on his own supernatural abilities. Though I have never met Lala personally, a few of his followers attended a televised public debate on Malagasy Jewish heritage to which I was invited (apparently a regular occurrence in the pre-conversion days of normative Judaism on the island) and in which I participated. I was warned in advance by my hosts that Lala's people were coming. They would ask me 'trick questions' on behalf of the *kohen*, so I should be on my guard. So why not prevent them from coming in? I asked. My hosts responded that they feared a confrontation. So why not let them simply join the community? They would never, my hosts asserted, agree to respect the principles of democratic governance, let alone agree to follow normative-style Judaism.

When Lala's followers entered the room, I spotted them right away. Each wore a large skullcap and flowing tunic in the style of an Arabian *thawb*. Several appeared to be hired thugs working as security for the others. They introduced themselves to me, in Hebrew, as disciples of *hakohen hagadol* (the high priest), and said that their leader was pleased about my presence in Madagascar. My being there had been prophesied long ago, they said, and my presence was a sign that 'Hebrew Judaism' would one day become the official state religion of Madagascar. Besides a few bizarre questions intended to buttress support for the astrological leanings of their leader ('Can you show me a text that proves no Jewish witches exist?'; 'Was Gershom Scholem not a soothsayer?'; 'Why did God allow the *nefilim* [the 'fallen ones' spoken of in Gen. 6: 5] to be led astray with witchcraft [a reference to Enoch 7] if it was not his will?'), and an uncomfortably long kiss planted on my cheek by one of the men, their rhetorical strategies seemed quite ineffectual, and, as a result, harmless. A member of the normative community who had studied kabbalah rather seriously was able to answer most of their questions with little difficulty, and I was called upon several times to supply clarifications. In one of my remarks to the crowd, I affectionately dubbed the relentless questioners 'the Cohen brothers', but nobody got the joke. I am told that they still come occasionally to services and report back to their leader (who, as of this writing, is again in prison) about the goings-on within the normative Jewish community.

The second group of onlookers interested in the goings-on of the formalized Jewish community who attended the televised debate is perhaps the most contentious: Messianic Jews. As most readers are aware, there is often a knee-jerk reaction among Western Jews to the activities of Messianic Jews, whom they mistakenly confuse with the group known as Jews for Jesus. Among the members of many Judaizing movements in the developing world, however, Messianic Jews are seen as assets to burgeoning Jewish movements. In their eyes, Messianic Judaism is considered a logical step on the path to normative Jewish practice—a bridge between Christianity and Judaism, and a way for people to ease out of the former into the latter: a kind of slow slide towards the desired destination, if you will, as opposed to a riskier plunge or leap.

That said, the self-defining Jews in Madagascar dissent from the stances taken by other Judaizing movements with which I am familiar on the subject of Messianics. They see Messianic Judaism as a sort of backsliding Malagasy Judaism: a movement that purports to resurrect the lost Malagasy heritage, but, like an abused dependent, still clings to the debasing habits of the old colonial master. More importantly, as many of them are former Messianics themselves, they see Messianic Judaism as a potential thorn in their side as they seek recognition from overseas Jews who would not look favourably on such an affiliation.

A brief explanation about the differences between the aforementioned movements is in order. Messianic Jews are Christian believers who attempt to remain faithful to the Hebrew Scriptures while retaining the central messages of what they call the 'New Covenant' (i.e. the New Testament). Most acknowledge that the New Testament contains some Hellenistic corruptions surrounding the martyrdom of Yeshua (Jesus) the messiah. In principle, they do not seek to proselytize Jews. Rather, they wish to emulate them in their own attempt to become the 'spiritual Israel'. For its part, Jews for Jesus is an evangelical Christian organization made up mainly of Jewish converts to Christianity.[16] The policy of Jews for Jesus is actively to seek the conversion of Jews to Christianity, often through means that some consider to be deceitful, such as the incorporation of Jewish customs and/or Hebrew language into their ritual practice. Those whose movements I reference in this section are Messianic Jews.[17]

In hindsight, it now seems quite logical that the organized Jewish Community of Madagascar would have some trepidation about the enthusiasm of Messianic Jews, since, as mentioned, many members of the normative community originally came from Messianic congregations. What is more, the second major split within the community took place when a group of 'closet' Messianics—purportedly, approximately half of those who remained after the first split—finally admitted their unease with following a religion that categorically denies that the messiah has already appeared. This group accused the others of being too strict in their adherence to 'European' Jewish theology. One frequent insult whispered about the normative community was that they had become 'competitive capitalists', besmirching the image of the others with their overzealous devotion to normative Jewish minutiae. During my fieldwork in Madagascar, I had ample opportunities to discuss Jewish topics with people from the Messianic community, as they attended many different events at which I spoke, including this particular public debate. Throughout all of this interaction, I sensed a great frustration on their part for what they see as their unnecessary exclusion from the growing participation in Jewish life in Madagascar.

Some of the reactions at the televised debate should function as a proper illustration of this expressed displeasure. The same evening that I met the 'Cohen brothers', a number of Messianic Jews wanted to conduct an open discussion on how to establish criteria for recognizing the Jewish messiah. When asked, I repeated what the normative Malagasy members had listed as the standard touchstones according to Jewish law, but emphasized to the Messianics that I had no desire to change their opinions or influence the trajectory of their religious lives. I was, I said, simply reciting what the criteria were according to normative Jewish thought. They responded with a series of carefully executed argumentative strategies intended to counter the idea that Jewish theology was monolithic.

They began by referencing the Karaites, who practise only 'biblical' Judaism and deny the authority of the Talmud. Was not the Talmud the Oral Law, according to normative Judaism? How could one call Karaites Jews but not Messianics, when Messianics at least take into consideration the opinions of the rabbis? And what about the Samaritans, the ethno-religious group whose members claim to possess sacred, pre-Babylonian exile texts (the 'Samarian Pentateuch') not included in the Hebrew Scriptures, and whom conventional Judaism regards as members of a 'Jewish sect', but Jewish, all the same? (Although the Israelite descent of Samaritans is not in dispute, the Israeli Rabbinate nonetheless requires a 'precautionary conversion' process for those Samaritans who wish to be integrated into the rabbinic Jewish framework.) Their clearly articulated assault on the logic of exclusion was astute. It made everyone in the room uncomfortable—especially the leadership of the normative Jewish community, who had never heard of Karaites or Samaritans, and who therefore had no idea how to counter these arguments. While the 'Cohen brothers' were not much more than a spectacle at this debate, the Messianic Jews chalked up a relatively uncontested victory during their portion of the evening. Was this because they had been coached by Messianic Jewish missionaries (mainly from France and South Africa), who have operated on the island since the 1990s, and who provide in-depth training on the doctrines of Messianic Judaism, in order to cultivate local leadership? It seems quite likely. Distance learning may be paradigm-changing, but it sometimes does not trump face-to-face interaction.

Considering subsequent correspondence with members of the Messianic group, it seems that their knowledge about these subjects stems from lessons (whether imparted by missionaries or not) taken from some of the more prominent advocate-scholars of Messianic Judaism. For instance, they frequently cited arguments that I later confirmed come from the so-called 'Bible Code' scholars Grant R. Jeffrey and Yacov Rambsel, according to whom prophecies of the coming of Jesus and other events are encoded in the Hebrew numerology of the Bible.[18] They are also deeply familiar with the ideas of Messianic teachers like Michael Rood, who 'exposes' the Graeco-Roman falsehoods implanted in the New Testament by later 'pagan' editors (Rood 2007). Their familiarity on these topics extends to the work of established non-Messianic scholars like Bart D. Ehrman, who deals with the problems of canonization (see, for instance, Ehrman 2012). Based on other comments made during the debate, it appears that they supplement their conventional instruction with constantly updated online learning tools available from Messianic Jewish websites, especially the French version of the Sukkat David (David's Tabernacle) online seminary, originally founded as a Messianic outreach tool in Holland (Soucat David n.d.).

Conclusion: Discursive Technologies and Jewish Identity

In this essay, I have analysed the ways in which normative Judaism as a hereditary signifier has been recently embraced by Malagasies across a wide ethnic and socio-economic divide. Through the revived and ritualized practice of this supposed bio-racial heritage, disenfranchised peoples in Madagascar have discovered a way to return to a perceived 'pristine' precolonial past that serves both to preserve and to perpetuate native pride in an era of unprecedented levels of globalization. It is indicative of our interconnected age that, because the public discussions over the adoption of normative Judaism were conducted both in the forms of television and radio broadcasts, individuals unable to attend the events in person and engage in face-to-face contact were still made part of the conversation.

This case study of the formation of one specific neo-Jewish community in the Global South is instructive in that it demonstrates the extent to which specialized knowledge, notions, and means of engendering community belonging, and transformative encounters with the loci of Global Northern Jewry are products of as well as dependent upon the mediated culture of new digital media. In fact, in the absence of such globalized modes of communication, the Jewish community of Madagascar might have simply remained Messianic, or, conversely, developed along the lines of other Old Testament-centred ideologies common to so-called 'African Independent Church' movements. Among such movements, the best-known include organizations such as the Hebrew Roots Apostles, various Sabbatarian denominations, or the hyper-legalistic African strains of the Seventh Day Adventist movement.[19] They might also have developed into something akin to a Karaite sect. That is to say, without the aid of the Internet and other digital media to fill in the gaps of their knowledge, they might well have translated their mistrust of mission-based Christianity and their desire to return to the religion of the ancestors into a new mode of ritual observance based solely on the Hebrew Scriptures, but completely free of rabbinic Judaism and its influence on post-exilic Jewish life, due to the lack of appropriate print materials in Madagascar. Moreover, it is almost certain that, four years after their association's official founding, they would not have benefited from the arrival of an Orthodox rabbinical court that converted them, largely on the basis of online interviews, conversations, materials, and study sessions that had taken place 'virtually' for the preceding three years. In other words, in the late twentieth century, even if the overseas volunteers had been willing, conducting such a project using the traditional mail service would have taken much, much longer. In fact, given Madagascar's lack of functioning infrastructure, this method would probably have proved unworkable.

To be clear, I use the aforementioned term 'benefited' from the perspective of those future converts who desired formal recognition and inclusion. As mentioned, many of those who initially joined the 'Judaist' association formed by Andrianarisoa and his cohort wanted no such thing. For those who simply wished to rectify the shortcomings of their Judaic/Malagasy knowledge (a situation brought about, according to them, by the colonial project) in order to better practise the religion of the ancestors, the connection to the matrix of globalized media was a means, not an end. Continuing on a path where white, European-descended Jews from the Global North persisted in instructing them about what was right and what was wrong not only reminded them of the bad old days of colonial rule; it smacked of neocolonial hegemony couched in terms of assistance.

Will the recent 100-plus converts to Orthodox Judaism on the island of Madagascar succeed in bringing about a religious revolution in their country, whereby hundreds of thousands—even millions?—of individuals who already feel a genealogical connection to the Jewish people will endeavour to follow rabbinic Judaism and receive the blessings of their overseas coreligionists? Or will their efforts stall, causing this episode to be remembered simply as a momentary flash in the proverbial pan of yet another new religious movement in the developing world? Whatever happens, one thing is certain: just like its genesis, normative Judaism's eventual standing in Madagascar will be mediated by discursive technologies that, by their very nature, fundamentally shape both the content and the form of the discussion.

Notes

1   For popular news coverage of this event, see, for instance, Berkowitz 2016; Josefson 2016; Kestenbaum 2016; Sussman n.d. For the only pre-conversion news article on this community, see Miles 2015.

2   Kulanu means 'All of Us' in Hebrew. For more on this organization, see Kulanu n.d.

3   For background on the Cameroonian and Nigerian communities, see Bruder 2014: 216–23; Ilona 2004, 2014; Lis 2009: 21–38; Lis 2015; Miles 2013, 2014.

4   For the most compelling examples of such scholarship (in addition to the above), see the following: Brettschneider 2015; Bruder 2008, 2011, 2013; Egorova 2015; Egorova and Perwez 2012a, 2012b, 2013; Parfitt 1987, 2002a, 2002b, 2007, 2008, 2012, 2013; Parfitt and Egorova 2006.

5   According to Tudor Parfitt, the foremost scholar of neo-Jewish studies to date, the estimated number of non-recognized 'shadow Jews' worldwide may be between 13.5 million and 14 million. This, of course, is a rough figure, corresponding only to those people who entertain notions of Jewish identity, not a number that points to the individuals who currently practise or wish to someday embrace normative Judaism. (That number is quite likely much lower; how much lower, it is impossible to establish.) Cited in Maltz 2014.

6   Thus far, the only contemporary research on the possible Jewish origins of Madagascar's native inhabitants, including a compilation of oral heritage narratives, has been published in Bruder 2008: esp. 124–32, 178–84; Bruder 2013. However, due to the time of its composition, Bruder's pioneering scholarship does not deal with the formation of the community profiled here.

7   Per the determination of the University of Utah's Institutional Review Board, this study has received an exemption, under 45 CFR 46.101(b), Category 2, from the federal regulations governing human subjects research. Ethnographic methods employed in this study include informal interaction, theme-based and free-flowing discussions with individuals and groups, participant observation, unobtrusive direct observation, naturalistic observation of public behaviour, overt observation, and unstructured, semi-structured, or structured interviewing. As mandated by the appropriate human subjects research protocol, all the individuals quoted in this essay provided their oral consent before being interviewed. In all but one instance, I have kept the identity of these individuals anonymous (the main

community leader's name has been repeatedly identified in open-source materials related to the community, and so is given here). All oral exchanges took place in French, but I have provided only the English translation for these exchanges. For print and e-correspondence, I have listed both the original French quotation as well as the English translation.

8 For genetic studies on origins of the population, see, for example, Regueiro et al. 2008.

9 For specificities about these systems of worship, see Dahl 1999.

10 Such descriptions, as well as sources for and versions of local legends about Israelite descent, may be found in the following: Colby and Williams 1916; Copeland 1822: 56; de Flacourt 1661: 308; Grandidier 1908: 74; Keane 1901: 48; Sibree 1870: 169.

11 Previously articulated iterations of this rather dubious claim may be found in Razakandrainy 1949; 1954: 11.

12 In a strange twist of fate, the May 2016 conversions facilitated by Kulanu occurred approximately two weeks short of the 76th anniversary of the plan's conception. On the Madagascar Plan, see Browning 2007: 81–9.

13 The full text of Genesis 12: 2–3 reads: 'And I will make of thee a great nation, and I will bless thee, and make thy name great; and be thou a blessing. And I will bless them that bless thee, and him that curseth thee will I curse; and in thee shall all the families of the earth be blessed.'

14 For the mission statements of Be'chol Lashon and Shavei Israel, see, respectively, Be'chol Lashon n.d.; Shavei Israel n.d.

15 The most accessible study on this genre is Horowitz 2010.

16 Unfortunately, there is little recent scholarship of value on the Jews for Jesus movement. For an early study, see Lipson 1978. For a current manifesto, see Jews for Jesus n.d.

17 Two excellent studies on Messianic Judaism are the following: Cohn-Sherbok 2000; Rudolph and Willitts 2013.

18 The discussions to which I was privy relied heavily upon Jeffrey 2002, esp. ch. 11, 'The Name of Jesus Encoded in the Old Testament'.

19 On African Independent Church typologies, see Ndungu 1997; Turner 1979: 92; Venter 2004: esp. 13–43.

References

ANDRIANTSOA, PASCAL, NANCY ANDRIASENDRARIVONY, STEVEN HAGGBLADE, BART MINTEN, MAMY RAKOTOJAONA, FREDERICK RAKOTOVOAVY, and HARIVELLE SARINDRA RAZAFINIMANANA, 2005. 'Media Proliferation and Democratic Transition in Africa: The Case of Madagascar'. *World Development*, 33: 1939–57.

BE'CHOL LASHON. n.d. 'Vision: A Global Jewish People'. Be'chol Lashon website <http://www.bechollashon.org/about/mission.php> (accessed 2 Apr. 2015).

BERKOWITZ, ADAM ELIYAHU. 2016. 'Mysterious Madagascar Community Practicing Jewish Rituals Officially Enters Covenant of Abraham'. *Breaking Israel News* (30 May) <http://www.breakingisraelnews.com/68765/100-members-of-lost-jewish-community-of-madagascar-enter-covenant-of-abraham-05-16> (accessed 31 May 2016).

BRETTSCHNEIDER, MARLA. 2015. *The Jewish Phenomenon in Sub-Saharan Africa: The Politics of Contradictory Discourses*. Lewiston, NY.

BROWNING, CHRISTOPHER R. 2007. *The Origins of the Final Solution: The Evolution of Nazi Jewish Policy, September 1939–March 1942*. Lincoln, Nebr.

BRUDER, EDITH. 2008. *The Black Jews of Africa: History, Religion, Identity*. Oxford.

—— 2011. 'The Beit Avraham of Kechene: The Emergence of a New Jewish Community in Ethiopia'. In Emanuela Trevisan Semi and Shalva Weil, eds., *Beta Israel: The Jews of Ethiopia and Beyond: History, Identity, and Borders*, 181–96. Venice.

—— 2013. 'The Descendants of David in Madagascar: Crypto-Judaism in Twentieth-Century Africa'. In Efraim Sicher, ed., *Race, Color, Identity: Rethinking Discourses About 'Jews' in the Twenty-First Century*, 196–216. New York.

—— 2014. *Black Jews: Les juifs noires d'Afrique et le mythe des tribus perdues*. Paris.

CAMPBELL, HEIDI A. 2012. 'Understanding the Relationship Between Religion Online and Offline in a Networked Society'. *Journal of the American Academy of Religion*, 80: 64–93.

COHN-SHERBOK, DAN. 2000. *Messianic Judaism*. New York.

COLBY, FRANK MOORE, and TALCOTT WILLIAMS, eds. 1916. 'Masudi'. In *The New International Encyclopedia*, 2nd edn., vol. xv, 228. New York.

COPELAND, SAMUEL. 1822. *A History of the Island of Madagascar, Comprising a Political Account of the Island, the Religion, Manners, and Customs of Its Inhabitants, and Its Natural Productions*. London.

DAHL, ØYVIND. 1999. *Meanings in Madagascar: Cases of Intercultural Communication*. Westport, Conn.

DE FLACOURT, ÉTIENNE. 1661. *Histoire de la grande isle Madagascar*. Paris.

Diagram Group. 2000. 'Madagascan People'. In The Diagram Group, *Encyclopedia of African Peoples*, 138–40. New York.

EGOROVA, YULIA. 2015. 'Redefining the Converted Jewish Self: Race, Religion, and Israel's Bene Menashe'. *American Anthropologist*, 117: 493–505.

—— and SHAHID PERWEZ. 2012a. 'Old Memories, New Histories: (Re)discovering the Past of Jewish Dalits'. *History and Anthropology*, 23: 1–15.

—— —— 2012b. 'Telugu Jews: Are the Dalits of Coastal Andhra Going Caste-Awry?' *South Asianist*, 1: 7–16.

—— —— 2013. *The Jews of Andhra Pradesh: Contesting Caste and Religion in South India*. Oxford.

EHRMAN, BART D. 2012. *Forgery and Counterforgery: The Use of Literary Deceit in Early Christian Polemics*. Oxford.

FISHER, DANIEL. 2011. 'The World's Worst Economies'. *Forbes* (5 July) <http://www.forbes.com/sites/danielfisher/2011/07/05/the-worlds-worst-economies> (accessed 5 Mar. 2014).

GRANDIDIER, ALFRED. 1908. *Histoire physique, naturelle et politique de Madagascar*, vol. iv. Paris.

HOROWITZ, AMY. 2010. *Mediterranean Israeli Music and the Politics of the Aesthetic*. Detroit.

ILONA, REMY. 2004. *The Igbos: Jews in Africa?* Abuja.

—— 2014. *The Igbos and Israel: An Inter-cultural Study of the Largest Jewish Diaspora*. Washington, DC.

JEFFREY, GRANT R. 2002. *The Signature of God: Astonishing Bible Codes Reveal September 11 Terror Attacks*. Colorado Springs, Col.

Jews For Jesus. n.d. 'Our Mission Statement'. Jews for Jesus website <http://jewsfor jesus.org/about-jews-for-jesus/categories> (accessed 5 June 2006).

JOSEFSON, DEBORAH. 2016. 'In Remote Madagascar, a New Community Chooses to Be Jewish'. *Jewish Telegraphic Agency* (5 June) <http://www.jta.org/2016/06/05/news-opinion/world/in-remote-madagascar-a-new-community-chooses-to-be-jewish> (accessed 6 June 2016).

KEANE, AUGUSTUS HENRY. 1901. *The Gold of Ophir: Whence Brought and by Whom?* London.

KESTENBAUM, SAM. 2016. '"Joining Fabric of World Jewish Community," 100 Convert on African Island of Madagascar'. *Forward* (24 May) <http://forward.com/news/341106/joining-fabric-of-world-jewish-community-100-convert-on-african-island-of-m> (accessed 24 May 2016).

KULANU. n.d. 'Welcome to Kulanu, Inc!' Kulanu website <http://www.kulanu.org> (accessed 5 Apr. 2015).

LIPSON, JULIENE. 1978. 'Jews for Jesus: An Anthropological Study'. Ph.D. diss., University of California, San Francisco.

LIS, DANIEL. 2009. '"Ethiopia Shall Soon Stretch Out Her Hands": Ethiopian Jewry and Igbo Identity'. *Jewish Culture and History*, 11: 21–38.

—— 2015. *Jewish Identity Among the Igbo* of Nigeria: Israel's 'Lost Tribe' and the Question of Belonging in the Jewish State. Trenton, NJ.

MALTZ, JUDY. 2014. 'Number of Wannabe Jews Equals That of Recognized Jews' *Haaretz* (4 Nov.), <http://www.haaretz.com/jewish-world/.premium-1.624585> (accessed 30 Mar. 2015).

MILES, WILLIAM F. S. 2013. *Jews of Nigeria: An Afro-Judaic Odyssey*. Princeton, NJ.

—— 2014. *Afro-Jewish Encounters: From Timbuktu to the Indian Ocean and Beyond*. Princeton, NJ.

—— 2015. 'The Malagasy Secret'. *Jerusalem Report* (3 Sept.) <http://www.jpost.com/Jerusalem-Report/The-Malagasy-secret-415164> (accessed 17 Sept. 2015).

NDUNGU, NAHASHON. 1997. 'The Bible in an African Independent Church'. In Hannah W. Kinoti and John M. Waliggo, eds., *The Bible in African Christianity*, 58–67. Nairobi.

PARFITT, TUDOR. 1987. *The Thirteenth Gate: Travels Among the Lost Tribes of Israel*. Bethesda, Md.

—— 2002a. 'Judaising Movements and Colonial Discourse'. In Tudor Parfitt and Emanuela Trevisan Semi, eds., *Judaising Movements: Studies in the Margins of Judaism in Modern Times*, 1–16. New York.

—— 2002b. *The Lost Tribes of Israel: The History of a Myth*. London.

—— 2007. 'Tribal Jews'. In Nathan Katz, Ranabir Chakravarti, Braj M. Sinha, and Shalva Weil, eds., *Indo-Judaic Studies in the Twenty-First Century: A View from the Margin*, 181–96. New York.

PARFITT, TUDOR. 2008. *The Lost Ark of the Covenant: The Remarkable Quest for the Legendary Ark.* New York.

——2012. '(De)Constructing Black Jews'. In Edith Bruder and Tudor Parfitt, eds., *African Zion: Studies in Black Judaism*, 12–30. Cambridge.

——2013. *Black Jews in Africa and the Americas.* Cambridge, Mass.

——and YULIA EGOROVA. 2006. *Genetics, Mass Media, and Identity: A Case Study of the Genetic Research on the Lemba and Bene Israel.* London.

POINDEXTER, MARK. 2001. 'Radio in Madagascar: Pluralism in an Economically Underdeveloped Country'. *Journal of Radio Studies*, 8: 175–90.

RAZAKANDRAINY, FRANCIS XAVIER. 1949. *Étude comparative du malgache et de l'hébreu: Le Malgache est une langue sémitique plus proche de l'hébreu que de l'arabe.* Antananarivo.

——1954. *Parenté des hovas et des hébreux: D'après leurs proverbes et leurs mœurs et coutumes.* Antananarivo.

RAZAFIMBELO-HARISOA, MARIE SOLANGE. 2005. 'Radio in Madagascar: Roles and Missions'. *Radio Journal: International Studies in Broadcast & Audio Media*, 3: 35–44.

REGUEIRO, M., S. MIRABAL, H. LACAU, J. L. CAEIRO, R. L. GARCIA-BERTRAND, and R. J. HERRERA. 2008. 'Austronesian Genetic Signature in East African Madagascar and Polynesia'. *Journal of Human Genetics*, 53: 106–20.

ROOD, MICHAEL. 2007. *The Pagan-Christian Connection Exposed.* Orlando, Fl.

RUDOLPH, DAVID J., and JOEL WILLITTS. 2013. *Introduction to Messianic Judaism: Its Ecclesial Context and Biblical Foundations.* Grand Rapids, Mich.

SHAVEI ISRAEL. n.d. 'Our Goals'. Shavei Israel website <http://shavei.org/about-us/our-goals> (accessed 30 Apr. 2016).

SIBREE, JAMES. 1870. *Madagascar and Its People: Notes of a Four Years' Residence. With a Sketch of the History, Position, and Prospects of Mission Work Amongst the Malagasy.* London.

SOUCAT DAVID. n.d. 'Yeshiva Soucat David'. Soucat David website <http://www.soucat-david.net/node/207> (accessed 30 May 2014).

SUSSMAN, GERALD. n.d. 'A Wild and Crazy Day'. Kulanu blog <http://kulanu.org/b2/a-wild-and-crazy-day> (accessed 30 May 2016).

Tana News. 2013. 'Je peux faire revenir Marc Ravalomanana au pays'. *Tana News* (24 Apr.) <http://www.tananews.com/asides/kohen-rivo-lala-je-peux-faire-revenir-marc-ravalomanana-si> (accessed 20 June 2016).

Temple Mount and Land of Israel Faithful Movement. n.d. 'Our Goal'. Temple Mount and Land of Israel Faithful Movement website <http://www.templemountfaithful.org> (accessed 20 Nov. 2013).

TURNER, HAROLD W. 1979. *Religious Innovation in Africa: Collected Essays on New Religious Movements.* Boston, Mass.

VENTER, DAWID. 2004. *Engaging Modernity: Methods and Cases for Studying African Independent Churches in South Africa.* Westport, Conn.

World Bank. n.d. 'Madagascar: Poverty Assessment'. The World Bank website <http://web.worldbank.org/WBSITE/EXTERNAL/TOPICS/EXTPOVERTY/EXTPA/0,,contentMDK:20204495~menuPK:435735~pagePK:148956~piPK:216618~theSitePK:430367,00.html> (accessed 2 Feb. 2015).

Worldometers. n.d. 'Madagascar Population (Live)'. Worldometers website <http://www.worldometers.info/world-population/madagascar-population> (accessed 31 May 2016).

SEVEN

Telling Jokes: Connecting and Separating Jews in Analogue and Digital Culture

SIMON J. BRONNER

NOTICING IN THE 1990s that the behaviour of 'playing on the computer' (often perceived by office managers as 'misusing' the computer) primarily involved sharing jokes, folklorist Paul Smith dubbed the computer 'The Joke Machine' and predicted the exponential growth of its humour-generating function. This label implied that the machine was more than a storehouse of information. If the Internet merely provided a cabinet to file one's favourite joke, it would not brandish the expressive, interactive features or cultural functions of folklore that frequently lodge as commentary on popular culture. More than being a reproductive medium, however, the computer, as it became more of a home appliance, fostered the creation of new material that, in Smith's words, could only exist 'within the machine' (Smith 1991: 274; see also Foote 2007; Fox 1983; Jennings 1990: 120–41). Users at home and work manipulated images and adapted texts, often commenting on the technology and inviting social feedback that distinguished the humour as 'computer lore' (Bronner 2009; Preston 1996).

Why joke in and around the machine? Smith implied that it is a natural process for humans to appropriate new technology for folkloric transmission, and he drew an evolutionary pattern from user-controlled media of the typewriter to the photocopier, fax machine, and computer. Yet the high volume of traffic on the Internet and the creative, interactive forms therein suggest something more at work (and play) on the computer. In its personalized consumer version, the computer promised more self-reliance in a growing culture of modernistic individualism, but at the same time risked alienation and corporate, mass cultural control over individual users and appeared to threaten social interaction in traditional communities. As a result, I contend that joking became associated with digital transmission for several reasons: first, it serves emotionally and psychologically to respond to anxieties concerning diminished human control and competency for users; second, it signals for them an intimate social connection that questions a dominant corporate order; third, it creates symbols that provide or project a satisfying transgressive or aggressive effect; and fourth, its brief and often visual form adapts well to the physical screen frame.

The Internet is also appealing for enabling cultural agglomeration without the user being publicly visible. Users can usually amass news of their own ethnic communities without confronting them physically, and at the same time investigate cultures from around the world without being intrusive or noticed by those groups. Yet some computer lore taken out of context or reframed with the productive capacities of the computer can be disturbing to the communities that generated them. A prime example is ethnic joking, typically meant in oral tradition to be shared privately between one person and another. And for a number of Jewish Orthodox groups, the Internet and computerized devices should be used for work, and not play. Yet twenty years after Smith made his observations, a Google search of 'jokes' resulted in an astounding figure of 329 million hits that clearly indicate a development well beyond the adaptation of lore transmitted by fax machine or photocopiers. Most of the Internet sites are lists of texts and cartoons arranged by categories, and among the most common jokes are those identified as 'Jewish jokes' or 'Jew jokes'. For the most part the jokes are about Jews rather than jokes provided by Jews, and they fit the characterization of Jewish humour as deprecating material related to the characteristics and characters of Jewish life, often deriving from the legacy of persecution in eastern Europe and immigrant experience in countries in the West (see Ziv 1998: 12). Although jokes about Jews were especially conspicuous as ethnic humour in Europe and the Americas in the late nineteenth and early twentieth centuries, the extent of Jewish sites in the twenty-first century, as the Internet became a global phenomenon, is still surprising. One cause for amazement is the perception of Jewish jokes as 'period pieces', related to their historical association with mass immigration in the early twentieth century rather than to the assimilation of the twenty-first century.

With the emphasis in the discourse of the twentieth century over the effect of joking in oral and print circulation, questions remain for the twenty-first century about the role of technological mediation, such as what happens to the characterization of Jews as agents of joking when the category of 'Jewish jokes' goes online in such a massive number of sites. Over 25 million hits come back from a Google search for 'Jewish joke', and many websites, such as 'Old Jews Telling Jokes' (www.oldjewstellingjokes.com), 'Jewish Jokes' (www.jewishjokes.net), and 'A Word in Your Eye' (www.awordinyoureye.com) are devoted exclusively to the Jewish joke as a genre. The number of hits for Jewish jokes is the largest among ethnic-religious categories apart from racialized 'black jokes' and 'Chinese jokes' (receiving over 42 and 46 million hits respectively), and the figure has grown steadily since Smith's early inventory of ethnic jokes as an integral part of computer lore. An indication of the pervasiveness of Jewish jokes in my Google search is that the number of sites coming back as 'Jewish' or 'Jew jokes' amounts to double the number of sites listed for Polish, Irish, Catholic, and Mexican jokes combined.

Once pronounced dead (or at least out of oral circulation) by Jewish public intellectuals such as Irving Kristol (1951), Jewish jokes abound on the Internet, in citation if not performance. Does that mean the jokes enjoy a second, more robust life in digital culture than in oral tradition or photocopied lore? Broadly speaking, this query provides a basis for theorizing not only the representation and expression of Jewishness in mass society, but also more generally the shift of narrative communication in the twenty-first century from analogue culture (face-to-face, oral, corporeally based) to digital (reliant on mediated communication by individual users) (see Blank 2009, 2012; Bronner 2009; Howard 2011; Jenkins 2008; Turkle 2011). Indeed, what happens in the move from a back-slapping rendition of a joke in person to a text read on an Internet site, or from an inside joke to a video gone viral in emails and downloads?

One answer to the question of the ubiquity of Jewish jokes on humour sites is that the texts are essentially archived and then selected for oral re-enactment or private amusement. Readers can imagine a process by which the texts are extracted from their performative social contexts and are 'posted', as if the webpage were an enormous bulletin board for passersby to browse. The Internet, then, is a massive storehouse rather than a stage for performance or a folk frame for play 'just among ourselves'. In an archival transformation (or what some may see as a conversion experience), many webmasters take pride in, or show their technological mettle by making available historic or formerly analogue forms in long digital lists. Another view is that the Internet transforms folkloric genres by providing a different communicative medium and a novel play frame. From this perspective, digital media are not simulating or stirring a face-to-face interactive context; instead, they serve to redefine the social setting and reorganize the cultural frame, thus allowing users to create a fresh expressive form.

Although it is tempting to lump Jewish jokes together with the ethnic humour that pervades the Internet, Jewish jokes are distinctive because of their special connection to Jewish culture derived from east European heritage, their historical association with oral and print forms, and the scholarly presumption that they should not grow in digital culture because of their association with oral perform-ance in Jewish community contexts (Oring 2016: 129–46, 165–81; Wisse 2013). Rising in oral tradition with mass emigration from eastern Europe in the late nineteenth century, Jewish jokes enjoyed immense popularity on the theatre stage as well as in print in the early twentieth century. With the assimilation of subsequent generations, the repression of material that could be twisted into antisemitic barbs, and an aversion to self-degradation, American Jews especially discouraged the circulation of Jewish jokes. With their heavy reliance on Yiddish terminology and references to the immigration period, Jewish jokes were often contextualized, and consequently distanced, as old, 'classic', or relic humour (see Biro 2001; Eilbert 1981; Minkoff 2005). Although many of the jokes were report-edly told by Jews to one another, and were enjoyed as a form of ethnic bonding, many Jews became uncomfortable when they 'went public' in print, especially on the global Internet. If we accept the view that Jews are symbolic targets for ridicule and marginalization in host societies, either because their social difference needs to be reinforced as they integrate or because their minority status raises suspicion among members of the dominant society, then the jokes inevitably raise the question of whether stereotyping and racism are evident.

As a minority group in a dominant Christian context, though not easily distinguished by physical difference, American Jews both championed and were victims of humour that commented on their alleged physical differences and social aspirations. Many critics thought that Jewish jokes, more than other types of ethnic humour, demanded symbolic decoding with knowledge gained from being in a primarily Protestant culture (Fischman 2011: 48). When presented by Jewish humorists, the jokes were usually intended for Jews to 'poke fun at themselves', but Jews increasingly expressed concern that the narratives appeared malicious when told outside the group. A counterargument is that the Internet deflates the prejudicial impact of ethnic humour by rendering jokes in mummified form. Throughout this essay, I contend that digital culture has made Jewish jokes visible, if not audible, by recontextualizing them from esoteric folk culture into an exoteric memory piece.[1] Just as oral practice can signal a baleful or benevolent intent, so does the Internet have an open 'design', a visual frame for interactive discourse that affects the projection of anxiety and consequent communication of meaning on the fictive plane of humour.

The Form of the Joke, Jewish and Otherwise

For the comparison of analogue and digital versions of jokes to be valid, I should first establish that the forms are equivalent. Jokes usually take the form of brief, fictional narratives, usually told in the present. Complicating this description is the proliferation of joking questions (also called 'riddle-jokes') that are often included in lists of jokes in Internet humour sites, as well as in oral performances. Listed as a 'Daily Jew Joke' on a Facebook community page, for instance, is 'What do you get when you lock 2 Jews in a room?' with the answer, '3 opinions'.[2] It can also be rendered as a proverb by stating a condition and a result: 'Two Jews, three opinions' (Telushkin 1992: 17). If 'Jews' structurally constitutes a motifeme (a unit of action that is a variable building block of a plot or linguistic sequence), then other groups could conceivably fill the slot, as in a light bulb joke with the formulaic question 'How many (group) does it take to screw in a light bulb?' (Dundes 1962; 1981). Yet a Google search for 'two three opinions' comes back with hardly any variations of 'two Jews, three opinions', suggesting a Jewish rhetorical frame. Even results such as 'two lawyers, three opinions' and 'two economists, three opinions' refer to the primary use of the phrase in a Jewish context (Michaels 2006; Michaelson 2006).

In uttering the saying or spinning a story around 'two Jews, three opinions', the question arises whether the characterization of Jews is deprecatory inside as well as outside the play frame of humour. The Internet can be a location to offer a textual interpretation of the characterization, suggesting a metafolklore of the Jewish joke—that is, traditionalized narrative that comments on a tradition. Although folklorist Alan Dundes suggested the term metafolklore in a pre-digital age for 'oral literary criticism', the expectation of commentary, often interactive, on the Internet invites an expansion of metafolkloric discourse (Dundes 1966). For example, under the title of 'two Jews, three opinions', a rabbi online shares the following narrative:

A new rabbi comes to a well-established congregation. Every week on the Sabbath, a fight erupts during the service. When it comes time to recite the Shema prayer, half of the congregation stands and the other half sits. The half who stand say, 'Of course we stand for the Shema. It's the credo of Judaism. Throughout history, thousands of Jews have died with the words of the Shema on their lips.' The half who remain seated say, 'No. According to the Shulchan Aruch (the code of Jewish law), if you are seated when you get to the Shema you remain seated.'

The people who are standing yell at the people who are sitting, 'Stand up!' while the people who are sitting yell at the people who are standing, 'Sit down!'. It's destroying the whole decorum of the service, and driving the new rabbi crazy. Finally, it's brought to the rabbi's attention that at a nearby home for the aged is a 98-year-old man who was a founding member of the congregation. So, in accordance with Talmudic tradition, the rabbi appoints a delegation of three, one who stands for the Shema, one who sits, and the rabbi himself, to go interview the man. They enter his room, and the man who stands for the Shema rushes over to the old man and says, 'Wasn't it the tradition in our synagogue to stand for the Shema?'

'No', the old man answers in a weak voice. 'That wasn't the tradition.'

The other man jumps in excitedly. 'Wasn't it the tradition in our synagogue to sit for the Shema?'

'No', the old man says. 'That wasn't the tradition.'

At this point, the rabbi cannot control himself. He cuts in angrily. 'I don't care what the tradition was! Just tell them one or the other. Do you know what goes on in services every week—the people who are standing yell at the people who are sitting, the people who are sitting yell at the people who are standing—'

'That was the tradition,' the old man says. (Zauderer 2011)

'This is a joke', the rabbi affirms at the story's conclusion, but he connects the fiction of the joke to a disturbing reality with the metafolkloric comment that 'Jews tend to fight with each other, especially with regard to matters religious, and how they establish one breakaway synagogue after another.' The rabbi narrates the joke in the present and frames it as a distinctively Jewish type, but it has been traced to a non-ethnic precedent in the nineteenth century with the rabbi being replaced by a judge (Raskin 1992: 14–17). To be sure, the rabbi's narrative strategy is to engage his presumably Jewish readers with a story, but he also acknowledges it as a way to deal with what he calls a 'troubling issue'. He expects to arouse commentary on the issue with the story, because, in his words, 'Recognizing that problems exist is the first step in the healing process—not only between husband and wife, but within the entire Jewish community as well' (Zauderer 2011).

Under the title 'Two Jews Three Opinions', a non-rabbinical blogger visualized the joke by using photo editing software to create and subsequently post an image showing the backs of two Orthodox Jews (identified by full beards and dark skullcaps). The blogger put in English call-outs that viewers would read from left to right as one would read an English sentence rather than the Hebrew, which would be scanned from right to left. The first one states 'It's a valid point but I must disagree.' The second shows a cloud above a man who states, 'But you're the only one who has spoken so far.' The blogger further clarifies that the intent of the blog is to 'provide fun, healthy and constructive debate about Jewish issues' (Brad 2008). The reference that might be lost on non-Jewish viewers is the association of Orthodox Jews with an agonistic learning style in which students argue over interpretations of sacred texts. The implication of the cartoon, though, is that this style extends into daily life. The blogger featured the image's 'joke' to promote feedback, indeed heated 'debate' on a broad array of topics. Instead of seeing the screen as something to be passively read, he encouraged viewing the 'frame' established by the 'two Jews, three opinions' image as highly interactive.

The shared characteristic between riddle-joke, narrative, and image humour is the presence of a punchline. According to folklorist Elliott Oring,

The punchline is a device that triggers the perception of an appropriate incongruity. It reveals that what is seemingly incongruous is appropriate, or what is seemingly appropriate is incongruous. In any event, the recognition brought about the punchline must be *sudden*. The punchline must bring about an abrupt cognitive reorganization in the listener. As such, the punchline is not a necessary element of humor but a literary device that characterizes the particular form of humor we label 'joke'. (1992: 83; see also Oring 2016: 16–32)

I would add to Oring's characterization that the punchline can be a visual device as well as a literary one. In the image on the blog 'Two Jews Three Opinions' the picture establishes that Jews are talking without a narrative stating so. An incongruity is set up by the first Jew apparently arguing with another person, but the 'punchline' is that he is arguing with himself. In the riddle-joke, the punchline is the answer to the question which brings an unexpected or incongruous statement. In the riddle-joke, the twist is often word-play. In the visual material more common in digital culture, the convolution is conveyed visually either by an incongruity between what is seen and what is read, or between the fiction of the composed image and its reality. Understanding the punchline, or 'getting' the incongruity of the joke, depends on a shared, typically unstated cultural understanding of the references in the text or image (Correll 1997). Although some strict structuralists might view the production of humour mechanically as the setup of the incongruity, my point for further analysis is that the cultural understanding of references suggests a perceptual psychology used to unpack meanings as well as identify processes of enactment. When a punchline falls flat and the teller responds with the apology of 'I guess you had to be there', there is an indication that participants in the play frame do not relate to the joke in the same way. If the listener or reader mutters 'I don't get it', more than a miscomprehension of the structural incongruity is implied. The suggestion is that the joke is not relevant (or is even repulsive), and this situation raises questions about social perceptions and psychological issues often wrapped around the joke.

Both analogue and digital cultural forms of jokes have punchlines, but a difference in ritualization can be discerned in oral performances. Someone may say 'I've got a joke for you' at a place and time that the teller and listener perceive to be appropriate. Setting up a joking frame on a fictive plan outside everyday time signals a play on forms, an expectation of symbols and associated references, and a ritualized sequence of narration and punchline that often invites comment or a reversal of listener and teller (see Douglas 1968: 370). The content, too, needs to be considered appropriate, or the references understood, for it to be effective. If participants in a play frame perceive the joke with the expectation of being brief, biting, and funny, the joke will be contextualized in the moment for teller and listener, and the separation in time and place as joking will allow for reordering or subversion of reality. According to anthropologist Mary Douglas, 'Social requirements may judge a joke to be in bad taste, risky, too near the bone, improper, or irrelevant. Such controls are exerted either on behalf of hierarchy as such, or on behalf of values which are judged too precious and too precarious to be exposed to challenge' (1968: 366). All jokes, she observes, express the social situations in which they occur: 'The one social condition necessary for a joke to be enjoyed is that the social group in which it is received should develop *the formal characteristics of a "told" joke*: that is, a dominant pattern of relations is challenged by another. If there is no joke in the social structure, no other joking can appear' (1968: 366; emphasis added).

If the joke is not *told* online, then, is it, perceptually, a joke? On the Internet, the poster of the joke is probably not aware of a listener, but nonetheless uses the design of the page to render the joke appropriate or implicate an audience. With most sites providing space for comments and ratings, the user expects a response, but it is fair to say that online the joker has more opportunity to joke and more leeway to post questionable material. The anonymity or disguise allowed by the new medium encourages broader participation because the risk of rejection is reduced. Thus, jokes posted online still depend on a contextualized appropriateness within the design of the electronic 'page'. In print within the spate of joke books that appeared during the early twentieth century, and later on the Internet, attention shifts from oral delivery to textual form.

An indication of the anxiety caused by the status of the Jewish joke is humour about its definition. Richard Raskin calls defining the Jewish joke a 'risky enterprise' and cites an attempt to draw ethnic boundaries in the metafolkloric statement 'A Jewish story is one which no *goy* [Yiddish: 'non-Jew'] can understand and which a Jew says he has heard before' (Raskin 1992: 181). Implying that the text of the joke is not as significant a marker as the response of the listener is another joke, typically set in eastern Europe, that associates Jews with joking:

You tell a joke to a peasant and he laughs three times: when you tell it; when you explain it; and when he understands it. A landowner laughs only twice: when he hears the joke and when you explain it. For he can never understand it. An army officer laughs only once: when you tell the joke. He never lets you explain it—and that he is unable to understand it goes without saying. But when you start telling a joke to another Jew, he interrupts you: 'Go on! That's an old one,' and he shows you how much better he can tell it himself. (Friedlander 2011; see also Olsvanger 1965; Raskin 1992: 181)

The story set in eastern Europe raises a question of whether the Jewish joke is historically defined by the Jewish Old World and immigrant experience, not only by its content but also in reference to the typical location in which it was delivered (Jason 1967: 49). In other words, as a performance, is Jewish joking a re-enactment from the view of tellers of what Jews in shtetls might have done, or is it a modern urban practice that connects Jews who feel caught between their distant heritage and the assimilative pressures of a mass society that appears to diminish the functions of community?

As a type, the Jewish joke can be told, or posted, by both Jews and non-Jews, but for Jews there is typically a reference to a Jewish character or behavioural trait with roots in eastern Europe. Writing in a folkloristic journal, Ed Cray tried to broaden the experience that informs Jewish jokes with the assertion that the joke is 'one which intrinsically deals with the Jew and one which would be pointless if the Jewishness of a character were removed' (1964: 344). For sociologist Christie Davies, the key to the distinctiveness of the Jewish joke type is one of social boundaries that can be expressed positively or negatively, and for that matter orally or online: 'Jewish jokes are unique in the way in which they refer explicitly to the problematic nature of the boundaries of a people and focus on the blurring of this boundary not by similar or related outsiders but by assimilating insiders' (Davies 1990: 309). The trouble with this perspective is that it does not address the perception of the joke's content or transmission. Fernando Fischman connects, for example, South American Jewish jokes (*chiste judío*) with their North American cognates by identifying key components of 'a humorous narrative whose dramatis personae are Jewish and act according to socially shared stereotypical images—the Jewish mother, the greedy businessman, the stingy Jew' (Fischman 2011: 48). Of significance to the perception of the historicity of the jokes is Fischman's observation that the tradition-bearers he interviewed generically classified the jokes as of immigrant origin. The label 'Jewish joke' in this perspective suggests an emic category of an orally delivered deprecatory, humorous narrative, whether told by Jews or non-Jews, deriving from Jews' immigrant experiences of the late nineteenth and early twentieth centuries.

Dead or Alive? Observations on the Vitality of the Jewish Joke

Noting the rapid rise of the Jewish joke in the nineteenth century as a distinctive historic genre, *Commentary* editor Irving Kristol proclaimed its demise, boldly declaring: 'What we call Jewish humor is Yiddish humor' and 'with the wiping out of the Yiddish-speaking communities, the creative source of this humor is gone' (1951: 433). The American-born son of Yiddish-speaking immigrants from eastern Europe, Kristol assumed that the Jewish joke was esoteric knowledge; it was a lore shared privately among Jews. This is not to say that the Jews stopped telling jokes, but to Kristol, in post-immigrant America neither Jews nor jokes should be defined by the lore of the east European shtetl. Formerly, he claimed, 'the European Jew, achieving self-consciousness in the Enlightenment, found himself at the point of intersection of faith and reason, in a comic situation he could only master with a joke' (1951: 436). From Kristol's mid-twentieth century vantage point, Jews had moved past arguing for their place in civilization and had joined modernity. In this agenda, he responded to the categorization by Sigmund Freud early in the twentieth century of the Jewish joke as 'stories created by Jews and directed against Jewish characteristics' (Freud 1960 [1905]: 111). Unlike Freud, who thought that Jewish humour was unusual because the narrator is the object of mockery rather than an 'other', Kristol reflected that American Jews no longer wrung their hands over the distressful 'Jewish situation'. Instead, he observed that Jews used humour as Americans generally did, to confront the challenges of modernization.

When Kristol suggested the end of the Jewish joke, he referred to the passing of the standard comic folktype of the bearded, backward Jewish immigrant on the vaudeville stage and in many joke books published in the late nineteenth and early twentieth centuries (Erdman 1997). He shared with Jewish civic and religious leaders disapproval of material that moved from private conversations among Jews to public consumption and misinterpretation. Well before Kristol's famous column, the Central Conference of American Rabbis (CCAR), in 1912, objected to the publication of the fast-selling *Hebrew Jokes*. The CCAR

entered a strong protest, requesting the discontinuance of the publication and sale of the book, because of its vilification, and insisted that the jokes are not harmless fun, but dangerous libels. We regret to state that the firm in a letter received March 13, 1912, replied that it was at a loss to understand our criticism, and it assigned the conventional excuse of holding the Jew in high esteem, and of making him 'the target of the same good-humored raillery as the Scotchman and Irishman'. (Friedman 1912: 107)

The CCAR's Committee on Church and State observed 'a large national movement' featuring the 'Jewish Comedian', often a non-Jew spouting jokes in a costume lampooning the Orthodox Jewish immigrant from eastern Europe. Often the theme of the jests concerned Jews involved in business as pedlars or merchants trading with non-Jews. The committee declared that 'We are not supersensitive, but our pride must resent the burlesquing of the Jew, of his religion or traditions' (Friedman 1912: 103). Although recognizing that Jews had told such jokes among themselves, the committee bristled at the mockery of Jews in the popular culture movement of Jewish jokes to the stage and print.

If not accused of being 'supersensitive' to ethnic teasing in the turn-of-the-century era, the same Jews who laid claim to a long folkloric tradition of the self-deprecating jest were accused of being humourless. In 1893, in the article, 'Jewish Wit and Humour', Chief Rabbi of the British Empire Hermann Adler responded to the criticisms of French historian Joseph Ernest Renan and Scottish philosopher Thomas Carlyle that Jews lack the capacity to laugh and create witticisms. The sources he gave for the placement of Jews among civilized groups with a humorous repertoire was not in the earthy material of the Yiddish speakers from eastern Europe, but rather in the ancient texts of the midrash, a genre of compilations of homiletic teachings on the Hebrew Bible (Adler 1893: 370–1). He recognized wit conveyed by Jews in Yiddish, but noted that the humour was more esoteric and couched in the 'vernacular', presupposing 'a very accurate knowledge of the Bible—ay, even of the labyrinthine intricacies of the Talmud— in order to be fully appreciated. And when once you attempt to explain and to interpret, all the sparkle and effervescence of the witticism are irretrievably lost, and the savour thereof is like unto that of a bottle of champagne that was uncorked yesternight' (1893: 531). He maintained to his non-Jewish audience that Jews, as a downtrodden people, use humour as a tool for survival: 'I would rather liken it [humour] to the weapon which a beneficent Maker has provided his feeble creatures, whereby they have been enabled to survive in the fierce struggle for existence' (1893: 530–1). While he cited examples of British Jewish figures such as Moses Montefiore and Abraham Solomon contributing wit that entered into popular culture, he thought that humour in Yiddish stayed within the Jewish community (1893: 537).

The Yiddish language, and especially the Yiddish 'accent' in a host country's language, represented the expressive inflection of Jews as distinct from non-Jews, and for many immigrants it signified amusement (Fischman 2011: 47–9). It also caused some embarrassment to religious leaders such as Hermann Adler, who wanted to show the contribution of Jews to modern Western civilization in the form of fine arts and literature. He called Yiddish 'that strange degeneration and uncouth blend of the two languages [Hebrew and German]' (1893: 531). Older civic leaders, many from German backgrounds, viewed the use of Yiddish among immigrants from eastern Europe as a sign of minority or folk status that created a barrier between Jews and popular or mainstream British or American culture. Yet reporters also noticed the mixture of ethnic and popular culture on stage and screen. In 1913 Viola Paradise reported in *Survey* magazine that the typical Jewish immigrant went to the theatre for amusement, where he or she 'hears Yiddish jokes and songs and American popular music, and she marvels at the wonders of the moving-pictures' (Paradise 1913: 701). The historical association of Yiddish with the immigrant generation led to the presumption that as Jews became assimilated and lost their inflection in the second and third generations, Yiddish humour would drop away in favour of the de-ethnicized popular culture of the host society.

Despite the predictions of the demise of the Jewish joke by the mid-twentieth century, exoteric forms of humour identified as Jewish jokes enjoyed great popularity in oral circulation and print during the boom of ethnic jokes in the midst of the 1960s and the civil rights movement (Blumenfeld 1965; Dundes 1971). Besides being reported in folkloristic field collections (Baker 1986; Barrick 1970; Cray 1964; Dundes 1997), a spate of mass-market books under titles such as the *Official Jewish Joke Book* by Larry Wilde (1980), *Truly Tasteless Jokes* by Blanche Knott (1982), and *Gross Jokes* by Julius Alvin (1991) flew off bookstore shelves. Much of the content of these texts was not about the *shlemiels* (awkward, unlucky persons) and *shlimazls* (inept persons) of Kristol's Yiddish humour, but the narcissistic, spoiled Jewish American Princesses and their doting, neurotic mothers of a post-immigrant generation (Dundes 1985). The theme of a group using commercialism to advance themselves despite social prejudice and physical obstacles became channelled into queries of the impact of success on ethnic identity and social relations, epitomized by the non-normative family and sexual mores. The new topics also included more comparisons to African Americans, with whom Jews were connected as persecuted minorities (Boyer 1993). Moreover, the structure of the civil rights-era texts appeared different. Instead of the joke being related as an episodic story, the new forms offered a humorous answer to a question, such as the opener of the 'Jewish' chapter of *Truly Tasteless Jokes*: 'What's the Jewish version of foreplay? Half an hour of begging' (Knott 1982: 19).

Although these books suggest that jokes were being silently read as relics of an earlier era, Henry Eilbirt in *What Is a Jewish Joke?* (1981) insisted that the printed Jewish joke was still 'an orally told genre'. He argued that placing jokes on a printed page did not destroy their fundamental orality. 'When we read them', he wrote of the jokes, 'we are really listening to them in our heads' (Eilbirt 1981: 5). Folklorist Dan Ben-Amos countered that the Jewish joke, like many folkloric forms, is performed and therefore depends on physical delivery and an appropriate social context; they are, in his words, 'communicative events' (1973: 122).

The social context to which Ben-Amos refers is an encounter between teller and listener in which Jewish identity was shared. Compilers of Jewish joke books from the 1960s and 1970s drew their materials from oral tradition, but unlike the earlier period, they did not rely solely on Jewish tellers. Placing the jokes on the printed page encouraged a suspension of the social frames in oral performances. The jokes selected were those that did not need knowledge of the biblical and talmudic contexts that Hermann Adler thought essential to a vernacular Jewish humour. No longer framed as a communicative event 'just between us', the printed joke drew more cognitive attention to the meaning of words rather than to the contextualized inflected delivery or identity of the teller. Seeing the joke in print gave the text a fixity and permanence that it did not have in oral tradition. As reading material, the jokes encouraged individualistic, silent consumption.

The ambiguity of cultural effect as Jewish jokes moved from esoteric to exoteric expression became especially evident in the research of folklorist Alan Dundes, who documented the burgeoning technological mediation of Jewish humour through the facsimile machine and photocopier. Together with Carl R. Pagter, Dundes identified cartoons and texts distributed through the technology of reproduction that in the corporate 'paperwork' empire appeared to contain more antisemitic sentiments, or at least relied on Jewish stereotypes, particularly on commercial associations, as ethnic icons to convey their humour (Dundes and Pagter 1978). For instance, he claimed that the Jewish American Princess cycle did not consist of Jewish jokes per se, but that it used the symbol of the Jewish female to reference mainstream American society's anxiety over the effects of consumerism (Dundes 1985). Dundes in fact identified the 'begging' joke as a joke told by Jews, but differentiated their poking fun at 'the alleged proclivities of Jewish women, either the Jewish mother or the Jewish wife' from what he called antisemitic folklore, or the ethnic slur of Auschwitz and other Holocaust jokes that Jews eschewed (1997: 20).

Along with other analysts, Dundes also implied that the primary transmitters of jokes generally, and ethnic jokes specifically, were men, and further speculated that technological mediation by technology such as the fax machine, often managed by women, allowed females to express more 'complaints about the males with whom they live' (1997: 94; see also Mitchell 1985). In popular culture, the tendency toward insulting or transgressive humour by women and the spread of the joking context to non-Jews became evident in the fame accorded to edgy Jewish comics, many of whom were women. Their coarse use of sexual references and insults appeared to cross the line of genteel or gentile propriety for humorous effect. The humour performed in night clubs or on comedy records countered the image of self-deprecating Jewish humour with a post-immigrant aggression (Del Negro 2010). In the digital age, the computer 'joke machine' further altered the significance of gendered performance by removing or disguising the identities of posters. What appeared to rise in importance with anonymity of posters was the transgressive act of joking and the textual focus on the content of, and response to, the joke.

Posters often leave clues with their monikers to their identities or the identities they want others to perceive. One psychological statement is the assumption of Yiddish labels such as *shmendrik* (neurotic bumbler), *kibitzer* (busybody), *nudnik* (nag), and *payats* (clown) to emphasize effectiveness as a joker. This association with Old World Yiddish characters (and later, Jewish comedians such as Jerry Seinfeld, Rodney Dangerfield, and Woody Allen) derives from the characterization of joke-telling as a distinctive Jewish trait. Echoing the sentiment of journalist Leo Rosten (1968), folklorist Elliott Oring (1983) interpreted the purported Jewish reliance on humour in everyday discourse as a turn from characterization of Jews in religious terms as the ancient 'people of the book' to a modern secular classification as 'people of the joke'. This ascription raises the possibility that the modern, post-immigrant popularity of Jewish jokes comes from the perception that Jewish jokes or Jews who tell them are supposed to be funny, at least in part because they have a background of struggle out of which they lampoon the disrespect and uncivil responses they receive. The Jewish persona can be perceived to set up a play frame in a workaday world. Although this perception underlines an ethnic difference, objectifying Jews as consumable entertainment, it nonetheless tethers Jews more closely to mainstream society as a group that shares in the everyday experience of a good laugh (Miller 1993; Spalding 1976: p. xv; Telushkin 1992: 19–20).

Behind the attribution of joking as a Jewish trait is the view that with many Jewish material-culture and religious practices fading from view in twentieth-century America, joke-telling became a primary marker of Jewishness. Although assimilated, Jews could disclose their ethnicity through the esoteric and linguistic references in jokes or their very fondness for telling jokes. If the idea of the 'Jewish joke' is lodged in the topical context of European immigration to America and to an extent in Western Europe, the modern Israeli experience was difficult to fit into the self-deprecatory, mobile world of the Jewish joke. Some commentators claimed that 'Jewish humour got lost in transit to Israel' or at least that Jewish humour in Israel, as part of a majority, nationalistic culture, is not self-aimed and universalized (Nevo and Levine 1994: 126; Saper 1993: 81; see also Telushkin 1992: 173–84). Their argument is that Israeli humour was nationalistically based rather than being associated with Jews globally.

In sum, the Jewish joke in its narrative form could be identified through at least seven thematic criteria:

1. A historical reference in humour to the experience of east European or Yiddish-speaking Jews (Katz and Katz 1971; Spalding 1976: pp. xiii–xiv; Ziv 1998).

2. The use of humour to deny harsh conditions and to find advantage in disadvantage (Adler 1893: 530–1; Eilbirt 1981: 277–8; Spalding 1969: p. xiv).

3. The delineation of what is special about Jews in contrast to others, often stressing the uniqueness of Jewish society and culture, including reference to Jewish communal characters (turned into folktypes) such as the *rebbe* and *rebetsn* (Yiddish terms for an esteemed rabbi and his wife, respectively), *ḥazan* (cantor), and *shames* (synagogue sexton). The distinctiveness of Jewish society also is conveyed with reference to religious traditions such as the *brit* (circumcision), reciting the Shema prayer, and synagogue worship (Cray 1964: 335–43; Oring 2016: 165–81).

4. The criticism by Jews of other Jews, often with the implication that Jews could criticize themselves better than anybody else (Spalding 1969: p. xvi; Telushkin 1992: 17).

5. The use of humour as a kind of parable to elucidate a moral and teach a lesson. Related to this use is the textual or intellectual content of the joke related to the cerebral or inconspicuous nature of Jewish character. In Kristol's (1951) view of what Jewish jokes are *not*, for instance, Jewish humour contains 'no pranks, no slapstick, no practical jokes—nothing that reduces the spiritual and human to the mechanical.'

6. A propensity for using joke-telling to manifest social differentiation, particularly of the denominations of Judaism such as Orthodox, Conservative, and Reform. In this view the fact that Jews tell jokes about each other demonstrates not so much self-hatred as the internal segmentation of their society (Ben-Amos 1973: 129).

7. A concern for stereotypical Jewish attributes or collective cultural personality such as answering questions with questions, concern for money, argumentativeness of Jews among themselves, and a propensity to joke (Nevo and Levine 1994: 127). Folktypes of community characters such as the *yente* (talkative female busybody), *shlimazl*, and *shlemiel* mark esoteric versions of Jewish traits, whereas in exoteric versions the identification of the Jew (often in contrast to other ethnic types of the 'black man' and 'Chinaman') signals behavioural stereotypes.

Although the emphasis in oral performances of Jewish themes had been on the historical context of immigrant and merchant life, the rise of print versions of Jewish jokes influenced a referential move to the last theme of stereotypical Jewish attributes or collective cultural personality. An implication of this move was that Jews were in fact less recognizable as an assimilated group in host countries. The play frame of the jokes, especially when contextualized by popular culture, appeared to mock Jewish foibles and implied the maintenance of a Jewish identity defining individuals and the solidity of their community. In so doing, the jokes raised the question of whether 'Jewish' was in fact a significant ethnic or even racialized category of modern life.

In the nineteenth century, Jewish advocates were concerned that a purported lack of humour among religious Jews discredited them from being part of an advanced civilization. Efforts in print and on stage were made to promote an ethnically distinctive humour among Jews to merit joining progressive, modern countries (Oring 1992: 116–21). In the twentieth century, a collective humorous tradition associated with the past could be read as a sign of integration, but it ran the risk of fuelling stereotypes that erected barriers between Jews and non-Jews. Scholars pointed out the decline of the Jewish joke as more than a loss of *yidishkeyt* ('Jewishness'); they correlated this decline with Jewish mobility out of separate communities and the subsequent loss of Jewish social bonds (Golden 1965: p. x; Telushkin 1992: 125–41; Zeitlin 1997: 17–24). Jewish civic leaders still worried about the persistence of antisemitic humour, but also postulated that with the increase of tolerance for, or deracialization of, Jews in middle-class society, the Jewish joke would go the way of stigmatized blackface minstrelsy (Rubin and Melnick 2006: 17–48; Telushkin 1992: 21–5). The remoteness of the Yiddish-speaking community from eastern Europe also contributed to the erosion of the dialect story, a mainstay of the post-immigrant Jewish generation. However, for many observers, the dialect joke was not Jewish anyway because its reliance on the immigrant malapropism could be located among many groups (Brandes 1983; Bronner 2006). These signs could be read to mean that the Jewish joke engine would stall on the global superhighway of the future-oriented Internet in the twenty-first century. Instead, posting of Jewish jokes by all measures has accelerated in digital media (Berger 2006: p. xii; Davies 2011: 4; Schachter 2008: p. x; Serracino-Inglott 2001).

Jewish humour, even for the unassimilated Orthodox, is hardly remote or esoteric on the Internet (Heilman 2006: 184). With a quick search, millions of jokes can be obtained. Although true for humour generally, the *Forward*, the largest American Jewish newspaper (now a magazine), saw fit to feature a news story on the growth of sites for Jewish jokes. 'From riddles and one-liners to satires and comic strips', the article proclaimed, 'the Internet's trove of Jewish humor goes on and on.' The author viewed the trend positively, with the comment, 'This is instant gratification at its best, funnies at your fingertips' (Solomont 2005). Nonetheless, he was careful to note those sites such as 'Bangitout' (www.bangitout.com) constituting 'a place where Jews can laugh at themselves'. The jokes selected to exemplify 'Bangitout', as in other sites such as 'A Word in Your Eye' (www.awordinyoureye.com), referred to revealing Jewish identity in popular culture: 'How do you know you are at a Jewish Thanksgiving meal?

Leftover vegetable kugel [baked casserole, usually with potato] is suddenly titled "stuffing".' According to the *Forward*, the 'Jewish Humor Yahoo! Group' (groups. yahoo.com/ groups/JewishHumor) was especially adept at poking fun at modern Jewish life, and one could note larger issues referenced, such as the recession at the time (an exemplary joke was 'Why did the man getting an *aliyah* [a ritual honour in synagogue] say his name was Sarah bat Moshe? He's having financial trouble and put everything in his wife's name.'

The Jewish Telegraphic Agency (JTA), the main international Jewish news agency, also took notice of the transmission of Jewish humour on the Internet, but expressed greater worry about whether this humour in an open, public medium would be perceived negatively. The digital-age story pointedly raised the question, 'What is the line between lighthearted parody and wicked satire? Between being "good for the Jews" and "bad for the Jews"?' (Klein 2009). Although not a new question aimed at non-Jewish appropriation of, and even Jewish production of humour for a wide audience, the query took on a new immediacy because, according to the JTA article, in the twenty-first century, 'people hang out . . . on Web sites'. Rather than the image of the silent reader taking in a joke book, on websites users produce and consume, and the result is often folkloric. An indication of the interactive process is in the response to the circulation of one video based on jokes about Jews eating Chinese food on Christmas. When asked for the source, a viewer commented, 'Oh my cousin from Argentina got it from his uncle in Israel who sent it to his doctor in California' (Klein 2009; see also Blank 2007). It is to the placement of 'Jewish jokes' on sites in the twenty-first century, where users in digital culture live, work, and play, that I now turn my analytical attention and answer the questions raised by the journalists noticing people connecting anew to Jewish jokes online.

Three Sites of the Jewish Joke in Digital Culture

Whether or not the Jewish joke continues to be told in the twenty-first century, it is arguably more evident than ever before because of the global visual medium of the Internet. A key feature of the Internet in digital culture is the ability to retransmit material without necessarily taking the role of 'teller'. The 'forwarding', 'retweeting', or 'reposting' of humour allows for a distancing of the teller from the material (Frank 2009; Hathaway 2005; Perz 2009). Users might even reinforce this transmittal objectivity with the introductory comment (or subject line) of 'FYI' (For your information) or 'Thought you'd be interested'. Although the computer eases the process of transmittal mechanically by taking away the pressure to perform, the question remains: why do so many users choose Jewish jokes to transmit, especially non-Jews who after all constitute the vast majority of computer users? One possibility is that the perception of Jewish jokes as historical artefacts or non-racialized material takes away the stigma of joke texts for some users. For many users, Jewish jokes are not as highly charged as the other major sources of ethnic humour in African American and Chinese material. One could also point to symbolic reasons for their circulation: many of the attributes of characters in Jewish jokes are visible in commercial culture (such as an obsession with money), feminization (in the roles of the Jewish mother and Jewish American Princess), and the witty or creative individual struggling in a dominant society (Baker 1986: 148–55; Dundes 1985; Foxman 2010; Reik 1962: 66–74).[3] These characterizations relate to the mass culture that acts as a foil for many computer users working within a transgressive play frame. In choosing the Jewish joke, users can project their concerns about massification, represented by the computer, to an external source that is relevant to their status. Indeed, many sites for Jewish jokes online differ from earlier print sources by having fewer references to the shtetl folktypes and more to the ordinary figure in a larger society who feels unjustly marginalized.

Even if this symbolic explanation holds, the spread of Jewish jokes online still seems curious in light of predictions of the decline or obsolescence of the defensive, self-deprecating Jewish joke and dialect story. Often torn from a performative context, Jewish jokes online convey ambiguous meanings (even more than in books, which have connections to an author or editor). As Elliott Oring points out, a website for humour is more like an archive than a repertoire or event, but it is an influential one because of its visibility in digital searches (2003: 129–30). Oral tradition operates editorially; jokes become transformed or eliminated from a repertoire (Oring 2003: 139). In a face-to-face communicative event, jokes frequently invite a 'comeback' and a narrative exchange. Jokes can be customized and selected for specific social conduits. In oral tradition, observers have assumed that the lines between antisemitic or exoteric lore could be clearly distinguished from esoteric or Jewish humour. Online, many joke sites labelled 'Jew jokes' are actually hate sites, while others are presented in conjunction with ethnic humour sites (Billig 2001; Weaver 2011). The division appears to signal a new era and definition for the non-performative Jewish joke.

To identify varieties of the frames or designs used for Jewish jokes in digital culture, I will discuss three renowned Jewish joke sites in an effort to identify patterns in online communication of ethnic humour and Jewishness. With digital culture, it is prudent not only to contemplate the intentions of a Jewish joke, if that is what the genre can be called, but also the response of a remote and disembodied viewer. A broader thesis than Freud's self-deprecation postulate based on the Jewishness of joke-tellers needs testing in online communication—especially because of the uncertain relation of a narrator to his or her subject, and the removal of context in drawing attention to a text or image.

One analytical strategy is to adapt anthropologist Gregory Bateson's contribution of frame theory to explain transgressive play (Bateson 1955; 1956). According to frame theory, the Jewish joke online can be viewed as metacommunicative by referring to an inherent paradox of its framed or stylized play, characteristic of structural incongruity: messages in the play frame deny the very rules that make play possible. People listen to jokes because they accept the idea that the material is located in time and place within reality, but will subvert that reality in the end. The fragile play frame is especially critical for jokes because the action of joking may often be interpreted as offensive and aggressive. As I have previously discussed, Internet sites foster metafolklore because of their interactive and visual features and therefore use metacommunication to provide a discourse of meaning in the absence of a 'real' material and social context.

In the physical frame of the computer screen, Jewish jokes online are arguably not about the Jewish joke. As metamessages, they use the ambiguity of the Internet frame to question Jewish joking, and ultimately Jewishness as a category between reality and fantasy. Frames are constructed by social actors who cognitively establish boundaries or symbolic oppositions of allowable 'play' and 'not play'. When the stylized actions of a group are challenged, the frame may be used to ask if this is 'play' and confront the need for, and meaning of, the play in relation to behaviour outside the frame (Bronner 2010; 2011; Mechling 2008; 2009). The Internet poses this kind of challenge because the actors involved may be invisible to one another and do not constitute a group in the usual sense, or because the ability to restrict a frame within the Internet's openness presents an obstacle to social construction.

For the purposes of a frame analysis, let me proceed from the most textual to most contextual of popular Internet sites featuring Jewish jokes. 'Jewish Jokes' was the top-ranked Jewish joke site retrieved from my Google search. The compiler is anonymous, but the site conveys its Jewish context by its welcoming rhetoric of 'Shalom', its traditional blue and white colour scheme, and a variety of Jewish networking links, including the Jewish online dating and social networking sites, 'Jdate', 'JewishSingles', and 'JewSchool'. Whether as an editorial statement or a sign of Jewishness, the prominent image next to the welcoming message is of a bearded, tallit-wearing man beckoning the viewer with his index finger in one hand and scissors in the other. When I asked a college-level class what this figure represented, my Jewish students recognized him as a *mohel*, a ritual circumciser, while the non-Jews thought of him as an 'old country' stereotype.[4] The difference was significant because the Jewish students interpreted the figure as signalling that the site contained 'insider' jokes relating to *yidishkeyt*, whereas the non-Jewish students anticipated stereotypical or antisemitic material, especially related to the traits of financial stinginess and ethnic difference. Gender was not as much of a predictor of perception as religious–ethnic identity.

Under the 'add a joke' tab, the site invites password-protected members to contribute jokes and then subject the texts to ratings. The joke-tellers are thus identified, although they can use monikers that disguise their ethnic background. In the listing of the latest jokes, Jewish references can be discerned from screen names such as 'moish' (a Yiddish nickname for the Jewish biblical patriarch Moshe or Moses), 'funnyJew', and 'alte kaker' (Yiddish: 'old shit' and idiomatically a 'geezer'), while there are other participants whose identity remains masked through less revealing handles like 'Tony', or 'chihuahualady'. Still, viewers scrolling through the lists get the impression that overall these are Jewish jokes from Jews. The pre-established categories for humour listed in alphabetical order are: 'American Jewish', 'Blue-Ish Jewish', 'British Jewish', 'European Jewish', 'Food', 'General Jewish', 'Health', 'Israeli', 'Jewish Mother', 'Rabbi', and 'Yiddish'.

'Jewish Jokes' presents a user-influenced voting forum that displays the site's top ten rated jokes on a scale of 1 to 5 (with 5 representing 'very good', while 1 stands for 'very poor'). The only perfect score is surprisingly not awarded to a joke in narrative form. It goes to a humorous image deriving from *The Simpsons* that depicts a scene of Krusty the Clown walking his dog through his old neighbourhood, which also happens to feature store windows that advertise for the barber, 'Fantastic Schlomo's: Payos Trims Two for One' (referring to bargain rhetoric of 'two for one' on an ultra-Orthodox Jew who has earlocks, or *peyes* in Yiddish), and a grocery store bearing an advertisement for 'I Can't Believe It's Not Trayfe' (a parody of a commercial advertisement for the margarine 'I Can't Believe It's Not Butter'). All of the other jokes rated in the range of a '4' rating are narratives involving Jewish denominationalism, Jewish figures such as rabbis, or Jewish/non-Jewish relations, often in an Old World context. Many of the low-rated jokes are in the Israeli category. The lowest-rated joke, for example, required esoteric information on the double meaning of falafel as food or as pips on a soldier's uniform:

There are two Israelis in the front of a car and an American in the back. One Israeli says to the other, look at that man and his falafels. So the American says, falafels, where? I am hungry.

Needing esoteric explanation of Hebrew slang, the joke falls flat. The content of the joke indicates a high-context frame because the knowledge necessary to appreciate the humour does not permeate the social conduit. The site distances narrator and viewer by not allowing comments on individual jokes, but it implies that humour can be key to social networking by facilitating the emailing of posted jests 'to a friend' and receiving jokes by email.

In 2017 'Jewish Jokes' went offline without warning, but 'A Word in Your Eye' increased in popularity , with 15,686 monthly unique visitors, according to data monitoring on SitePris.com. Like 'Jewish Jokes', 'A Word in Your Eye' has a rhetorical reference to its Jewishness with its welcoming message of 'Mazeltov, you have arrived at the best website for Jewish jokes and Jewish humour available today.' The homepage screen is multicoloured but contains no visual icons. The site has the look of an archive with enumerated sets of jokes. However, unlike

'Jewish Jokes', 'A Word in Your Eye' has a clear back-story and moderator behind its production. The site began in 2000 when David Minkoff, a Jew from London, established the site to share, in his words, 'what I feel are the best Jewish jokes around'. He claims oral sources for his jokes, including schoolmates, family, friends, co-workers, the changing rooms at the Maccabi football club,[5] friends at his Israeli dance class, and his rabbi. Minkoff does not identify his sources, but implies that his Jewish jokes in fact represent Jewish tellers. As of May 2017, the site contained over 2,900 jokes organized into 171 sets of jokes under the categories: 'Jewish Jokes', 'Naughtier Jewish Jokes', 'Kosher Lateral Thinking', 'Material for Speeches', 'Jewish Jokes for Children', and 'Non-Jewish Jokes'.[6] With the framing device of designating Jewish jokes by what they are not, one notices that the three sets of Jewish jokes mostly concern modern institutions or situations, such as finance, education, marriage, and health. A few are about priests to act as a counterpoint to the rabbi jokes contained within the Jewish jokes.

The establishment of humour in 'A Word in Your Eye' outside the Jewish play frame also brings up another rhetorical strategy in the presentation of the jokes. Minkoff insists that the jokes' selection be made on the basis of their funniness, but couches them in nostalgia for a past world of *yidishkeyt*. From the site, he published two joke books with the Yiddish 'Oy!' in the title: *Oy! The Ultimate Book of Jewish Jokes* (2005) and *Oy Vey: More! The Ultimate Book of Jewish Jokes Part 2* (2008). His introduction in the first volume nostalgically connects the Jewish joke to life in the Jewish community and a past age:

I grew up in a Jewish household (my father was a kosher butcher and poulterer) so I was surrounded by Jewish culture. I started collecting jokes from the age of thirteen. Don't all boys get a book on Jewish customs and folklore as one of their Bar Mitzvah presents (as well as umbrellas, a *siddur*—or prayer book—and fountain pens)? (Minkoff 2005: p. ix)

His pride in the number of jokes compiled on the site insists on the value of the Jewish label while also representing the relic nature of its community in modern life.

More than the previous two sites, 'Old Jews Telling Jokes' takes advantage of the visual quality of the Internet's capability of uploading and subsequently streaming. The site contains videos of Jews over 60 years of age telling jokes. Although not all the jokes are about Jewish topics, they associate Jews with being funny because of their heritage, culturally induced delivery, or collective personality. Animated tellers set against a plain white background are introduced by klezmer music associated with *yidishkeyt*. Belying the site's modern media look, however, is the notion that the prime transmitters of the Jewish joke are 'old people'. The performers are presented in contrast to 'digital natives', who are assumed to be young, assimilated, and cosmopolitan rather than ethnic and non-technologically oriented (Prensky 2010). The aged performers often inflect their stories with a Yiddish accent and conclude with a laugh track, thereby reinforcing the Jewish joke as a product of nostalgia.

The producer, director, and editor of 'Old Jews Telling Jokes' is Sam Hoffman, who garnered notice with directorial credits behind mass-market hits such as *It's Complicated* (2009), *The Producers* (2005), *School of Rock* (2003), *The Royal Tenenbaums* (2001), and *Dead Man Walking* (1995). Hoffman describes the twenty-first century beginnings of the site in his hometown of Highland Park, New Jersey, with twenty of his father's friends and relatives. Emphasizing the narrative of the Jewish joke, he cast people he thought could 'tell a good story'. Hoffman decided that no joke teller could be younger than 60 years old because he 'wanted a lifetime of experience to infuse these jokes' (Hoffman 2010: p. viii). He filmed individuals in technologically advanced studios in Los Angeles and New York City. Within a year, he claimed that the jokes had been seen six million times and had gone viral, which he had to explain to the pre-digital tellers (labelled 'digital immigrants' by Prensky (2010)) was a 'good thing'. Implying the metamessage of the Jewish jokes within the play frame, Hoffman notes that on the archival, instantaneous Internet, the videos represent the performative memory of Jewish jokes. According to Hoffman, Jewish jokes as old jokes 'get passed around and around, sometimes for decades. The jokes themselves become time capsules, revealing the fears and anxieties and celebrating the joys of all aspects of life, including its end' (p. viii). In Hoffman's book (2010) describing the success of the website, he proceeds from the immigrant age topics of the Jewish mother and coming to America to modern situations of the suburbs and retirement in Florida. The last two situations exemplify the representativeness with Jewish symbolism of a broader pattern of commercialism, individualism, and modernization.

As if to question the vibrancy of Jewish culture with the fading of the Jewish joke, Hoffman ends his book with jokes about death. An exemplary joke in Hoffman's collection refers to the transition of authentic Jewish artefacts to nostalgia in the post-Jewish context. Considering the title of the site is 'Old Jews Telling Jokes', the opening line is startling—'The old man is dying.' It continues:

He calls his son into his bedroom. 'Sammy', he says, 'I can smell all the way up here that your mother is downstairs in the kitchen, baking rugelach. You know that your mother's rugelach is my favorite thing in the world. I'm sure that this will be the last thing I'll ever eat. Would you please go downstairs and get me some?'

Sammy leaves the room. Five minutes go by. Ten minutes.

Fifteen minutes later, Sammy returns to this father's bedroom. Empty-handed.

'Sammy', the old man says, 'where's the rugelach?'

'Pop', Sammy says sheepishly, 'Mom says they're for after the funeral.' (Hoffman 2010: 225)

In a version that demands more esoteric Jewish knowledge, the *rugelach* are for the *shiva* (seven-day period of mourning) (Lowitt 2006; Platt 2011; Rozakis 2007: 92). The food is associated with eastern European cuisine, and the joke uses this detail for the significance of nostalgia as the younger generation contemplates the passing of Sammy (in oral versions the character is often rendered as the *zayde*, or grandfather). The old man, and his *yidishkeyt*, is a thing of the past. His pleasure in eating *rugelach* has been transferred into a symbol by the dominating Jewish mother of the New World for the broader society. The mother reverses the expectations of evoking memory with a future orientation characteristic of modern culture.

In one featured joke at the close of 'Old Jews Telling Jokes', the text appears to make a reference to the listing of jokes on the Internet. The joke raises the question of whether an archived joke still has life. In the metamessage of a joke about jokes, folklorists will recognize a migratory narrative adapted for a Jewish, or modern, context:

This guy goes to prison. He's very scared. The first day he's eating lunch, and when lunch is over he sees one of the inmates get up on the table and say, 'Thirty-two!' and everybody in the whole place laughs. And then he says, 'Sixty-eight!' and people are roaring. The new prisoner says to the guy next to him, 'What's going on?' The guy next to him says, 'Well, you know, we've all been here so long, we've heard all the jokes. We've memorized them, so we don't have to retell them. We just say the number, and people remember it, and then they laugh.' Well, this guy just thinks that's terrific. So he spends the entire next year memorizing and practicing all of the jokes. He's finally ready and he gets the nerve to try it. He stands up on the table and shouts, 'Fifty-five!' Dead silence. He can't believe it. He thinks for a moment and says, 'Seventy-four!' Again the room is completely still. The other inmates stare at him. He starts to panic. So he picks the surefire one. He says, 'One hundred and three!' Nothing happens. He goes back to his seat. He says to the guy next to him, 'What happened? What went wrong?' The guy says, 'Well, some people can tell a joke, and some people just can't.' (Hoffman 2010: 237; M. Miller 2010; see also Barth 1987: 70–2; Dundes 1989: 34)

One might question how this narrative is a Jewish joke if there is not a single reference to a Jew or Jewish object. I have collected variants of this joke with the punchline/motifeme of 'some people can tell a joke, and some people can't' in other socially contextualized settings (such as a hunting camp or university dormitory). Indeed, the joke emphasizes the importance of oral delivery, but placed within the context of 'Old Jews Telling Jokes', it additionally questions the passing of a Jewish community in which 'we've all been here so long, we've heard all the jokes.' The 'new guy' cannot replicate the fantasy of the jokes or the reality of their experience in community. The website constructs a play frame on the site with old Jews, who are presumed to be funny, to create symbolic distance between old and new, and therefore create a paradox of a figure being connected to a group while being disconnected from its heritage. The new guy can recall the action but cannot maintain its practice.

Simcha Weinstein, author of *Shtick Shift* (2008), thinks that the Jewish joke of yore may be gone because of its struggle with the past need to disguise one's Jewish identity. In his view, a 'twenty-first century humor' has emerged with the Internet that honestly and often brutally declares narrators' Jewishness as an attitude rather than as an appearance, belief, or practice. Referring to Jon Stewart and Sacha Baron Cohen as popular, edgy performers who do not tell Jewish jokes but act 'Jewishly', Weinstein claims that these 'performers are firmly rooted in reality—or at least a twisted sense of reality that includes themselves in their parody of anti-Semitism. All very post-modern' (2008: 33). Considering the Jewish joke originally appeared as a response to oppression, in the context of the digital age he asks, 'What happens when the oppression largely disappears?' Weinstein's claim is that Jewish humour with its *shtick* (style of performance or distinctive content) of neurosis from the burdens of being rich and famous projects anxieties of being American. Jewish success is narratively used to reference the paradox of America being the wealthiest and most powerful nation in history, while suffering at home and abroad. This pattern of symbolizing Jews as success-oriented Americans may have been presaged by the Jewish American Princess joke and the comical figure of the nervous, feminized, '*nebbish*' Jewish male as commentaries on American consumerism and feminization (Dundes 1985).[7]

A way to categorize the paradoxical perception of the Jewish joke's meta-message in emerging digital play frames of the twenty-first century is in the concept of 'allosemitism'. The term emphasizes perception of otherness, from the Greek root *allos*, 'other', rather than hostility or adulation towards Jews. Sociologist Zygmunt Bauman characterizes the consumption of expressive material about Jews as affectively ambivalent, especially in a modern environment of tolerance, meaning that while use of the material can show either positive or negative emotion that is 'intense and extreme', it contains evidence of the opposite (Bauman 1998: 143–4; V. Weinstein 2005: 497–8). According to Bauman, the emerging psychology of allosemitism refers to the 'practice of setting the Jews apart as people radically different from all the others, needing separate concepts to describe and comprehend them and special treatment in all or most social intercourse—since the concepts and treatments usefully deployed when facing or dealing with other people or peoples, simply would not do' (Bauman 1993: 143). The possibility in this usage is that 'the Jew' in the postmodern or digital age becomes a cognitive category for a non-racialized other, a type close to, or actually part of, the normative culture, but one that needs differentiation, or at least projection onto the category of 'the Jew' from one's own social and economic anxieties about a differential identity within mass culture.

The dark side of projecting Jews as a broadly American malaise is apparent in the use of joke sites by hate groups to criticize moral decline and multiculturalism in America. The 'Jew Jokes' site at www.nazi-lauck-sdapao.com is sponsored by the neo-Nazi NSDAP (the Foreign Organization branch of the neo-Nazi National Socialist German Workers Party) based in Lincoln, Nebraska. In making the rhetorical move from 'Jewish' to 'Jew' in its adjective for the jokes, the site is establishing the Jew as a racial type possessing physical differences rather than an ethnic background. The site emphasizes joking questions similar to those found in *Truly Tasteless Jokes* (Knott 1982), but they are framed in a succession that follows more traditional racial slurs such as 'Why is the rhinoceros jealous of Jews? Jews have bigger noses.' They may also include propagandistic, antisemitic messages, such as 'What caused the Jew's biggest problem? The greatest man who ever lived, Adolf Hitler.' The site verifies Elliott Oring's contention that humour may appear on the Internet (Oring 2016: 129–46), but that its enactment or performance is not an unconscious sublimation of aggression as is often interpreted in oral tradition; instead, such humour is in fact deliberately and consciously used to exaggerate hostility (Oring 1992: 41–57). The play frame and its metamessages of paradox break down in hate-group sites because their design rarely mentions laughter or a concept of a fictive plane. Unlike the other sites, Jews are depicted not as integrating into society but as being in need of removal. According to rhetorical critic Simon Weaver, the racist site operates on the logic of exclusion and segregation, based on the observation of threat (Weaver 2011: 421). More paradoxical is the arrangement of jokes around the observation of integration and inclusion, such as 'Old Jews Telling Jokes', that rhetorically employs allosemitic strategies of simultaneous inferiorization and aggrandizement, to bring out the difference of the otherwise hidden minority group.

Not all humour sites are as overtly antisemitic and exclusive as the 'Jew Jokes' site, but many do manipulate their presentation in popular search engine results by framing their sites' content as humour to lure in visitors and incite racial hatred. An exemplar of the humour of hate is 'Racist-Jokes.com', set against a solid black background. The site's home page prominently displays its proud slogan: 'The face of Hate on the net!' Like the 'Jew Jokes' site, 'Racist-Jokes.com' again concentrates on joking questions and cartoons with stereotypical icons to 'spread the hate', in its words. The home page leaves little doubt about the illiberal agents of its creation when it clearly states that their provision of 'jokes based on race' is due to the fact that 'we're racist' (Weaver 2011: 418). The jokes are not categorized by content, but by group—'Jews', 'Arabs', 'Gooks', and 'Spics'. Additionally, a strong theme of homophobia runs through much of the content, along with support for what Simon Weaver categorizes as 'the hard right, white power, neo-Nazism and the Ku Klux Klan' (2011: 418). Trying to normalize the site's content, the designers include a traffic rank of over half a million visitors spread across the globe. These 'visitor counters' rhetorically reinforce the acceptability of visitors perusing the profane content on the website. Moreover, a high visitor count also helps to validate the site's very existence by creating an illusion of vernacular authority regarding its contents' acceptability as a legitimate storehouse for controversial or hate-inspired joke repertoires.

Appropriating the Jew in Digital Jewish Jokes

My survey of popular sites with Jewish joke content demonstrates the ambiguity of the Internet when dealing with humour. Sites often simulate the presence of a Jewish narrator to evoke an esoteric experience, even as the texts tend toward an exoteric understanding of the material. Being in an open cyberspace, however, such sites still appear to struggle with the difficulty of conveying stereotypes to an audience that may not share the same frame of reference. One way that such sites often deal with this virtual dilemma is to couch Jewish jokes as nostalgia for a past era and people. Without the Jewish narrator and in the absence of narrative, the Jewish joke online appears unsublimated and contemporary. Hence it is clearer in conveying antisemitism on hate-group sites, and even on normal humour sites that decontextualize jokes as metafolklore about American or modern conditions. Online, Jewish humour often comprises jokes without Jews and arguably is not about Jews. In contrast to Sigmund Freud's view of 'stories created by Jews', the Jewish joke online engages the transgressive qualities of cyber-modernity and signals a change in the Jew as cultural symbol in the twenty-first century from forms consistently expressed in the nineteenth and twentieth centuries. Jewish joke sites display the paradoxical features of allosemitism by appropriating the figure of Jews full of *yidishkeyt* and implicating them as the everyman lost in postmodern mass culture, a dumpy or neurotic character who is both revered and reviled.

Theodor Reik, who elaborated on Freud's ideas on Jewish projection of self-degradation in humour (Freud 1960), theorized a psychology of Jewish joking based on Jews' isolation in society and their wish for integration. Reik observed that many joke-tellers intentionally operate in the region 'between fright and laughter' to deal with difficult subjects (1962: 233). In a compact play frame, the effective joke evokes unconscious alarm, which is weakened by sharing social anxiety (equated with feelings of guilt) with the listener by the time the punchline rolls around. Reik speculated that the 'intensity of response' to Jewish jokes, at least among Jews, is due to the 'severity of Jewish moral notions, by the strict inhibitions and suppressions induced by religious education' (1962: 234). More than other jokes, he contended, Jewish jokes presuppose a 'certain emotional solidarity'. In other words, the modifier of Jewishness suggested a communal connection in the midst of the alienating or individualizing forces of modernization (Spalding 1969: p. xiv). In Reik's psychological take on oral performances of esoteric Jewish humour, 'the telling of Jewish jokes also has the unconscious aim of cementing the bond that was originally founded on certain common values, and on the awareness of the Jewish isolation within the nations in which they live' (Reik 1962: 236). Countering Kristol's disdain for Jewish jokes gone public, Reik was of the opinion that Jewish jokes spreading to widening circles of non-Jews should be read as social progress, because possession of the jokes in their play repertoire meant that boundaries had been broken down. Reik hypothesized that attitudes of self-hatred represented a 'masochistic-paranoid attitude' as a result of Jews' concealed desire to suffer (so to remain a community was at the root of Jewish humour) (1962: 227). With assimilation and social progress, Reik predicted, self-deprecatory humour would disappear (Booker 1992; Falk 1993; Gilman 1990).

The explosion of Jewish jokes in digital culture plays out a process in which non-Jews appropriate Jewish jokes because of what psychologist Patricia Wallace describes as their provision of 'socioemotional thaw' to the isolating 'chill' of individualized, often alienating work on the computer (1999: 18–19; see also Bronner 2009; Smith 1991). Jewish jokes are not alone as expressive material in this process, as folklorist Paul Smith observed at the dawn of the digital age, but the symbolism of Jewish jokes regarding secluded, enervated individuals, who negotiate between integrating into a large society and retaining a sense of membership in a group, is psychologically compelling in response to the anxieties of a growing digital culture. To be sure, Jewish jokes online still can serve the purposes of bigotry and hostility, but the dominant frame for digital play refers to the symbolic acquisition of Jewishness as a way to access membership of a group in a commercial, mass culture. The Internet has also facilitated the visualization, as well as the virtualization, of Jewish identity for Jews troubled by a loss of community. Jewish jokes, with their socio-emotional reference to *yidishkeyt*, have re-emerged online even more than on the street or stage to address the tradeoffs of assimilation and commercial success. Despite Kristol's obituary, the Jewish joke in the twenty-first century has not yet been laid to rest.

Notes

1   I use the concepts 'esoteric' and 'exoteric' in the sense suggested by Franz Boas of a cultural process involving the movement of specialized knowledge within a community (esoteric) to a dominant society (exoteric). See Boas 1902; 1938. William Hugh Jansen's (1959) problematic usage of the terms refers more to relative expressive content: esoteric refers to a group's folklore about itself and exoteric refers to a group's folklore about other groups (Bronner 1986: 109–10).

2   This particular joke can be found in the 'Off-Topic' forum on 'I'm not a racist, that's what's so insane about this' at the 'Civilization Fanatics Center' website, posted by 'jeps' on 2 June 2007 <https://forums.civfanatics.com/threads/im-not-a-racist-thats-whats-so-insane-about-this.225199/page-4> (accessed 21 Dec. 2017).

3   An indication of this thematic shift is a relative absence of six jokes identified as 'classic' in Richard Raskin's *Life is Like a Glass of Tea* (1992). With the exception of the Jewish mother joke (taken from Wilde's *Official Jewish Joke Book* (1974)) in Raskin's list, the classic jokes involve religious themes of rabbinical characters questioning the relationships of humans to God. Raskin cites publication histories of the individual jokes but does not chronicle their circulation on the Internet.

4   A *mohel* is a Hebrew-Yiddish term for a specialist trained in the practice of *brit milah* (circumcision for boys eight days after birth, as specified in Gen. 17: 1–4). The anxiety over circumcision and the view that the *bris* (Yiddish: circumcision) is a distinctive mark of Jewish identity have led to a large number of jokes in Jewish tradition, and may possibly constitute the reason for the website using the figure as a symbol for Jewish humour generally. For example, 'A Word in Your Eye' has a separate page for 'bris, circumcision, mohel jokes' (<http://tinyurl.com/87k7bb>). The 'naughtier' versions are visually represented in red type, in contrast to the tamer jokes in black. Jewish students also thought the Yiddish pronunciation of the figure sounded funny: *moyel* (perhaps because it sounds similar to the English mole or a Brooklyn accent pronouncing 'girl' as 'goil'; a comic song title, for example, is 'I Lost My Goil to a Mohel and Now I'm All Cut Up'). Most of the jokes involve wordplay such as the confusion of 'castration' and 'circumcision', or variable meanings of 'cut' and 'tips'. For example, riddle-jokes that were familiar to my Jewish students were 'Why did the *mohel* retire? He just couldn't cut it anymore', and 'Why did the rabbi want to be a *mohel*? The tips were good.' One *mohel* joke about the Internet requires esoteric knowledge: 'What is the proper blessing to recite before logging on to the Internet? *Modem anachnu lakh*.' One Jewish context for this joke is the reference to many blessings for everyday activities in Jewish tradition. Another is the familiar blessing of gratitude from the Amidah prayer, which begins *modim anaḥnu lakh* ('We shall thank you'). In relation to my thesis about commentary in the jokes about commercial mass culture, the replacement of modem for *modim* represents the replacement of God with the machine in modern digital culture.

5   Maccabi football clubs are Jewish soccer organizations. They take their name from the Maccabees, a nickname for the Hasmonaean dynasty who rebelled against the Seleucid empire to take control of Judaea in the second century BCE. For an example of a London Maccabi football club, see <http://www.londonlions.com> (accessed 31 Aug. 2017).

6   The site was active in the period I checked between December 2010 and January 2012. In that time Minkoff added 140 texts and included a banner stating 'The 135th set of Jewish jokes was added on 22nd December 2011.'

7   The demasculinized Jewish man as a *nebbish* (Yiddish: a fearful, scrawny, or unfortunate person) is often portrayed as dominated and intimidated by women, although he might be intelligent. In the modern American context, the Jewish *nebbish* is often equated with the technological or educated nerd (Brod 1995; Desser 2001: 278).

References

ADLER, HERMANN. 1893. 'Jewish Wit and Humour'. *Eclectic Magazine of Foreign Literature, Science, and Art*, New Series 57 (April): 530–8.

ALVIN, JULIUS. 1991. *Gross Jokes*. New York.

BAKER, RONALD L. 1986. *Jokelore: Humorous Folktales from Indiana*. Bloomington, Ind.

BARRICK, MAC. 1970. 'Racial Riddles and the Polack Joke'. *Keystone Folklore Quarterly*, 15: 3–15.

BARTH, JOHN. 1987. *The Tidewater Tales: A Novel*. Baltimore, Md.

BATESON, GREGORY. 1955. 'A Theory of Play and Fantasy: A Report on Theoretical Aspects of the Project for the Study of the Role of Paradoxes of Abstraction in Communication'. In American Psychiatric Association, *Approaches to the Study of Human Personality*. Psychiatric Research Reports 2, 39–51.

BATESON, GREGORY. 1956. 'The Message "This Is Play"'. In Bertram Schaffner, ed., *Group Processes: Transactions of the Second Conference on Group Processes*, 145–242. New York.

BAUMAN, ZYGMUNT. 1998. 'Allosemitism: Premodern, Modern, Postmodern'. In Bryan Cheyette and Laura Marcus, eds., *Modernity, Culture, and 'the Jew'*, 143–56. Stanford, Calif.

BEN-AMOS, DAN. 1973. 'The 'Myth' of Jewish Humor'. *Western Folklore*, 32: 112–31.

BERGER, ARTHUR ASA. 2006. *The Genius of the Jewish Joke*. New Brunswick, NJ.

BILLIG, MICHAEL. 2001. 'Humour and Hatred: The Racist Jokes of the Ku Klux Klan'. *Discourse & Society*, 12: 267–89.

BIRO, ADAM. 2001. *Two Jews on a Train: Stories from the Old Country and the New*. Chicago.

BLANK, TREVOR J. 2007. 'Examining the Transmission of Urban Legends: Making the Case for Folklore Fieldwork on the Internet'. *Folklore Forum*, 37: 15–26.

—— 2009. 'Toward a Conceptual Framework for the Study of Folklore and the Internet'. In Trevor J. Blank, ed., *Folklore and the Internet: Vernacular Expression in a Digital World*, 1–20. Logan, Utah.

—— ed. 2012. *Folk Culture in the Digital Age: The Emergent Dynamics of Human Interaction*. Logan, Utah.

BLUMENFELD, GERRY. 1965. *Some of My Best Jokes Are Jewish!* New York.

BOAS, FRANZ. 1902. 'The Ethnological Significance of Esoteric Doctrines'. *Science*, 16: 872–74.

—— 1938. 'Mythology and Folklore'. In Franz Boas, ed., *General Anthropology*, 109–26. Boston, Mass.

BOOKER, JANICE L. 1992. *The Jewish American Princess and Other Myths: The Many Faces of Self-Hatred*. New York.

BOYER, JAY. 1993. 'The *Schlemiezel*: Black Humor and the *Shtetl* Tradition'. In Avner Ziv and Anat Zajdman, eds., *Semites and Stereotypes: Characteristics of Jewish Humor*, 3–12. Westport, Conn.

BRAD. 2008. *Two Jews Three Opinions*. Weblog. <http://tinyurl.com/2Jews3Opinions-Blog> (accessed 24 Oct. 2017).

BRANDES, STANLEY. 1983. 'Jewish-American Dialect Jokes and Jewish-American Identity'. *Jewish Social Studies*, 45: 233–40.

BROD, HARRY. 1995. 'Of Mice and Supermen: Images of Jewish Masculinity'. In T. M. Rudavsky, ed., *Gender and Judaism: The Transformation of Tradition*, 279–93. New York.

BRONNER, SIMON J. 1986. *American Folklore Studies: An Intellectual History*. Lawrence, Kans.

—— 2006. 'Dialect Stories'. In Simon J. Bronner, ed., *The Encyclopedia of American Folklife*, 307–10. Armonk, NY.

—— 2009. 'Digitizing and Virtualizing Folklore'. In Trevor J. Blank, ed., *Folklore and the Internet: Vernacular Expression in a Digital World*, 21–66. Logan, Utah.

—— 2010. 'Framing Folklore: An Introduction'. *Western Folklore*, 69: 5–27.

—— 2011. 'Framing Violence and Play in American Culture'. *Journal of Ritsumeikan Social Sciences and Humanities*, 3: 145–60.

CORRELL, TIMOTHY CORRIGAN. 1997. 'Associative Context and Joke Visualization'. *Western Folklore*, 56: 317–30.

CRAY, ED. 1964. 'The Rabbi Trickster'. *Journal of American Folklore*, 87: 331–45.

DAVIES, CHRISTIE. 1990. *Ethnic Humor Around the World*. Bloomington, Ind.

—— 2011. *Jokes and Targets*. Bloomington, Ind.

DEL NEGRO, GIOVANNA P. 2010. 'From the Nightclub to the Living Room: Party Records of Three Jewish Women Comics'. In Simon J. Bronner, ed., *Jews at Home: The Domestication of Identity*, Jewish Cultural Studies 1, 188–216. Oxford.

DESSER, DAVID. 2001. 'Jews in Space: The "Ordeal of Masculinity" in Contemporary American Film and Television'. In Murray Pomerance, ed., *Ladies and Gentlemen, Boys and Girls: Gender in Film at the End of the Twentieth Century*, 267–82. Albany, NY.

DOUGLAS, MARY. 1968. 'The Social Control of Cognition: Some Factors in Joke Perception'. *Man*, 3: 361–76.

DUNDES, ALAN. 1962. 'From Etic to Emic Units in the Structural Study of Folktales'. *Journal of American Folklore*, 75: 95–105.

—— 1966. 'Metafolklore and Oral Literary Criticism'. *Monist*, 50: 505–16.

—— 1971. 'A Study of Ethnic Slurs: The Jew and the Polack in the United States'. *Journal of American Folklore*, 84: 186–203.

—— 1981. 'Many Hands Make Light Work or Caught in the Act of Screwing in Light Bulbs'. *Western Folklore*, 40: 261–6.

—— 1985. 'The J.A.P. and the J.A.M. in American Jokelore'. *Journal of American Folklore*, 98: 456–75.

—— 1989. *Folklore Matters*. Knoxville, Tenn.

—— 1997. *Cracking Jokes: Studies of Sick Humor Cycles and Stereotypes*. Berkeley, Calif.

—— and CARL R. PAGTER. 1978. *Work Hard and You Shall Be Rewarded: Urban Folklore from the Paperwork Empire*. Bloomington, Ind.

EILBIRT, HENRY. 1981. *What Is a Jewish Joke? An Excursion into Jewish Humor*. Northvale, NJ.

ERDMAN, HARLEY. 1997. *Staging the Jew: The Performance of an American Ethnicity, 1860–1920*. New Brunswick, NJ.

FALK, AVNER. 1993. 'The Problem of Mourning in Jewish History'. In L. Bryce Boyer, Ruth M. Boyer, and Stephen M. Sonnenberg, eds., *The Psychoanalytic Study of Society, Volume 18: Essays in Honor of Alan Dundes*, 299–316. Hillsdale, NJ.

FISCHMAN, FERNANDO. 2011. 'Using Yiddish: Language Ideologies, Verbal Art, and Identity among Argentine Jews'. *Journal of Folklore Research*, 48: 37–61.

FOOTE, MONICA. 2007. 'Userpicks: Cyber Folk Art in the Early 21st Century'. *Folklore Forum*, 37: 27–38.

FOX, WILLIAM S. 1983. 'Computerized Creation and Diffusion of Folkloric Materials'. *Folklore Forum*, 16: 5–20.

FOXMAN, ABRAHAM H. 2010. *Jews and Money: The Story of a Stereotype*. New York.

FRANK, RUSSELL. 2009. 'The *Forward* as Folklore: Studying E-Mailed Humor'. In Trevor J. Blank, ed., *Folklore and the Internet: Vernacular Expression in a Digital World*, 98–122. Logan, Utah.

FREUD, SIGMUND. 1960 [1905]. *Jokes and Their Relation to the Unconscious*, trans. James Strachey. New York.

FRIEDLANDER, JUDITH. 2011. 'Typical Jokes in the Shtetl'. *Jews and Mexicans: Here and There*. <http://tinyurl.com/6y79vfc> (accessed 24 Oct. 2017).

FRIEDMAN, WILLIAM S. 1912. 'Report of Committee on Church and State'. In Samuel Schulman and Solomon Foster, eds., *Yearbook of the Central Conference of American Rabbis, Volume XXII*, 101–18. New York.

GILMAN, ANDER L. 1990. *Jewish Self-Hatred: Anti-Semitism and the Hidden Language of the Jews*. Baltimore, Md.

GOLDEN, HARRY. 1965. 'Introduction'. In Immanuel Olsvanger, ed., *Röyte Pomerantsen: Jewish Folk Humor*, pp. vii–xv. New York.

HATHAWAY, ROSEMARY V. 2005. '"Life in the TV"': The Visual Nature of 9/11 Lore and its Impact on Vernacular Response'. *Journal of Folklore Research*, 42: 33–56.

HEILMAN, SAMUEL C. 2006. *Sliding to the Right: The Contest for the Future of American Jewish Orthodoxy*. Berkeley, Calif.

HOFFMAN, SAM. 2010. *Old Jews Telling Jokes*. New York.

HOWARD, ROBERT GLENN. 2011. *Digital Jesus: The Making of a New Christian Fundamentalist Community on the Internet*. New York.

JANSEN, WILLIAM HUGH. 1959. 'The Esoteric-Exoteric Factor in Folklore'. *Fabula: Journal of Folktale Studies*, 2: 205–11.

JENKINS, HENRY. 2008. *Convergence Culture: Where Old and New Media Collide*. New York.

JENNINGS, KARLA. 1990. *The Devouring Fungus: Tales of the Computer Age*. New York.

KATZ, NAOMI, and ELI KATZ. 1971. 'Tradition and Adaptation in American Jewish Humor'. *Journal of American Folklore*, 84: 215–20.

KLEIN, AMY. 2009. 'YouTube Jews'. *Jewish Chronicle* (31 Mar.) <http://thejewishchronicle.net/view/full_story/2210743/article-YouTube-Jews> (accessed 31 Aug. 2017).

KNOTT, BLANCHE. 1982. *Truly Tasteless Jokes*. New York.

KRISTOL, IRVING. 1951. 'Is Jewish Humor Dead? The Rise and Fall of the Jewish Joke'. *Commentary*, 12 (1 Jan.), 431–6 <http://www.commentarymagazine.com/viewarticle.cfm/is-jewish-humor-dead-br-em-the-rise-and-fall-of-the-jewish-joke-em–1367> (accessed 31 Aug. 2017).

LOWITT, BRUCE. 2006. 'They're for the Shiva'. *Jewish Sightseeing* (4 July) <http://www.jewishsightseeing.com/jewish_humor/punchlines_and_their_jokes/2006-07-04-Number%2093.htm> (accessed 24 Oct. 2017).

MECHLING, JAY. 2008. 'Gun Play'. *American Journal of Play*, 1: 192–209.

——— 2009. 'Is Hazing Play?' In Cindy Dell Clark, ed., *Transactions at Play: Play & Culture Studies*, 45–62. Lanham, Md.

MICHAELS, RALF. 2006. 'Two Economists, Three Opinions? Economic Models for Private International Law—Cross-Border Torts as Example'. *Duke Law Faculty Scholarship*. Paper 1234 <http://scholarship.law.duke.edu/faculty_scholarship/1234> (accessed 31 Aug. 2017).

MICHAELSON, JAY. 2006. 'Two Lawyers, Three Opinions: On the Jewishness of Law, and Vice Versa'. *Jewish Daily Forward* (3 Nov.) <http://www.forward.com/articles/7395/.> (accessed 31 Aug. 2017).

MILLER, CAROLYN. 1993. 'Are Jews Funnier than Non-Jews?' In Avner Ziv and Anat Zajdman, eds., *Semites and Stereotypes: Characteristics of Jewish Humor*, 13–28. Westport, Conn.

MILLER, MICHAEL. 2010. 'Jokes in Prison'. *Old Jews Telling Jokes*. Posted 10 March <http://www.oldjewstellingjokes.com/2010/03/11/michael-miller-jokes-in-prison/> (accessed 31 Aug. 2017).

MINKOFF, DAVID. 2005. *Oy! The Ultimate Book of Jewish Jokes*. New York.

—— 2008. *Oy Vey: More! The Ultimate Book of Jewish Jokes Part 2*. New York.

MITCHELL, CAROL. 1985. 'Some Differences in Male and Female Joke-Telling'. In Rosan A. Jordan and Susan J. Kalčik, eds., *Women's Folklore, Women's Culture*, 163–86. Philadelphia, Pa.

NEVO, OFRA, and JACOB LEVINE. 1994. 'Jewish Humor Strikes Again: The Outburst of Humor in Israel during the Gulf War'. *Western Folklore*, 53: 125–45.

OLSVANGER, IMMANUEL, ed. 1965. *Röyte Pomerantsen: Jewish Folk Humor*. New York.

ORING, ELLIOTT. 1983. 'The People of the Joke: On the Conceptualization of a Jewish Humor'. *Western Folklore*, 42: 261–71.

—— 1992. *Jokes and Their Relations*. Lexington, Ky.

—— 2003. *Engaging Humor*. Urbana, Ill.

—— 2016. *Joking Asides: The Theory, Analysis, and Aesthetics of Humor*. Logan, Utah.

PARADISE, VIOLA. 1913. 'The Jewish Immigrant Girl in Chicago'. *Survey*, 30 (6 Sept.): 700–4.

PERZ, SALLY ANNE. 2009. 'Are You Forwarding Folklore?' *Family Times*, 2 (Nov./Dec.), 1–2.

PLATT, ROBERTA. 2011. 'Shloime is Dying'. *Old Jews Telling Jokes*. Posted 4 May <http://www.oldjewstellingjokes.com/?s=shloime+is+dying> (accessed 31 Aug. 2017).

PRESTON, MICHAEL J. 1996. 'Computer Folklore'. In Jan Harold Brunvand, ed., *American Folklore: An Encyclopedia*, 154–5. New York.

PRENSKY, MARC. 2010. *Teaching Digital Natives: Partnering for Real Learning*. Thousand Oaks, Calif.

RASKIN, RICHARD. 1992. *Life Is Like a Glass of Tea: Studies of Classic Jewish Jokes*. Aarhus, Denmark.

REIK, THEODOR. 1962. *Jewish Wit*. New York.

ROSTEN, LEO. 1968. *The Joys of Yiddish*. New York.

ROZAKIS, LAURIE. 2007. *The Portable Jewish Mother*. Avon, Mass.

RUBIN, RACHEL, and JEFFREY MELNICK. 2006. *Immigration and American Popular Culture: An Introduction*. New York.

SAPER, BERNARD. 1993. 'Since When Is Jewish Humor Not Anti-Semitic?' In Avner Ziv and Anat Zajdman, eds., *Semites and Stereotypes: Characteristics of Jewish Humor*, 71–86. Westport, Conn.

SCHACHTER, STANLEY J. 2008. *Laugh for God's Sake: Where Jewish Humor and Jewish Ethics Meet*. Jersey City, NJ.

SERRACINO-INGLOTT, PETER. 2001. 'To Joke or Not To Joke: A Diplomatic Dilemma in the Age of Internet'. In Jovan Kurbalija and Hannah Slavik, eds., *Language and Diplomacy*, 21–38. Msida, Malta.

SMITH, PAUL. 1991. 'The Joke Machine: Communicating Traditional Humour Using Computers'. In Gillian Bennett, ed., *Spoken in Jest*, 257–78. Sheffield.

SOLOMONT, E. B. 2005. 'Point, Click, Chuckle: Jewish Humor Goes Online'. *Jewish Daily Forward* (4 Feb.) <http://www.forward.com/articles/2879/> (accessed 31 Aug. 2017).

SPALDING, HENRY D. 1969. 'Preface'. In Henry D. Spalding, ed., *Encyclopedia of Jewish Humor: From Biblical Times to the Modern Age*, pp. xiii–xix. New York.

——1976. 'Introduction'. In Henry D. Spalding, ed., *A Treasure-Trove of American Jewish Humor*, pp. xiii–xvii. Middle Village, NY.

TELUSHKIN, JOSEPH. 1992. *Jewish Humor: What the Best Jewish Jokes Say About Jews.* New York.

TURKLE, SHERRY. 2011. *Alone Together: Why We Expect More from Technology and Less from Each Other.* New York.

WALLACE, PATRICIA. 1999. *The Psychology of the Internet.* New York.

WEAVER, SIMON. 2011. 'Jokes, Rhetoric and Embodied Racism: A Rhetorical Discourse Analysis of the Logics of Racist Jokes on the Internet'. *Ethnicities*, 11: 413–35.

WEINSTEIN, SIMCHA. 2008. *Shtick Shift: Jewish Humor in the 21st Century.* Fort Lee, NJ.

WEINSTEIN, VALERIE. 2005. 'Dissolving Boundaries: Assimilation, and Allosemitism in E.A. Dupont's *Das alte Gesetz* (1923) and Veit Harlan's *Jud Süs* (1940)'. *German Quarterly*, 78: 496–516.

WILDE, LARRY. 1974. *The Official Jewish Joke Book.* New York.

——1980. *The Last Official Jewish Joke Book.* New York.

WISSE, RUTH. 2013. *No Joke: Making Jewish Humor.* Princeton, NJ.

ZAUDERER, DAVID. 2011. 'Two Jews, Three Opinions'. *Torah from Dixie* <http://www.tfdixie.com/parshat/korach/013.htm> (accessed 24 Oct. 2017).

ZEITLIN, STEVE. 1997. 'Introduction'. In Steve Zeitlin, ed., *Because God Loves Stories: An Anthology of Jewish Storytelling*, 17–24. New York.

ZIV, AVNER. 1998. 'Introduction to the Transaction Edition'. In Avner Ziv, ed., *Jewish Humor*, 5–16. New Brunswick, NJ.

PART III

Virtual Spaces for Jews in a Digital Age

Going Online to Go 'Home': *Yizkor* Books, Cyber-Shtetls, and Communities of Location

RACHEL LEAH JABLON

'The production of hereness in the absence of actualities depends increasingly on virtualities.' (Kirshenblatt-Gimblett 1998: 169)

ONLINE *yizkor* (memorial) books and shtetls—'cyber-shtetls'—give access to the places where Jewish life once flourished that are otherwise inaccessible, primarily because of the Holocaust. These resources attract users who seek information about a specific place, generating Jewish communities based on location. These communities draw attention to changes in contemporary Jewish identity formation and the mediation of Jewish social connection in the digital age. Instead of focusing on a Jewish way of life or Jewish lineage, these communities are based on their members' geographical origin. From as microcosmic an issue as which street in which neighbourhood, to as macrocosmic a concept as the region in which a particular dialect is spoken, the site where a person considers 'home' to be leads to a sense of community that may supersede kinship as a defining feature, especially in the wake of the Holocaust when the concept of family changed irrevocably. Accordingly, online *yizkor* books and cyber-shtetls give people who are searching for 'home' a place to go. My contention in this essay is that the space that they occupy on the Web is a surrogate for the real thing.

Benedict Anderson (1991) argues that the metropolitan daily newspaper representing a convergence of market capitalism and print technology emerging at the start of the Industrial Revolution served to forge communities (1991: 25–8). Similarly, with the advent of the Digital Age, cyber-shtetl websites offer users an experience that, to use Anderson's words, is 'replicated . . . by thousands (or millions) of others of whose existence [they are] confident, yet of whose identity [they have] not the slightest notion' (1991: 35). The resulting 'communities of location' are so salient in Jewish life and culture that Yiddish has a set of words to describe people who come from one geographic place. A person who comes from the same place as another person is called a *landsman*; the community of people coming from the same place is a *landslayt*; and an organization of all the people who come from the same place is a *landsmanshaft*. *Landsmanshaftn*—more than one *landsmanshaft*—were central to the development and well-being of Jewish immigrant communities from the late nineteenth to the late twentieth centuries in the United States, Israel, and other places where Jews relocated (Bronner 2001; Kliger 1989: 406). Regardless of kinship, the fact that two people could have had the same teacher or gone to the same butcher or shared the same idiomatic expressions made them feel more comfortable in their new and often difficult surroundings. For some *landsmen*, in fact, these communities based on place came to replace communities based on kinship. Gershon Zik, for example, writes in a description of the global network of *landsmanshaftn* from Rozhishche, Ukraine, that '[i]t is as though we were all one family' (Zik 1976: 53). For a *land-slayt*, the common experiences in or memories of a particular place are founda-tions for communal identity. *Landsmanshaftn* thus develop their social activities and other programmes out of a sense of this communal identity.

Jewish Communities of Location

The issue of geography is nothing new in Jewish life and culture. Some of the most basic alignments among Jews pertain to where those Jews are 'from'. Jews often navigate through the Jewish world by determining if someone is Ashkenazi or Sephardi, or from the American South or the Lower East Side. By playing 'Jew-ish geography', Jews better understand each other's perspectives and personali-ties. Communities of location suggest cultural practices, language and slang, foodways, dress, and even behaviour. The appeal of *landsmanshaftn*, indeed, is this very idea that places affect ways of life. Jews from Siedlce, a medium-sized Polish industrial town close to the Polish–Belarusian border (Yasni 1956), for example, lived differently from Jews in Flonheim, a small rural town in south-western Germany (Borut 1992). These differences are significant enough for each community to establish a *landsmanshaft* devoted to its members living in exile. The members of a *landsmanshaft* understand each other's customs and dialects, because they came from the same place.

  Part of what raises the 'Jewish question' (historically a phrase used primarily in Europe to pose the vexing questions of what makes a Jewish community and who is Jewish) is the way in which Jews claim their Judaism. According to Michael Fishbane (1987), there are two primary ways that Jews can be Jews: belief and ethnicity. Belief refers to the covenants between God and Abraham in Genesis 17 and God and Moses in Exodus 20 that lay out God's expectations of Abraham's and Moses' descendants, who will eventually be known as Jews. If someone believes in and adheres to the covenants, however interpreted, then that person is Jewish. Ethnicity, on the other hand, suggests that someone born into Judaism is also Jewish. However, ethnicity has two components: biology and geography (Sokolovskh and Tishkov 1996: 190–1). Being born into Judaism satisfies the biological component. In other words, according to most streams of Judaism, someone with a Jewish biological mother is also Jewish. A presumption is that Jewish mothers will transmit Jewish belief and practices to their children, thereby raising children who are Jewish both through ethnicity and belief. Other streams of Judaism, it should be noted, maintain that Jewish fathers and Jewish grandparents can also determine someone's membership in a Jewish community. In this way, biology—being born of Jewish parentage—generally satisfies a criterion for being Jewish.

The second component of ethnicity—geography—makes an appearance in Fishbane's work, although he does not make a direct link between being born into Judaism and where that person is born. He emphasizes that the word 'Judaism' comes from the region of the Mediterranean where Judaism as a system originated. Judea as a location is just as important to the development of Judaism as the expulsions from it. Bordered by hills and bodies of water, Judea was under the control of various empires that regulated its religious expression and day-to-day activity. Many aspects of Judaism developed in direct response to this territorial management. In fact, Judaism can still be seen as a direct response to its geographical centres. Delineations between Ashkenazi and Sephardi Judaism begin with differentiating between place and then distinguishing among consequent practices. In as much as Judaism is based on the belief in the Torah as the leading authority on Jewish tradition and law and on ancestry, it also depends on place as a characterizing feature. This issue of location as satisfying a criterion of being Jewish becomes more important as the Internet makes explorations of those locations easier and more illuminating.

Landsmanshaftn exemplify the concept of community of place; their reason for being is, in fact, to foster communities of location. Known as mutual aid or benevolent societies, they organized social events, provided health insurance, held fundraisers, offered burial plots, and sent money and other resources to their *landslayt* 'back home'. Eventually, according to Hannah Kliger, members of *landsmanshaftn* realized that efforts to help their communities in Europe were futile because of the devastation wrought by the Second World War and the Holocaust (Kliger 1989: 407). They then turned their attention to publishing items that would remind them of home, that would preserve in some small way what Hitler and his supporters sought to eradicate. As Rosemary Horowitz writes, '[t]he books are proof that Hitler's final solution to exterminate the Jews failed' (2002: 41). *Landsmanshaftn* took it upon themselves to mitigate the damage caused by the Holocaust, the decreased numbers instigated by emigration, and the changes in lifestyle triggered by modernity.

Before the ubiquitous use of the Internet to find such information, *landsmanshaftn* maintained and offered the most complete information about their communities. Because many of the physical communities in which Jews lived before the Holocaust have been destroyed, they cannot be visited or experienced.

Nobody can see how Jews lived their lives, learn about developments in those places, or experience what Jewish life is like there now. Vivian M. Patraka calls this phenomenon 'goneness' (1999). It is the feeling that the destruction of the communities and the people living in them has far greater ramifications, that the destruction precludes any kind of reconstruction, renovation, or reparation, that there will be no later generations to carry on. Patraka quotes performance artist Leeny Sack as someone who performs the 'gone'—that which really cannot (or should not?) be performed: 'I sit inside the memory of where I was not' (Patraka 1999: 5). Sack's statement refers to the idea that later generations feel the trauma induced by the Holocaust, even though they did not experience it directly. What existed before and during the Holocaust is gone, never to 'be' again. 'Goneness' is different from 'absence' in that absence implies the possibility of reappearance, whereas 'goneness' negates such a possibility. In light of 'goneness', communities of location that arise from online *yizkor* books and cyber-shtetls are even more special because there are no physical points of reference. All of these communities are based on virtualities.

There are materials, though, that provide insight into the lives of Jews over the centuries. First are visual depictions. These representations depend entirely on the technology of the times, and are thus limited in scope. The Yiddish film industry, for example, reached its peak in the 1930s (Hoberman 1991) and by and large produced no 'period pieces', depicting contemporaneous scenes instead of reconstructions of the past. Photography was limited by the bulkiness and expense of the equipment. Families had portraits taken when they could afford to do so, usually at times of joyous life-cycle events, such as when a couple married or a child was born. The scarce family photographs that still exist offer a lot of information if viewers know what they are looking at. The clothing worn by subjects alone may provide clues to date, location, climate, and social class, all of which Jewish genealogy enthusiasts often long to know about their ancestors. However, these signs are hard to decode because there are so few references to help, particularly for viewers who are unfamiliar with them. Other visual media, such as newsreels and postcards, are driven by a different kind of rhetoric, so are often harder to decipher. For example, the films were made for people who were probably 'in the know'. Film-makers do not seem to have been intent on educating their audiences or propagandizing Jewish life. Photographs also targeted viewers who knew what or who they were looking at. Newsreels, on the other hand, were usually designed for mass consumption. News stories were supposedly represented with journalistic objectivity, yet depictions of shtetl life or Jews in cities may have been exaggerated, in order to elicit sympathy from viewers for war efforts or for some similar deliberate effect. Postcards may have exoticized Jewish life to make a point of the difference between the senders' and recipients' circumstances. In any event, there is not nearly enough of these materials to enable a thorough understanding of Jewish life, especially without the subjects present to explain their experience.

The second kind of information that provides clues to how Jews lived before the Holocaust is written material. It often comprises documents that shaped or recorded Jews' day-to-day activities: town charters, meeting minutes, school records, health records, personal diaries, contracts, invoices, and other materials. These documents are priceless resources, but many were destroyed along with the buildings that contained them, many have sustained damage over time, and many lack explanation or cultural contextualization.

Online *Yizkor* Books

A third resource, and one of the foci of this chapter, falls under the generic title 'Jewish memorial book', or *yizkor* book. Although the two kinds of sources mentioned above—visual and written material—are contemporaneous with the communities they document, *yizkor* books are mostly retrospective in nature. They combine visual images and documentary sources with explanations and are a unique type of source material. Though sometimes considered faulty by historians because of their reliance on personal narrative, the wealth of information contained in *yizkor* books is unparalleled. Peppered with nostalgia, *yizkor* books attempt to flesh out, at least on paper, the communities they memorialize. *Yizkor* books do come with limitations—of 'authenticity', of language, of the number that exist—but they are significant enough for the New York Public Library and the National Yiddish Book Center to have devised a system to digitize hundreds of them and make them available through the Internet (New York Public Library n.d.). These texts provide their readers with memories of places where they have never been, since most readers have no direct experience with the contents of *yizkor* books, and are reliant on them for knowledge. In this way, *yizkor* books epitomize and mediate the effects of 'goneness'.

Most of the extant 1,600 *yizkor* books belong to special collections in museums and libraries around the world, further limiting access to them. With the advent of the New York Public Library and National Yiddish Book Center's digitization project, one need not visit the United States Holocaust Memorial Museum, the British Museum, or Yad Vashem. Instead, one can visit the website of the Yizkor Book Project and browse over 600 *yizkor* books. Granted, the system is somewhat inconvenient: pages can be enlarged only if users download a special plug-in, for example. Nonetheless, every page, including blank pages, has been scanned and is accessible free of charge. The project not only gives unprecedented access to *yizkor* books, but raises awareness of their existence, which also raises consciousness of the existence of the former Jewish communities.

Yizkor books are a phenomenon of Jewish culture. Few, if any, other groups publish records like these, especially with such strong effects on their cultural memory. They enable readers to mourn for the loss of life and culture while perpetuating their memory. They traverse the spectra of sacred and profane; anguish and pride; life and death; destruction and perpetuation; and personal experience and communal memory. Characterized by these paradoxes, *yizkor* books have two main purposes, encapsulated by the opening of the 1976 English addendum to the *yizkor* book of Rozhishche, which includes a quotation from Psalm 78:

May the pages of this book speak to the generations to come:

'That they should make them known to their children;

That the generations to come might know them, even the children
   which should be born;

Who should arise and declare them to their children.' (Zik 1976: 5–6)

The citation of Jewish liturgy intimates that the *yizkor* book is a text to be taken as seriously as any other liturgical text. In addition, the references to children and generations advise that the book contains an inheritance to be bequeathed perpetually. Thus, *yizkor* books are a 'liturgical–martyrological' form of Jewish literature (Baumel 1995: 150), and they perpetuate the memory of communities that, for all intents and purposes, no longer exist.

Following in the tradition of liturgical-martyrological literature, *yizkor* books both sanctify the Jewish communities destroyed by the Holocaust and revere them. David Sohn, in his foreword to a Bialystoker *yizkor* book—there are three *yizkor* books dedicated to this city—writes that the book is

not alone a chronicle of our Bialystoker martyred dead that brings to the reader the annihilated hometown in all its phases; the book is also the 'Tree of Bialystoker Life', which blooms and flourishes the world over. If but this alone is attained—if this volume enables the reader to experience in his memory the resurrection of the Bialystok hometown and to continue, in day-to-day living, our glorious Bialystoker heritage—then, indeed, has my goal been achieved and my endeavors in having realized this collosal [*sic*], difficult undertaking amply rewarded. (Sohn 1951: 10)

In this excerpt, references to martyrs, the tree of life, and resurrection imply the cultural significance of Sohn's initiative in putting the book together, and he obviously considers Bialystok to be worthy of celebration. The language used in this *yizkor* book and others has a religious quality, matching the artwork of their covers, frontispieces, and title pages. The imagery in the Chelm *yizkor* book's frontispiece, for example, reflects the themes of martyrdom and worship (Figure 1) (Kantz 1981: 6). From the top of the page to the bottom, every image conjures Jewish religiosity: the hands reaching out of the flames, which convey the sacrifice made by the people of Chelm; the scroll showcasing the title of the book, which recalls a Torah scroll; the candles on either side of the scroll, which are reminis-

Figure 1 Frontispiece to the 1981
Chelm *yizkor* book

cent of the candles lit on the sabbath and other holidays; and the aged man in
the cemetery, who resembles Moses reading the Torah. *Yizkor* books thus reflect
a liturgical-martyrological approach to remembering Jewish communities and
memorializing the effects of the Holocaust.

However, their effects on communal memory are probably the most significant. With so little known about their communities, *yizkor* books shape what is
remembered about them. For instance, the *yizkor* book for Lomza, Poland, tells a
story about a rabbi who fled the town for Vilnius instead of staying to comfort his
community when the Russians arrived (Lewinsky 1952: 120). The book depicts
the rabbi as a selfish coward. Chaim Shapiro, a critic of the book and a Lomza
landsman, challenges the story by stating that the rabbi's flight was merely a ruse
to thwart Russian soldiers from killing him for forsaking Stalinist values (Shapiro
1980: 20). According to Shapiro, the rabbi stayed in Lomza, hiding from the Russians and Nazis. Without anyone to substantiate Shapiro's version, readers cannot possibly know which is the true version. However, one can assume that the
rumour mill was so strong that either the Lomza *landsmen* who compiled
the *yizkor* book or Shapiro was willing to pass on a fabricated story. If Shapiro had
not challenged the veracity of the *yizkor* book, readers would have no idea that

there are conflicting versions, leaving Lomza remembered as its *yizkor* book portrays it, potential inaccuracies and all.

That there may be conflicting views of how a community functioned signifies that *yizkor* books are not necessarily the most historically judicious. Indeed, Shapiro instructs, 'on reading a *yizkor* book, first check the ideology of the editors and writers. You can be sure that they will twist the facts to their fancy, to suit their ideology' (1980: 25). Perhaps such editorial bias seems obvious, given the method of publishing *yizkor* books, which usually places an editor in charge of anthologizing submissions collected from *landslayt* at the behest of a *landsmanshaft*. However, for people who seek to immortalize the homes to which they can never return or replicate, or for whom the books provide their only insight, the biases of the individual spearheading a *yizkor* book project are probably difficult to discern and reconcile. As a way to lessen any effects of bias, some communities have multiple *yizkor* books compiled by different editorial committees and thus providing an alternative communal history; other *yizkor* books are published in multiple editions that contain revisions or amendments. The Baranowicze *yizkor* book, for example, corrects mistakes by including errata (Fuksman 1964: 107).

Despite any controversies in or challenges to the content of *yizkor* books, *yizkor* books are designed to indicate the importance of community. In addition to the socio-religious rhetoric described above, *yizkor* books contain rhetoric highly evocative of communality, bringing their readers together to connect to the communities. The forewords and other prefatory comments in *yizkor* books demonstrate how important the communities were to the people who wrote them. Additionally, there are whole sections in many *yizkor* books devoted to rituals and traditions of specific communities. For example, the Ratno *yizkor* book includes a photograph of its community's *tashlikh* ceremony (Tamir 1983: 39), performed by the Pripyat River in Ukraine. Although the photograph obscures the faces of the participants in the ceremony, readers see how central the river was to the community, as well as how vibrant the religious life was. Similarly, a photograph and description in Dobrzyn's *yizkor* book depicts the community's amateur theatre company (Harpaz 1969: 118). One sees both men and women on stage, as well as varying styles of clothing. The play they are rehearsing is Jacob Gordin's *God, Man, and Devil*, according to the caption, which suggests that a segment of the community held progressive perspectives on religion and the secular art of Yiddish theatre (Harpaz 1969: 117–18). By including glimpses of the social fabric of their communities, *yizkor* books attest to the importance of communal life. Rhetorically, *yizkor* books show that *landsmen* valued being part of their *landslayt*, evoking a similar pride in community in readers.

Because one of the directives of *landsmanshaftn* is to maintain records of their communities—of births, marriages, community leaders, and other significant events and people—they were in tune with the 'essence' of the communities: the dynamics and mores known only from personal experience. This familiarity on the part of *landsmanshaftn* became a great comfort after the Holocaust, when the imperative to mourn for the dead was felt more keenly. In this way, *yizkor* books are not just commemorative texts but also repositories for community activity, records of what happened when and to whom. Censuses, such as the one in the Nowy-Targ *yizkor* book (Veltzer-Pas 1979: 31), indicate that *landsmanshaftn* were organized enough to compile and preserve the information and that they had their fingers on the pulse of their communities. In the same vein, one of the most sought-after sections of *yizkor* books is the necrologies: lists of people, organized by family name, who died during the Holocaust. The necrology listed in the Gorzd *yizkor* book (Alperovitz 1980: 351), for instance, lists family name, first name, and family members. For those family members whose names are unknown, their roles in the family are stated. As an example, the twelfth line reads 'Srulovitz Elkhanan, his wife and two children'. This family, like the others on the list, died in the Kovno ghetto and in concentration camps. The necrologies provide the proof of death, albeit without details, that some Holocaust survivors needed for closure. They also allow the dead to be mourned as appropriate in Jewish tradition. In short, for those researchers who want to know about the communities, *yizkor* books are the obvious primary source, despite any shortcomings as described above.

One reason why researchers largely ignore *yizkor* books as viable sources is that most *yizkor* books are published in Yiddish—a language not commonly spoken nowadays, especially by generations of Jews who grew up in non-Yiddish-speaking societies. Other languages, such as Hebrew, Polish, Russian, Hungarian, Czech, and German, pose similar problems. Many Jewish immigrants who fled European persecution chose not to speak the languages of their assailants, which also may have been one of their native languages. Instead, they spoke the languages of their new homes, whether English, French, Hebrew, or Spanish. With so many potential users unable to read *yizkor* books, the texts get set aside.

Of course, this linguistic limitation reveals an irony of *yizkor* books. If younger generations are unskilled in the languages in which *yizkor* books are published, how are *yizkor* books able to teach them about their ancestral homes? For whom are *yizkor* books published, if the languages of publication only alienate future generations? The Targowica *yizkor* book, like many others, has a dedication in English, although the rest of the book is in Hebrew and Yiddish (Siegelman 1967). At least with the dedication, readers will learn of the potential of the book's usefulness, hopefully piquing their interest enough to learn the languages. The dedication reads:

> To Our Children,
> To you, our children and grandchildren, who have not heard very much about your parents' past—a world unknown to you, and sometimes strange, even odd.
> To you, most of whom did not have the privilege to see and know your grandparents, to hear from their mouths stories about their world, about sorrow and grief, troubles

and hardships, that were afflicted upon them in the darkness of the Diaspora:
...

It brings out from the depths of oblivion the happenings of your forefathers and tells of their spiritual, social, and cultural world. In this book you will find also a description of the Holocaust in which every Jewish family in the Diaspora suffered, and about which the survivors rescued from hell, relate. Indeed, this townlet and this way of life no longer exist.
Please, look through this book.
    Your Parents
(Siegelman 1967: 452)

Almost every other *yizkor* book is multilingual, like Targowica's, representing an identity politics even more complicated than that implied by turning to the languages of places of refuge. Jewish immigrants faced questions about which language to use, particularly after the Holocaust, but their descendants do not. As is usual in any immigrant community, use of the 'native' language diminishes over time, in favour of the 'host' language, which becomes the native language of later generations. Accordingly, most descendants of contributors to *yizkor* books are illiterate in the languages of publication. How, then, are they to understand the material in *yizkor* books in order to pass the knowledge on to their descendants? A direct result of post-migration Yiddish and Hebrew illiteracy is that these books frequently sit unrecognized as the goldmines that they are.

However, as the New York Public Library and the National Yiddish Book Center make *yizkor* books—and their translations on JewishGen.org—available online, more readers realize their significance and make use of them, bringing vanished Jewish communities to light and substantiating their near-mythological status in contemporary Jewish life. According to JewishGen.org, the project to translate *yizkor* books has enabled the publication of 'hundreds of completed or partially completed translated books online' (JewishGen 2011). Many of the translations were commissioned by researchers who could not understand the original languages and either found volunteers to donate their time and language skills or paid someone to translate the necessary sections. As *yizkor* books average 600 or so pages, translating them requires time, energy, and dedication. However, the value of these translations is immeasurable as more and more potential readers are unable to access the originals because of language barriers.

Cyber-Shtetls

Similarly, volunteers have donated countless hours to developing websites dedicated to the 'vanished communities'. A 'cyber-shtetl' (not to be confused with Bruno Kempel's defunct website of this name for Ladino and Spanish-language Jewish culture), resembles a *yizkor* book in the way that it hosts an array of information, including virtual tours, photographs, descriptions, travelogues, cemetery maps, and some personal narratives. The tables of contents of *yizkor* books and cyber-shtetls do look similar: histories and descriptions of the towns during the First World War, between the two world wars, during the Holocaust, and after liberation. However, unlike *yizkor* books, these sites present more current data obtained by volunteers who often travel to the places. For example, the cyber-shtetl for Dusetos, Lithuania, features photographs of the town's lake that were taken by Ruth Stern in 2007 (Gamsu 2007). By seeing these photographs, supplemented with an explanation that the town has a yearly event on the lake, visitors to the site gain an understanding of what life is like in Dusetos now. Ironically, the pictures sit between a series of photographs that commemorate the dead: above the Lake Sartai photographs are pictures of the grave markers of two Jews—a father and his son—who died while trying to cross the lake when it was frozen, and below is the photograph of a memorial to Dusetos Jews who died during the Holocaust. Placing the beautiful and calming Lake Sartai pictures between these photographs breaks up the funereal tone that they evoke.

As users make more trips to the actual towns, they can continue to take pictures of the lovelier parts of the towns, like the Lake Sartai photographs, and upload other information. If they take more photographs, if they chart more of the cemeteries, if they meet current residents—all of these can be added and shared. Cyber-shtetls allow for virtual travel to these communities. They give as full a picture as possible of what Jewish communities are like so that people do not need to make the trips themselves, avoiding the effort and expense of finding flights, tour guides, accommodation, translators, archives, and other components of these pilgrimages (Cuckle 2000; Posner 2009; Salinger n.d.).

Although many websites detail history and life in various places around the world where Jewish life thrived, the largest compendium of such sites is hosted by JewishGen.org. Its project, called 'KehilaLinks' as of May 2017,

facilitat[es] web pages commemorating the places where Jews have lived. KehilaLinks provides the opportunity for anyone with an interest in a place to create web pages about that community. These web pages may contain information, pictures, databases, and links to other sources providing data about that place. (JewishGen 2017b: para. 1)

Before August 2011, JewishGen.org used 'ShtetLinks' as the project's title. Fearing that users would prioritize Ashkenazi communities over Sephardi or other Jewish communities, JewishGen.org was careful to remind its users on the ShtetLinks webpage that shtetls—the insular communities in which Jews lived—are not just an east European phenomenon, but that similarly insular Jewish communities exist in other regions of the world. These non-east European sites are just as remarkable in their generation of communities of location as traditional shtetls. The KehilaLink for Harbin, China, for instance, includes several transcripts of interviews with Jews who lived in Harbin and their descendants, photographs of families and community activities, maps of the city as its borders and sovereignty changed, and even some audio clips of sounds of Harbin (Clurman and Prichard 2017). This site evokes the same sense of community of location as the *yizkor* books discussed above, appealing to users who have some kind of interest in learning more about the communities.

In fact, cyber-shtetls—a name which also comes with the disclaimer that not all Jewish communities immortalized online are Ashkenazi and that 'shtetl' is being used to describe any Jewish community that exists within a greater non-Jewish community—may serve as a substitute for *yizkor* books in certain situations. Not only is publishing online easier than publishing a *yizkor* book in hard copy, but the information is more easily verifiable, and much more widely accessible. The British Isles section of KehilaLinks solicits assistance in 'record[ing] details of all Jewish communities and congregations that have ever existed in the United Kingdom . . . in order to preserve the information for posterity, and to make this information freely available via the Internet' (JewishGen 2017a). While this KehilaLink offers more information on non-extant communities, it wishes to increase its offerings on current communities. Its webmaster—David M. R. Shulman—maintains that members of the communities themselves are able to expand on the information already posted. This philosophy leads to a certain similarity between cyber-shtetls and *yizkor* books: former members of communities are the best sources of information about them, as they live the communities' histories and can corroborate each other's memories. However, the immediacy of having something posted online, versus the length of time taken by the publishing process, makes cyber-shtetls a more convenient outlet for this kind of information.

KehilaLinks, although an extensive collection of cyber-shtetls, does not hold a monopoly on online communities of location. Indeed, non-KehilaLinks sites are just as interesting and evocative of a sense of a community. The cyber-shtetl for Luboml, Poland, provides a 'virtual exhibit' of what Jewish life was like by hosting photographs that take users through the town, showcasing both special and mundane places, both of which are important to day-to-day lives (*Remembering Luboml* 2017). These websites, as with other cyber-shtetls, create a sense of community that surrounds what life must have been like, highlighting the towns' pasts while bringing them into the present. Visitors to the sites come to them to learn about their ancestral homes, and the sites offer as much as possible, which is sometimes all that is available.

The Lampert Family Foundation's site for Oradea, Romania, represents another model of a cyber-shtetl. It is not only devoted to narrating the past and present of the Jewish community in that city; it also looks to the city's future. It is a rallying point for people concerned with reinvigorating Jewish life in Oradea (Lampert 2017). The site has pages dedicated to educating Romanians about its Jewish history, creating a Jewish museum and learning centre in Romania, and raising funds and awareness about the Foundation's initiatives in Oradea. In this way, Oradea's cyber-shtetl attempts to secure its future by making itself integral to the Oradea *landslayt*.

Many of the places immortalized by cyber-shtetls do not currently have a Jewish presence, let alone knowledge of their Jewish legacies. The Lampert Family Foundation seeks to change the situation, and so does the now-'retired' 'Jews of Cuba' website (Smith 2017). They emphasize the places' pasts, but they also speak to their futures, especially the future of Jewish life. 'Oradea Jewish Community' expresses a hope for donations to build museums and memorials. A purpose of all three sites is to see Jewish life return to the communities. For these cyber-shtetls, documenting the past is not enough; they must also predict a future for Jewish life. Once they memorialize their origins and their futures, they can, in the words of anthropologist Margaret Mead, describing the remembrance and purposeful forgetting of European ancestry in America, 'dwell in the present which is assumed to be part of one continuous way of life' (Mead 2000: 19). There happen to be Jews still living in each of these places—though fewer and fewer—and, while some cyber-shtetls may end up ignoring whatever Jewish presence remains in favour of recording their histories, Oradea's and Cuba's respective cyber-shtetls take them into account by addressing their needs too.

By hosting images and descriptions of the towns, narratives about life in the towns, and other materials, cyber-shtetls offer a safe space for Jews to visit—even if the space is on the Internet. As physical places, the shtetls are awkward to visit, uncomfortable, perhaps, because of the ghosts of the past. Cyber-shtetls, on the other hand, more than acknowledge the histories of the towns. Their Jewish heritage is a jumping-off point for cyber-shtetls' development, even if the towns' current residents ignore their heritage. Cyber-shtetls base their existence on 'goneness'—on the Jewish legacies that have been silenced and neglected after having been destroyed by the Holocaust. Websites that trace these pasts and maintain records of them for posterity respond to 'goneness' by putting the legacies online, making sure that people searching for information will find what they seek.

What's Gone Is Here

Patraka's concept of 'goneness' implies the need for representation: that which is incomprehensible almost begs for attempts at making it comprehensible (1999: 4). Representations of the 'gone', according to Patraka, adhere to roughly three principles. First, they reveal deliberations over what exactly is being represented, as well as how it is being represented. They show that the representers are conscious of the emotional and intellectual intensity of what is being represented, and they recognize the sociopolitical factors that influence them. Second, representations of the 'gone' distinguish between history and memory as epistemological categories, as they may appear to be incongruous or at odds with each other. Third, they reflect a tension between the tangibility of representation and the intangibility of the 'gone', of what the Holocaust, in this case, made 'gone'. *Yizkor* books and cyber-shtetls enact these principles and complicate them, fulfilling Patraka's conception of representations of 'goneness'.

In terms of the first principle, that of deliberating over the content of the texts, *yizkor* books and cyber-shtetls show that they are self-conscious about what they memorialize, as well as how they memorialize it. The 'gone' is the places where Jewish people lived, as well as the Jewish people themselves. Because of the attachment between the people and the places, *yizkor* books and cyber-shtetls cannot represent the places without including the people too. They depict both the lost geography of Jewish life and the lost demography of Jews. They portray the people who lived in the communities, as well as their daily activities. They showcase the towns in terms of their social significance to the countries, empires, nation-states, or territories that taxed, registered, or otherwise controlled the shtetls. They express the essence of the *landslayt* in as many of their own words as possible. Moreover, almost all *yizkor* books and cyber-shtetls follow the same structure. There are sections on the beginnings of communities, pre-First World War and inter-war histories, Second World War experiences, and a section asking 'Where are they now?' The last section contains updates about the status of *landslayt* around the world, including marriages, deaths, births, graduations, careers, and locations. Using a template indicates that editors make conscious decisions to conform, that their process of representing the communities signals a distinct choice. The rhetoric, too, indicates a choice to portray the communities through lenses of religiosity and martyrdom. The artwork, the language, and the structure all convey an understanding of what is being represented and how.

Yizkor books and cyber-shtetls, as in the second principle of distinguishing between history and memory, problematize distinctions between history and memory. Many sections appear to be historical in nature: they provide chronologies of earlier times, and reflect a sense of objectivity absent in other sections. Those other sections are very clearly reflections on certain parts of the community and are couched as memoirs. Maurice Halbwachs calls this latter approach a 'remembrance', for it is 'a reconstruction of the past achieved with data borrowed from the present, a reconstruction prepared, furthermore, by reconstructions of earlier periods wherein past images had already been altered' (1980: 69). In other words, in order to imagine the 'gone', especially for people who lived it, one must consider the past based on what information is available in the present, which, of course, has been influenced by the past. Both *yizkor* books and cyber-shtetls represent communities with the information that is available, creating a mediated narrative of Jewish life that is probably accurate but might not be. The memories published in *yizkor* books and cyber-shtetls become history because there is no way of verifying them. Editors of *yizkor* books and cyber-shtetls bring the past to light by blurring the boundaries between history and memory, and by doing so consciously.

The third principle entails describing the indescribable. *Yizkor* books and cyber-shtetls exhibit just how complicated the situation is. One of the defining features of 'goneness' is the lack of ability to understand what is gone. The effects of the Holocaust, for example, are incomprehensible. However, because of 'goneness' and because of just how unfathomable the Holocaust is, there is an urge to find some way to comprehend it. Patraka writes: 'It is the goneness of the Holocaust that produces the simultaneous profusion of discourses and understandings; the goneness is what opens up, what spurs, what unleashes the perpetual desire to do, to make, to rethink the Holocaust' (1999: 7). The sections in which writers recount what happened to the communities during the Holocaust is one way that *yizkor* books and cyber-shtetls manifest as a rethinking of the Holocaust, as a way of understanding what happened. *Yizkor* books and cyber-shtetls represent the 'gone' of Jewish communities, attempting to recreate lives and lifestyles that are impossible to recreate fully. This tension encapsulates the spirit of *yizkor* books and cyber-shtetls.

In fact, *landsmanshaftn* intended *yizkor* books to be 'relics' of their communities, and cyber-shtetls are well on their way to act as relics, too (Horowitz 2002: 40). They—and especially *yizkor* books—are an unchanging representation of Jewish communities, and they are, for all intents and purposes, all that is left of the communities. Horowitz maintains that '[i]n addition to their value as texts, these books [are] valued as icons. They [are] seen as a tangible representation of the hometowns' (2002: 40). Without any other way of knowing what the communities were like, readers have only *yizkor* books and cyber-shtetls on which to rely. The films and other resources described above may fictionalize social norms, may not reference a particular ancestor, or may pose too many unanswered questions. *Yizkor* books depict life in these communities in the words of the people who lived it, while cyber-shtetls add a picture of the communities' contemporary life.

Such publications have 'fixed and unchanging meaning or value' (Hall 1981: 237) because they are an unalterable representation of Jewish communities that no longer exist. Although websites are relatively easily amended, making cyber-shtetls alterable, there is little material with which to make changes. Perhaps more material on the communities will come to light as archives are made available, but, for the most part, there is nothing else to add to *yizkor* books, and no one to add it even if there were. Barbara Kirshenblatt-Gimblett confirms the static nature of online *yizkor* books and cyber-shtetls, suggesting that the way in which these volumes represent the communities is how those communities will be remembered (Kirshenblatt-Gimblett 1998: 76).

Yizkor books and cyber-shtetls exemplify Kirshenblatt-Gimblett's concept of 'hereness', which stands, at least semantically, in direct opposition to Patraka's 'goneness'. 'Hereness' implies the existence of an object—in this case, a location—that can never really be experienced. It means that an encounter in or with that place depends on the encounter's context, that *yizkor* book readers or cyber-shtetl visitors are different at each instant of their lives, and that their 'visits' are the sums of their life experiences and the communities' histories. This instantaneity means that their perspectives on the locations vary according to what is available to them at any given moment. In other words, 'hereness' recommends that the reader, viewer, or visitor appreciate the object for what it is, rather than what it was. *Yizkor* books and cyber-shtetls are what is 'here', and what they represent is 'gone'. Therefore, Kirshenblatt-Gimblett's 'hereness' breathes life into the communities of location that result from *yizkor* books and cyber-shtetls, bringing them into the present. To Patraka, however, this effect is an impossibility, because 'goneness' precludes the ability to be in the present.

Taken together, Kirshenblatt-Gimblett's 'hereness' and Patraka's 'goneness' allow for the ambiguities of how *yizkor* books and cyber-shtetls represent communities. *Yizkor* books attempt to reconstruct the past, while cyber-shtetls attempt to shed light on the past by exhibiting the present. The reliance of *yizkor* books on memory leads to questions of exigence, such as 'What is important to note for posterity? What power does the present have to explain the past?' For Alex Gisser (2003), who travelled to Lunna, Belarus, in 2003, the ambiguous relationship between the past and present in the shtetls results in a sense of 'hereness' in the wake of 'goneness'. Gisser writes that he is 'convinced that Lunna still has . . . a significant amount of Jewish karma' (2003: para. 12), that despite the current lack of a Jewish physical presence, the vibrancy of Lunna's Jewish community still resonates. He feels a presence—the 'hereness'—even though the Jewish community is actually gone. 'Goneness' and 'hereness' complement each other, particularly in the context of the Holocaust and the communities it destroyed.

Given the synergy between Patraka's 'goneness' and Kirshenblatt-Gimblett's 'hereness', online *yizkor* books and cyber-shtetls allow communities to regain and retain significance in Jewish life and culture. Users of the websites pursue information about the communities they represent, and this information is often of a personal nature. Where did my ancestors come from? Which rabbi did my grandfather follow? Was my aunt involved in a Zionist youth group? In what industries could my family possibly have been involved? *Yizkor* books and cyber-shtetls offer answers to these questions, expanding the borders of their communities to encompass an infinite number of members worldwide. The communities based on place generated by these websites offer Jews and others a new, technology-dependent way of identifying with each other. These mediated communities of location change the face of Jewish communality from actual to virtual, from what is here to what is gone and vice versa.

Jack Kugelmass and Jonathan Boyarin caution that '[o]ne should not confuse the memorial books [or cyber-shtetls] with the towns they commemorate' (1998: 41). Because of the effects of 'goneness' and 'hereness', there really is no danger of such confusion. Visitors to the websites know that there are no other options for learning about the Jewish communities, and they enter the sites with enough awareness to realize that no text can repair the damage caused not just by the Holocaust, but also by migration and modernity. That said, as online representations of the communities, *yizkor* books and cyber-shtetls do provide a place to go, a site to visit, and a community to join. In sum, while these texts cannot be substitutes for the communities that no longer exist, they forge a new kind of Jewish community—one based on virtualities instead of actualities, as noted in my epigraph, taken from Kirshenblatt-Gimblett (1998: 69).

References

ALPEROVITZ, YITSHAK, ed. 1980. *The Book of Gorzd (Lithuania): A Town in Its Beginnings and Its Extinction* [Sefer gorzd (lita): ayarah beḥayeiha uvekilayonah]. Tel Aviv.

ANDERSON, BENEDICT. 1991. *Imagined Communities: Reflections on the Origin and Spread of Nationalism*. Revised edn. New York.

BAUMEL, JUDITH TAYLOR. 1995. '"In Everlasting Memory": Individual and Communal Holocaust Commemoration in Israel'. In Robert Wistrich and David Ohana, eds., *The Shaping of Israeli Identity: Myth, Memory, and Trauma*, 146–70. London.

BORUT, JACOB. 1992. 'Flonheim'. In Henry Wassermann, ed., *Pinkas Hakehilot: Encyclopedia of Jewish Communities, Germany*, vol. 3, trans. Avi Zucker, 278–89. Jerusalem <http://www.jewishgen.org/Yizkor/Pinkas_germany/ger3_00278.html> (accessed 6 Sept. 2017).

BRONNER, SIMON J. 2001. 'From *Landsmanshaften* to *Vinkln*: Mediating Community Among Yiddish Speakers in America'. *Jewish History*, 15: 131–48.

CUCKLE, HAROLD. 2000. 'How I Came to Visit My Grandparents [*sic*] Shtetl'. <http://kehilalinks.jewishgen.org/igumen/igumen_webmap.htm> (accessed 6 Sept. 2017).

CLURMAN, IRENE, and VINCENT PRICHARD. 2017. 'Harbin, Heilongjiang Province, China'. <http://kehilalinks.jewishgen.org/harbin/> (accessed 6 Sept. 2017).

FISHBANE, MICHAEL A. 1987. *Judaism: Revelation and Traditions*. New York.

FUKSMAN, YOSEF, ed. 1964. *Baranowicze: In Destruction and Resistance* [Baranovitch: in umkum un vidershtand]. New York.

GAMSU, ADA, ed. 2007. 'Dusetos Lake Sartai'. <http://kehilalinks.jewishgen.org/Dusetos/> (accessed 6 Sept. 2017).

GISSER, ALEX. 2003. 'Reflections from a Visit in Lunna'. <http://kehilalinks.jewishgen.org/Lunna/visits-2001.html> (accessed 6 Sept. 2017).

HALBWACHS, MAURICE. 1980 [1950]. *The Collective Memory*, trans. Francis J. Ditter Jr. and Vida Yazdi Ditter. New York.

HALL, STUART. 1981. 'Notes on Deconstructing "the Popular"'. In Raphael Samuel, ed., *People's History and Socialist Theory*, 227–40. London.

HARPAZ, M., ed. 1969. *My Town: Memorial Book for the Communities Dobrzyn-Gollub* [Ayarati: Sefer zikaron le'ayarot dobzhyn-golub]. Tel Aviv <http://yizkor.nypl.org/index.php?id=2393> (accessed 6 Sept. 2017).

HOBERMAN, J. 1991. *Bridge of Light: Yiddish Film between Two Worlds*. Philadelphia.

HOROWITZ, ROSEMARY. 2002. 'The Transformation of Memory in On-line *Yisker Books*'. *Proteus: A Journal of Ideas*, 19: 39–42.

JewishGen. 2011. 'Research'. <http://www.jewishgen.org/JewishGen/Research.html> (accessed 6 Sept. 2017).

——2017a. 'Jewish Communities and Records—United Kingdom'. <https://www.jewishgen.org/JCR-UK/ > (accessed 6 Sept. 2017).

——2017b. 'KehilaLinks'. <http://kehilalinks.jewishgen.org/> (accessed 6 Sept. 2017).

KANTZ, SIMON, ed. 1981. *Yizkor Book in Memory of Chelem* [Sefer hazikaron likehilat khelem]. Tel Aviv.

KIRSHENBLATT-GIMBLETT, BARBARA. 1998. *Destination Culture: Tourism, Museums, and Heritage*. Berkeley, Calif.

KLIGER, HANNAH. 1989. 'The Continuity of Community *Landsmanshaftn* in New York and Tel Aviv'. In U. O. Schmelz and S. DellaPergola, eds., *Papers in Jewish Demography 1985*, 405–15. Jerusalem. <http://www.policyarchive.org/handle/10207/bitstreams/9962.pdf> (accessed 6 Sept. 2017).

KUGELMASS, JACK, and JONATHAN BOYARIN, eds. 1998. *From a Ruined Garden: The Memorial Books of Polish Jewry*, 2nd edn. Bloomington, Ind.

Lampert Family Foundation. 2008. 'Oradea Jewish Community'. <http:// www.oradeajc.com> (accessed 6 Sept. 2017).

LEWINSKY, YOM-TOV. 1952. *Memorial Book for the Community of Lomza/Lomza: A Yizkor Book* [Sefer zikaron likehilat lomzah / Lomza: a yizker bukh]. Tel Aviv <http://yizkor.nypl.org/index.php?id=2393> (accessed 6 Sept. 2017).

MEAD, MARGARET. 2000 [1965]. *And Keep Your Powder Dry: An Anthropologist Looks at America*. Oxford.

NEW YORK PUBLIC LIBRARY. n.d. 'Yizkor Books'. <https://www.nypl.org/collections/nypl-recommendations/guides/yizkorbooks> (accessed 6 Sept. 2017).

PATRAKA, VIVIAN M. 1999. *Spectacular Suffering: Theatre, Fascism, and the Holocaust*. Bloomington, Ind.

POSNER, BARRY. 2009. 'Travelogues'. <http://kehilalinks.jewishgen.org/Zagare/visits.html> (accessed 6 Sept. 2017).

Remembering Luboml: Images of a Jewish Community. 2017 <http://www.luboml.org> (accessed 6 Sept. 2017).

SALINGER, RALPH. n.d. 'In and Around Vilkaviskis'. *Vilkaviskis: A Small Town in Southern Lithuania Where the Jewish Community Is No More* <http://www.jewishvilkaviskis.org/In_and_around_Vilkaviskis.html> (accessed 22 Oct. 2017).

SHAPIRO, CHAIM. 1980. 'How Not to Write a "Yizkor Book"'. *Jewish Observer*, 14(8): 18–25.

'ShtetLinks'. 2010. *JewishGen.org* <http://www.shtetlinks.jewishgen.org> (1995–2010).

SIEGELMAN, ISAAC, ed. 1967. *Memorial Book of Targovica* [Sefer trovits/Trovitzer yizker-bukh]. Kiryat Motzkin <http://yizkor.nypl.org/index.php?id=2393> (accessed 6 Sept. 2017).

SMITH, RICHARD, ed. 2017. 'The Jews of Cuba'. <http://www.jewishcuba.org> (accessed 6 Sept. 2017).

SOHN, DAVID, ed. 1951. *Bialystok: A Picture Album of a Famous City and Its Jews throughout the World* [Byalistok: Bilder album fun a barimter shtot un ayre iden iber der velt]. New York.

SOKOLOVSKH, SERGEY, and VALERY TISHKOV. 1996. 'Ethnicity'. In Alan Barnard and Jonathan Spencer, eds., *Encyclopedia of Social and Cultural Anthropology*, 190–3. New York.

TAMIR, NAKHMAN, ed., 1983. *Ratneh: Story of the Destroyed Jewish Community*. Tel Aviv.

VELTZER-PAS, MICHAEL, ed. 1979. *Book of Nowy-Targ and Surroundings* [Sefer novi-targ vehasevivah]. Tel Aviv <http://yizkor.nypl.org/index.php?id=2393> (accessed 6 Sept. 2017).

YASNI, A. V., ed. 1956. *Memorial Book for the Community of Siedlce: From the 1940s until the Holocaust* [Sefer yizkor likehilat shedlits: lishenat arba-esreh leḥurbanah]. Buenos Aires.

ZIK, GERSHON, ed. 1976. *Rożyszcze: My Old Home*. Tel Aviv.

NINE

The Second Life of Judaism: A History of Religious Community and Practice in Virtual Spaces

JULIAN VOLOJ AND
ANTHONY BAK BUCCITELLI

IN 2003 the San Francisco-based company Linden Lab launched Second Life. Despite its similarities to other Massive Multiplayer Online Role Playing Games (MMORPGs), the company insisted that Second Life was not a game, but rather 'an online digital world, built, shaped, and owned by its participants' (Linden Lab 2004).[1] Although now in decline, for a short period Second Life was seen as the next big Internet phenomenon and was the focus of attention by investors and media alike.

Like all virtual worlds, Second Life (SL) exists in a complex relationship with 'real life' (RL), a relationship which is defined both by the encoded parameters of the virtual space and by the social and cultural practices of the people who use the platform. Although the kinds of clearly constructed virtual experiences available to people in worlds like SL have often been taken as merely representational at best, or ersatz at worst, scholars have slowly begun to shed light on the creative ways in which humans construct their social and cultural worlds, not just online but offline as well. As the anthropologist Tom Boellstorff has observed, for instance:

Second Life culture is profoundly human. It is not only that virtual worlds borrow assumptions from real life; virtual worlds show us how, under our very noses, our 'real' lives have been 'virtual' all along. It is in being virtual that we are human: since it is human 'nature' to experience life through the prism of culture, human being has always been virtual being. (Boellstorff 2008: 5)

Boellstorff's comments make a case that an equivalent ontological weight should be accorded to both 'virtual' and 'real' experiences. They also suggest that scholars must study digital virtual contexts both as existing in relation to offline contexts and simultaneously as distinct in specific ways from offline settings. Like our 'virtual' offline lives, we experience life online not only through a digital platform but 'through the prism of culture'. Just as this prism is dynamic and varied in offline settings, so are online settings structured by diverse and ever-shifting cultural constructions.[2]

These insights hold true no less for religious cultures than for any others. SL, as a broad platform encompassing many cultural constructions, quickly developed a rich and diverse set of religious cultures. By 2007 its most prominent religious group was 'Javatars', a term Julian Voloj introduced and that became widely accepted for Jewish users of SL (Voloj 2007a, 2007b; Shandler 2009: 277–8). As the platform grew in popularity, dozens of Jewish sites across the grid emerged, created both by individual users and by offline institutions that established SL presences. And in short order a visitor to this virtual world could spend hours on Jewish sightseeing tours, interacting with other Javatars in Jewish social spaces, or engaging in certain aspects of ritual practice.

Yet these sites, interactions, and practices emerged in an intriguing relation to offline Jewish cultures. 'In a milieu in which reinvention has limitless potential', media scholar Jeffrey Shandler asks of SL Judaism, 'why is this virtual Jewish world so indebted to the actual one?' (Shandler 2009: 280). As Shandler's question suggests, in many cases Javatars seemingly did not use the possibilities of the medium to invent wholly new Jewish places in SL, but rather to create virtual copies of existing sacred or religiously significant sites in actual spaces. Yet, importantly, these sites function within the specific context of the virtual space and established traditions of media practice, while also existing in a particular relationship to their offline counterparts. As Boellstorff further observes:

Many places were designed by residents to have tight referential relationships with the actual world . . . Such forms of imbrication have been a source of confusion in the literature on virtual worlds because of the assumption that such traffic blurs or even erases the gap between the virtual and actual, rather than working to define and sustain that gap. (Boellstorff 2008: 200)

In this essay we offer, not a single response to this confusion or to Shandler's question, but several. By tracking the relationship between SL and RL Jewish culture, we will show that the relations which Shandler and Boellstorff note existed in a variety of configurations in SL's short-lived Jewish community. Moreover, these relations were configured somewhat differently when connected with identity, place-making, commemoration, and religious observance.[3]

Virtual Worlds and the Origins of Second Life

While the idea of 'virtual' experiences arguably extends back millennia (Boellstorff 2008: 33–4; Boellstorff et al. 2012: 22; Shields 2003; Tofts et al. 2002: 105–41), the emergence of virtual worlds in digital spaces is much more recent. Depending on how it is accounted, digital virtual worlds either began with the emergence of single-screen, multiplayer video games such as *Tennis for Two*

(1958) and *Spacewar!* (1961) or with the emergence of more experientially immersive online games such as the text-based *MUD1* (1979) or the graphical world *Habitat* (1986) (Boellstorff 2008: 39; Boellstorff et al. 2012: 23; Brand 1974; Pearce and Artemisia 2009: 8–9).[4]

While science fiction writers like Bruce Sterling and William Gibson were popularizing ideas about 'cyberspace' in the 1980s,[5] in 1992 Neal Stephenson published the cyberpunk novel *Snow Crash*, a thriller set in a futuristic Los Angeles that proved deeply influential on the development of SL. The book became a cult classic among science fiction fans, especially for Stephenson's description of a virtual-reality-based Internet he named 'The Metaverse', which users experienced from a first-person perspective.

While Linden Lab's founder Philip Rosedale claimed that he already had the idea for this virtual world before reading the book, he admitted that '*Snow Crash* certainly painted a compelling picture of what such a virtual world would look like in the near future, and I found that inspiring.' Along these lines, Linden Lab insisted that its virtual world was not just another game but, like the Metaverse, 'a popular virtual space for meeting friends, doing business, and sharing knowledge' (Dubner 2007).

To document the creation of this alternate world, Linden Lab hired Wagner James Au, a technology reporter, to record the developments in this virtual environment. Au became SL's 'historian, ethnographer, and sole reporter' (Au 2008: p. xvii). His *New World Notes*, a blog first published under the SL umbrella, later independently, became the first main news source of this virtual world and later inspired other publications, including at least three regular newspapers: the *Alphaville Herald*, the *Metaverse Messenger*, and the *Second Life Newspaper*. Even prior to the wide RL media attention then, developments in SL were well documented. While several major RL media institutions, including CNN and Reuters, established virtual presences in SL, they tended to focus on the novel or sensational aspects of the world (Boellstorff 2008: 72; Brennen and dela Cerna 2010: 547; Newman 2006), so in many ways the in-world media represent some of the best sources of information about SL before the emergence of significant scholarly works on the topic.

Creationist Capitalism and the Popularity of Second Life

A unique feature introduced by Linden Lab was that users were enabled to modify their virtual environment independently, making them co-developers of the world (Rymaszewski 2007: 2). SL therefore allowed real commercial interactions that distinguished it from other virtual worlds at the time. By 2007, users were spending 'close to $5 million there every month', and this was money not spent on goods created by Linden Lab, but on 'things that other users have created and added to the world' (Rosedale 2007: p. iii).

This business aspect was one of the main reasons for the wide RL media attention to SL, including the famous cover story of the 2006 *Business Week*'s edition titled 'Virtual World, Real Money'. The cover featured Anshe Chung, the avatar of Chinese German entrepreneur Ailin Graef, an SL real-estate developer who was called 'the virtual Rockefeller' by CNN (Sloan 2005). Graef was the first person in SL to achieve a net worth exceeding one million US dollars entirely with transactions in the virtual world (Hof 2006). With the increased media coverage, the number of registered users in SL skyrocketed. SL reached its tipping point on 18 October 2006 when the millionth user signed up. By the end of 2006, the number had already doubled, and by mid-2007, the virtual world had 8 million 'residents' and boasted a growing grid size.

At the same time, the logic of 'creationist capitalism' was an important guiding principle in the sociocultural life in-world. In terms of earning money, Linden Lab offered a virtual currency that could be earned in SL and exchanged for RL currency, and in interacting socially, personal creativity became the 'primary asset' in SL (Boellstorff 2008: 205–11).

Entering Second Life: The Basics of Avatars, Aesthetics, and Interaction

This essay is primarily based on ethnographic fieldwork conducted by Voloj between 2006 and 2009. In September 2006, Adam Pasick introduced Voloj to SL.[6] Pasick was then preparing the launch of Reuters' SL bureau, which was officially announced a month later. Voloj became an active participant in the SL Jewish community during its period of peak activity and he wrote about the community in his role as a journalist for *2Life Magazine*. He also conducted interviews with members of the community between 2006 and 2009, and again in 2009, after a majority had left SL. In most cases, the interviews were conducted in-world, as avatars via SL's chat system. After Linden Lab introduced Voice over Internet Protocol (VoIP), interviews were also done verbally, but still only in form of avatars. In a few cases, Voloj was able to meet these SL users in real life for face-to-face interviews.[7]

When they registered, SL users were not required to enter any personal information, unless they intended to purchase virtual real estate, for which a credit card was necessary. After installing the SL software, users had to create their 'avatar'.[8] Here we generally use RL names to refer to participants, but because of the central importance of in-world identity, we note SL avatar names as well.

In SL, users were able to choose their own first name and could then select the second name from a number of pre-set surnames that were changed on an ongoing basis. The next step was to create the avatar, choosing between female and male, human and furry (anthropomorphic animal characters) templates that could be edited in all aspects, from skin colour to height and weight. SL avatars were never final, and users were always able to modify them at any given point. While basic avatars were free, there were more advanced features available for purchase, such as skin texture or accessories, a main part of SL's economy. The more time users spent in SL, the more they were willing to invest in their avatars, modifying the given templates in creative ways.

Entering the virtual world, users could toggle between first-person or third-person perspectives, the latter being an elevated camera view from behind the avatar. By using the SL directory, users could identify interest groups they wanted to join, or find locations, so-called 'sims' they wanted to visit. To visit, users had simply to click on a link in the directory, or they could save the location in their inventory for later visits. If other avatars were in the proximity of the user's avatar, communication via text chat was possible. Later a voice chat was introduced as well. Avatars could befriend others and add them to their network, allowing private chats.

Second Life's Introduction of Judaism

Although it eventually came to incorporate some offline institutions, SL's Jewish community began as a grassroots creation that depended on a few highly engaged individuals who came from very different backgrounds. They ranged from Jews living in *ḥaredi* ('ultra-Orthodox') communities that shun the Internet to secular Jews living in isolated areas with no Jewish community nearby. While a few ambitious individuals drove the creation of a community, it also depended on them.

The Hebrew term *am hasefer* ('people of the book') underlines the historical importance of the written word in Judaism.[9] In SL, during the founding phase of the community, Jews connected with each other solely through written communication. In a way, SL presented an extreme of a virtual social network since its members had no face-to-face, but solely avatar-to-avatar, interaction mediated through writing. The particular prominence of the SL Jewish community was therefore perhaps due in part to this historical feature of Jewish culture that spanned the diverse backgrounds of the earliest participants in SL Judaism.[10]

In August 2006 the first synagogue of SL, Temple Beth Israel, was created by Beth Odets, avatar of then 33-year-old Beth Wollanow Brown (Figures 1 and 2). The classically trained concert violinist had joined SL in 2005 and eventually become a very experienced builder, owning her own region on the grid. Until the creation of Temple Beth Israel in SL, Brown had not been particularly religiously active, either in SL or in RL. Thus, perhaps surprisingly, the creation of this first Jewish space in SL had an aesthetic rather than a religious origin.

On one of her excursions through SL, Brown found a virtual Torah scroll, 'a rather weak replica', she recalled. She recounted what happened next: '[I] knew that I could do better, and started building. Before I knew it, I was on the Web

Figure 1 Beth Odets, the avatar of Beth Wollanow Brown, in Second Life. *Photograph by Julian Voloj*

looking for a Hebrew texture and half an hour later the Torah was done. Now, having a Torah, I needed a place to put it, and I started to build the Ark. . . . what started as correcting a Torah became the whole Temple Beth Israel' (Odets 2007; see Figure 2). Since the first virtual Torah had nothing indicating its creator, the origins of this replica were never discovered, and the story of Odets' encounter became the aetiological myth of SL's Jewish community.

Shortly after completing the structure, Brown listed the synagogue in the SL directory, allowing users to visit it by clicking on the teleport button. Within a day, the first avatars discovered the synagogue, transforming Temple Beth Israel from a simple virtual structure to the first Jewish destination in SL, and turning its creator into the matriarch of virtual Judaism.

Brown's introduction of a Jewish destination into the SL directory also came at a turning point in SL's virtual geography. Initially, Linden Lab only allowed users to teleport themselves via telehubs, which functioned like stops in an RL public transportation system. After landing at a telehub, players had to walk or fly, depending on the granted abilities of the area, to their exact destination. Linden Lab abolished this system in November 2005, replacing it with point-to-point

Figure 2 Temple Beth Israel in Second Life, the first synagogue in the virtual world, January 2007.
Photograph by Julian Voloj

teleports (Zheng 2009: 98). While this move caused wide protests, since it decreased real-estate value in areas close to telehubs, it also made more remote areas such as Nessus, where Brown built the synagogue, more accessible. Everyone who found the synagogue in the directory could teleport his or her avatar directly to the building's entrance by simply clicking on the listing.

The accidental introduction of Judaism into the virtual world was part of a general trend to initiate spiritual experiences in SL. As the number of SL Jewish sites grew, so did Buddhist temples, cathedrals, mosques, and other places associated with RL religions, as well as religious parodies such as the Church of Elvis (Grossman 2007).

Blogger Drown Pharaoh, who was documenting religion in SL in 2007, believes that the success of the synagogue had 'something to do with the increasing self-confidence of SL avatars. When you're in SL for a while, your avatar becomes more and more your real self, and you start looking in SL for a place that really means something to you.' Jewish users searching for something Jewish in SL therefore found with this virtual synagogue a place where they could connect with other Jews in this virtual environment.

Brown decided to use the interest in her creation to build a network among Jewish SL users and created the 'Second Life Synagogue' (SLS) group; membership was free and by signing up, avatars would receive information about any planned activities. In less than two months, this mailing list already had more than one hundred members. Jewish residents who wanted to socialize with other Jewish residents therefore joined SLS to be able to identify them.

The first Jewish event in SL was held in October 2006. Brown created a sukkah and invited other avatars to 'hang out' with her in this virtual hut. The event had no ritual or ceremony but offered a chance for Javatars to socialize at a common location in-world. Motivated by the interest in the virtual Sukkot gathering, Brown organized a Hanukah celebration in December 2006. Unlike the Sukkot gathering, which replaced ritual with socialization, during each day of the Hanukah celebration, Brown would type the prayer for the candle lighting, as did the participants, and then light virtual candles. Being aware that participants from different time zones might want to participate, Brown organized several lighting ceremonies, reflecting these geographical differences. Dozens of avatars participated and these events became the forerunner for the 'Shabbat Around The World' candle-lighting ceremonies that Brown started in January 2007.

The Rise of Jewish Journalism in Second Life: *2Life Magazine*

Julian Voloj was not only a participant in these first 'Shabbat Around The World' ceremonies, but also the first journalist to report on Judaism in SL, eventually becoming editor of the only magazine covering exclusively Jewish aspects of SL (Harp 2007). The magazine was dubbed *2Life*, a play on the words SL and the Hebrew expression *leḥayim* ('to life'); its reporters were, like Voloj, residents of SL. Each issue featured interviews and portraits of Javatars, points of Jewish interests, event listings, and other news. Fourteen issues of the magazine were published, the first in April 2007, the last exactly two years later in April 2009.

Parallel to the launch of the first issue of *2Life Magazine*, a virtual Jewish community centre inspired by Bauhaus design was opened near Temple Beth Israel (Figure 3). Beth Brown was commissioned to create this building, which served as a place where avatars could obtain the latest copy of the magazine, and where a number of art exhibitions were held, as a way to bring RL art into the virtual world.[11]

Jewish Sites in Second Life

In addition to *2Life Magazine*, Jewish media outlets from around the globe started to report on Temple Beth Israel, which in turn brought more Jews into SL and to

Figure 3 The cultural centre of the Jewish community in Second Life was the 2Life Gallery, an art space located near Temple Beit Israel that offered real-life artists the opportunity to present their art to an online community. The name 2Life was a play on words, referring both to the expression *leḥayim* and to 'Second Life'. *Photograph by Julian Voloj*

the virtual synagogue. As the number of active Javatars increased, so did the number of in-world Jewish sites they created.

After Brown, the first Javatar to create Jewish sites was GruvenReuven Greenberg, the avatar of Reuven Fischer. In January 2007, less than a month after the weekly 'Shabbat Around The World' celebrations were initiated, Fischer, a *ba'al teshuvah* (newly religious Jew) then in his mid-forties, from rural Pennsylvania, created a replica of Jerusalem's Western Wall. At the SL Kotel (*kotel* being the Hebrew word for the Western Wall) visitors were able to download the weekly *parashah* (section of the Torah) and the teachings of Rabbi Menachem Mendel Schneerson of the Chabad-Lubavitch movement.

Over the nearly three years that he was active within SL's Jewish community, Fischer organized a variety of programmes, starting with the materials on Chabad that he made available at the virtual Western Wall. In 2008, he began organizing regular gatherings of Javatars in a recreation of the former residence of Schneerson, in Crown Heights, Brooklyn. The three-storey, gothic-style, red-brick building at 770 Eastern Parkway has been reproduced materially around the world as a spiritual centre and community icon for Lubavitch members and guests (Berlinger 2010), but in SL, students in a yeshiva instructed by an RL rabbi could dress as hasidim and engage in role play (Figure 4). During larger assem-

Figure 4 Chabad-Lubavitch used the voice function in Second Life for education. Here a rabbi from Philadelphia interacts in a virtual yeshiva with students. Many of the students were secular in real life, but dressed as hasidim in a form of role play. *Photograph by Julian Voloj*

blies or *farbrengens* (Yiddish: 'gatherings'), Javatars gathered in the common space to discuss issues of religious significance and to learn about the Chabad movement.

Fischer's creations were notable for a couple of reasons. First, unlike Brown, whose buildings, while identifiably Jewish spaces, were not intended to invoke specific RL spaces, Fischer mainly recreated spaces that were keyed to important sites in the RL geography of Judaism, and Chabad-Lubavitch hasidism in particular. Second, Fischer's use of the SL platform to connect visitors with information about the Chabad movement and the teachings of Rabbi Menachem Mendel Schneerson is also consistent with what Jeffrey Shandler has argued is a distinguishing characteristic of Lubavitcher hasidism in the post-war United States: its approach to media. Tracing this orientation through Schneerson's tenure as the seventh Lubavitcher Rebbe, Shandler argues that Schneerson's advocacy for media such as print, television, and video recording as methods both to connect non-Lubavitchers with the movement and to draw together geographically dispersed Lubavitchers, created conditions in which media texts related to the Rebbe have taken on additional significance for his followers after his death in 1994. 'As some of his disciples have argued', Shandler observes, 'the Rebbe may be a more powerful spiritual leader as an invisible, dematerialized presence—or

Figure 5 A New Jersey artist created this virtual Tabernacle in Second Life on the basis of information from the Hebrew Bible. *Photograph by Julian Voloj*

rather, as a virtual reality—for his followers, exemplified by his legacy of media-tions and media practices' (Shandler 2009: 264). Shandler notes that this legacy of media work tends to bring together new media practices with existing commu-nicative traditions within Chabad-Lubavitch to constitute a virtual, though not just digitally virtual, community (Shandler 2009: 270).

In this respect, Fischer's deployment of his creative capital to replicate RL sites in SL was structured by a specific set of relations. These recreated sites did attempt, in certain ways, to replicate RL spaces, but only within the context of a specific tradition of virtualized and mediated experiences that had already been established through the historical media practices established by Schneerson and the Chabad-Lubavitch community.

Around the same time that Fischer was recreating existing Jewish sites as points of entry to Chabad-Lubavitch, other Javatars were exploring the creative possibilities of the medium to re-create vanished objects and spaces in the his-torical geography of Judaism. For instance, New Brunswick-based Javatar Marc Shoulson, known in-world as Ever Student, recreated the Tabernacle, the sanc-tuary that protected the Ark of the Covenant, using biblical references for the blueprint (Figure 5). A Dutch builder with the avatar name Rabbi Writer went even further, rebuilding Jerusalem's Second Temple (Figure 6). Later, Rabbi Writer reconstructed the birthplace of the Ba'al Shem Tov, the founder of the hasidic movement (Figure 7).

This last site was also part of a second trend to recreate Jewish sites in eastern

Figure 6 The creation of Temple Beth Israel and the 2Life Gallery in Second Life inspired historical reconstructions of Jewish icons such as this replica of the Second Temple in Jerusalem. *Photograph by Julian Voloj*

Figure 7 Rabbi Writer, an avatar for a Dutch artist, used Second Life to reconstruct the birthplace and synagogue in western Ukraine of the Ba'al Shem Tov, the founder of the hasidic movement. *Photograph by Julian Voloj*

Europe that had been destroyed or lost as a result of antisemitic persecution. As part of this trend, in March 2007, Carter Giacobini, the avatar of 33-year-old Keith Dannenfelser from Indiana, created SL's first 'real' Jewish museum, which also included the first Holocaust memorial (Shoffman 2007). The memorial became a central location for commemoration ceremonies for the Jewish community in SL, but also a space for socialization among its members.

In early 2008, Attila Seres, a Hungarian 'tax consultant with unusual hobbies', became one of the first Javatars to use his creative capital in SL, and the social connections it facilitated, to raise awareness about an RL issue of concern among Hungarian Jews, the disappearance of the former Jewish quarter in his home city, Budapest. Under his avatar name Sofar Shepherd, Seres used photographs to build a three-dimensional virtual copy of the neighbourhood. As a kind of performance piece, which he titled 'Saving Budapest's Jewish quarter', he used a virtual bulldozer to attack and destroy his own creation. Despite its striking imagery, however, the installation seemed to generate little activism, if any.

The activist uses of site creation in SL continued to broaden outwards, however, to include pro-Israel creations as well. For example, Chaim Landau, an American living in Jerusalem, spearheaded an initiative to bring Israel into SL. By September 2007, a group of French Jews had created Tel Aviv-Yaffo, a virtual site resembling the Israeli port city. But SL Israel, as envisioned by Landau, was meant to extend from this beginning to include sites from all over the country and to 'present Israel beyond the conflict to an international audience'.

Landau's project is particularly interesting not just because it focused on pro-Israel activism, but also because Landau's entire SL presence was predicated upon his activism. Unlike the other site creators, Landau was not an active Javatar prior to the start of his SL Israel project. Instead, he was only interested in using the virtual world for *hasbarah* (Hebrew: 'explanation', 'propaganda') or creating a positive portrayal of Israel. 'In 2007 SL was the hottest new Internet phenomenon', he told Voloj in 2012. 'Established companies were racing to establish a presence in SL. I thought the medium should also include an Israel in it.'

Landau secured funds for the project and commissioned Brown to create an island, highlighting Jewish as well as non-Jewish sites in the country. SL Israel held a number of events in 2008, celebrating the sixtieth anniversary of the founding of RL Israel. These events were well attended, but the attendees were mostly the same Javatars attending regular events at Temple Beth Israel. A more expansive Jewish space did not necessarily create a broader engagement with Jewish users in SL.

Religious Practice, Education, and Commemoration

Besides the educational and commemorative aspects that were built into many Jewish sites in SL, the building boom of Jewish sites fuelled interest in

Figure 8 This image is from a commemoration of Yom Hashoah at the Holocaust Memorial in Second Life. The avatars in the centre and on the right are holding *yahrzeit* candles. This space, created by Javatars, was separate from a later simulation created by the United States Holocaust Memorial Museum in Second Life. *Photograph by Julian Voloj*

expanded religious observances, educational efforts, and commemorative cere-monies, which were some of the best-attended events in the Javatar community, in their own right. Some of these efforts were expressly spiritual in their inten-tions. Cryptomorph Lake, an avatar of Jeremy Finkelstein of Sydney, Australia, for example, organized a Passover Seder in SL in 2007 (Levi 2007). Later that year, Finkelstein and Boston-based Benjamin Dauer, who was known as the avatar Malachi Rothschild, founded the Beit Binah Jewish Intentional Commun-ity. Dauer explained that he wanted to create a community of 'people who want to dedicate time in the metaverse to God [and to] explore Judaism in a deep, personal, and meaningful way'.[12]

By contrast, the commemoration of the Shoah was for more secular Javatars an event with greater resonance with their Jewish identities. On 15 April 2007, Keith Dannenfelser organized the first Yom Hashoah (Holocaust Day) ceremony in SL, concurrent with the RL observances of this commemoration (Figure 8). Similarly to the shabbat ceremonies at Temple Beth Israel, participants lit virtual candles and typed out the words of the Kaddish prayer in their text chats. A day later Dannenfelser held a second ceremony using a similar format to memorial-ize Liviu Librescu, a Holocaust survivor killed in the Virginia Tech shootings on 16 April. Participants created a memorial for Librescu in front of the SL Jewish Historical Museum, where avatars were able to leave virtual candles.

In 2009, the US Holocaust Memorial Museum opened an educational simulation, designed by high school students, of the infamous Kristallnacht pogrom (Trezise 2011: 401). However, while previously most Jewish sites and events had been created by individuals active in the Javatar community, this simulation was initiated by an institution, which gave it a very specific context and orientation. The simulation allowed avatars to walk through a variety of scenes depicting the aftermath of Kristallnacht, interactively encountering 'performed' information about historical events. As Bryoni Trezise has argued, however, the exhibition, 'Through its emphasis on embodied knowledge . . . participates in the circulation of a range of "wound culture" affects in ways that serve the moral certitude of the spectator/participant *as* witness over the subject being recollected.' In other words, 'virtual traumas', such as that presented by the Kristallnacht simulation, '(re)structure that which was not known the first time around as knowable, feelable and experiential, at the same time as they perform that very perceptual blind spot as a knowable, feel-able and experiential origin' (Trezise 2011: 393–5). The exhibition, Trezise concludes, in an attempt to establish authenticity and empathy, thus gives primacy to the subjects experiencing it, rather than to the subjects to which it is supposedly dedicated: the victims of the pogrom.

Perhaps for this reason, Javatars generally identify their most powerful, Holocaust-related experiences in SL not as their experiences with virtualized historical recreations, but rather as events in which community participants came together to memorialize or remember specific experiences of the Shoah. For instance, many speak of the significance of a series of lectures initiated in 2008 by Helen Starr, known as the avatar Explorer Dastardly. Starr brought her mother Fanny, a Holocaust survivor from Poland, into SL, using VoIP technology to let Fanny tell her story. While her mother was speaking, Starr managed her mother's avatar and showed photographs in a virtual auditorium.

In an interview in 2012, Starr explained that with this project she wanted to give as many people as possible the opportunity to hear her mother's survival story in a time when fewer and fewer survivors are left alive. In this way, engaging the memory of the Holocaust virtually, but directly through the experience of RL historical subjects, Javatars created a personally and socially relevant experience of Holocaust memory that was meaningful within the context of the virtual community.

Virtual Hate and Anti-Israel Protests

On 20 April 2007, coinciding with the anniversary of Adolf Hitler's birthday, the first reported antisemitic incident occurred in SL. Anonymous attackers littered the SL Kotel with swastikas (Messmer 2007). As a consequence of this attack, Javatar Binyomin Etzel founded the Jewish Defence League of Second Life (JDLSL), inspired by Meir Kahane's RL organization. Using different avatars, or 'alts', members of the JDLSL infiltrated virtual hate groups, documenting avatars who were wearing Nazi or Ku Klux Klan uniforms, distributing antisemitic and racist literature, and selling White Power accessories at in-world stores.

One of the most prominent hate groups that had come together in SL by that time was 'Nazi Furs'. 'Furzi' members, as they called themselves, claimed that they were simply role-playing the Second World War in the role of Nazis.[13] When JDLSL agents reported Furzi activities to Linden Lab, the company's response was slow and conflicted. At first tolerating Furzi activity as freedom of expression, Linden Lab later deleted the avatars of some Furzi instigators in response to pressure from in-world media outlets. Ironically perhaps, in the same way that JDLSL agents made use of 'alts' to infiltrate the Nazi Fur organization, deleted Nazi Furs simply created new avatars and continued their in-world activities.

In 2009, SL Israel became the centre of a different kind of political activism when it was used as the venue for anti-Israel protests. Dozens of protesters teleported themselves into SL Israel, waving Palestinian flags, 'slurring obscenities about murderous Israeli forces', according to Odets, and posting signs with images of dead Arab children. Odets felt forced to close the SL Israel sim to outsiders temporarily, since 'people weren't wanting to be logical, or talk' (Au 2009).

The Reorganization of Jewish Spaces in Second Life

Shortly after the antisemitic attack on SL Kotel, Fischer decided to move his site from Choi to Nessus, a different land area in the SL spatial grid. Nessus was already home to Temple Beth Israel and the 2Life Building. Around the same time, Matzohenge,[14] a large clock tower with matzah-like 'texture', also moved to the vicinity in Nessus. With four major Jewish sites, Nessus became SL's first Jewish neighbourhood.

In RL, from a practical vantage point, Jewish neighbourhoods have historically meant proximity to kosher food, walking distance to synagogues, and access to Jewish education for the children. In short, these areas developed out of a need for proximal religious and cultural resources in urban spaces.[15] Yet in SL, especially after the 2005 reform of the telehub system, users could teleport themselves directly from one place to another instantaneously. Thus, in terms of ease and time of travel between sites, there was no advantage to grouping Jewish sites together in SL space. Instead, this growing trend underlined the cultural rather than pragmatic values that SL spaces encode; the virtualized experience of meaning that has long shaped cultural spaces, including Jewish spaces, in RL was similarly restructuring the virtualized space of SL.[16]

Taking this a step further, in May 2007 Carter Giacobini opened Ir Shalom, a virtual island. Unlike Nessus or Choi, this area had no borders shared with other neighbourhoods on the grid, but was surrounded by virtual water, giving it a sense of isolation and protection. Ir Shalom's main attraction was Temple Beit Shalom, a modernist synagogue building created by Cryptomorph Lake. The *New World Notes* blog named Temple Beit Shalom 'one of the best places to visit in Second Life' (Au 2007). Over the next few months, more Jewish sites, such as the Jewish Historic Museum, moved onto the island, making it SL's second Jewish neighbourhood (Munro 2007).

Jewish Identity in the Virtual and 'Real' Worlds

Misha Kobrin, a then 32-year-old computer programmer from Germany, explained his fascination with SL in 2007: 'you create a different identity. It does not matter how you look or where you come from. You reinvent yourself.' Unlike other digital environments, such as Facebook or other social networking sites, where correspondence between online and offline identities is structurally favoured, SL is a space in which users are given wide latitude to formulate virtual identities that in no way correspond to their offline identities. In an environment in which the central form of capital is personal creativity, users often display this creativity in both the visual formation of their avatar, and in the types of activities in which they engage in-world. As is the case with more explicitly 'game' programmes, especially MMORPGs, SL users also engage with one another in digital spaces external to the SL platform. Hundreds of SL avatar profiles, for example, can be found on social network sites like Facebook or Flickr, and a group of entrepreneurs even created a social network website exclusively for SL avatars, SL Profiles.

Yet, as Tom Boellstorff has observed, by 2007 'Second Life was already so large that there were many subcultures within it' (2008: 7). Thus it is notable that while the structural features of the platform allow a great deal of freedom to users to define their identities creatively, the cultural practices that developed within specific 'subcultures' in SL often established an acceptable range of identity formations.

While SL users in-world interacted in the form of avatars, virtual bodies that move through SL space, the platform also allowed users to create a static profile, similarly to social network websites. Users were free to provide information about their RL identities and lives in this space, but the general trend in practice across the SL platform was to focus the profile on virtual rather than actual identity and experience. SL profiles could be viewed by clicking on the avatar, which pulled up a profile window. 'The distinction between actual and virtual self', as Boellstorff points out, 'was encoded in the Second Life platform with the tab entitled "1st Life"' and another labelled "2nd Life"'. While the former was often left without substantive information, the latter was often more extensively filled with information on the users' main online interests, groups joined, favourite sites, and friends made in SL (Boellstorff 2008: 158). The friends list in particular was 'an indication of a reciprocated formal partnership', enabling players to see which of their contacts was online and where on the grid these friends were currently located (Krotoski et al. 2009: 52). Additionally, users could communicate with friends through their profile via an Instant Messenger, even when in different locations.

If users rarely shared RL information in their profiles, however, they often shared very personal details about their lives when interacting with other users in-world. This information included RL personal relationships, backgrounds, and issues (Heider 2009: 138). While SL users were more heavily involved in other SL subcultures and sometimes came to the virtual world expressly to decouple their RL and SL identities through role-play (Boellstorff 2008: 120–2), individuals who participated in SL's Jewish community more often saw their virtual alter egos as an extension of their RL identities. 'I wouldn't know how not to be a Jew anywhere', explained Moshe Dreyfuss, known by his avatar RebMoshe Zapedzki. An observant Jew from RL Baltimore, then in his mid-fifties, Dreyfuss created an avatar that resembled an Orthodox Jew, visually identifying himself as Jewish in-world.[17] Derek Goldman, then in his early twenties, from Austin, Texas, whose avatar was Avram Leven, echoed Dreyfuss: 'I am not someone who lives his life any differently in real life versus Second Life, so being Jewish in SL is a natural thing for me. My virtual Judaism is simply an extension of my RL practices and beliefs.'

This trend is consistent with research on the disclosure of religious identities in digital social media more generally. In a 2011 study, for example, Piotr Bobkowski and Lisa Pearce found that nearly 80 per cent of religious affiliations disclosed on MySpace were consistent with the offline religious affiliations of users. Instead, they noted that it was more likely for users to control their self-presentation by simply not identifying with religious culture than by identifying inconsistently. Additionally, they observe that users whose closest online friends are openly religious are also more likely to identify as religious and to engage in religious discussion openly (Bobkowski and Pearce 2011: 757–8).

In most cases, Javatars did not meet each other in real life, but had emotional connections (often defined by them as 'close friendships') with people with whom they only interacted in the form of avatars. As communications scholar Don Heider has observed, 'relationships formed in a virtual world, even when they stay virtual, can have emotional impact on people quite similar to the impact of relationships in the flesh . . . The fact that it takes place in a virtual environment does not diminish the value or meaning. In daily life we may have trivial or meaningful contact with people in a variety of settings. It is not the surroundings that define the relationship or exchange, it is the meaning we ascribe to these relationships and exchanges that define their relative value and importance to us' (Heider 2009: 134–5; see also Boellstorff 2008: 151–78; Marshall 2014: 110; Welles et al. 2014: 11).

The number of people who regularly attended Jewish events in SL was never more than 80 to 120, although there were hundreds of members of the various Jewish groups in SL, and assuredly more users with RL Jewish backgrounds. The vast majority of active Javatars came from North America, followed by Israelis, a statistic that reflects perhaps both the demographic centres of the RL Jewish population as well as differential geographical access to the Internet. Despite these patterns, Javatars came from all over the world, many from areas where there was no organized Jewish community.[18]

Other than RL geographic concentrations, there was no typical RL demographic profile of a Javatar. They represented a diverse group in terms of RL age, affiliation, and geography. As Tamara Cogan, an educator from California whose avatar name was TamaraEden Zinnemann, pointed out in 2007: 'The beautiful thing about Second Life's Jewish community is that I've met people of literally every stream of Judaism . . . Perhaps a place like Second Life will be the start of many communities, from both ends of the spectrum, to reach out and step outside their worlds, embracing and learning about the most beautiful part of Judaism: our diversity.'

The Decline of Second Life Judaism

SL's next-big-thing status was short-lived. Although a 2012 estimate placed the user base at 1.5 million (Boellstorff et al. 2012: 10), there have been clear signs of decline in user as well as economic activity. By the end of 2009, many companies and media organizations started to close their SL locations (Thomas 2009). Less publicity also meant fewer new users, and at the same time Linden Lab struggled to maintain its clientele. This economic and social decline of SL caused internal disputes at Linden Lab. On 11 December 2007, the company's CTO Cory Ondrejka resigned (Money 2007). He was later hired by Facebook. On 14 March 2008, SL founder Philip Rosedale announced plans to step down from his position as Linden Lab CEO (Golson 2008). His successor, Mark Kingdon, only survived in this position for less than two years. In June 2010, the company announced layoffs of 30 per cent of its workforce (Kawamoto 2010).

Even if Linden Lab's internal struggle was not visible inside SL, it coincided with the decline of its Jewish community. The first victim was Ir Shalom. Carter Giacobini had based Ir Shalom's business model on SL's successful real-estate developer Anshe Chung, who created themed spaces, such as Japanese gardens with apartments for rent or purchase. After initially offering free spaces on his island, he tried to generate rent income to maintain it, but was never able to fill the space. Ir Shalom had to close down for financial reasons in March 2008, and many Jewish sites followed, including SL Israel in August 2012.

In addition to the diminishing economic potential of SL, Javatars less experienced with virtual worlds sometimes became frustrated with the relatively complicated building tools and abandoned their avatars. 'SL as a medium was laggy, not intuitive', explains Chaim Landau of his frustration with SL. 'Linden Lab did not make the experience smooth; instead it demanded a steep learning curve. Eventually SL became a niche market, one that was not growing' (cf. Boellstorff 2008: 101–6).

Reuven Fischer, however, believes that SL was a good opportunity for 'exposing Judaism to others in a non-in your face type of way. It allowed others to learn in a fun manner making Judaism seem current and relevant.' However, he agrees with Landau that 'its challenges were . . . the limitation in technology'. Fischer eventually left SL for good in spring 2009: 'The lure of Twitter & Facebook pulled me away due to their ubiquitous nature. That is the inherit [sic] problem with Second Life. You have to be in front of your fat-client to interact with others in Second Life. The mobility of Twitter, Facebook, Skype allows folks to connect and conversion [sic] anywhere.'

Fischer believes that, when it comes to Jewish learning, many lessons learned from the Javatar experience in SL have already been applied to other platforms. 'The learning I was doing in Second Life in 2006 was novel for its time. Today it's commonplace', he explained. 'I fully embrace the internet and social media in regards to the total flood of Jewish information.'[19]

SL continues to exist, but rather as a fringe phenomenon of the Internet. From the hundreds of SL users who regularly participated in Jewish events, only a dozen or so remain in-world. Brown and other volunteers at Temple Beth Israel continue to organize the 'Shabbat Around The World' gatherings most Fridays, but struggle to maintain a virtual *minyan*.[20]

At the peak of its popularity, SL users were able to find dozens of groups, sites, and individuals who used the term 'Jewish' in their listing on the SL directory, in addition to a number of Israeli groups. However, the total number probably never exceeded 800, with only a few dozen very active individuals. These key players were the ones who connected the Jews of SL. The majority of Javatars were only passive visitors. There is no doubt that by creating virtual Jewish environments, even creating a Jewish avatar for oneself, these users acknowledged and embraced a Jewish identity; for some this may also have been an act of faith, even if this did not reflect their actions in the real world (Shandler 2009: 280).[21]

Yet the fact that Jewish sites, events, practices, and identity in SL often related to RL in specific ways underlined that Judaism in this virtual world relied on certain knowledge and practices brought to SL from outside.[22] Landau therefore believes that 'Judaism is predicated on involvement in a real life Jewish community. No virtual community can ever replace that. The best a virtual Jewish community can do is augment Jewish life for those who already spend a lot of time in virtual worlds or for those who live very far from a real life Jewish community.' But at the same time, as we have shown in a variety of ways in this study, the relationship between virtual and actual Judaism was characterized by a 'tight referential relation' that was importantly contextualized in the virtual particularities of various aspects of Jewish culture, both digital and otherwise.

Notes

1   While a number of structural features of the SL platform make it distinct from virtual world MMO video games, it does share certain aesthetic features with these games. For interesting discussions of the aesthetic features of video games, especially their formal aesthetics, see Bogost 2007, 2011; Galloway 2006.

2   Theorizing Boellstorff's observations in the context of work by Slavoj Žižek, Gunkel points out that 'For Žižek ... the real is already a virtual construct ... this means explicitly recognizing the way what comes to be enunciated is always and already conditioned by the situation or place of enunciation. ... The strategic advantage of this particular approach, then, is not that it provides one with privileged and immediate access to the object in its raw or naked state but that it continuously conceptualizes the place from which one claims to know anything and submits to investigation the particular position that is occupied by any epistemological claim whatsoever' (Gunkel 2010: 138).

3   In this sense, we are responding to E. Gabriella Coleman's argument that an ethnographic study of the digital 'must involve various frames of analysis, attention to history, and the local contexts and lived experiences of digital media' (Coleman 2010: 488–9).

4   See also Shields 2003: 54–69 for a historical discussion more focused on digital 'virtual reality' developments.

5   The term 'cyberspace' was introduced in Gibson's 1984 novel *The Neuromancer*. For further discussion of Gibson's work, see Shields 2003: 51–4.

6   Incidentally, Buccitelli entered the world at about the same time as the avatar Virpa Tuominen, but only informally.

7   Some of these real-life interviews were documented in *tachles*, a weekly that also published *2Life Magazine*.

8   The Sanskrit word literally means 'incarnation' and was popularized by Stephenson's *Snow Crash* as term for the user's graphical representation in games and online communities (Boellstorff 2008: 128).

9   The historian Martin Jay has argued for the historical connection between Hebraic culture and the heard or written word (Jay 1993: 33, 269). In a more contemporary media context, Liebes-Plesner (2010) argues that the historical orientation towards verbal expression in Jewish culture partly accounts for the reason that radio, rather than television, played such a key role in the formulation of modern Israeli nationalism.

10 As an interesting counterpoint, in a 2014 study of online friendships in virtual worlds, Welles et al. have argued that 'while immersive virtual worlds can provide enjoyable activities for friends to participate in together, there is nothing about virtual worlds that make them *uniquely* well suited for friendship formation. Our results suggest that it is the ability to make a personal connection via communication (a feature of, but not specific to, immersive virtual worlds) that enables true friendships to emerge' (Welles et al. 2014: 11–12).

11 The magazine was also available for download at the now closed website <www.2lifemaga zine.com>.

12   Notably, Dauer and Finkelstein never met in real life.

13   'Furzi' is short for 'fur Nazi' but also a word play for the German term for 'little fart'.

14   Matzohenge was the creation of Crap Mariner, avatar of Texas-based user Laurence Simon. Although parodic, Jeffrey Shandler points out that 'its effectiveness assumes multiple cultural literacies and an understanding of their interrelation as provocatively amusing' (Shandler 2009: 278).

15   It should be noted, of course, that some European neighbourhoods were also the result of historical antisemitic ghettoization of Jews, policies often encoded in the laws of municipalities.

16   For representative discussions of the virtualization of RL Jewish spaces in the context of the Lower East Side neighbourhood of New York City, the most significant memory site in American Jewish life, see Diner 2000; Diner, Shandler, and Wenger 2000; Rottenberg 2010; Wenger 1997. This point is also interesting in light of Marilyn Halter's argument, in the early days of Web 2.0, that online Jewish spaces 'throw into question the fundamental meanings of community and of ethnic enclaves' (Halter 2000: 102).

17   In a 2015 study of age identity representation in SL, Martey et al. interestingly conclude that, while the visual age appearance of avatars in SL does not generally correspond to offline identity (i.e. older people tend to create younger-looking avatars), they do reflect certain visual patterns that run along RL age lines. In other words, while most users create younger-looking avatars, certain patterns of visual markers, while not the same markers that encode offline age identity, are consistent in corresponding to certain RL age groups. One example they note, for instance, is the use of 'furry' avatars, avatars with animal features, which were never employed by users whose RL age was over 35 (Martey et al. 2015: 53).

18   Among the North Americans, it is interesting to note that many came from ultra-Orthodox backgrounds.

19   Celia Pearce and Artemesia have already called significant attention to the migration of social groups between virtual world platforms (Pearce and Artemisia 2009). While it is beyond the scope of the present study, it would be interesting to examine the extent to which Javatars have congregated in other digital spaces.

20   Jack Kugelmass, in his classic study *The Miracle of Intervale Avenue*, has shown the maintenance of a *minyan* to be both a central concern and, at times, a point of significant cultural adaptation in declining RL congregations (Kugelmass 1996). Interesting, Jeffrey Shandler's study of the media practices of the Chabad-Lubavitch movement stresses that virtual presence is not sufficient to form a *minyan* in that community, given the tradition of spiritual emphasis on the physical body in hasidism (Shandler 2009: 272).

21   That SL practices could have emotional and spiritual significance is not only suggested by the data collected by Shandler and the authors of this study, but also by a 2014 study conducted by Kathleen Gabriels, Karolien Poels, and Johan Braeckman, which demonstrated that in-world actions in SL that had significant moral content, in their case engaging in infidelity in a digital virtual space, 'triggered emotions that were equally intense compared to a similar situation in the material world' (Gabriels et al. 2014: 464).

22   As Stromer-Galley and Martey have observed on SL place-making, 'in online worlds, visual settings activate spatial schemas related to player experiences both on- and offline. These schemas contribute to the social meanings players attach to that space, which in

turns helps to shape the social norms that emerge' (Stromer-Galley and Martey 2009: 1050). See also Marshall 2014: 110.

References

AU, WAGNER JAMES. 2007. 'Best of Second Life'. *New World Notes* (23 Nov.) <http://nwn.blogs.com> (accessed 7 Sept. 2017).

——2008. *The Making of Second Life: Notes from the New World*. New York.

——2009. 'Disputed Territory: War in Gaza Provokes Protest (and Conversation) in Second Life Israel'. *New World Notes* (7 Jan.) <http://nwn.blogs.com> (accessed 7 Sept. 2017).

BERLINGER, GABRIELLE A. 2010. '770 Eastern Parkway: The Rebbe's Home as Icon'. In Simon J. Bronner, ed., *Jews at Home: The Domestication of Identity*, Jewish Cultural Studies 2, 163–87. Oxford.

BOBKOWSKI, PIOTR S., and LISA D. PEARCE. 2011. 'Baring Their Souls in Online Profiles or Not? Religious Self-Disclosure in Social Media'. *Journal for the Scientific Study of Religion*, 50: 744–62.

BOELLSTORFF, TOM. 2008. *Coming of Age in Second Life: An Anthropologist Explores the Virtually Human*. Princeton, NJ.

——BONNIE NARDI, CELIA PEARCE, and T. L. TAYLOR. 2012. *Ethnography and Virtual Worlds: A Handbook of Method*. Princeton, NJ.

BOGOST, IAN. 2007. *Persuasive Games: The Expressive Power of Videogames*. Cambridge, Mass.

——2011. *How to Do Things with Videogames. Electronic Mediations*. Minneapolis, Minn.

BRAND, STEWART. 1974. *II Cybernetic Frontiers*. New York.

BRENNEN, BONNIE, and ERIKA DELA CERNA. 2010. 'Journalism in Second Life'. *Journalism Studies*, 11: 546–54.

COLEMAN, E. GABRIELLA. 2010. 'Ethnographic Approaches to Digital Media'. *Annual Review of Anthropology*, 39: 487–505.

DINER, HASIA. 2000. *Lower East Side Memories: A Jewish Place in America*. Princeton, NJ.

——JEFFREY SHANDLER, and BETH S. WENGER, eds. 2000. *Remembering the Lower East Side: American Jewish Reflections*. Bloomington, Ind.

DUBNER, STEPHEN J. 2007. 'Philip Rosedale Answers Your Second Life Questions'. *Freakonomics* (13 Dec.) <http://freakonomics.com/2007/12/13/philip-rosedale-answers-your-second-life-questions/> (accessed 7 Sept. 2017).

GABRIELS, KATHLEEN, KAROLIEN POELS, and JOHAN BRAECKMAN. 2014. 'Morality and Involvement in Social Virtual Worlds: The Intensity of Moral Emotions in Response to Virtual Versus Real Life Cheating'. *New Media & Society*, 16: 451–69.

GALLOWAY, ALEXANDER R. 2006. *Gaming: Essays on Algorithmic Culture. Electronic Mediations*. Minneapolis, Minn.

GOLSON, JORDAN. 2008. 'Linden Lab CEO Stepping Down'. *Gawker* (14 Mar.) <http://www.gawker.com>. [Article no longer available since the Gawker website has been shut down.]

GROSSMAN, CATHY LYNN. 2007. 'Faithful Build a Second Life for Religion Online'. *USA Today* (1 Apr.) <https://usatoday30.usatoday.com/tech/gaming/2007-04-01-second-life-religion_N.htm> (accessed 23 Dec. 2017).

GUNKEL, DAVID J. 2010. 'The Real Problem: Avatars, Metaphysics and Online Social Interaction'. *New Media & Society*, 12: 127–41.

HALTER, MARILYN. 2000. *Shopping for Identity: The Marketing of Ethnicity*. New York.

HARP, DUSTIN. 2009. 'Virtual Journalism and Second Life'. In Don Heider, ed., *Living Virtually: Researching New Worlds. Digital Formations*, 271–89. New York.

HEIDER, DON. 2009. 'Identity and Reality: What Does It Mean to Live Virtually?'. In Don Heider, ed., *Living Virtually: Researching New Worlds. Digital Formations*, 131–43. New York.

HOF, ROBERT D. 2006 'My Virtual Life'. *Business Week* (30 Apr.) <https://www.bloom berg.com/news/articles/2006-04-30/my-virtual-life> (accessed 7 Sept. 2017).

JAY, MARTIN. 1993. *Downcast Eyes: The Denigration of Vision in Twentieth-Century French Thought*. Berkeley, Calif.

KAWAMOTO, DAWN. 2010. 'Second Life Owner Linden Lab to Lay Off 30% of its Workers'. *Daily Finance* (9 June) <https://www.aol.com/2010/06/09/second-life-owner-linden-lab-to-lay-off-30-of-its-workers/> (accessed 7 Sept. 2017).

KROTOSKI, ALEKSANDRA, EVANTHIA LYONS, and JULIE BARNETT. 2009. 'The Social Life of Second Life: An Analysis of the Social Networks of a Virtual World'. In Don Heider, ed., *Living Virtually: Researching New Worlds. Digital Formations*, 47–65. New York.

KUGELMASS, JACK. 1996. *The Miracle of Intervale Avenue: The Story of a Jewish Congregation in the South Bronx*. New York.

LEVI, JOSHUA. 2007. 'Aussie Hosts Seder in Cyberspace'. *Australian Jewish News* (13 Apr.) http://www.ajn.com/au/news/news.asp?pgID=2971 [Website has since disappeared.]

LIEBES-PLESNER, TAMAR. 2010. 'The Voice of Jacob: Radio's Role in Reviving a Nation'. In Chris Berry, Soyoung Kim, and Lynn Spigel, eds., *Electronic Elsewheres: Media, Technology, and the Experience of Social Space*, 137–56. Minneapolis, Minn.

LINDEN LAB. 2004. 'What is It?' Second Life website, 29 Mar. Internet Archive Wayback Machine, <https://web.archive.org/web/20040401193715/http://secondlife.com:80/about> (accessed 10 Feb. 2017).

MARSHALL, AMBER. 2014. 'Sensemaking in Second Life'. *Procedia Technology*, 13: 107–11.

MARTEY, ROSA MIKEAL, JENNIFER STROMER-GALLEY, MIA CONSALVO, JINGSI WU, JAIME BANKS, and TOMEK STRZALKOWSKI. 2015. 'Communicating Age in Second Life: The Contributions of Textual and Visual Factors'. *New Media & Society*, 17: 41–61.

MESSMER, MANTA. 2007. 'Nazi Attack on Jewish Sim'. *AvaStar* (16 May), 6.

MONEY, MOO. 2007. 'Was Cory Linden Fired, or Did He Quit?' *Massively* (11 Dec.) <https://www.engadget.com/2007/12/11/was-cory-linden-fired-or-did-he-quit/> (accessed 7 Sept. 2017).

MUNRO, MIRALEE, 2007. 'A New Homeland for the Jews'. *SL Newspaper* (22 May).

New World Notes. 2017. <http://nwn.blogs.com> (accessed 7 Sept. 2017).

NEWMAN, ANDREW ADAM. 2006. 'The Reporter Is Real, but the World He Covers Isn't'. *New York Times* (16 Oct.) <http://www.nytimes.com/2006/10/16/technology/16 reuters.html?mcubz=3> (accessed 7 Sept. 2017).

PEARCE, CELIA, and ARTEMESIA. 2009. *Communities of Play: Emergent Cultures in Multiplayer Games and Virtual Worlds.* Cambridge, Mass.

ODETS, BETH. 2007. 'A Torah Got Carried Away'. *2Life Magazine*, 1 (Apr.), 4.

ROSEDALE, PHILIP. 2007. 'Foreword'. In Michael Rymaszewski, ed., *Second Life: The Official Guide.* Indianapolis, Ind.

ROTTENBERG, CATHERINE. 2010. 'Affective Narratives: Harlem and the Lower East Side'. *Journal of American Studies*, 44: 777–93.

RYMASZEWSKI, MICHAEL, ed. 2007. *Second Life: The Official Guide.* San Francisco.

SHANDLER, JEFFREY. 2009. *Jews, God, and Videotape: Religion and Media in America.* New York.

SHIELDS, ROB. 2003. *The Virtual.* London.

SHOFFMAN, MARC. 2007. 'Virtual Shoah Museum Opens'. *Totally Jewish* (5 Mar.). <http://www.totallyjewish.com>. [Website has since disappeared.]

SLOAN, PAUL. 2005. 'The Virtual Rockefeller. Anshe Chung is Raking in Real Money in an Unreal Online World'. *CNN Business* (1 Dec.) <http://money.cnn.com/maga zines/business2/business2_archive/2005/12/01/8364581/index.htm> (accessed 2 Oct. 2017).

STEPHENSON, NEAL. 1992. *Snow Crash.* New York.

STROMER-GALLEY, JENNIFER, and ROSA MARTEY. 2009. 'Visual Spaces, Norm Governed Places: The Influence of Spatial Context Online'. *New Media & Society*, 11: 1041–60.

TOFTS, DARREN, ANNEMARIE JONSON, and ALESSIO CAVALLARO. 2002. *Prefiguring Cyberculture: An Intellectual History.* Cambridge, Mass.

TREZISE, BRYONI. 2011. 'Touching Virtual Trauma: Performative Empathics in Second Life'. *Memory Studies*, 5: 392–409.

THOMAS, OWEN. 2009. 'The End of Second Life'. *Gawker* (22 Feb.) <http://gawker.com/ 5158190/the-end-of-second-life> (accessed 7 Sept. 2017).

VOLOJ, JULIAN. 2007a. 'Javatar Finds Javatar'. *2Life Magazine* (May), 6.

—— 2007b. 'Virtual Hate—Real Danger?' *2Life Magazine* (May), 7f.

WELLES, BROOKE FOUCAULT, TOMMY ROUSSE, NICK MERRILL, and NOSHIR CONTRACTOR. 2014. 'Virtually Friends: An Explorations of Friendship Claims and Expectations in Immersive Virtual Worlds'. *Journal of Virtual Worlds Research*, 7: 1–15.

WENGER, BETH S. 1997. 'Memory as Identity: The Invention of the Lower East Side'. *American Jewish History*, 85: 3–27.

Wikifur. 2017. *en.wikifur.com* <http://en.wikifur.com/wiki/WikiFur_Furry_Central/ 800> (accessed 2 Oct. 2017).

ZHENG, NAN. 2009. 'When Geography Matters in a Virtual World: In-Game Urban Planning and Its Impact on the Second Life Community'. In Don Heider, ed., *Living Virtually: Researching New Worlds. Digital Formations*, 93–110. New York.

Rethinking Jewishness in Networked Publics: The Case of Post-Communist Hungary

ANNA MANCHIN

MANY SCHOLARS viewed the fall of communism in 1989 as a potential turning point for east European Jewish communities. They noted that political freedom promised new possibilities for organizing religious and secular Jewish life and for representing individual Jewish identities and communities (Gitelman and Kovács 2003; Gruber 2000; Papp 2004; Webber 1994). Could political change lead to a new flourishing of Jewish religion and culture, and if so, what form would it take? Hungary's Hungarian-born Jewish population in Budapest, estimated at between 80,000 and 150,000, constituting between 3 and 8 per cent of the residents of the capital, represents the largest such community in any central European city, and thus was thought to hold great potential for community building. Yet by the early twenty-first century, most observers had concluded that despite some experiments in alternative religious communities, a lasting religious revival was not likely to materialize in Hungary. As several scholars have noted, the greatest change was happening in the cultural field instead, where Jews were partaking in 'new manifestations of cultural ethnicity such as an interest in Jewish history[,] culture [and] tradition' (Kovács 1996–9; Mars 1999 and 2001). New forms of Jewish cultural expression notwithstanding, a redefinition of the Hungarian Jewish community would be difficult, if not impossible, due to the historical discourse, dating from the nineteenth century, of not treating Jews as a separate, ethnically defined group (Kovács 1996–9; Mars 1999; Papp 2004).

In this essay, I argue that while political change alone did not lead to a redefinition of the Hungarian Jewish community, cultural changes, specifically the technological and social effects of networked publics and their blurring of the boundaries between public and private, have led to changes in Hungarian public discourse on Jewishness. To show this, I examine the challenge of two social-networking sites, one a Facebook group called 'The Holocaust and My Family', and the other a blog called 'Judapest', both of which posed challenges to the way Jewishness was being discussed among Hungarians. Although there are other 'Jewish' blogs and 'Jewish' Facebook groups in Hungary, the ones I discuss here are the best-known and most successful examples in that they drew large readerships and were widely discussed in other media as well. Furthermore, they were both concerned with topics of Jewish interest and the place of Jewishness in Hungarian society, and explicitly sought to disrupt and shape Hungarian public discourse on Jewishness.

My analysis shows that the blog and the Facebook group's intervention came not only from their explicit content, but also through the effects produced by the medium. In other words, it was a result of interaction between the technology, the architecture of the public forum, the intention of the creators, and the contribution of their participants; these were all shaped by the specific cultural, social, and political context and the multimedia environment in which they emerged. I contend that new social media, as used in Hungary, pose a challenge to the prevailing idea that Jewish identities and experiences are private, rather than public or national, issues. Social media have thus enabled new ways of imagining Hungarian Jewish communities by shifting the boundaries of what is private and what is public. In this essay I begin by discussing the historical discourse on Jewishness in Hungary and explain why the fall of communism failed to change it radically. Using theories of a 'networked public' in the Digital Age, I then turn to the analysis of the two social networking sites, working towards an assessment of their effects on the Hungarian Jewish community.

Jews and the Hungarian Public Sphere: A Historical Overview

The idea that democratization would transform the Jewish community and discourse on Jewishness in Hungary was a reasonable expectation, because as elsewhere in communist eastern Europe, the state suppressed public discussion of Jewishness and Jewish identities. Any Jewish community that could be seen as a political organization or an interest group outside the Communist Party threatened to introduce internal divisions in the workers' state. As a result, in communist Hungary, as in Czechoslovakia, the only acceptable forms of Jewish expression in public were religious. Political, ethnic, or cultural expressions of Jewishness threatened to undermine both the communist narrative of anti-fascist resistance and that of communist unity. As elsewhere in eastern Europe, neither the Holocaust nor its Jewish victims could be part of official public memory.

In Hungary, however, the pressure against discussing Jewishness in anything other than a religious context originated in the nineteenth century, and had to do with the specific circumstances of Jewish assimilation. After emancipation in 1867, Jews were considered Hungarians of the Jewish faith, rather than an ethnic or national minority. This reflected the hope and expectation shared by both Jewish assimilationists and liberal nationalists that Jews would be fully integrated into Hungarian society linguistically, culturally, and socially, and that the only difference would remain religious. This benefited Hungary politically by adding to the numbers of Hungarian nationals (important in a multi-ethnic empire shaken by rising nationalist movements) and by allowing Jews to contribute to Hungary's much-needed modernization. It was also appealing to assimilationist Jews, as it gave them formal access to new areas of economic, cultural, and political life and assurance of protection against antisemitism by the state. From the last third of the nineteenth century, Jews participated actively and successfully in most areas of Hungarian public life, but they did so as Hungarians, not as Jews. The suggestion that Jews were ethnically or culturally different from non-Jews seemed to question both the possibility of assimilation and Jews' membership and equal rights in the Hungarian nation—and by extension the nation's boundaries as well. It was therefore seen as dangerous, not only by Jews but also by the liberal political elite, which, while it remained in power until 1918, suppressed political antisemitism. Discussing Jewishness in public was considered indecorous; it was supposed to have no bearing on how a person was seen or treated.

Although Jews were participating in formal political life by the last decades of the nineteenth century, they carefully avoided appearing to represent any particular Jewish interest in their politics. The Hungarian Jewish community had no formal political representation, and this remained the case for much of the twentieth century as well. Hungarian Jews famously rejected international intervention on their behalf in the 1920s, when Hungary passed antisemitic laws, preferring to maintain that they were not a minority in need of protection but citizens who could protect their equal rights. This was challenged but ultimately remained unchanged by state-supported antisemitism from 1920 onwards and during the Holocaust. Hungary, a somewhat reluctant ally of Nazi Germany, passed antisemitic laws and, after German occupation in March 1944, it ultimately deported the majority of some 460,000 Jews from rural Hungary, most of whom were murdered in Auschwitz in the summer of 1944. Yet under communism Jews continued their earlier strategies of assimilation and integration, and the regime continued the historical approach of recognizing the Jewish community as a religious group.

The communist state, conscious of the thin line between anti-communism and antisemitism in Hungary, was eager to repress public antisemitism, and did not allow the anti-Zionist campaigns in Poland and the USSR to gain traction in Hungary. As historian András Kovács has argued, however, the public statements of politicians and political essayists in the 1970s and 1980s made it clear that 'Assimilation, identification with the nation, meant identification with the communist political system and its program, and it was acceptance of this that established the right to protection from antisemitism' (Kovács 2010: 51). As a result, discussion of Jewish culture and history was also shunned until the mid-1980s.

To be sure, the fall of communism removed some barriers for Jews as well as for public discussions of Jewishness (Fritz 2015).[1] As Kovács has shown, however, it did not change the historical discourse surrounding Jews and Jewishness, and in response, in 1988 the Shalom Hungarian Jews' Independent Peace Group offered to provide a secular ethnic alternative to the religious framework of Hungarian Jewry (Kovács 1996–9). But in 1990, when the Hungarian government offered a chance for Hungarian Jews to be officially classified as an ethnic minority, most Jews opposed this and the representative body of Hungarian Jewry declined the offer, choosing to remain categorized as Hungarians of the Jewish faith—the National Association of Hungarian Israelites.[2] This remains the dominant way of discussing Jewish identity in Hungary to the present day (Gitelman 1996–9). Most Jews in Hungary continue to prefer the traditional model of individual assimilation and Hungarian identity, and reject both ethnic affiliation and political representation for Jews as an ethnic community. Hungarian law on the rights of ethnic and national minorities (Act LXXXVII/1993) makes it possible for a group to be officially added to the list of minorities in Hungary if at least a thousand members of that community sign a petition to parliament; that the Jewish community was never added indicates that fewer than 1,000 people support such a redefinition (Kovács 1994). This is not only due to fear that such a redefinition would support the arguments of antisemites vying for their exclusion, but also because if Jews are not an ethnic group, and most do not belong to a religious community either, there would be no commonly shared Jewish culture, tradition, or identity that could form the basis of such a community.

At the same time, throughout the entire historical period, the official, or public, way of talking about Jewishness (that designated Jews as ethnically Hungarian, and Jewishness a private, religious matter) coexisted with an unofficial, private way of discussing Jewishness that was shared by Jews and non-Jews alike. Outside official discourse, Jewishness not only mattered a great deal, but was seen as permeating all aspects of culture, and, when it came to individuals, it was an immutable, implicitly ethnic or racial category that no amount of assimilation—not even religious conversion—could change.

On the other hand, antisemitism, and especially the impact of the Holocaust (specifically the fear of being perceived as a separate group with interests in conflict with those of the majority society), led most Jewish families in Hungary to adopt various strategies to 'pass' in Hungarian society and to manage the stigmatized identity associated with Jewishness. According to Kovacs, they acquired 'different behavior and communication strategies' for Jewish and for non-Jewish audiences (Kovács 1996–9). That the significance of Jewishness never really disappeared from Hungarian culture and unofficial discourse became clear after 1989, when antisemitism re-emerged both in popular culture and as part of the political right's rhetoric. But the unspoken rule against mentioning Jewishness in public outside the religious context remained, not only in political life but in public life more generally. Neither one's Jewish background nor its relevance for cultural representations in public life are considered appropriate topics for public discussion.

What was also new in the post-communist period was that, as elsewhere in post-communist eastern Europe, a central question of national memory and identity in post-1989 Hungary was the place of the interwar period and the Holocaust in Hungarian history, especially vis-à-vis the communist period. In Hungary, this has coincided with a search for a new Jewish identity, especially among a young generation of Jews, typically the grandchildren of Holocaust survivors, who rejected the stigmatized identity, silence, and shame of their parents' and grandparents' generations. These two issues became the subject of intense public discussion after 1989, and are the subjects of the blog and Facebook group discussed below. My approach therefore uses discourse analysis to examine not only the content of the two online spaces but also their place in the larger context of communication that connects participants to shared public concerns.

Public and Private in Networked Publics

My goal in the remaining portion of this essay is to analyse how two specific online communities or public spaces have functioned in a wider public field as part of a historical discourse in a specific place and time. On the basis of Nancy Fraser's and Michael Warner's critique of sociologist Jürgen Habermas's theory of the bourgeois public sphere, I understand both 'community' and 'public' not as natural categories, but as ideological and political divisions and historically specific cultural constructs that change over time, shaped by particular social, cultural, and political contexts (boyd 2011; Habermas 1989; Fraser 1990; Warner 2002). Public, in this understanding, is both a space in which discussion and interaction takes place and a collection of people defined by their shared engagement with a text—a community. In terms of networked publics, I follow recent digital media scholarship that has argued that 'digital media has come to be understood not just as a form of material exchange, but also as a site of social and cultural production, supporting new forms of social connection, the maintenance of social ties and identity expression' (Lindtner et al. 2011: 2).

I build on danah boyd's theory of networked publics, which she defines as publics that are restructured by networked technologies (boyd 2011: 41). boyd has argued that, although networked publics have much in common with other publics, they are distinctive because of being shaped by technology, which introduces some special characteristics, with new possibilities for interaction that frame participation (2011: 39). boyd argues that social networking sites are defined by users having public profiles, a list of 'friends', and the possibility for interaction and, in addition, they have four key new characteristics: online expressions are recorded and archived; they can be easily duplicated; they are scalable, potentially allowing for much greater visibility; and are searchable. Although these possibilities, according to boyd, 'do not determine social practice', they 'can destabilize people's assumptions about engaging in social life and can reshape publics both directly and indirectly'. The blog I discuss shares the features boyd describes and functions in much the same way (Renninger 2015). According to boyd, changes in the social environments in which people communicate influence how people think and behave.

boyd identifies the three central dynamics of networked publics as collapsed contexts, the blurring of public and private, and invisible audiences. She argues that 'the lack of spatial, social and temporal boundaries [for public acts in networked publics] makes it difficult [for participants] to maintain distinct social contexts'. As sociologist Erving Goffman has argued, people perform different public selves depending on who their audience is; in other words, context determines what it is appropriate to reveal to whom. Also relevant is Goffman's notion of front and back stage, where 'front' means the presentation of self for others as if 'on stage' and 'back' means the sphere 'typically out of bounds to members of the audience' (Goffman 1959: 124). Participants lack full control over the context in which their performance will be received, so maintaining the different ways in which they communicate in formerly distinct social settings and groups they participate in becomes difficult. When contexts are collapsed, people are unable to adjust their behaviour to make it appropriate for different audiences. They may indeed not be aware that their audience includes different contexts, and thus may overlook the need for adjustment.

Networked publics make it possible for individuals to have private and intimate conversations online, including with strangers on the other side of the world, but they also facilitate communication becoming public, and indeed shared with an unprecedentedly wide public. This makes it difficult for people to control what is private, and to keep 'private' and 'public' things separate and distinct. Third, the invisibility of audiences means that the potential audience in networked publics is usually different from and much larger than the audience imagined by participants. None of these features is unique to networked publics but they are intrinsic to them (boyd 2011: 50). The discourse on Jewishness in Hungary has relied on the distinction between public and private, and the separation of different contexts and audiences. The dynamics of networked publics that blur and undermine these boundaries can therefore contribute to the breakdown and transformation of that discourse.

Judapest: A Jewish Blog's 'Semantic Guerrilla War'

Judapest, a blog about 'Jewish popular culture', written by Bruno Bitter and a handful of other bloggers, ran from 2004 to 2008. Its name, as a post explains, is the moniker that Karl Lueger, Vienna's antisemitic mayor, gave to Budapest at the turn of the last century. At the time, close to a fifth of Budapest's population was Jewish, and Theodor Herzl described Hungary as an 'oasis in the antisemitic world'. The blog attracted several thousand unique visitors a day and tens of thousands a month. Over four years, it produced over 1,500 posts, some with several hundred substantive and thoughtful comments. Judapest was not only influential but was also viewed by many users as the definitive Jewish blog. Its success and significance were discussed in major on- and offline media, and it won the Hungarian Goldenblog awards' silver and gold medals for outstanding content, in 2007 and 2008 respectively. Initially a virtual community, Judapest eventually also organized offline social and cultural events and even staged a political performance. Most critics agreed that the blog injected a new voice into the stalled discourse on Jewishness in Hungary.

As its introductory page explains, the blog had two explicit, related goals: to change, or at least disrupt, Hungarian public discourse on Jewishness, and to offer Jewish culture an identity for the twenty-first century. Bruno Bitter (Shadai), the blog's editor, explains that he hoped 'to lift talk about Jews/Jewishness out of the context of antisemitism' by 'waging a semantic guerrilla-war' (Shadai 2007). This war would be waged, he explains, by popularizing and supporting 'progressive, alternative Jewish self-expression in culture, politics and religion' (Shadai 2008). In an interview for an article on 'alternative Jewish movements', Bitter explained:

We created Judapest in part because it bothered us that Jewishness is discussed in Hungary in connection with antisemitism and the Holocaust, in a victim role. For us, this is not the only Jewish experience, this does not define Jewish existence and at first we explicitly avoided these topics, as well as Mazsihisz [the association of Hungarian Jewish communities], and politics. A lot of the editors traveled regularly, and I too acquired a lot of experiences that I wanted to share. On my travels, I encountered a living, current, relevant Jewish culture, defined as much by a variety of lifestyles, pop culture and gastronomy, as through a broad range of religious options. This is what I wanted to show. (Miklósi 2008)

In other words, this approach reflected the specific cultural and political experiences and outlook of the 'third generation' after the Holocaust, who came of age in a democratic context; the cultural restrictions against discussing Jewishness in public seemed to them to have little relevance. They rejected their parents' (and the 'official' Jewish community's) focus on antisemitism and the Holocaust, but had little knowledge of Jewish tradition and religion and were eager to search for a new way of being Jewish.

As participants in a more global culture, the creators of Judapest had access to the products of global capitalism offline and online, in Hungary and abroad, where they saw examples of 'alternative' Jewish culture and public figures who discussed their Jewish background publicly. This blog was not the only place where a new understanding of Jewishness could be expressed; it also happened in public meeting places and social movements. They could point, for instance, to the cultural space of Sirály and Auróra, alternative religious groups, and cultural festivals. But as this example shows, the mission was amplified by the medium in important ways.

Beyond showing a diverse range of positive expressions of Jewish identity and culture, the blog also changed Hungarian discourse surrounding Jewishness by blurring the boundaries of public and private ways of speaking about Jewishness. By speaking publicly about various social and cultural actors as Jews, and by posting messages about the 'private' experience of Jewishness as having public relevance, Judapest consciously tried to change the discourse surrounding Jewishness by lifting it out of the private realm and into public culture. The bloggers referred to what they were doing as 'creative (anti)semitism' in pointing out that a public figure was Jewish, and discussing non-religious culture as Jewish. This was in response to the social expectation that Jewishness was discussed privately, and was, to most citizens, unacceptable in public, and risked being perceived as antisemitic. It was not simply the topic and content of the blog, however, but also the technological aspects, architecture, form, and style that helped blur the boundaries between public and private, and in particular between public and private discourse on Jewishness. That the authors shared their opinions on social media meant that they created a public space where anyone willing to create a profile could also participate in this activity.

The blog format, with short journal entries appearing in reverse chronological order, suggested personal, private musings. This was underlined by a public statement that it was not connected to any organization or institution, but created by private individuals. Furthermore, the style of the discussion, which was decidedly informal and popular, in the sense of being unauthorized by religious, academic, or political establishments, encouraged people to contribute material in a private, informal, and familiar tone. It is important that the blog focused on popular culture and everyday life, because it encouraged people to participate based not on their expertise but on their personal experiences and everyday lives. Some of the posts that garnered the most interaction encouraged readers to contemplate and share their own understanding and experience of their Jewishness. One of these, titled 'Are you Jewish?', featured sixteen points of Hungarian Jewish experience, a tongue-in-cheek list titled 'You know you're Jewish when . . .', which was then amended by readers in the 682 comments (Tet 2008). The comments led to individuals sharing their private experiences regarding the public discussion of the symbolic markers of Jewishness in everyday life (often verbalized as such for the first time). This made it possible to share what was seen as the behaviour, gestures, cultural tastes, linguistic turns, and fashion choices that marked the performance of Jewish group belonging. Consequently, conversation ensued about topics rarely discussed in public, such as the fact that Hungarian Jews have remained, in many ways, a distinct social and cultural group rather than an ethnic community. By posting these personal musings about private lives in a public forum, the blog also showed, implicitly, that Jewishness, however one understood it, was not just a private identity but something that mattered a great deal for people in their everyday life, even if they did not participate in Jewish religious life or organizations.

The blog was free and accessible to anyone with an Internet connection; its potential audience was the general public, but as with most other social networking sites (the blog started before Facebook came into wide public use with its current features), participants had to register and have a profile to comment. Profiles were not required to have any specific information: users did not have to use their real names or photographs, and could, if they chose, remain anonymous to the larger public while revealing their offline identities to the smaller group. The blog's audience, conjured in its introduction, was 'Jews and philosemites'—in essence a counter-public with 'different assumptions about what can be said or what goes without saying', in this case with regard to Jewishness and Hungarianness (Warner 2002: 424). The 'invisible' wider public notwithstanding, then, this made it inviting for others to contribute as if they were speaking merely to a Jewish counterpublic.

The blog provided a continuous public space because it was updated on a nearly daily basis, drawing a loyal readership for whom reading it could become an everyday experience. As one commenter noted, 'I've been reading Judapest daily for the last month . . . I check more than once a day to read any new comments' (Ruauch, 14 November 2007). The collection of posts and the evolving discussions that followed them provided a place and a community for contemplation. That the posts were searchable by keyword and topic allowed readers to peruse the discussion easily, even if they joined in later. It became a regular virtual meeting-point for people interested in the question of how to make sense of Jewishness in twenty-first-century Hungary, and in how to make sense of various (Jewish and non-Jewish) events and experiences.

In effect, the public forum also created a sense of community. As the comments in the forum noted, those who participated in the discussion felt they had become members of a virtual community and, over time, an offline one: they organized several community brunches, city walks, and other activities.

One comment on the closing of Judapest noted, 'I'm sad . . . It was decidedly inspiring to be part of a—initially virtual—community, that is concerned with fundamentally different issues than Mazsihisz, Szochnut, and Joint-groups, one that is in the present, is open, multicoloured, and has a sense of humour. It was good to contribute here: it was the first time I felt that I am happy to be part of some kind of Jewish community' (Vadjutka 2008). The community the blog invoked was an open-minded, liberal, pluralist, multicultural Jewish group open to all kinds of Jewish expression. The community that appeared in the comments was composed of Jewish young adults from Budapest. It was a fairly homogenous group in terms of religion, political views, and even socio-economic status. Most of the bloggers reflected a completely secular interest in Jewishness; as one Orthodox participant noted, this secularism shaped the values and perspective of the community that the blog had created. This person complained that the blog represents a 'loud and proud' disregard for Jewish tradition (both on the blog and in offline community activities) that made it difficult for more religious or traditional-minded Jews to identify with and participate in it. In response, Shadai (Bruno Bitter) argued that

you are also part of the Judapest-Jewry, just as I or sdw or other editors who are not even halachically Jewish. Your values, style, choices and Jewishness are represented here to the exact extent that you actively post here. In the first year, you and miou wrote a lot: so Jewish orthodoxy was far overrepresented. This wasn't a problem. The offline events are not organized by some Central Committee: they are the initiatives of private individuals. Just as I have come up with and organized things, you can do the same. These can also be Judapest events. . . . But Prezzey (and Charlie, if you're still here) I totally understand how you feel. You're a minority within a minority: doubly disadvantaged. (15 November 2007)

That this change in the way Jewishness was publicly discussed and imagined would bring into being a new kind of Jewish community in public life was made particularly clear in December 2007, when Judapest addressed a wider public in the form of a clever political performance. When Hungary's president László Sólyom did not sign a hate-speech bill into law, something that the leadership of the 'official' Jewish organization (Mazsihisz), had supported, the organization protested by refusing to attend the annual interfaith luncheon hosted at the president's official residence. Judapest's writers, disagreeing with Mazsihisz, decided to express their public dissent by sending the president a *flódni* (a traditional Hungarian Jewish pastry), accompanied by a letter saying that Hungarian Jewry, like Hungarian tradition, 'has always been a pluralistic entity: we are diverse and multifaceted'. The president thanked Judapest and served the *flódni* at the luncheon.

Judapest's point was that Hungary's contemporary Jewry is no longer adequately represented by a religious organization (if it ever was), or indeed in view of its diversity in religious, cultural, and political outlook, by any single organization (Judapest 2007; Sanders 2007). Since this political interaction clearly undermined the authority of the official Jewish representative body to speak for all Hungarian Jews, its leadership reacted angrily to the stunt. The act ruptured the idea that Mazsihisz represented the 'Hungarian Jewish community' in political life, arguing instead for a multiplicity of Jewish views, perspectives, and communities that are not adequately represented by a religious organization. More interesting, if seemingly obvious, was the suggestion that a Jewish community could, in fact, exist and is compatible with Hungarian social and political life. In other words, Jewishness is not only a private identity and interest that needs to remain outside the public sphere, but it is also a public issue appropriate for consideration in the public sphere.

The Holocaust and My Family Facebook Group

The Facebook group was started in February 2014 by Mátyás Eörsi, a liberal politician and former member of Parliament, with the main purpose of collecting personal stories from the Holocaust period, not only from Jews but all segments of society, and archiving them for posterity. More ambitiously, the group hoped to change the attitude of Hungarian Jewish survivors and their children regarding the Holocaust by ending silence, hiding, and the suppression of Jewish memory. Finally, it hoped to have an impact on public discourse on the Holocaust, to help Hungary come to terms with its past by including the voices of the victims in the discussion.

The Holocaust and My Family project situated itself in the wider public discourse on Jewishness that had been dominant in Hungarian public life since 1948. In Hungary, discussion of the Holocaust was not entirely precluded under communism, especially by the 1980s. But Hungary's role was usually examined only on the level of official politics and the choices of Hungary's political leadership. Until the 1990s, most historical investigations tended also to focus on political and diplomatic history, asking if and what the political leadership could have done differently. In the official narrative, the Hungarian fascist regime and Arrow Cross hooligans were responsible for the carnage and chaos. The links between interwar antisemitism and discriminatory government policies against Jews and the responsibility and agency of ordinary people never became the subjects of wide public debate.

More specifically, the group's aim was to intervene in public discussion of the Holocaust in Hungarian public life, including the official (state-sponsored) discourse on the Holocaust in 2014, the seventieth anniversary of the Holocaust in Hungary and designated by the government as 'Holocaust Memorial Year'. Although since 1989 both the Holocaust and its Jewish victims have been a part of official commemorations, public acknowledgement of this past remains divided, and in official and popular public memory of the interwar years, Hungarian society is usually represented as a unified whole, where the experiences of Jews, often different from those of the majority, are excluded. In 2014, the government distributed public funding for commemorative projects to many different non-governmental organizations and also created public events and memorials. Critics of the government's efforts saw them as minimizing and relativizing the role of the Hungarian government and Hungarian society in the Holocaust.

The group was successful in quickly attracting attention and a large membership: by autumn 2014 there were nearly 5,000 members, and over 7,000 in November 2016. The project also had wide public visibility across media; its significance was discussed in online and offline news sites, newspapers, journals, books, radio, television, and theatre. It led to the publication of a book containing individual contributions, and public readings in various settings, in both Jewish and non-Jewish contexts, including theatres and synagogues.[3]

According to the Facebook group's mission statement, it collected individuals' private stories, most of them about members' own families. These were published as individual posts (some appeared in several parts). Discussion of all other issues was rerouted to a linked group. 'Family stories' from the time of the Holocaust could, theoretically, mean any narrative from the time, with a wide range of narrative arcs and styles, beginnings, and endpoints. In practice, however, most of the posts are about individuals considered Jewish by Hungary's wartime anti-Jewish laws. Most stories range from a few sentences to several paragraphs; many start with a brief description of life before (mostly before 1944, or sometimes before 1938), and then describe what happened during the Holocaust, including how, when, and where family members were taken (or hid); where they were killed or how they survived and returned; and what they did afterwards. The group's language is Hungarian, and accordingly, since most though not all of those postings to the group are Hungarians living in Hungary, their stories often contain brief indications of their experience and, sometimes only implicitly, the family's view of identity under communism. Some of the posts also include family photos, and others contain administrative documents related to survival or death.

This was, of course, neither the first nor the only place where Hungarian Jews' experiences of the Holocaust were recorded and made public. In the following, I will briefly summarize how the technology linked to Facebook and networked publics influenced the impact that these stories had on public discourse and the social structure of the Jewish community in Hungary. In the case of this Facebook group, the effects of technology were the source both of some of its success and some of its setbacks.

Using Facebook promised to expand the potential public of contributors enormously, expand the visibility of the posts, and invite unprecedented discussion. The advantage of Facebook was that it is a popular social media tool, used by nearly all segments of the younger population with access to the Internet. This made it easy to make the group visible, by inviting potentially interested 'friends', who could in turn invite their friends. Upon joining the group, people already knew how it worked; they knew how to read, comment, post, and had some control over privacy. The dissemination of the posts was, in a sense, automated: since Facebook was already integrated into everyday media consumption habits, and was already a way of reading about issues and news, and of maintaining and building social connections, Facebook users would find updates from the group in their newsfeeds and have access to the private stories and the comments without any extra effort. The posts could be replicated and shared both on Facebook and across other types of media almost indefinitely. Importantly, Facebook also provided a platform for people to react and reflect on the posts. Facebook's platform suggests that the public group one joins will be the public of one's communication: a virtual, but limited, community.

On the other hand, Facebook and the Internet were not ideally suited for the group's purposes. It is a medium that is most widely used by younger generations; the generation of Holocaust survivors who could share first-hand stories are often unfamiliar with the technology, although, as Zsuzsa Hetényi, one of the group's administrators and a long-time moderator, mentioned, in some cases, some Holocaust survivors asked them for help in registering with Facebook with the express purpose of joining the group (personal communication, 2016). Many did not in fact want to share their stories beyond the limited public of the Facebook group, and explicitly asked others not to repost or share their posts. Although some privacy settings do exist, in the end, contributors do not have complete control. Participating in the group required a reconsideration of what to share in public and what to keep private, and accepting an overlap of audiences made up of individuals' contacts from different social contexts. Although the group's goal was to encourage public discussion of the Holocaust from the perspective of its victims, not all the group members were comfortable discussing their family's persecution in public under their own names.

A distinctive aspect of the project was the opportunity to comment on the stories and to interact with the people who posted them. As seems to be the case with many social media platforms, only a small percentage of group members actively shared content; most were passive readers, and most of the reactions and comments came from a small subgroup. It is perhaps significant from the perspective of the participants' experience that this can be seen only from analytics, and is not obvious to the casual observer. What was obvious to members (and confirmed by analytics provided by Hetényi) is that nearly every post (99 per cent) garnered a reaction from the group, and 87 per cent also received comments. The comments that follow the posts are most often emotional reactions to the story, offering condolences and sympathy. Examples are 'I am sorry for your loss', 'I am crying as I read this', or 'so tragic', and emoticons (for example, a crying face). They rarely enter into any kind of substantive debate about the context, or initiate any discussion of historical or theoretical questions raised by the posts. Although they do not compose a rational discussion, the comments and emoticons may serve important public functions. First, they affirm that this is indeed an active listening public; such reactions are also acknowledgement that the stories were read and that they were read by a sympathetic audience. They allow the victims (and their families) to be publicly mourned, in their specificity and individuality, and reassert their concerns as within 'the universe of moral obligation' for Hungarians. As contributor Éva Vámos noted, the group was particularly helpful for the second generation, since writing and reading these stories can be therapeutic:

'[The project] fills a void for the [second] generation who had no forum where they could fully discuss, share and mourn their loss.' This is of course also true of most first-generation survivors, who were rarely able to share their experiences even in the private sphere of their families (Breuer 2015).

Although the originators of the Facebook group envisioned it as contributing to a larger public discussion in Hungarian public life, and invited all members of the Hungarian public, regardless of ethnicity, to participate, it soon became clear that most members, at least those who post, are from Jewish or mixed families. Nevertheless, as the group was 'public', most of the posts were publicly shared and visible to anyone on Facebook, including non-members. Furthermore, as the book based on the group is sold in large national bookshop chains, the potential public in fact becomes the general Hungarian reading public. Although Facebook records and archives posts, it is not ideal for making the posts accessible over time. The posts are generally organized in reverse chronological order and posts beyond the first page are often difficult to access. As media journalist and producer Bryce Renninger notes, this is because posts are 'curated by an individually calculated social algorithm that privileges new posts over old ones and assumes one only wants to see posts that garner a lot of interactions or are from certain people or organizations that one interacts with regularly' (Renninger 2015: 10). Users cannot effectively search and discover older posts or discussion threads. The posts are difficult to search, as they are not indexed by keyword or topic and follow no thematic organization. The discussion unfolds in real time, and latecomers to the group will not have the same experience, especially because the group's level of activity peaked in the first year and became much less frequent later.

The use of Hungarian made it difficult for those survivors and especially their family members who left Hungary to become aware of the project or to participate in Hungarian. However, it also had the effect of keeping the group relatively homogenous, both in terms of their awareness of the wider political and cultural discourse surrounding Jewishness (in post-1948 Hungary) and also in the more immediate political context. The understanding of Jewishness (and Hungarianness) that emerges from the group is thus shaped by these discourses. For the most part, participants seem to agree that individuals should be free to define themselves and their own identities. This is partly the result of the group's composition—mostly survivors, who were more likely to be from Budapest (a largely Neolog and secularizing, assimilationist, highly integrated community), since almost the entire rural Jewish population was murdered. Thus members seem to reject both a religious and an 'ethnic' definition of Jewishness. Many comments argue that, as far as this group goes, anyone whose family was targeted as Jewish by racial laws is Jewish, regardless of halakhah, and also point out again and again that their ancestors were and felt very much Hungarian.

The stated goal of the group's founders and members was not to redefine the Jewish community itself, or the place and meaning of Jewishness in Hungary. Rather, it was to get Jews to speak out in public, and for others to witness the stories. But giving voice to previously suppressed private stories posed a challenge to public memory of the Holocaust, and, specifically, the role of non-Jewish society. The way the group used the platform provided by Facebook was not for a discussion of topics between Jews and non-Jews, but for the acknowledgement of these stories as having public relevance, even if the majority of the participants believed they were speaking to a limited, Jewish, public. The private stories also made it clear that private ways of thinking about Jewishness shaped peoples' actions and public events. This validates the idea that Jewishness is an important part of everyday and private experience, both before, during, and after the Holocaust. In short, Hungarian Jewish experience matters and needs to be part of the wider public discourse.

Conclusion: Talking about Jews and Jewishness

The case studies of Hungarian Jewish networking on social media have pointed to the importance of using a historical perspective for understanding the construction of communities online. The examples I have described expand on Fraser and Warner's theoretical models for countercultural publics, and on boyd's idea of networked publics, by connecting online Jewish publics both to the historical construction of the Hungarian public which excluded Jews as Jews, and to the immediate context of post-communist debates on Jewish identities and communities.

Sociologists and anthropologists have suggested that the burgeoning expressions of Hungarian Jewish 'cultural ethnicity' were not likely to lead to a political redefinition of Jews as an ethnic group (Kovács 1996–9; Mars 2001). But in Hungary, as in other post-communist central European societies, cultural expressions of Jewishness, as well as reflections on the place of Jewish history and the Jewish community in Hungarian history, are inextricably intertwined with political debates on public memory and national identity. I have argued that social networking sites, like other areas of public and popular culture, have also participated in this debate, and that they did so in interaction with other public discourses taking place in a polymedia environment.

By shifting perceptions of what is public and what is private, social networking sites in Hungary have blurred public and private ways of talking about Jews and Jewishness, with important implications for how Jewish communities can be conceptualized. In other words, besides political and social actors with particular agendas, digital technology has also had an effect on shaping Jewish identities, and, by changing norms of discussing Jewishness, has created new possibilities for imagining Jewish communities, including their role in the political sphere.

Notes

1   Perhaps most obviously, it removed the taboo on discussing the Holocaust, that is, of talking about Jews as anything other than a religious community. In 1989, at the 45th anniversary of the Holocaust in Hungary, the Hungarian parliament's ceremony specifically mentioned Jewish victims and on 10 May 1989, Mátyás Szűrös, the president of Parliament, used the word 'Holocaust' in his address.

2   Gitelman makes the point that in 1991, the association's name was changed to reflect an ethnic understanding, using the word 'Jew', 'an ethnic term' in place of 'Israelite'. I would argue that 'Jew' is also a religious term and is in this case explicitly used as such: *zsidó hitközség* means Jewish religious community.

3   The public readings, which in turn spurred further public discussion on various media, included a performance at the Rumbach Street Synagogue (not a functioning synagogue) on 4 May 2014, a reading which also functioned as a memorial event at the Central Theatre on 13 May 2014, and a book launch and reading at the Atrium Theatre on 12 November 2015, all of which filled the venues.

References

BOYD, DANAH. 2011. 'Social Network Sites as Networked Publics: Affordances, Dynamics and Implications'. In Zizi Papacharissi, ed., *A Networked Self: Identity, Community, and Culture on Social Network Sites*, 39–58. New York.

BREUER, PETER. 2015. 'Holokauszt és a családom: Vámos Éva' [Interview with Éva Vámos]. *Breuerpress*. <http://www.breuerpress.com/2015/12/09/holokauszt-es-a-csaladom-vamos-eva/> (accessed 14 Sept. 2017).

FRASER, NANCY. 1990. 'Rethinking the Public Sphere: A Contribution to the Critique of Actually Existing Democracy'. *Social Text*, 25/26: 56–80.

FRITZ, REGINA. 2015. 'Nyilvános Emlékezet, Személyes Emlékezet' [Public Memory, Personal Remembering]. In Katalin Fenyves, ed., *A Holokauszt és a Családom*, 43–68. Budapest.

GITELMAN, ZVI. 1996–9. 'Reconstructing Jewish Communities and Jewish Identities in Post-Communist East Central Europe'. *Jewish Studies at the CEU Yearbook*, 1 <http://web.ceu.hu/jewishstudies/pdf/01_gitelman.pdf> (accessed 14 Sept. 2017).

——and ANDRÁS KOVÁCS, eds. 2003. *New Jewish Identities: Contemporary Europe and Beyond*. Budapest.

GOFFMAN, ERVING. 1959. *The Presentation of Self in Everyday Life*. Garden City, NY.

GRUBER, RUTH ELLEN. 2000. *Virtually Jewish: Reinventing Jewish Culture in Europe*. Berkeley, Calif.

HABERMAS, JÜRGEN. 1989. *The Structural Transformation of the Public Sphere*. Cambridge, Mass.

Judapest. 2007. 'Flódni-gate'. *Judapest.org* <http://web.archive.org/web/20080820050706/http://www.judapest.org/faq/flodni-ugy/> (accessed 30 Dec. 2017).

KOVÁCS, ANDRÁS. 1994. 'Are Hungarian Jews a National Minority? Remarks on a Public Debate'. *East European Jewish Affairs*, 24: 63–71.

—— 1996–9. 'Jewish Assimilation and Jewish Politics in Modern Hungary'. *Jewish Studies at the CEU Yearbook*, 1 <http://web.ceu.hu/jewishstudies/pdf/01_kovacs.pdf> (accessed 14 Sept. 2017).

—— 2010. 'Jews and Jewishness in Post-War Hungary'. *Quest: Issues in Contemporary Jewish History*, 1: 34–57 <http://www.quest-cdecjournal.it/files/KOVACS.pdf> (accessed 14 Sept. 2017).

LINDTNER, SILVIA, JUDY CHEN, GILLIAN R. HAYES, and PAUL DOURISH. 2011. 'Towards a Framework of Publics: Re-encountering Media Sharing and its User'. *ACM Transactions on Computer-Human Interactions* (TOCHI), 18: 1–23 <http://www.ics.uci.edu/~lindtner/documents/lindtner_frameworkofpublics_2011.pdf> (accessed 14 Sept. 2017).

MARS, LEONARD. 1999. 'Discontinuity, Tradition and Innovation: Anthropological Reflections on Jewish Identity in Contemporary Hungary'. *Social Compass*, 46: 21–33.

—— 2001. 'Is There a Religious Revival among Hungarian Jews Today?' *Journal of Contemporary Religion*, 16: 227–38.

MIKLÓSI, GÁBOR. 2008. 'Alternatív zsidó mozgalmak: Önépítkezés' [Alternative Jewish Social Movements: Self-Building]. *Magyar Narancs* (10 Apr.). <http://magyarnarancs.hu/belpol/alternativ_zsido_mozgalmak_-_onepitkezes-68595> (accessed 14 Sept. 2017).

PAPP, RICHÁRD. 2004. *Van-e Zsidó Reneszánsz?* [Is There a Jewish Renaissance?] Budapest.

RENNINGER, BRYCE J. 2015. 'Where I Can Be Myself . . . Where I Can Speak My Mind: Networked Counterpublics in a Polymedia Environment'. *New Media & Society*, 17: 1–17.

SANDERS, GABRIEL. 2007. 'Pastry Diplomacy'. *Forward* (12 Dec.) <http://forward.com/articles/12242/pastry-diplomacy-/> (accessed 14 Sept. 2017).

SHADAI. 2007. 'Judapest Schmudapest' *Judapest.org* (13 Nov.) <http://web.archive.org/web/20081204153321/http://www.judapest.org/judapest-schmudapest/> (accessed 30 Dec. 2017).

—— 2008. 'Zsidónak lenni jó' [It's Good to be Jewish] *Judapest.org* (10 July) <http://web.archive.org/web/20090312082828/http://www.judapest.org:80/zsidonak-lenni-jo/> (accessed 30 Dec. 2017).

TET. 2008. 'Zsidó-e Vagy?' *Judapest.org* (16 Jan.) <http://web.archive.org/web/20100225024037/http://www.judapest.org/zsido-e-vagy-2/> (accessed 30 Dec. 2017).

VADJUTKA. 2008. [Comment.] <http://vadjutka.hu/bezart-a-judapest/> (accessed 30 Dec. 2017).

WARNER, MICHAEL. 2002. 'Publics and Counterpublics—Abbreviated Version'. *Quarterly Journal of Speech*, 88: 413–25.

WEBBER, JONATHAN, ed. 1994. *Jewish Identities in the New Europe*. London.

Contributors

Caspar Battegay teaches modern German literature at the University of Basel (Switzerland). He received his D.Phil. from the Hochschule für Jüdische Studien/University of Heidelberg (Germany) in 2009. Since then he has taught modern German literature and Jewish studies at the universities of Graz (Austria), Basel (Switzerland), and Berne (Switzerland). Between 2014 and 2017 he was 'Ambizione' (Research Fellow) of the Swiss National Foundation for Scientific Research (SNF) in the German Department of the University of Lausanne (Switzerland). He is the author and editor of several books on German and Jewish literature and cultural history, including *European-Jewish Utopias* (De Gruyter, 2016). He also contributed 'German Psycho: The Language of Depression in Oliver Polak's *Der jüdische Patient*' to *German Jewish Literature after 1990: Beyond the Holocaust?*, edited by Katja Garloff and Agnes Mueller (Camden House, 2018). He is a member of Die Junge Akademie der Berlin Brandenburgischen Akademie der Wissenschaften (Young Academy of the Berlin-Brandenburg Academy of Sciences), funded by the German Federal Ministry of Education and Research.

Simon J. Bronner is Maxwell C. Weiner Distinguished Professor of Humanities at Missouri S&T and Distinguished University Professor Emeritus of American Studies and Folklore at Pennsylvania State University, Harrisburg, where he was founding director of the campus's Holocaust and Jewish Studies Center. He has also taught at Harvard, Leiden, and Osaka universities. He is the author and editor of over forty books, including *Greater Harrisburg's Jewish Community* (Arcadia, 2011), *Explaining Traditions: Folk Behavior in Modern Culture* (University Press of Kentucky, 2011), and *Encyclopedia of American Folklife* (Routledge, 2006). He edits the Material Worlds series for the University Press of Kentucky and has published on Jewish cultural studies in the *Journal of Modern Jewish Studies*, *Jewish History*, *Yiddish*, *Markers*, and *Chuliyot: Journal of Yiddish Literature*. As well as editing the Littman Library's Jewish Cultural Studies series, he leads the Jewish Folklore and Ethnology Section of the American Folklore Society and has been president of the Fellows of the American Folklore Society. He has received the Mary Turpie Prize from the American Studies Association and the Kenneth Goldstein Award for Lifetime Academic Leadership from the American Folklore Society.

Anthony Bak Buccitelli is Associate Professor of American Studies and Communications at Pennsylvania State University, Harrisburg, and has served as director of Penn State's Center for Holocaust and Jewish Studies. He is the author of *City of Neighborhoods: Memory, Folklore, and Ethnic Place in Boston* (University of Wisconsin Press, 2016) and editor of *Race and Ethnicity in Digital Culture: Our Changing Traditions, Impressions, and Expressions in a Mediated World* (Praeger, 2017).

He served as co-editor of *Cultural Analysis: An Interdisciplinary Forum on Folklore and Popular Culture* from 2006 to 2014, and is the founding editor of *SOAR: The Society of Americanists Review*. In 2013, he represented the American Folklore Society as part of its Forum on Intangible Cultural Heritage Professional Exchange with the China Folklore Society. His essays have appeared in the *Journal of American Folklore*, *Oral History*, *Culture and Religion*, and *Western Folklore*, among others.

Nathan P. Devir is Assistant Professor of Jewish Studies, Religious Studies, and Comparative Literary and Cultural Studies at the University of Utah, where he also serves as director of the Middle East Centre. Previously, he was Visiting Assistant Professor of Modern Hebrew and International Studies at Middlebury College. He is the author of *New Children of Israel: Emerging Jewish Communities in an Era of Globalization* (University of Utah Press, 2017). He has published essays on Jewish studies in *Biblical Reception*, *Jewish Culture and History*, *Journal of Feminist Studies in Religion*, *Journal of Modern Jewish Studies*, *Nashim*, *Religion and the Arts*, *Studies in American Jewish Literature*, and *Journal of the Middle East and Africa*. He has received numerous honours for his research on worldwide Judaizing movements, including awards from the Association for the Study of the Middle East and Africa, the Centre for Advanced Holocaust Studies, the Council of American Overseas Research Centers, the Earhart Foundation, the Lucius N. Littauer Foundation, the National Endowment for the Humanities, the Posen Foundation, the Reed Foundation, and the Tauber Institute for the Study of European Jewry.

Rachel Leah Jablon is an affiliate of the Meyerhoff Center for Jewish Studies at the University of Maryland. She has taught at the universities of Maryland, Denver, and Delaware; Arapahoe Community College in Littleton, Colorado; and Montgomery College in Silver Spring, Maryland, and served as the inaugural scholar in residence of the University of Denver's Holocaust Awareness Institute. Her research has appeared in *Academic Exchange Quarterly*, the *Journal of Popular Culture*, and *Legacy: A Journal of American Women Writers*.

Anna Manchin has held the Ray D. Wolfe Post-Doctoral Fellowship in Jewish Studies at the University of Toronto, an Aresty Visiting Scholarship at Rutgers University, a Prins Post-Doctoral Fellowship at the Center for Jewish History in New York, and a Fred and Ellen Lewis Fellowship at the Joint Archives in Jerusalem. She has published articles on Jewish history and culture in *East European Jewish Affairs*, *Hungarian Quarterly*, *Polin*, and *Shofar*, among others.

Amy K. Milligan is the Batten Endowed Assistant Professor of Jewish Studies and Women's Studies at Old Dominion University (USA), where she is also the director of the Institute of Jewish Studies and Interfaith Understanding. She is the author of *Hair, Headwear, and Orthodox Jewish Women: Kallah's Choice* (Lexington,

2014), as well as a number of scholarly articles exploring the intersections of hair, body, gender, sexuality, and religion. She has received the Raphael Patai Prize in Jewish Folklore and Ethnology from the American Folklore Society.

Diana I. Popescu is a Research Fellow at the Pears Institute for the Study of Anti-semitism, Birkbeck, University of London. Previously, she was a lecturer at the James Parkes Institute for the Study of Jewish/Non-Jewish Relations, University of Southampton, where she completed her doctoral degree in Holocaust studies (2013). She has published essays in *Holocaust Studies* and *Jewish Renaissance Quarterly*. She is the co-editor (with Tanja Schult) of *Revisiting Holocaust Representation in the Post-Witness Era* (Palgrave Macmillan, 2015). In 2015 she received a grant from the Swedish Research Council for the research project 'Making the Past Present: Performative Holocaust Commemorations since the Year 2000', led by Tanja Schult of Stockholm University. She currently serves on the editorial board of *Genocide Studies and Prevention: An International Journal*.

Tsafi Sebba-Elran is Lecturer in Hebrew Literature and Folklore at the Department of Hebrew and Comparative Literature at the University of Haifa in Israel. She has also taught at Indiana University. She is the author of *In Search of New Memories: The Aggadic Anthologies and Their Role in the Configuration of the Modern Hebrew Canon* (Yad Ben-Zvi Research Institute, 2017). Her research interests and publication topics include the formation of cultural memory in Israel, the contribution of national anthologies (including humoristic anthologies) to the construction of modern Jewish identities, and the social as well as the epistemological changes those anthologies reflect. She has received a grant from the Israeli Science Foundation for an inter-university project at the Israeli Folktale Archives.

Pavel Sládek is Associate Professor of Hebrew Studies in the Faculty of Arts, Charles University, Prague. He is a co-founder of the Prague Centre for Jewish Studies and serves as the director of the Institute of Near Eastern and African Studies. He has published several studies on sixteenth-century rabbinic culture and the history of Jewish books and practices of reading, including 'A Sixteenth-Century Rabbi as a Published Author: The Early Editions of Rabbi Mordekhai Jaffe's *Levushim*', in *Connecting Histories: Jews and Their Others in the Early Modern Period*, edited by David Ruderman and Francesca Bregoli (University of Pennsylvania Press, 2019), 'Early Modern Ethnographies of Jews: An Unpublished Book on Jewish Mores by the Czech Catholic Priest Karel Jugl', in a special issue of *Frankfurter Judaistische Beiträge* (2015), and 'Typography and the Strategies of Reading: The Lesson of *Tzemah David* (1592)', in *Judaica Bohemiae* (2016). In 2013 he was a fellow at the Herbert D. Katz Center for Advanced Judaic Studies, University of Pennsylvania. He is a member of the executive committee of the European Association for Jewish Studies.

Julian Voloj is a writer and photographer known for exploring Jewish diversity in his work. He is the author, contributor, and editor of over twenty books, including *Jewish Topographies: Visions of Space, Traditions of Place* (Ashgate, 2008) and *Jews of Gotham: New York Jews in a Changing City, 1920–2010* (NYU Press, 2012). Voloj was the first to document the Jewish community in the virtual world of Second Life. From 2007 to 2009 he was the editor of *2Life Magazine*, a publication focusing exclusively on virtual Judaism in Second Life.

Index